THE ILLUSTRATED HISTORY OF THE

AIR
FORCES
OF WORLD WAR I
& WORLD WAR II

THE ILLUSTRATED HISTORY OF THE
AIR FORCES
OF WORLD WAR I
& WORLD WAR II
BY CHRIS CHANT

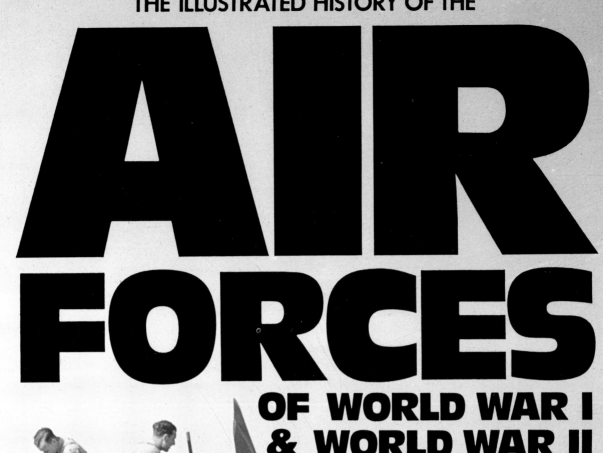
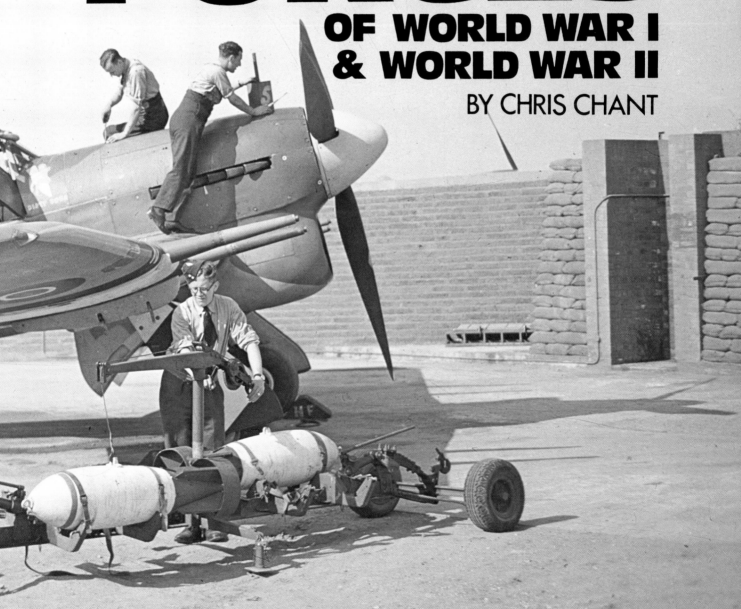

Galley Press

A QUARTO BOOK

Published in this edition by Galley Press,
an imprint of W. H. Smith and Son Limited,
Registered No 237811 England. Trading as
WHS Distributors, St John's House,
East Street, Leicester, LE1 6NE

ISBN 0 86136 792 8
First published in 1979

© Copyright 1979 Quarto Limited

This book was designed and produced by
Quarto Publishing Limited,
32 Kingly Court, London W1
Designers: Clive Hayball, Marian Sanders
Editor: Corinne Molesworth

Typeset in Britain by Filmtype Services Limited
Printed in Hong Kong

Endpapers
Engines being installed in RAF SE.5s (Scouting Experimental No.5s)
at the Wolseley factories in England.

CONTENTS

INTRODUCTION

The object of the present book is to examine in greater detail than before the genesis and nature of the air forces which fought in World Wars I and II. Although it would have been easier to state what each belligerent country in the two World Wars had in the way of air services and then merely to work backwards towards their origins, this could not adequately reflect the role of national resources, the endless planning and re-planning, the industrial factors, the manpower concerns and all the other contributory aspects to the background of the air forces. It seemed sensible, therefore, to combine a narrative of the general course of air war from 1911 to 1945 with an account of how such air operations were possible, given the air forces in existence, and conversely how the conduct of those air operations affected the future growth and organisation of the air forces.

The history of air warfare can be likened to human growth. From 1903 to 1914 is its infancy, with events such as the Italo-Turkish War indicating the strength the child may possibly have, if only it can be harnessed and controlled to grow in a constructive manner. From 1914 to 1918 is its puberty, the newly emerged air arms showing, at first hesitantly, and then with growing vigour, that they are entities in their own right, and can play a man's part in the world, despite the evident gangliness of some parts of their anatomies resulting from the haphazard growth of the period. From 1919 to 1939 is adolescence, with general growth of the body's skills and strengths, though at times certain developments seem to accelerate more swiftly than they should, and others seem extraordinarily late. And 1939 to 1945 is the beginning of maturity, with the physical and intellectual pretensions of adolescence being put to the

Samuel Franklin Cody, an American, made the first officially recognised aeroplane flight in Britain, in 1908. Pictured below is the *British Army Aeroplane No. 1*, designed and built by Cody, in which he made the historic flight.

test and found to a certain extent wanting, until finally in 1943 it began to appear that at last the ambitions of youth were about to be realised, as indeed they were in the second half of 1944 and 1945.

This analogy may appear strained but closer examination will reveal this not to be the case, either physically or intellectually. During the adolescence of air warfare in the 1920s and 1930s, for example, while its 'head' was developing grandiose ambitions for its role in manhood, governments were keeping very watchful eyes on it, checking over-ambition and using the threat of financial and prestige losses, just as a parent might. With the passing of years since the end of World War II, it is perhaps possible to look back with a certain dispassion to this early period in the history of air warfare, and decide that although the continuity of air warfare remains unbroken to the present, the dropping of the two atomic weapons on Hiroshima and Nagasaki at the end of World War II mark the end of air warfare's early life.

Although air power played a dominant part in the naval history of World War II (as attested by the emergence of the aircraft-carrier as the capital ship of the day in place of the battleship) it existed almost in a vacuum of its own in maritime affairs. And while there can be no denial of the absolute importance of air power in defeating the menace of the German U-boats in the Atlantic Ocean, and in defeating the Imperial Japanese Navy (and to a lesser extent the Imperial Japanese Army with tactical air operations by the US Navy and US Marine Corps), the main effect of air power has been over the land battlefields, and in taking the war to the civilian populations backing the fighting men with political resolve and industrial output. The majority of the present work is devoted to the air forces involved in these seminal aspects of air warfare, especially the planning and organisational effort that went towards making these air forces the weapons they were.

WAR—As Germany Saw It 40 Years Ago

Above War as envisaged by a German cartoonist early this century.
Left This remarkable French painting depicts an idea to invade Britain, conceived by the German military expert Rudolf Martin, soon after the first successful aeroplane flight in Europe in 1908. He suggested building a fleet of 50,000 aircraft, of the type used by the Wright brothers, to land 100,000 men in Kent.

CHAPTER ONE

THE GERMAN AIR SERVICES 1900·18

Like most other nations that were to evolve air services in the years prior to World War I, Germany obtained her first experience with military aviation with observation balloons – the *Luftschiffer Detachement* (Lighter-than-air Detail) of the *Eisenbahntruppe* (Railway Troops) was formed as early as 1884 to assess the work of balloons as a means of observation. By 1887 this *Detachement* had become an independent *Luftschiffer Abteilung* (Unit) and by 1901 a *Luftschiffer Bataillon* of two companies. From 1896 the earlier round balloons were replaced by the more familiar 'sausage' or kite-balloons pioneered by *Major* von Parseval and *Hauptmann* von Sigsfeld.

In the lighter-than-air field, the next step was the dirigible, of which the *Graf* Ferdinand von Zeppelin may be considered the father. This controllable, free 'balloon' captured the imagination of the German people, and was greatly favoured by the German Army and the German Navy for long-range reconnaissance purposes. It is interesting to note that of the twenty-six airships in the world in 1910, fourteen were German. The others were possessed by France (five); Italy (two); and Austria-Hungary, Belgium, Great Britain, Russia and the United States (one each).

Heavier-than-air aviation had got off to a slow start in Germany, but the German Great General Staff, always ready to consider the military possibilities of advanced technology, had been keeping a careful eye on the steady progress of the aircraft as a reliable, speedy, long-range and load-carrying means of transport.

On 1 October 1908 the general staff took the far-sighted step of forming a special section to watch and report on developments in radio, road transport and aviation – all these factors would play vital parts in any future fast-moving mobile operations, as the Germans were to prove with their *Blitzkrieg* tactics in World War II. The establishment of this Technical Section was a direct result of recommendations by *Hauptmann* Thomsen of the Fourth Section of the General Staff, previously entrusted with this work. In this, Thomsen was fully supported by *General* Erich Ludendorff, head of the Second Section of the General Staff.

Soon after its formation, the Technical Section reported that in the near future aircraft would become useful as offensive weapons and as observation platforms. In this conclusion the Technical Section was backed by *Major* Gross and *Hauptmann* de le Roi, aeronautical advisers to the War Ministry and *Luftschiffer Abteilung der Versuchsabteilung der Verkehrstrappen* (Lighter-than-air Unit of the Experimental Detachment of the Transport Troops) respectively.

Gross had in 1906 pressed for the War Ministry to subsidise German aircraft designers, but up to 1910 this programme had yielded no design of promise. But while the Ministry was unwilling to disburse large sums on what was as yet of unproven worth, it was willing to let officers learn to fly at another's expense – in this case Dr. Walther Huth of the Albatros aircraft company. Huth had bought a Farman biplane and paid for his chauffeur to learn to fly. He in turn taught army officers

The Albatros D.V (foreground) and D.Va were Germany's most numerous fighters of 1917 and 1918, and the Gotha G.V was the mainstay with the G.IV of the campaign against London.

from 4 July 1910 at *Flieger Kommando* Döberitz (Döberitz Aviation Detachment).

By the end of March 1911 some ten pilots had been trained: *Hauptmann* de le Roi, *Oberstleutnants* Geerdt, Bercio and Erler, and *Leutnants* Mackenthun, von Tarnoczy, *Freiherr* von Thüna, Stein, Förster and Canter. Although the General Staff remained sceptical of the real use of aircraft in war, and so permitted only small sums of money and few personnel to receive any form of training to do with heavier-than-air flight, de le Roi persevered in his propagandising efforts, and gradually made headway with the authorities.

There was thus held in September and October 1910 an investigation into the suitability of certain aircraft types for military use. Amongst these were Albatros, Aviatik, Etrich and Wright types. After searching tests, the War Ministry allowed 150,000 marks for the purchase of seven aircraft   (one Etrich *Taube*, two Frey biplanes, one Farman, one Albatros-built Farman, one Aviatik-built Farman, and one Albatros-built Sommer biplane).

The purchase of these aircraft at last gave the German Army some heavier-than-air machines, and so the organisation of the *Verkehrstruppen* had to be altered to accommodate the new machines. The previous *Inspektion* (Inspectorate) was replaced by a *Generalinspektion des Militärvekehrswesens* (Inspector-General's Department of Military Transport) under which came the *Inspektion des Militär Luft und Kraftfahrwesens* (Inspectorate of Military Aviation and Transport). As yet, however, the aviation service was not considered 'worthy of being included in the military budget', and thus survived only in straitened circumstances even after the establishment of the *Generalinspektion* on 1 April 1911. But the War Ministry and General Staff were well aware that such a situation could not continue indefinitely, and a commission allocated an additional 500,000 marks for expansion and more aircraft. Some thirty aircraft were bought during 1911 (nineteen B-type single-engined unarmed biplanes, and eleven Rumpler-built Etrich *Taube* monoplanes). By the end of the year the army had purchased thirty-seven aircraft in all and there were thirty pilots on strength. More importantly, aircraft had taken part in the 1911 manoeuvres, and pilots had begun to see the real possibilities of aircraft in war.

Further progress was made in 1912, when the inadequacy of the army training school at Döberitz (*Lehr und Versuchsanstalt für Militärflugwesen* or Training and Experimental Establishment for Military Aviation) meant that new pilots had to be trained by civilian schools and then brought up to military standards at the *Fliegerstationen* (Air Stations) at Strassburg and Metz. Special courses were also run for observers, who did not have to be pilots.

The *Fliegertruppen* were now growing apace, and there was some controversy between the War Ministry and the General Staff about what should be done with them. *Generaloberst* Helmuth von Moltke, the Chief of the General Staff, thought that they should be organised along French lines, as France was the likely enemy that Germany would have to face; the War Ministry felt that no further reorganisation or expansion was desirable. In September, however, von Moltke put forward a major scheme for *Fliegertruppe* reorganisation.

According to this scheme, each army command (*Armee Oberkommando* or AOK) should have in time of war two or three *Feldflieger Abteilungen* (Field Aviation

Units) and one *Etappen Flugzeugpark* (Aircraft Supply Depot on the Lines of Communication). Moreover, every corps command (regular, reserve or cavalry) should also have a *Feldflieger Abteilung* as soon after the outbreak of war as possible. Moltke also suggested that each corps should also have an artillery co-operation unit. By 1 April 1914, von Moltke concluded, there should be thirty-four *Feldflieger Abteilungen*, one for each of the eight AOKs and twenty-six corps. Von Moltke also thought that each corps should have a *Fliegerstation* to facilitate the distribution of the *Fliegertruppen* within the army. Finally, von Moltke suggested, the *Fliegertruppen* should be divorced from the overall control of the *Verkehrstruppen* and provided with their own *Inspektion*.

Both the War Ministry and *General Inspektion* expressed disapproval with von Moltke's plans, claiming that aviation was too young and unknown a quantity to receive the amount of care and independence that was being lavished upon it.

On 1 October 1912, however, the *Fliegertruppen* began to move in the direction suggested by von Moltke, when the War Ministry began to remodel their structure. Döberitz became an 'ordinary' *Fliegerstation* like Strassburg, Metz and Darmstadt, and a *Fliegertruppe* of twenty-one officers and 306 men was attached to the élite *Gardekorps* (Guards Corps). All this re-

Above Anthony Fokker (with wing collar) with one of his Spin monoplanes and German officers.
Right An assortment of Rumpler-built Taube monoplanes.

organisation meant that more money was needed, and an additional budget demand had to be placed before the Chancellor at the end of 1912.

Military aviation was also helped indirectly by the *Nationalflugspende* (National Fund for the Promotion of Aviation) run by Prince Heinrich of Prussia. This collected over 7,000,000 marks, money which was used to further civilian flying, finance aeronautical research, provide loans for expansion to German aircraft constructors and other aspects of civilian flight, all of which benefited the *Fliegertruppen* in the long run.

Despite the War Ministry's scepticism of the use of aircraft for reconnaissance, the General Staff during 1912 decided to replace the non-rigid and semi-rigid airships it had previously used for tactical reconnaissance with aircraft. The fifteen rigid airships used for bombing and strategic reconnaissance by the *Obersten Heeresleitung* or OHL (Army High Command) were to be kept, however, and further expansion of the *Luftschiffertruppen* thus became necessary.

The move towards adoption of von Moltke's plans for aircraft continued during 1913, and on 1 October 1913 an *Inspektion der Fliegertruppen* or *Idflieg* (Inspectorate of Military Aviation) was set up. Its head was *Oberst* von Eberhardt, with the title of *Inspekteur der Fliegertruppen*. Four *Flieger Bataillone* (*Nr* 1 to 4), each of three companies, were established: *Nr* 1 was located at Döberitz and Grossenhain; *Nr* 2 at Posen, Graudenz and Königsberg; *Nr* 3 at Cologne, Hanover and Darmstadt; and *Nr* 4 at Strassburg, Metz and Freiburg. As it was a semi-independent body, the Bavarian Army formed its own two-company *Flieger Bataillon* at Schleissheim. Each of the above *Fliegerstationen* was the home of a *Flieger Kompagnie*, which would in war form the basis of a *Feldflieger Abteilung*.

It was a good start, and went much of the way to meeting von Moltke's suggestions. The General Staff went further than von Moltke, however, and planned for a strong air service by April 1916, with an additional twenty-three *Feldflieger Abteilungen*. This meant another expansion of the *Fliegertruppen*, to provide a total of fifty-seven *Feldflieger Abteilungen*. Moreover, the General Staff plan also called for the formation of another forty-six *Artillerie Flieger Abteilungen* as soon after mobilisation as possible, one for each of the infantry divisions. It was realised, however, that the plan was impossible, and so the General Staff decided that by 1 April 1914 each of the twelve *Flieger Kompagnie* should be able to form four *Feldflieger Abteilungen*, each with a strength of six aircraft.

As it was impossible for the *Fliegertruppen* to provide a *Fliegerstation* for each corps, however, it was decided not to make the air service independent, and so it remained subservient to the *Verkehrstruppen*. At the same time, an accident to an aircraft during the main 1913 manoeuvres led to a 'rethink' about the structural integrity of aircraft. Whereas previously it had been essential for any aircraft to be easily dismantled and put together again, to facilitate the road or rail transport of the machine, it was now decided that much stronger aircraft were needed.

The *Versuchsabteilung der Verkehrstruppen* (Experimental Section of Transport Troops) became the *Verkehrstechnischen Prüfungskommission* (Technical Transport Examination Board), and spent the winter of 1913–14 strengthening existing aircraft, to the detriment of the pilot training programme. During the last few months of peace further training was pressed ahead as quickly as possible. And while good progress was

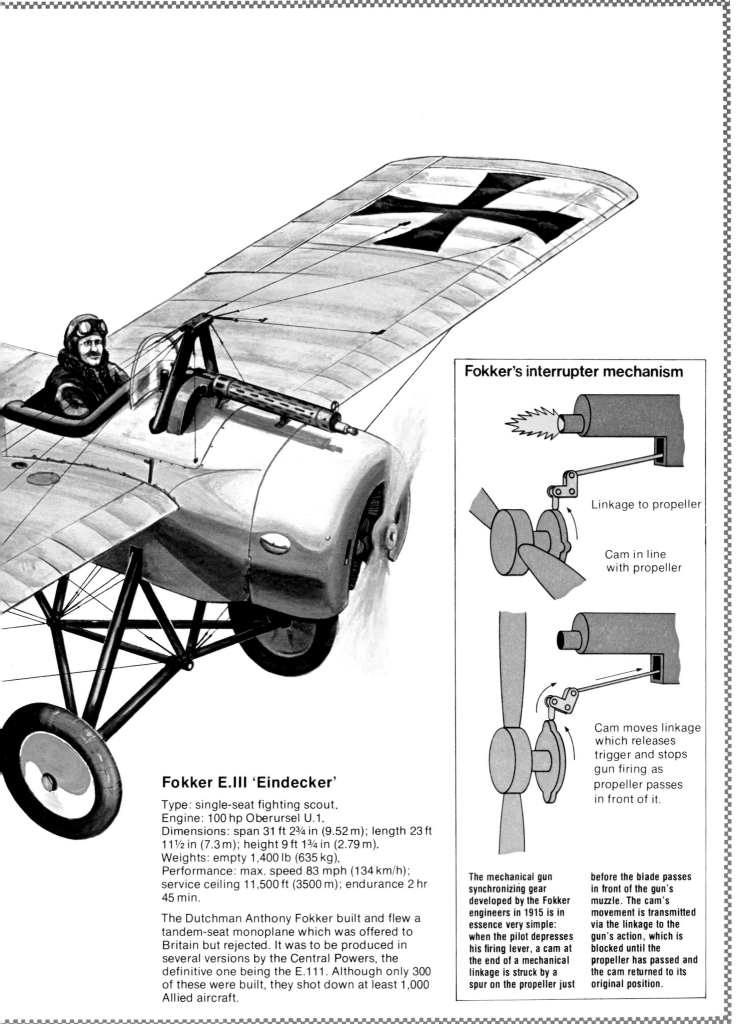

Fokker's interrupter mechanism

Linkage to propeller

Cam in line with propeller

Cam moves linkage which releases trigger and stops gun firing as propeller passes in front of it.

The mechanical gun synchronizing gear developed by the Fokker engineers in 1915 is in essence very simple: when the pilot depresses his firing lever, a cam at the end of a mechanical linkage is struck by a spur on the propeller just before the blade passes in front of the gun's muzzle. The cam's movement is transmitted via the linkage to the gun's action, which is blocked until the propeller has passed and the cam returned to its original position.

Fokker E.III 'Eindecker'

Type: single-seat fighting scout.
Engine: 100 hp Oberursel U.1.
Dimensions: span 31 ft 2¾ in (9.52 m); length 23 ft 11½ in (7.3 m); height 9 ft 1¾ in (2.79 m).
Weights: empty 1,400 lb (635 kg).
Performance: max. speed 83 mph (134 km/h); service ceiling 11,500 ft (3500 m); endurance 2 hr 45 min.

The Dutchman Anthony Fokker built and flew a tandem-seat monoplane which was offered to Britain but rejected. It was to be produced in several versions by the Central Powers, the definitive one being the E.111. Although only 300 of these were built, they shot down at least 1,000 Allied aircraft.

Above Fokker Dr.I of *Leutnant* Werner Voss, 4th highest German ace with 48 victories. The Dr.I was notable for great manoeuvrability and rate of climb.
Above right The Hansa-Brandenburg (K.D.W.) 1916.
Right Junkers J.I. 'Blechesel' (Tin Donkey) 1915. All-metal cantilever construction which first flew in December 1915. German authorities were sceptical of its strength and capabilities.

made with the theory and practice of reconnaissance for army and corps headquarters, artillery spotting failed to make progress for lack of a suitable method of communication between the ground and the air. Experiments had also been made with the arming of aircraft, but inconsistencies in machine-gun ammunition, resulting in 'hang-fire' rounds, had hampered aerial gunnery trials, and experiments with bomb-sights were progressing only relatively slowly. By the end of July 1914, the Germans had spent no less than 118,000,000 marks on military aviation from 1906.

General mobilisation was declared on 1 August 1914, and the next day the air service, in both its lighter-than-air and heavier-than-air forms, began to deploy for war. There were five *Flieger Bataillone* and six *Luftschiffer Bataillone*. The *Fliegertruppen* fielded thirty-three *Feldflieger Abteilungen*, numbered 1 to 30 (Prussian) and 1 to 3 (Bavarian); ten *Festungsflieger Abteilungen* for the defence of the fortress cities of Strassburg, Metz, Cologne, Posen, Königsberg and Graudenz, and the military centres at Boyen, Breslau and Glogau, numbered 1 to 9 (Prussian), and for the defence of the fortress of Germersheim, numbered 1 (Bavarian); eight *Etappen Flugzeugparke* for the replacement and supply

of aircraft and personnel in the field; and five *Flieger Ersatz Abteilungen* to take the place of the *Flieger Bataillone* in providing equipment and personnel for the mobile units.

The *Luftschiffertruppen* fielded eight *Feldluftschiffer Abteilungen*, each with a kite-balloon and a *Gaskolonne* to supply hydrogen, as well as a replacement balloon; fifteen *Festungsluftschiffer Truppen*, each equipped with one kite-balloon and several free balloons for use in fortress cities; eighteen *Lufschiff Kommandos* as crews for the twelve army airships; and six *Luftschiffer Ersatz Abteilungen* to take the place of the *Luftschiffer Bataillone* at home and provide equipment and personnel for the mobile units.

Mobilisation took some five days, as planned, and the various field formations were then assigned to their relevant army headquarters: one *Feldflieger Abteilung* was attached to each of the eight army headquarters and to each of the twenty-five regular infantry corps (the former also each having an *Etappen Flugzeugpark*); the OHL had no aircraft on which it could call directly. The *Feldluftschiffer Abteilungen* were allocated to each of the army headquarters, and the *Festungsluftschiffer Trupps* were allocated to fortress cities or kept in reserve

Right German Flying Officers and a Rumpler 6B.1 seaplane in front of the hangar of a German seaplane station at Zeebrugge. The Rumpler 6B.1 was developed from the Rumpler C.I land two-seater. *Below* A Friedrichshafen FF33 patrol floatplane seen from the deck of a U-Boat.

for deployment to captured fortresses. The airships played little part in the war after the first few days, and may be discounted on the whole.

On mobilisation, the *Fliegertruppen* totalled some 254 pilots and 271 observers, with 246 aircraft available. About half the aircraft were of the *Taube* type, and the rest were mostly parasol-wing monoplanes or Albatros and Aviatik B-type biplanes. *Feldflieger Abteilungen* each had six aircraft, and the *Festungsflieger Abteilungen* four each.

Early war operations revealed the deficiencies of the *Taube* type, but the B-types proved very successful, and a number of useful reconnaissance flights were flown on both the Eastern and Western Fronts, particularly the former. Then, on 19 October 1914, the German air service suffered a stroke of considerable luck when *Major* Wilhelm Siegert joined OHL to advise on any matter relating to aviation. His initial reports about the nature and state of the *Feldflieger Abteilungen* led to the almost immediate formation of the *Fliegerkorps der Obersten Heeresleitung*. This was a special unit under OHL control, commanded by Siegert and intended to undertake special bombing missions from Calais once this port had been taken.

In November the unit was given the cover-name *Brieftauben Abteilung Ostende* or BAO (Ostend Carrier Pigeon Unit), and its tasks were increased to include the bombing of targets in the region around London. Only the most experienced pilots and observers were accepted for service with the BAO. Calais never fell, and BAO turned its attentions to attacks on French railway junctions and other such targets.

The *Feldflieger Abteilungen* had performed their task of spotting enemy deployments and strengths well enough in the first months of the war, but the onset of static trench warfare from the end of October onwards presented them with new problems, for now they had to operate over short ranges to observe a well-prepared enemy in strong defences, and so suffered heavy losses, the more so after the removal of the better men for the BAO. Realising this, Siegert recommended alterations in organisation to OHL: the principal one of these was the need for a *Chef des Feldflugwesens* or *Feldflugchef* (Chief of Field Aviation) to control the activities of the air service in the field. Siegert's recommendation found favour, and the office he had recommended was established on 11 March 1915, with *Major* Hermann von der Lieth-Thomsen, Siegert's nominee, occupying it. The

Above centre The Albatross C.VII was developed in 1916 by adding a 200 hp Benz Bz.IV engine to the airframe of the unsuccessful C.V. 350 examples of the C.VII were in service in February 1917.
Above left The Halberstadt CL.IV, an excellent improvement on the CL.II ground-attack aircraft with more manoeuvrability.
Above The Hannover CL.IIIa two-seat ground-attack and escort biplane, in service 1917–18. The small span of the biplane tail gave the gunner a good field of fire.

Feldflugchef was responsible for all concerned with flying operations and military aircraft, and was answerable only to the OHL and the War Ministry. All concerned with field operations of both airships and aircraft fell within the province of Thomsen's department, although the actual operations themselves were still controlled by the army and corps staffs to which the *Feldflieger* and *Feldluftschiffer Bataillone* were subordinated.

So far the *Feldflieger Abteilungen* had operated in almost total isolation from each other. But again, with the onset of static warfare, the army realised the need for liaison between the various *Abteilungen*, and to meet this need a *Stabsoffizier der Flieger* or *Stofl* (Staff Officer for Aviation) was appointed in each army headquarters. Although these officers had no executive authority, their presence went much of the way towards ensuring adequate co-operation between the *Abteilungen*.

Most of the *Feldfliegertruppe's* aircraft at the beginning of World War I had been of the A (single-engined unarmed monoplane) and B (single-engined unarmed biplane) types, and had been entirely adequate. In the spring of 1915 this was most decidedly no longer the case, as was proved by the success of the machine-gun armed Morane-Saulnier Type L flown by Roland Garros.

To counter this threat the Fokker firm had by the summer of 1915 developed an adequate machine-gun synchroniser gear, thus allowing a machine-gun to be fitted along the upper decking of the forward fuselage, where it could be aimed by pointing the whole aircraft at the target, and fired through the disc swept by the propeller blades, the synchroniser gear preventing bullets from striking the blades. Such a gear was first installed on the Fokker M5k monoplane, which thus equipped became the Fokker *Eindecker* or E type (single-engined armed monoplane). A dire period for Allied aircraft was about to begin.

At first the E types were allocated singly to *Feldflieger Abteilungen*, but by the late summer of 1915 the Bavarians had formed three *Kampfeinsitzerkommandos* (single-seat fighter units), each with several E-type aircraft. Such groupings became almost standard during the early part of 1916, and did much to improve the overall success rate of the *Eindeckers*. Two of the pilots in the second of the Bavarians' *Kampfeinsitzerkommandos* were later to acquire fame as leading aces – Oswald Boelcke and Max Immelmann.

Right through the war so far, the *Fliegertruppen* had been growing, and in March 1915 totalled seventy-one *Feldflieger Abteilungen*. There was also the *Bombenflug-*

zeuggeschwader der Obersten Heeresleitung (Army High Command Bomber Wing). This was the old BAO, redesignated in March 1915: it had six *Staffeln* (Squadrons) each with six aircraft each. Another unit, similar to the original BAO, and known as the BAM, had been formed at Metz. Then three more *Geschwader* and six independent *Staffeln* had been formed.

After brief lives in this form, all these units were turned into *Kampfgeschwader der Obersten Heeresleitung* or *Kagohl* (Army High Command Battle Wings) Nr 1 to 5. Equipment was of the C type (single-engined armed biplane), and the five *Kampfgeschwader* under OHL's direct control, were shuttled around by train to whichever formation most needed support.

By March 1915 the supply of aircraft to the front was being bottlenecked by the indifferent lines of communications from home offered by the *Etappen Flugzeugparke*, and three of them had been turned into the more efficient *Armee Flugpark* (Army Aviation Supply Depot), with the products of eleven flying schools (twenty by the end of the year) being channelled to the front by three *Flieger Ersatz Abteilungen* (nine by the end of the year). To meet the need for artillery observation officers, four special schools were in operation by the end of 1915.

The nature of the static warfare that had developed since the end of October 1914 placed great emphasis on artillery observation, and the normal growth of these units could not keep pace with demand. Thus fourteen special *Artillerie Flieger Abteilungen*, each with four aircraft, were formed in the second half of 1915. These were allocated to army and corps headquarters, and so successful were they that during 1916 it was hoped to form enough of these units to supply one to each division.

Although there had been classes of aircraft right from the beginning of the war, by the middle of 1915 it was clear that the types needed fell into four broad categories (reconnaissance and observation, infantry support work, aerial fighting and bombing). These four classes were eventually to comprise aircraft of the C; C, CL and J; D and Dr; and G and R types. (C = single-engined armed biplane; CL = light C-type; J = two-seater armoured and armed biplane for infantry support work; D = single-engined, single-seat armed biplane; Dr = single-engined, single-seat armed triplane; G = multi-engined armed biplane; and R = three- to six-engined armed biplane)

Major Thomsen produced at the end of the year suggestions for a slight reorganisation of the *Feldflieger Abteilungen*, designed to develop more of an 'air force'

Opposite page On the back of the truck is the fuselage of a Halberstadt two-seater (probably a C.V) with the fuselage of a French Salmson 2A.2 reconnaissance two-seater under tow.
Below Bombardment during the Battle of the Marne, 1918. German biplane patrolling the forward trenches and British tank in the background.

out of what was at present merely a number of support bodies attached to the higher army formations. Thomsen suggested that the *Abteilungen* be removed from corps command and attached permanently to army high commands.

The advantages were obvious: AOKs would have the ability to call on a substantial number of *Abteilungen* at short notice when necessary, and as armies moved far less frequently than corps, it would allow the same *Abteilungen* to remain on the same sector of the front for longer than had been the case previously, thus making them more efficient. Thomsen also hoped that such an organisation would give his *Stofls* more executive authority. *General* von Falkenhayn, the commander-in-chief, sought the opinion of the AOKs before going further with Thomsen's idea, and when the army commanders said they saw no need for such a re-organisation, von Falkenhayn turned down Thomsen's scheme.

Early in 1916 Thomsen presented another scheme to von Falkenhayn, this time calling for the amalgamation of all flying services into an autonomous third service, but opposition from the military establishment led von Falkenhayn, who was otherwise favourably impressed with Thomsen's idea, into rejecting the plan.

Thomsen realised that in the short term he stood little chance of moving forward with his notions for a third service, and so spent the winter of 1915–16 strengthening his existing organisation as much as possible. Thus by March 1916 there were five *Kagohls* each made up of six *Kampfstaffeln* or *Kastas* (Combat Squadrons) with six C-type aircraft each. Then a sixth *Kagohl*, of three *Kastas*, was formed in April, and in August a seventh *Kagohl* emerged. Improvements in production of aircraft and aircrew during the winter and spring also resulted in the strengthening of other flying units: by August there were some eighty-one *Feldflieger Abteilungen* and forty-five *Artillerie Flieger Abteilungen*. In the same period the number of single-seat fighters in service had risen to about 175, including some of the newer Halberstadt D types, which promised much superior performance to the essentially *ad hoc* Fokker E types.

Farther afield, the *Flieger Abteilung Pascha* had in February been sent off to the Middle East to support the German-Turkish forces in the Sinai, and the first of the giant R-types was undergoing service trials over the Eastern Front with *Riesenflugzeug Abteilung* 500. Tactically, therefore, the German air service was in good shape for the 1916 campaigns, and much was expected of the *Kagohls*, the mobile 'fire brigade' force contain-

Three major leaders of the German air force.

Below right Oberstleutnant Siegert was the *Inspekteur der Fliegertruppe* during one of the German air force's most critical periods. He was responsible for the formation of the post of *Feldflugchef* and the appointment of *Oberstleutnant* von der Lieth-Thomsen, right, to do it. This office became part of the *Kogenluft's* department in 1916, von der Lieth-Thomsen thus becoming *Generalleutnant* von Hoeppner's chief-of-staff. Far right Von Hoeppner was appointed *Kogenluft* in 1915, and with von der Lieth-Thomsen was largely responsible for the growth and reorganization of the German Air Force in 1916–7.

ing some of Germany's ablest aircrew.

The *Kagohls'* test came in February 1916 and the following months during the Battle of Verdun, in which von Falkenhayn hoped to 'bleed France white'. The air forces deployed by Thomsen for the battle included *Kagohl* I and *Kagohl* II, each temporarily strengthened by the addition of two extra *Kastas*; ten *Feldflieger Abteilungen*; six *Artillerie Flieger Abteilungen*; twenty-one Fokker and Pfalz E types, formed into three *Kampfeinsitzerkommandos*; two G types; four airships; and twenty balloons.

Thus at first the German were able to secure air superiority over the Verdun battlefield, the *Kagohls* penetrating deep beyond it to bomb French railway junctions and so cause considerable disruption and damage. Such was the importance of Verdun, however, that the French rushed in every available aircraft and managed to wrest air superiority from the Germans, who had nothing to match the Nieuport 11 *Bébé* fighter. More significantly, the French began to take the air war to the Germans. This meant that the élite *Kagohl* aircrew had to be taken off offensive work to fly patrols over the front line in an effort to prevent French aircraft probing into the German rear areas. The *Kagohls*,

therefore, which had been developed as offensive units, were now used defensively. By April there were four *Kagohls* over Verdun, all in defensive roles and all suffering heavy casualties.

The Battle of Verdun bled the Germans almost as much as the French, and then the Germans had to face a combined British and French offensive on the Somme at the same time as the Russians' great summer offensive directed by General Brusilov.

Outnumbered in the air by something like three to one, the German 2nd Army on the Somme on 1 July 1916 had five *Feldflieger Abteilungen*; four *Artillerie Flieger Abteilungen*; two *Kampfeinsitzerkommandos*; one *Kampfstaffel*; *Kampfgeschwader* 1; and three balloon detachments. Just as important as the Allied numerical superiority, moreover, was the fact that they now deployed superior fighting aircraft, which allowed them to take the air war to the Germans with a vengeance. This should not be construed to mean that the Allies sent their offensive aircraft deep into the German rear areas, but rather that the Allied aircraft had an almost free hand over the German front line areas, playing a considerable part in disrupting life here and supporting Allied infantry attacks.

Reinforcements were needed as quickly as possible by the Germans, and by the end of August the air forces available had increased considerably: seventeen *Feldflieger Abteilungen*; twelve *Artillerie Flieger Abteilungen*; four *Kampfgeschwader*; two *Kampfstaffeln*; and some sixty fighter aircraft. Just as importantly, *Hauptmann* Haehnelt, previously *Stofl* of the 5th Army at Verdun, was appointed *Stofl* of the new 1st Army created on the Somme. His experience of defensive air fighting was to prove invaluable.

The scale of the fighting that continued on the Somme right into October may be gauged by the air strength needed to provide some measure of support to the twenty-five German infantry divisions engaged in the battle: twenty-six *Feldflieger Abteilungen*; twenty *Artillerie Flieger Abteilungen*; thirty-three *Kampfstaffeln*; and four *Jagdstaffeln*.

In August 1916 the German air service had seen important changes in command and structure, however. In the short term, perhaps the most significant of these had been the introduction of the *Jagdstaffeln* or *Jastas* (Fighter Squadrons) to replace the earlier

Kampfeinsitzerkommandos. Oswald Boelcke, one of the early aces and one of the great constructive tactical thinkers of air warfare, had long advocated the formation of such regular fighter units, and received command of the first, *Jasta 2*.

Just before the establishment of the first *Jasta*, the German air service introduced the appointment of *Gruppenführer der Flieger* or *Grufl* (Group Leader of Aviation). Officers holding this title were appointed in corps headquarters, where their tasks were to supervise the tactical use of the flying units attached to the corps in the best possible way. In a way, therefore, the *Grufls* were *Stofls* with executive power.

On the command side, August 1916 saw the departure of *Major* Siegert from the acting office of *Feldflugchef* to become *Inspekteur der Fliegertruppen (Idflieg)*. Here Siegert was to undertake the major task of planning for all the future equipment needs of the German air service or *Luftstreitkräfte*.

So far, the air service had not enjoyed the services of a single commander of general rank, its units being split up into penny packets and allocated to higher army commands, and its tactical and equipment needs being catered for by a number of middle ranking staff officers such as Siegert and Thomsen. In the second half of 1916, though, the army high command felt that the air service had grown so much that it required the services of a commanding officer of some seniority, and accordingly received one on 8 October 1916: *Generalleutnant* Ernst von Hoeppner was appointed *Kommandierenden General der Luftstreitkräfte* or *Kogenluft* (General Commanding the Air Service).

The office of *Feldflugchef* was incorporated into the new appointment, and von Hoeppner thus became responsible for the air services in the field and at home to the army commander-in-chief. *Oberstleutnant* Thomsen became von Hoeppner's chief-of-staff. Thus at last there was a true German air service under single command, although it was still not autonomous. The only elements that did not come under *Kogenluft* command were the naval air service and Bavarian units.

The appointment of von Hoeppner was followed by a wholesale reorganisation of the air service along more rational and centralised lines. First of all, most of the old unit designations disappeared. For a start, the designation *Feldflieger Abteilung* was abandoned in

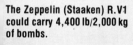

The Zeppelin (Staaken) R.V1 could carry 4,400 lb/2,000 kg of bombs.

favour of *Flieger Abteilung*, and *Artillerie Flieger Abteilungen* were redesignated *Flieger Abteilungen (A)*. Some forty-eight of the new *Flieger Abteilungen* thus appeared, the rest becoming *Flieger Abteilungen (A)*, of which there were thus ninety-three. The number of aircraft in each such unit was raised from four to six.

The *Kagohls* were reduced to three in number, their offensive use being now strictly limited, and they were re-equipped with aircraft of the G type, notably of Friedrichshafen or Gotha manufacture. The reduction of the *Kagohls* meant that there were now a number of surplus *Kastas*, and these were now converted into *Schutzstaffeln* or *Schustas* (Escort Squadrons). Their task was to protect the two-seaters of the *Fleiger Abteilungen (A)* and to attack front-line targets of opportunity.

Finally there were the *Jastas*. These remained essentially unchanged in nature, although it was planned to raise them to thirty in number, each squadron equipped with sixteen D-type single-seat biplane fighters.

The roles of the new units may therefore be defined as follows: the *Flieger Abteilungen* were to carry out reconnaissance over long ranges for army headquarters; the *Fligieger Abteilungen (A)* were to provide support for the infantry, and to offer artillery spotting services; the *Schustas* had the primary task of protecting the *Abteilungen (A)* aircraft, but were also on call from divisional commanders for tactical reconnaissance and artillery observation; the *Jastas* were to eliminate Allied fighters so that the German two-seaters could fulfil their tasks; and the *Kagohls* were to revert to their original role of bombing the enemy rear areas under OHL control. The reorganisation of the air services flying formations along these lines was to be completed by the spring of 1917.

While the actual flying units were being reorganised, the apparatus for their control was also being overhauled. For a start, the office of *Stofl* was replaced by that of *Kommandeur der Flieger* or *Kofl* (Commander of Aviation), who had authority over all flying units attached to his army. Under the *Kofl* came a *Stabsbildabteilung* or *Stabia* (Staff Photographic Unit) to assess the various photographs taken by the army's reconnaissance aircraft. The office of *Grufl* was retained, under the command of the *Kofl*, and worked in liaison with local anti-aircraft artillery and balloon commanders.

This reorganisation, combined with the arrival of new combat aircraft such as the Albatros D.III fighter, enabled the German air service to gain air superiority over the Allies in the spring of 1917 as the German forces made the careful strategic retreat to the 'Hindenburg Line'. But soon after this withdrawal, the Allies

launched a series of major offensives, forcing the German air service onto the defensive. At the same time the United States declared war on Germany, and although an initial panic about the military and industrial strength of the United States was soon followed by a more rational assessment that this strength could not be deployed in Europe until the spring of 1918, the Germans set about building up their forces to meet this future threat.

Kogenluft's ambitious plans were too great for *Idflieg* to meet for production reasons, and so the latter's *Amerika Programm* had to suffice. This allowed for the creation of forty new *Jagdstaffeln* and seventeen more *Flieger Abteilungen (A)*. Although quite a considerable programme in its own right, this was small compared with the production and training problem that would have to be overcome to provide the *matériel* and personnel requirements of the programme. Part of the trouble, excluding the shortages of manpower and raw materials, lay with the fact that the expansion programme of October 1916 had still not been fully implemented in the summer of 1917, despite the fact that it was meant to be completed by the spring.

Above Kaiser Wilhelm II visiting an aviation camp.
Below Fokker D.VIIs. This was almost certainly the best fighter of the war, with good performance, especially at altitude, good manoeuvrability and the ability to 'hang' on its propeller.

The increasing complexity of operations combined with the need for larger formations of aircraft to produce a new type of fighter formation in the summer of 1917. Realising that they had not enough fighters or good pilots to provide first-class protection all along the front, the Germans decided to form large fighter units on a mobile basis. These could then be deployed to the most important sectors of the front as the situation demanded. The first of these formations, *Jagdgeschwader Nr 1*, was formed by amalgamating *Jastas* 4, 6, 10 and 11 under the command of *Rittmeister* Manfred, *Freiherr von Richthofen*, commander of *Jasta* 11 on 23 June 1917. These *Jagdgeschwader* soon became known to the Allies as 'flying circuses'.

Aircraft of the *Flieger Abteilungen (A)* units, which had grown in number from ninety-three to ninety-nine, were increasingly finding themselves involved in direct support work for the ground forces, and gradually became known as *Infanterieflieger (Ifl)*. To meet the requirements of such work, in September 1917 the number of aircraft in each *Flieger Abteilungen (A)* was allowed to increase from six to nine C-type machines. By the end of the year, though, only thirty-seven units had been thus increased.

At about this time the role of the *Schustas* was changed from defense to offense, in the form of ground attack of enemy positions and troops with machine-gun and bomb attack. And to allow an increase in heavy bombing raids on targets such as London, the old *Kastas* were done away with, being replaced by *Bombengeschwader der Obersten Heeresleitung (Bogohl)*, each such formation consisting of three *Bombenstaffeln (Bostas)* with the exception of the main force attacking great Britain, *Bogohl* 3, which had six *Bostas*. By the

beginning of December the OHL thus had seven *Bogohls* with a total of 144 G-type bombers.

Operations continued throughout 1917, with the German air service being gradually outfought by superior Allied numbers. The tactical innovations had been considerable, and would continue to be so during 1918, with the introduction of newer fighters and armoured ground-attack aircraft from the end of 1917 onwards. But it was becoming increasingly apparent that Germany just did not have the manpower and the *matériel* to match Great Britain, France and the United States.

New types, such as the J- and CL-type machines, were entering service, and new fighters, such as the Fokker D VII, were entering service or were under development, but the prospects for 1918 looked poor. The German high command decided that their only chance was a series of co-ordinated blows against France and Great Britain before the full weight of the United States could be brought to bear. This resulted in the five great German spring offensives of 1918, which ultimately failed in their objectives and opened the way for the Allied offensives of late summer and auttmn of 1918 that brought the war to an end.

The winter of 1917–18 was a busy one for *Kogenluft*, his staff and the air service as preparations were made for the spring offensives. By February 1918 there were eighty-one *Jastas*, although many were understrength. On 2 February two new *Jagdgeschwader* were formed: Nr 2 (*Jastas* 12, 13, 15 and 19) under *Hauptmann Ritter von Tutschek*, and Nr 3 (*Jastas* 26, 27, 36 and Boelcke) under Hauptmann Bruno Loerzer.

In March 1918, on the eve of the offensives, the thirty-eight *Schustas* were renamed *Schachtstaffeln* or *Schastas* (Battle Squadrons) as being more appropriate to their offensive roles in the battles to come. *Schastas* were grouped into *Schlachtgruppen* and these latter into *Schlachtgeschwader*. At the same time, an eighth *Bogohl*, made up of Bavarian units, was formed. In March 1918, therefore, the front-line strength of the *Luftstreitkräfte* was 153 *Flieger Abteilungen*, thirty-eight *Schlachtstaffeln*, eighty-one *Jagdstaffeln* and seven (soon eight) *Bombengeschwader*.

Most of these units fought with distinction in the spring offensives, but no matter what their training and equipment, they could not prevail against the Allied overall superiority, despite the fact that time and time again they gained tactical victories. By the middle of the summer the Germans had finally been halted, and from August onwards it was the turn of the Allies. There was nothing that the *Luftstreitkräfte* could do but hamper final Allied victory, signalised by the armistice of 11 November 1918.

Strength of the German Air Service, November 1918

31 *Flieger Abteilungen* with 186 C types
10 *Flieger Abteilungen Lb* with 90 C type photographic reconnaissance aircraft
37 *Flieger Abteilungen (A)* with 333 C types
57 *Flieger Abteilungen (A)* with 342 C types
5 *Flieger Abteilungen (A) Lb* with 30 C type photographic reconnaissance aircraft
6 *Flieger Abteilungen Pascha* with 36 C types
38 *Schlachtstaffeln* with 228 CL types
81 *Jagdstaffeln* with 1,134 to 1,296 D types
8 *Bombengeschwadern* with 162 G types
2 *Riesenflugzeug Abteilungen* with 6 R types
56 *Feldluftschiffer Abteilungen*
186 *Ballonzuge* (Balloon Companies)

There were about 4,500 flying personnel available for these units, and war casualties had totalled 6,840 personnel killed, 7,350 wounded and 1,372 missing, plus 3,128 aircraft, 546 balloons and 26 airships.

CHAPTER TWO

THE FRENCH AIR SERVICES 1900-18

By the time the Wright brothers made the world's first truly successful flight in a heavier-than-air craft on 17 December 1903, like most other modern nations France had considerable experience of military aeronautics, though only with lighter-than air craft such as tethered balloons used for observation purposes. And although some years were to pass after the Wrights' triumph before the French and other European nations began seriously to consider the military application of heavier-than-air craft, it should nonetheless be noted that as early as the last decade of the nineteenth century the French War Ministry had shown sufficient interest in a 'flying machine' designed and built by Clément Ader (whom several eccentric aviation historians still consider to have been the first man to fly) to fund a development. The machine, named Avion III, was tested in 1897 and proved a dismal failure, although it did get off the ground!

Impressed with the rumours about the Wrights' 1905 aircraft, the Flyer III (in reality the world's first truly practical aircraft), the French Minister of War in 1906 sent off a mission to the United States with the object of securing a manufacturing licence for the Wright aircraft. For a number of reasons (one of them the Wrights' increasing desire for secrecy and unwillingness to show off their aircraft) the negotiations were protracted.

In 1908 the Wrights granted production rights to the commercial firm of *Compagnie Générale de Navigation Aérienne*, and it was from this company that the French War Ministry ordered its first machine, a Wright, on 12 July 1909. To a great extent this was in response to public demand that the War Ministry investigate the possibilities of military aviation, especially since Wilbur Wright had travelled to France during the summer of 1908 and there demonstrated the excellence of the Wright biplane compared with contemporary French machines. The purchase of an American machine definitely offended French *amour propre*, however, and it was decided at the same time to look for a French

design. Soon authority had been gained for the additional purchase of two Henry Farman biplanes, a Louis Blériot monoplane and an additional Wright biplane. The aircraft were all delivered in 1910, at about the time that the *Aéro-Club de France*, which controlled aviation in France, established its first regulations for the issue of pilots' licences.

In 1909, military aviation consisted of four army balloon sections, commanded by *Colonel* Hirschauer as part of *Général* Roques' Engineer Corps. Roques was in 1909 given overall command of the fledgling air service and set about finding the necessary pilots and aircrew. As other nations were to find, this was difficult, few commanders finding it easy to part with promising young men to what seemed an unnecessary extravagance with little real future.

The only pilot the French Army had was *Capitaine* Lucas-Girardville, who had been a pupil at the Wright school at Pau in 1908–9. In 1910, however, another ten started training: *Capitaine* Etévé at the Pau school; *Lieutenants* Camerman Sido and Féquant, and *Capitaine* Madiot at the Farman school at Châlons; *Lieutenants* Acquaviva and Bellenger and *Capitaine* Marie at the Blériot school at Pau; and *Lieutenants* Jost and Clavenad at the Antoinette school at Châlons. These novices started training in March 1910, and the first man to qualify was Camerman, who received brevet no. 33 on 7 March. Only a year later did the military start issuing its own brevets, the first going to *Capitaine* Tricornot de Rose on 7 February 1911. Until that time, trainee pilots received 2,500 francs for training at civilian schools.

The first aircraft for the military was the Wright, delivered on 10 June 1910 and test flown by *Capitaine* Etévé. Meanwhile, in August 1909 the world's first great aviation meeting had been held near Béthany, just outside Reims, under the auspices of the French champagne industry. This meeting is of seminal importance to the overall history of aviation, marking as it did the first time that large numbers of aircraft were seen by a

considerable attendance to be capable of sustained and useful flight over a number of days. Roques was present at Bétheny, on the look-out for likely military aircraft, and it was as a result of the meeting that the Farmans and the Blériot were ordered.

Yet something of a split in French military aviation developed here, as the meeting was also attended by a group of French artillery officers, their arm having seen the possibilities of aircraft as a means of spotting for the guns. *Général* Brun, the Minister of War, was then approached, and he authorised the artillery to buy a number of aircraft for experimental purposes. *Commandant* Estienne was appointed head of the *Etablissement d'Aviation* (Aircraft Establishment) set up at Vincennes. The existence of two aviation authorities within the army was bound to present problems, and it was only after a somewhat heated debate in the French Parliament that *Général* Brun put the *Etablissement d'Aviation* under the command of *Général* Roques in the latter's capacity of *Inspecteur-Général de l'Aéronautique Militaire*. This also brought the artillery's flying school, commanded by *Capitaine* Madiot, under the command of the engineer's flying school, commanded by *Lieutenant* Camerman since its establishment at Châlons in April 1910.

All this may be regarded as the truly formative stage of the *Aéronautique Militaire*, a stage which ended on 9 June 1910 with the service's first true cross-country 'reconnaissance' flight: taking off from Châlons at 0430 in a Henry Farman, *Lieutenant* Féquant flew his observer, *Capitaine* Marconnet, the 145 km (90 miles) to Vincennes in some two and a half hours. Although Marconnet had to hang on to his pilot to avoid falling out of the aircraft, a large number of interesting photographs of the route were obtained.

The *Aéronautique Militaire* was now going from strength to strength as was evidenced when Féquant took up *Général* Maunoury, commander of the key XX Corps, for an observation flight of his corps' front along the German border on 10 August. On the same day other aircraft spotted for the guns in an exercise near Nancy, and their corrections enabled far better results than normal to be obtained.

Choosing his moment well, *Général* Roques, supported by *Colonel* Hirschauer, his deputy, requested for aircraft to be used in numbers in the large-scale army manoeuvres planned for the Picardy region in September. Seeing the results gained in the two 10 August operations, the Army High Command agreed, and Roques prepared carefully for the exercise that

could make or break his command. Prominent civilian pilots such as Hubert Latham, Louis Breguet and Louis Paulhan were called up specially for the occasion.

The exercises proved the value of aircraft beyond the greatest hopes of Roques, Hirschauer and their pilots, although only a small number were allocated to the land forces: two Henry Farmans, one Sommer and one Blériot to II Corps; and two Henry Farmans, one Wright and one Blériot to IX Corps.

There were two immediate consequences to the aviation arm's success in the September manoeuvres. Firstly, the arm was allowed to order substantial numbers of new aircraft – twenty Blériots and twenty Henry Farmans. Some seventeen of the Blériots were two-seaters for observation, and all twenty had to be delivered in two months; seven of the Henry Farmans had to be capable of carrying two observers, and all twenty had to be delivered within three months. At the same time, a specification for a new machine was issued: it had to have a payload of 300 kg (661 lbs), possess a radius of action of 300 km (186 miles) and have a maximum speed of 60 km/h (37.3 mph).

Secondly, as a result of pressure from the French senate, the *Aéronautique Militaire* was given semi-autonomy within the army from 22 October 1910, under the command of *Général* Roques, who left the Engineer Corps to take up his official position as *Inspecteur-Général*.

Général Roques was now well placed to implement the two ideas he deemed most important for the future growth along the right lines for the aviation arm: proper flying training by the military for military pilots, and the acquisition of specifically military aircraft to replace the miscellany of civilian types then used. (In October 1910, the equipment of the *Aéronautique Militaire* consisted of the following, with aircraft on order in brackets: Henry Farman 11 (20); Maurice Farman 4 (6); Sommer 4 (6); Voisin 0 (6); Blériot 4 (20); Antoinette 2 (4); Nieuport 0 (3); Tellier 0 (2); Hanriot 0 (2); Breguet 0 (2); and Wright 5 (0). This gave a total of thirty aircraft in service, and seventy-one on order; no less than eleven types were in use.)

First of all came the flying schools, mention of which has been made above. These were formed in various places, and tended to specialise on single types: the *Ecole Militaire d'Aviation* at Pau specialised in Blériots, that at Châlons on Henry Farmans and that at Versailles on Maurice Farmans. At the same time, stringent flying and theoretical examinations were set, and even those who had previously qualified at civilian schools

Above Capitaine Eteve, graduate of the *Ecole Militaire d'Aviation* at Pau.
Below Farman M.F. II 'Shorthorn', derived from the M.F.7 'Longhorn' without forward elevators. Used for bombing and reconnaissance between 1915 and 1917, then as a trainer.

had to 'resit' and pass these if they wished to continue flying. Only thirty-one of the fifty-two pilots on strength in 1910 eventually passed for their military brevets. Civilians were also allowed to qualify in this way, so long as they joined the *Bataillon de Sapeurs-Aérostatiers* (Engineer Aviation Battalion) as reservists.

Of more importance, perhaps, was the *Aéronautique Militaire*'s need for purpose-built military aircraft. To give designers and manufacturers enough time in which to produce aircraft to the specifications issued, the first *concours militaire* was scheduled for October 1911, and the venue was fixed for Bétheny where the great Reims meeting had taken place. The specifications for entries in the *concours* included, apart from the performance parameters already quoted, that both engine and airframe be of French manufacture, that the aircraft should be able to carry a pilot, an observer, and a mechanic if necessary, that the aircraft should be capable of operating from grass fields and the like, and that each type should be capable of easy dismantling and assembly to facilitate transport by road or rail.

As judges for the *concours* were appointed *Général* de Division Roques, *Lieutenant-Colonel* Bouttieaux, *Directeur de Matériel Aéronautique* (Director of the Supply and Maintenance Command), *Lieutenant-Colonel* Estienne, head of the *Etablissement d'Aviation Militaire* at Vincennes, *Colonel* Hirschauer, Roques' deputy and *Commandant des Troupes de l'Aéronautiques*,

Above Voisin Type 4 (LB), with Salmson engine and fitted with a 47 mm Hotchkiss gun, 30 July 1915.
Left Blériot XI Monoplane, the type used in Blériot's Channel crossing of 1909 and by the Italians in Libya.
Right *Général* Roques became *Inspecteur-Général* of the *Aéronautique Militaire*, which was given semi autonomy within the army from 22 October 1910.
Below *Lieutenant-Colonel* Bouttieaux, one of the judges for the *concours militaire*.

plus other army officers and several civil servants. The British War Office sent over three officers as observers. The importance attached to the *concours*, not least by constructors, may be gauged by the fact that 140 aircraft, from forty-three builders, were entered. Yet most of these designs were wildly optimistic, and only thirty-one designs were left for the preliminary tests. These were whittled down to nine for the final trials: two Breguets, two Deperdussins, two Maurice Farmans, a Henry Farman, a Nieuport and a Savary Labor. Adjudged best was the Nieuport flown by Weymann and powered by a 100 hp Gnome rotary engine (this had carried the right payload over the right distance at very nearly double the required speed). Second was the Breguet flown by Moineau and powered by a 130 hp Gnome rotary, with a speed of 95 km/h (59 mph). Third was the Deperdussin flown by Prévost and powered by a 100 hp Gnome rotary, with a speed of 92 km/h

(57 mph). The winners all received financial prizes, and several orders were placed: for ten Nieuports, six Breguets and four Deperdussins. It should be noted here that the French aircraft industry was an especially strong one by the standards of the day. The figures of aircraft (and of engines) produced in 1911, 1912 and 1913 provide good proof of this: 1,350 (1,400) in 1911; 1,425 (2,217) in 1912; and 1,148 aircraft and 146 seaplanes (2,440) in 1913. In the same period over 30,000 propellers, notably breakable items, were built. A fairly large proportion of this output was for export, moreover.

The international crisis centring on France and Germany, as a result of the Agadir incident in the summer of 1911, gave added importance to the French manoeuvres of late summer. These were altered in concept quite considerably, and the two formations involved, VI and VII Corps, now took as their object the screening of the French frontier from an invasion from the east, to provide enough time for the French reserves to be mobilised – a prophetic exercise indeed! *Capitaine* Etévé, commandant of the Versailles flying school, commanded the twenty-five aircraft (ten of them civilian with civilian pilots specially called up) allocated to VI Corps. The VII Corps aircraft were commanded by *Capitaine* Félix, commandant of the Etampes flying school, but his unit's operations were severely hampered by a couple of fatal accidents.

Etévé's aircraft once again proved the utility of aerial reconnaissance, although further lessons had been learned, as *Général* Perruchon reported: reconnaissance machines should be two-seaters, with sturdy construction to allow them to operate from unprepared fields; it was also desirable to provide some type of protection for the aircraft's most vital components (including the crew); if possible flying controls should be duplicated; and it was also considered that to allow the observer to get the most out of his aerial vantage point he should have some form of staff training. These were all moves in the right direction, as was another – the decision to group together into homogeneous units aircraft of any one type. This would facilitate mainten-

ance, and would allow pilots of any one unit to fly any of the unit's aircraft.

These homogeneous units, known as *escadrilles* (squadrons), were first formed early in 1912, with an establishment of six aircraft commanded by a *Capitaine* with the title of *Chef d'escadrille* (Squadron Leader). Each *escadrille* was a self-contained unit, with permanent flying and ground personnel, motor transport and tented hangars.

Each *escadrille* was identifiable by its letter/number designation: thus *Escadrille* D6 was the 6th Squadron, and flew Deperdussin aircraft. Should the squadron then be re-equipped, the letter/number combination would normally alter also. By the middle of 1912 all five *escadrilles* were operational. These were HF1 with Henry Farmans at Châlons, MF2 with Maurice Farmans at Buc flying school, B13 with Blériots at Pau, D4 with Deperdussins at Saint Cyr and MF5 with Maurice Farmans at Saint Cyr as well.

As well as this organisational reshuffle, the *Aéro-*

Above A French air force squadron photographic truck, or mobile dark-room, at the Aviation Camp, St Amand (Aisne), November 1917. *Below* Caudron G.IV reconnaissance and light bombing aircraft, used operationally from 1915 to 1917. This was basically a larger, twin-engined version of the G.3. Caudron G.3/4/6 aircraft served with 40 *escadrilles*.

nautique Militaire also acquired a new head, *Colonel* Hirschauer, in April 1912. This was occasioned by the departure of *Général* Roques to take over command of the 7th Infantry Division. Hirschauer took over command just in time to implement a law passed on 29 March and enacted on 22 August. By this, which further removed the *Aéronautique Militaire* from central army control, the air arm was to be reorganised as three groups: *Groupe* I at Versailles under the command of *Lieutenant-Colonel* Bouttieaux, *Groupe* II at Reims under the command of *Lieutenant-Colonel* Breton, and *Groupe* III at Lyon under the command of *Lieutenant-Colonel* Estienne. These groups were entirely independent of each other, and each had their own logistic and other back-up elements. Each *groupe* was to be based on a number of *centres aéronautiques* where the flying units were to be based. Non-flying personnel were based at these *centres* or at other establishments such as the Chalais Meudon research station or rear area maintenance centres. At the same time as the *groupes* were formed, *Lieutenant-Colonel* Voyer became head of the *Matériel Aéronautique* (Aviation Supply Department), which later became the celebrated *Service des Fabrications de l'Aéronautique* or SFA. Voyer's headquarters were located at Chalais Meudon.

The growing independence of the air arm was also recognised in 1912 by the decision to provide a separate uniform. Hitherto officers had worn the uniforms of their previous corps, but now they were ordered into dark blue tunics with golden winged stars on the collar and golden rank insignia on the sleeves.

Hirschauer had been promoted to the rank of Général de Brigade on 12 December 1912, but was then in 1913 caught in the middle of a dispute between the artillery arm, on one side, and the engineer corps and other arms, on the other, about the ability of the *Aéronautique Militaire* to fulfil its designated tasks. A committee of enquiry, headed by *Général* Bernard, was set up, but in August Hirschauer resigned, to be succeeded by Bernard, although the latter knew nothing whatsoever of aeronautics. Nonetheless, it may fairly be said that Hirschauer had continued Roques' good work in the little time that he had, and had ordered over 400 new aircraft during the first six months of 1913. At the same time new *escadrilles* had been formed, and major air manoeuvres had been held at Agen near Toulouse. To reach this area, squadrons had flown in from all over France, some of them completing notable long-distance flights in the process. The air manoeuvres were notable in themselves, for the standards of aerial reconnaissance were high.

The success of the early reconnaissance flights in metropolitan France had succeeded in arousing the envy of military men in France's overseas possessions, who were plagued by the operations of dissident tribesmen whose movements could well be spotted by reconnaissance aircraft. First off the mark with a request for aircraft was the commander of XIX Corps in Algiers, in October 1910. He wanted the creation of a 'desert air corps', and at about the same time the governor of French West Africa demanded aircraft for operations in this wide-open area. Eventually six aircraft were voted for Algeria, and one of these made its first operational flight on 17 February 1912. The squadron's effect was immediate, and soon other commanders were calling for air support. Squadrons were then based at El Aouina in Tunis, at Biskra in Algeria and at Casablanca and Oujda in Morocco; four aircraft were bought by local residents in West Africa, shipped out there and manned by crews provided by the *Aéronautique Militaire*. Other overseas territories were still calling for aircraft as World War I broke out in August 1914.

Général Bernard called for general mobilisation of the air service soon after the assassination of the Archduke Franz Ferdinand of Austria-Hungary at Sarajevo on 15 June 1914. In a way this over-hasty reaction proved a blessing, for the air service's call-up plans had not been very well worked out, and the early mobilisation allowed time for the inevitable foul-ups to be corrected.

On mobilisation, the *Aéronautique Militaire* could field some twenty-one *escadrilles* of two-seaters: MF2, 5, 8, 16 and 20 with Maurice Farman biplanes; HF1, 7,

13 and 19 with Henry Farman biplanes; V14 and 21 with Voisin biplanes; C11 with Caudron G2 biplanes; Br17 with Breguet biplanes; B9, 10, 13 and 18 with Blériot XI monoplanes; D4 and 6 with Deperdussin monoplanes; REP15 with Esnault-Pelterie monoplanes; and N12 with Nieuport monoplanes. There were also two 'cavalry' *escadrilles*, BL C2 and BL C5, each equipped with three single-seat Blériot monoplanes.

The first-line strength of the *Aéronautique Militaire* at the end of July 1914 was then some 132 aircraft. Between 3 and 15 August, though, another five *escadrilles* were formed with reserve aircraft and others awaiting export. These were DO22 with Dorand biplanes destined for Russia; MS23 with Morane-Saulnier Type L parasol-wing monoplanes; V24 with Voisin biplanes; C25 with Caudron biplanes and MS26 with Type Ls. There had been 136 reserve machines available, so the removal of aircraft for these new *escadrilles* was of little importance. More importantly, though, *Général* Bernard thought that the war would be over quickly, and so towards the end of August closed down all the flying schools, posted the instructors to *escadrilles* and all groundcrew to infantry units. Moreover, he had decided that no more new aircraft would be ordered. Luckily for France and for the Allies, there were others who saw the fallacy of Bernard's actions.

Reconnaissance was the primary mission of the *escadrilles*, and to this end strategic flights were flown by the units attached to the information centres at Maubeuge, Mézières, Verdun, Toul, Belfort and Epinal, as well as other intermediate centres. The remaining *escadrilles*, meanwhile, were attached to army and corps headquarters to provide tactical reconnaissance. Soon the information began to flow in, and staff officers who had only peace-time experience began to grapple with the real problems of wartime intelligence gathered by a new means. Yet the results were encouraging and greater things could be expected.

By 1 October 1914 the *Aéronautique Militaire* had expanded to thirty-one reconnaissance units and three *escadrilles de cavalerie*. Yet important changes were in the wind, for the key information provided by aircraft during the 1st Battle of the Marne in September, in which the German advance had finally been halted and turned back, had persuaded *Général* Joffre, the French commander-in-chief, of the great role aircraft could play. Accordingly he summoned *Commandant* Barès, who had featured in the development of military aviation in North Africa, and instructed him on 25 September to set about preparing a reorganization and expansion programme for the *Aéronautique Militaire*.

Barès had for some time been considering such a programme, and was thus able to move quickly: by 8 October he had won Joffre's consent to a programme for sixty-five *escadrilles*. Although this would be only a small advance in numbers (hampered by Bernard's blunderings), it was advanced in other ways. For Barès had realised that aircraft could play other roles, and so ordered his scheme to provide sixteen *escadrilles de chasse* (fighter squadrons), thirty *escadrilles de corps d'armée* (corps squadrons, which would undertake reconnaissance and artillery spotting missions) and sixteen *escadrilles de bombardement* (bombing squadrons). There were also to be three *escadrilles de cavalerie*. Barès realised that specialised aircraft were needed for the three types of squadron, and fixed on the Morane-Saulnier Type L as the fighting aircraft, the Voisin as the bomber, and the remainder as reconnais-

sance/spotter aircraft.

Barès' programme highlighted several deficiencies in the air service's high command, and on 11 October Bernard was replaced as head of the service by *Général* Hirschauer, who was to hold this post until September 1915. Hirschauer immediately set about undoing some of Bernard's work, and ordered 2,300 aircraft plus 3,400 engines. He also encouraged the French aero industry to expand, and this is reflected in the immediate increase in production of aircraft (and engines): 100 (157) in October, 137 (209) in November and 192 (304) in December. Hirschauer also set about improving links between the *Section du Service aéronautique au Grand Quartier Général* (the air service liaison department at General Headquarters), headed by *Colonel* Voyer, an airship officer with little experience of heavier-than-air operations, and the aviation sections attached to the various army headquarters. At the same time, *Colonel* Stammler had been trying to speed up the supply of new aircraft to forward units, despite Bernard's restrictions.

Barès' work was to a certain extent forestalled, it should be noted, by the formation of the first French bomber group on 27 September. This contained three squadrons, V14, V21 and Br17, the last of which changed over to Voisin aircraft and was then redesignated. The SFA had meanwhile been evacuated to Lyon because of the German threat to Paris, but the factories in the capital continued to work flat out, deliveries to the squadrons increasing rapidly. Thus by October the French had reorganised their air service into specialised units by October, and the new era in air warfare was recognised when *Sergent* Frantz and *Caporal* Quénault in a Voisin of V24 shot down a German aircraft on 5 October – the first time an airborne aircraft had shot down another machine. Meanwhile new pilots were once again beginning to arrive from the flying schools that Hirschauer had reopened at Pau and Avord.

The beginning of 1915 was marked for the French air service by the formation of new bomber formations *(groupes de bombardement)*, each made up of three or more bomber *escadrilles*. The best known of these was GBI commanded by *Capitaine* de Göys, which flew a number of important missions into Germany.

Hirschauer, meanwhile, was trying with his staff to improve the equipment with which the now correctly organised air service had to fight. A new department was organised with the SFA, dealing with the whole question of armaments and weapons. At the same time a team was sent to Spain to try to acquire a building licence for his new engine from Marc Birkigt. This was eventually to win great fame as the Hispano-Suiza. But there were also outside pressures on Hirschauer, notably from the armed forces committee of the French parliament, which wished to see a specification for a heavy bomber. This finally emerged as a requirement for a machine capable of carrying 300 kg (661 lbs) at 120 km/h (74.6 mph) at 2,000 m (6,562 ft) over a radius of action of 600 km (372.8 miles). It was also decided that in future that armament for French aircraft should be of British manufacture – Vickers and Lewis guns. The pressures from outside the service failed to decline, though, and Hirschauer thus felt himself obliged to resign, his duties being assumed from 13 September 1915 by René Besnard, the Under Secretary for Military Aviation. This was not a happy choice, one of Besnard's worst decisions being that to divide the SFA into two parts. This caused no end of administrative

Left The Letord 5 bomber was one of a family of aircraft designed by *Colonel* Dorand of the STA, all with backward stagger of the wings. None was very successful.
Top Refuelling a Letord bomber.

problems, principally because Besnard's appointment was largely the result of a pro-artillery faction. Yet attempts to run the air service in the same way as the artillery were a dismal failure.

Before his departure, Hirschauer had supervised an expansion scheme (that of 6 July to 2 August 1915) whereby the air service was to grow to 119 *escadrilles*: fourteen of fighters, fifty of bombers (each *escadrille* having ten aircraft) and the rest reconnaissance/spotter *escadrilles*. A revision of 24 August provided for each corps squadron to have nine instead of six aircraft, and for one fighter to be allocated to each such unit for escort work.

In a programme of 21 November, Besnard called for the introduction of several new types, including the *type*

omnibus (all-purpose aircraft) by the spring of 1916. This was patently impossible, and Besnard's programme was investigated on 10 and 11 January 1916 by a conference headed by *Général* de Castelnau, army chief-of-staff. The conference roundly condemned many of Besnard's ideas, Besnard resigning on 8 February 1916. It decided that the *type omnibus* should be persevered with, but that more time should be allocated, and that the number of *escadrilles de combat* (as the fighter units were designated) should be raised to fifty.

Unfortunately, the resignation of Besnard and the abolition of the post he had held produced little improvement, his successor as head of the air service being *Colonel* Régnier, his erstwhile deputy. On

Régnier's assumption of power, the air service could muster some 1,149 aircraft (135 fighters, 826 corps aircraft and 188 bombers). Unfortunately, most of these were obsolescent, and with the opening of the Battle of Verdun on 21 February 1916, the only modern unit in the air service was the special fighter 'circus' created by *Commandant* Tricornot de Rose. This drew on other fighter *escadrilles* for their best pilots, and gradually *Les Cicognes* (the Storks) became France's most celebrated fighter force. At Verdun it was equipped with the neat little Nieuport 11 *Bébé* sesquiplane fighter that had just entered service and was proving more than a match for the otherwise invincible Fokker *Eindecker*.

During February it was also realised that all was not well with the aircraft procurement department, the SFA. In a reorganisation, the SFA had its tasks redefined as control of quantity production of aircraft types already chosen for service. The question of which aircraft and equipment should be chosen for service became the province of a new department, the *Section Technique de l'Aéronautique* (STAé). On 28 February 1916 *Commandant* Dorand, head of the research establishment at Chalais Meudon, became head of the STAé, and in May *Commandant* Raibaud was replaced as head of the SFA by *Lieutenant-Colonel* Stammler. Stammler was in turn replaced by *Commandant* Guiffart in February 1917, and Guiffart by *Commandant* Guignard on 8 August 1917. Both Guiffart and Guignard were able men.

After the Verdun battles there followed the equally

The Nieuport 17 appeared in service in March 1916, and was the definitive development of the Nieuport 11, with a synchronised gun.

Spad XIII

Type: single-seat fighter.
Engine: one Hispano-Suiza vee-8
water-cooled.
Dimensions: span 26 ft 6 in or 26 ft 10½ in
(8.20 m); length 20 ft 4¼ in or 20 ft 8 in (6.30 m);
height 7 ft 8½ in or 7 ft 11¼ in (2.42 m).
Weights: empty, typical, 1,255 lb (570 kg); max.
loaded 1,808–1,862 lb (820–845 kg).
Performance: max. speed 138 mph (220 km/h);
initial climb 1,500 ft (6,650 m); range 185–220
miles (300–350 km).

The Spad XIII, built in greater numbers than
any other Allied fighter, equipped 81 French
fighter squadrons, was the main type used by
16 pursuit squadrons of the American
Expeditionary Force in France, and later built
in vast numbers by Curtiss in the US. The
machine was a superlative fighter.
The illustration shows it in the markings of
SPA.15.

Above The Aviation Camp Villacoublay. The aircraft on the left is a Morane-Saulnier MS 30.E1. This was the trainer version of the MS Types 27C.1 and 29C.1 fighters, which served only at the end of 1917 and beginning of 1918 because of structural problems.

grisly 1st Battle of the Somme. During the course of this, *Capitaine* Brocard, who had fought with *Les Cicognes* (N3) at Verdun, formed the *Groupe de Combat* 12. This included N3, and soon acquired the illustrious reputation of this component, the whole *groupe* acquiring the soubriquet *Les Cicognes*. Such was the success of GC12 under the command of Brocard, promoted to commandant for his pains, that another *groupe*, GC13, was formed in the autumn under the command of *Capitaine* d'Harcourt.

It is worth noting that at this time a number of excellent new machines were entering service. Amongst these were the Nieuport 17 and Spad 7 fighters. Production and administrative problems were on the decline, but *Colonel* Régnier was not deemed fit to head the air service by the Minister of War, *Général* Lyautey, who ordered Régnier's supersession by *Général* Guillemin on 10 February 1917. Despite the opposition of *Général* Nivelle, the army commander-in-chief, Lyautey also wished to see the departure of *Commandant* Barès as *Chef du Service Aéronautique au Grand Quartier Général*, although Barès had much to his credit, including the formation of the first bomber *groupes*. Nonetheless Barès went on 15 February, and the air service was fortunate in that his replacement was *Commandant* du Peuty, an able and popular man who was a well-known fighter pilot and latterly head of the 10th Army's aviation department. The subsequent

scandal about these and other interferences in aviation matters was a considerable one, forcing Lyautey to resign. Soon afterwards the whole cabinet also resigned.

Luckily, the new cabinet enjoyed the services of Daniel Vincent, an ex-member of the air service who was appointed Under Secretary for Aviation on 20 March 1917. Vincent realised that the most important problem facing him was that of speeding up the introduction of newer combat types by the fast elimination of older types from production lines, and the securing of good types no matter what their country of origin. Vincent settled down to both these tasks with a will, and soon newer types began to emerge in quantity from the factories. The major 'foreign' type he selected for French use was the British Sopwith 1½-Strutter, an excellent single-seat bomber or two-seat escort fighter and reconnaissance machine. The Spad 13 fighter and Breguet 14 bomber were also selected for large-scale production. But that things were already moving in the right direction is indicated by the fact that production had risen from 832 aircraft in January 1917 to 1,225 in February.

After a disastrous ground offensive in April 1917, *Général* Nivelle was replaced as commander-in-chief by *Général* Pétain, who like his predecessor saw a change in the *Chef du Service Aéronautique au GQG*. On 17 August 1917 du Peuty was replaced by *Colonel* Duval. Vincent, meanwhile, was making great strides

Left The Breguet XIV, which in 1916 was an advanced prototype, having the engine in front, was constructed largely of the new light alloy Duralumin, had automatic flaps on the lower wing and a general performance far ahead of other French bombers.

French Air Force units, November 1918

10 *groupes de bombardement* (GB1 to 10), of which GB1, 2, 7, 8 and 10 were night bomber units, and GB3, 4, 5, 6 and 9. Night bomber equipment was the Farman F50, Caproni Ca 3 and Voisin 10; day bomber equipment was the Breguet Br14.

13 *groupes de combat* (GC11 to 23) of which GC14 to 21 each had five *escadrilles* and the rest four. All the GCs had Spad fighters as their primary equipment; the bomber-escort units had Caudron R11 twin-engined three-seat fighters.

12 independent fighter *escadrilles*.

124 observation *escadrilles* and twenty-four artillery observation *escadrilles* equipped with Breguet Br14 (forty *escadrilles*), Salmson 2 (forty-eight *escadrilles*), Spad 11 or 16 (twenty-nine *escadrilles*), Caudron R11 (two *escadrilles*) and Voisin Bn2 (five *escadrilles*) aircraft.

with the production services, reducing the friction between SFA and STAé and increasing production rates through careful control and encouragement.

Tricornot de Rose, who had seen the need for fighter units, and had formed the first such squadron, had been killed in an accident on 2 May 1915, but would have been glad to see the situation in the summer of 1917. There were now five *groupes de combat*, most of them equipped with the new Spad fighters. These *groupes* were playing an important role against the German air service.

Despite the successes of his tenure of office, Vincent did not last long, being replaced on 11 September 1917 by Jacques Dumesnil. But Duval was still at GQG, and Pétain took great heed of his advice. Luckily this was sound, and 1917 thus saw a considerable increase in the size of the *Aéronautique Militaire*, which had some 2,263 aircraft at the beginning of the year. Pétain's programme called for an air service of 2,870 aircraft, organised into sixty fighter *escadrilles* each with fifteen aircraft, twenty bomber *escadrilles* each with fifteen aircraft, 100 *escadrilles* of reconnaissance and observation machines, forty artillery-spotting *escadrilles* and eight special-purpose *escadrilles*. In the event, Pétain's target was exceeded, the *Aéronautique Militaire* deploying some 3,556 aircraft early in August. Despite this, a meeting of the War Committee of the cabinet on 8 October called for increased production yet again, and

also insisted on a specification for a new heavy bomber, both the Sopwith and Voisin types in production seeming inadequate.

November once again saw the onset of confusion when an order in council once again altered the role of the SFA, which was now neatly caught between dual responsibilities to the Under Secretary for Aviation on one side, and to the Armament Ministry on the other. At the beginning of 1918, though, rationality won, and the SFA and STAé were united. Plans for 1919 production were laid, and in the short term the development and introduction of the latest combat types were much improved by the closer cooperation of the SFA and STAé.

From the tactical point of view there were also improvements to the air service forces in the field. Up to 1918 the largest air formation had been the *groupe* of three or four *escadrilles*. There was now introduced the *escadre* (wing) to replace the earlier *groupe*. The *escadres* were in turn part of two major formations known as *groupements*, commanded by *Commandant* Ménard and *Commandant* Féquant and named after their commanders. Thus *Groupement* Ménard contained the *Escadre de Combat* No 1, with three *groupes* each of four Spad 13-equipped *escadrilles*, and the *Escadre de Bombardement de jour* No 17 with three *groupes* each of three Breguet 14-equipped *escadrilles* — a total of twelve fighter and nine day bomber squadrons under single command. *Groupement* Féquant had the *Escadre de Combat* No 2 with twelve fighter *escadrilles*, and the *Escadre de Bombardement* No 13 with six bomber *escadrilles*. Each fighter *groupe* had sixty aircraft, and the bomber *groupes* forty-five each. After 18 April 1918 these *groupements* were deployed together as a *Division Aérienne* under the command of Colonel Duval. This formation played a significant part in the battles that finally brought World War I to a conclusion with the armistice of 11 November 1918.

During the course of the war, the French aero industry had produced no fewer than 52,146 aircraft and 92,386 engines, of which 9,300 aircraft and 24,500 engines had been exported. Having started the war with 132 front-line aircraft, the French air service ended it with 3,222 deployed amongst the fighting *escadrilles*. The fighter arm alone numbered some 1,212 aircraft in sixty-six fighter and four escort *escadrilles* in France; eight home-defence units in France, one in Venice and one in Corfu; two fighter *escadrilles* were serving with the French Army in the Balkans, and one each with the Serbian and Greek armies.

CHAPTER THREE

THE BRITISH AIR SERVICES 1900·1918

The Sopwith Pup, perhaps the most delightful of the World War I aircraft to handle.

Early model of the Bristol Boxkite, one of the first British production aircraft.

Active British interest in military aviation reaches back as far as 1878, when the War Office allowed £150 in its budget for the purchase of a balloon for experimental observation purposes. Trials were encouraging, and in 1884 a balloon unit was set up within the basic Army structure. Thereafter the balloon enjoyed some measure of success and popularity as a means of observation in a number of late Victorian colonial wars and police actions. The success of the balloon was marked in 1892 by the permanent establishment of the balloon depot and factory, set up in 1883, at Aldershot, the 'home' of the British Army.

Despite this 'permanent establishment', in 1894 a Balloon Factory was set up at South Farnborough, near Aldershot, to make and repair the Army's lighter-than-air craft. At the turn of the century the balloon was supplemented as a means of observation by man-lifting kites, an idea devised by 'Colonel' S. F. Cody, an expatriate American. The kites were also built at the Balloon Factory, and in the first years of the twentieth century reached a fair peak of aerodynamic efficiency.

So impressed was Cody with the success of his kites, indeed, that he became convinced that the provision of control surfaces and motive power could turn the type into an aircraft. Hampered by lack of resources, Cody nonetheless persevered, being given considerable encouragement and support by Colonel J. E. Capper, Superintendent of the Balloon Factory since 1906. (Convinced of the value of the Wright brothers' work, Capper had in 1904 visited the United States to ask the brothers to work in Great Britain, but the Wrights' caution and Treasury parsimony brought Capper's endeavours to nought.) Cody was, to say the least, individualistic in his approach to flight, but was by 1908 making a number of experimental flights over Laffan's Plain at Farnborough in a machine of ungainly strength.

Whereas Cody enjoyed little financial help from the British authorities, Lieutenant J. W. Dunne of the Wiltshire Regiment had the fortune to receive slightly more support from the Treasury. Dunne had developed an interest in flight after being invalided home from the Boer War in 1900, and had evolved a fascinating design for an inherently stable flying wing aircraft by 1906. The British authorities were sufficiently impressed with Dunne's work and efforts 'which are of a highly scientific nature' to give him half a guinea a day extra money when he was actually at work on his aircraft. To prevent other powers getting to know of Dunne's work, though, he had to work in civilian clothes and preserve the utmost secrecy about the reasons for his attachment to the Balloon Factory. Dunne's first aircraft was tested in 1907, but so low was the power produced by its two engines that it failed to fly.

The third aircraft was tested in 1908, but as the Army refused to provide funds for enough linen to cover both the upper and lower surfaces of the wings, this aircraft too was a failure. Yet the soundness of Dunne's concepts was amply proved by his gliders, which made a number of successful flights piloted by Lieutenant L. D. L. Gibbs. Amongst the War Office's efforts to keep the whole programme secret was a provision for Dunne to test his machines in the highlands of Scotland, at the Duke of Atholl's estate at Blair Atholl. Naturally enough, the Army's heavy-handed security efforts had the effect of arousing intense interest amongst the Germans and others.

In April 1909, though, support for both Cody's and Dunne's efforts was cut off as the War Office 'had decided to cease making any experiments with aeroplanes as the cost had proved too great'. So far, the money spent on the two main experimenters' efforts had amounted to some £2,500; it is interesting to note that by this time Germany had spent some £400,000 on military aviation, and was currently preparing to expand her programme. France, too, had spent a great deal of money, supplied by the government or raised by public subscription.

Only three months after this absolute decision by the British Army, Louis Blériot flew his Type XI monoplane across the Channel, and the world came alight with the implications of the feat. Few thinking men in Great Britain could ignore the fact that Blériot's flight, in what was after all an undeveloped aircraft, heralded the effective end of Britain's insularity; yet both the War Office and Admiralty managed to do so. Airship programmes, such as those that had produced the army's *Nulli Secundus* in 1907 and the Navy's R.1 or *Mayfly* in 1911, were continued, but no further funds were allocated to heavier-than-air flight. It should be noted in the military establishments' favour, though, that they both kept a fairly close eye on continental developments in the field.

At this stage the further development of heavier-than-air military aviation owes an enormous debt to three officers of the Royal Field Artillery: Lieutenant Gibbs already mentioned in connection with Dunne's experiments, and who had subsequently learned to fly at the Farman school at Châlons; Captain Bertram Dickson, who had a Farman biplane; and Captain J. D. B. Fulton, who had a Blériot. In 1910 Dickson left the Army to join the British and Colonial Aeroplane Company (later Bristol), which had arranged for some of its aircraft to cooperate with the Army during the manoeuvres of September 1910. Despite the scepticism of the majority of Army officers, Dickson and Robert Loraine, flying Bristol Boxkites , and Gibbs flying his Farman made some useful reconnaissance flights. Loraine also had some success with radio experiments.

As a result of these manoeuvres, in October 1910 the War Office decided to 'enlarge the scope of the work hitherto carried out at the Balloon School ... by affording opportunities for aeroplaning'. By this time the Balloon School, part of the Royal Engineers, had been separated from the Balloon Factory. Colonel Capper continued in command of the school, and Mr. Mervyn O'Gorman became Superintendent of the factory. In fact it was at the factory that this fresh impetus towards heavier-than-air flight began to gather momentum, O'Gorman forming a design department under Frederick Green, an eminent car engineer.

Despite the fact that design was prohibited by the War Office, work got under way, spurred on in December by the arrival of Geoffrey de Havilland, whose unsuccessful first aircraft O'Gorman had been allowed to buy for £400. From this time on the factory began to produce original aircraft by means of the expedient of telling the War Office that these aircraft were merely extensive reconstructions of damaged aircraft that had been sent to the factory for repair.

During 1910 the War Office had also built an aircraft shed at Larkhill on Salisbury Plain. This was to be the base of the Hon. C. S. Rolls for the teaching of army officers to fly. In July, however, Rolls was killed when the tailplane of his Wright biplane collapsed in the air during an air display at Bournemouth, and the shed became the 'property' of Captain Fulton. Despite an edict that 'The Government were not as yet prepared to undertake any large expenditure upon aeroplanes; ... they had been advised by the Committee of Imperial Defence that the experiments with aeroplanes ... should be discontinued, but that advantage should be taken of private enterprise in this branch of aeronautics.'

In effect, this meant that officers could learn to fly at their own or others' expense, and this is exactly the service that Fulton provided, supported by Mr. G. B. Cockburn. The Navy was even more stingy with its money, and it was only because Mr. Francis McClean lent two aircraft, and Cockburn the training skills, that one Marine and three Navy officers learned to fly.

Such progress was being made with military aeronautics on the other side of the Channel, however, that in 1911 the War Office was at last prodded into positive action: on 28 February 1911 an Army Order was issued, creating with effect from 1 April the Air Battalion of the Royal Engineers, under the command of Major Sir Alexander Bannerman. The battalion was divided into two companies; No 1, under the Captain E. M.

Maitland, controlled airships, and No 2, under Captain Fulton, was responsible for aircraft. The initial equipment of the Aeroplane Company was one Blériot, one Wright, one Farman, one disastrous Paulhan and one FE 1. By the summer the Aeroplane Company had six Bristol Boxkites , the Farman, the Wright and another Blériot.

The Army's autumn manoeuvre of 1911 was cancelled, but the Aeroplane Company received permission to test its capabilities in the area of East Anglia designated for the manoeuvres. The whole exercise was a disaster, with four aircraft being written off, and only two getting to the exercise area and back in one piece. Such a fiasco was just what the War Office had been fearing, but such was the concern now being felt because of the great strides being made by French and German military aviation that in November 1911 the standing committee of the Committee for Imperial Defence debated the 'measures which might be taken to secure this country an efficient aerial service'. The conclusion reached was that a unified air service should be formed.

At the same time, the indifferent performance of several types that had taken part in the 'manoeuvres' fiasco led the Army to a decision that the new air service's aircraft should be of Army Aircraft Factory (as the Balloon Factory had just been redesignated) design. For here the aerodynamics of an inherently stable observation and reconnaissance machine were under investigation by the powerful intellects of Green, de Havilland and Edward Busk. At the time inherent stability seemed an admirable goal, but luckily the decision to equip the air service with such aircraft was never fully implemented, and the unstable (and therefore manoeuvrable) aircraft needed in combat were thus

Top The first two RFC squadrons sent to France, numbers 2 and 4, flew B.E. 2a aircraft and arrived on 13 August 1914. The observer occupied the front cockpit. *Above* Morane-Saulnier Type N fighter with deflector plates, used by 4 squadrons of RFC 1914–16.

Above   The Sopwith Snipe was the first production fighter to have electric heating and oxygen as standard equipment.

able to come to the fore after some early losses.

The recommendation of the standing committee of the Committee of Imperial Defence that a unified air service should be set up was strengthened by British fears of German aggressive intentions, especially after the Agadir incident of July 1911, settled by treaty in November. Germany, it was noted, had a large air service equipped with appreciable numbers of airships and aircraft; the British, on the other hand, had only 11 airmen in the Army and eight in the Navy, with only a few airworthy aircraft and two worn-out experimental airships. The prime minister, Herbert Asquith, had been instrumental in calling for the report, and now accepted its findings. Accordingly, on 13 April 1912 the Royal Flying Corps was established by Royal Warrant; an Army Order of 15 April set up the regulations under which the new corps would operate; and on 13 May the Air Battalion and its reserves were absorbed into the Royal Flying Corps. Allocated as an initial budget by Parliament was the sum of £308,000.

The Royal Flying Corps consisted of a Military Wing and a Naval Wing, a Reserve, the Royal Aircraft Factory (the Army Aircraft Factory renamed) at Farn-

Left   The Avro 504 started its long life as a reconnaissance aircraft. On the 21 November 1914, it was used by the RNAS to attack the Zeppelin sheds at Friedrichshafen, destroying one airship. Later in the war it was used as a trainer, in which role it continued until the 1930s.
Opposite page   The air force has always had a glamorous image which this early RAF recruitment poster helped to promote.

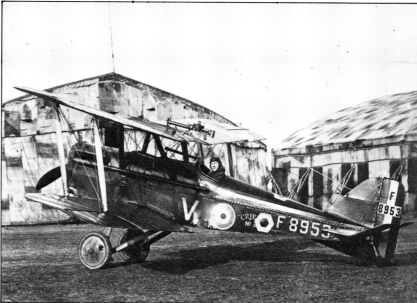

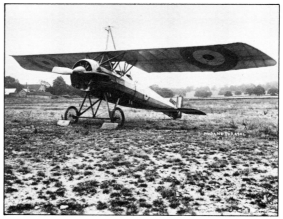

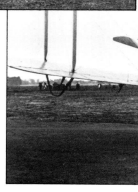

Above S.E.5A Scouts of 85 Squadron, at St Omer Aerodrome, 21 June 1918.
Top right S.E.5A with 200 hp Wolseley Viper engine. Britain's counterpart to the Spad fighters, these were fast, sturdy and had a good gun platform.
Above right The Morane 'Parasol' monoplane.

borough, and a Central Flying School to be established for the training of pilots for both wings. The Naval Air Service had been disbanded in January 1912 after the disaster to the navy's airship R.1 in the previous September, and so the Naval Wing at first had only twenty-two officers. It was a naval officer, Captain Godfrey Paine, who became the first commander of the Central Flying School. It should be noted, though, that the Navy also kept its own flying school at Eastchurch, and soon developed a fine disdain for the Army side of this joint service. Indeed, the official title of the Royal Flying Corps, Naval Wing, was almost never used, the naval element preferring to call their half of the corps the Royal Naval Air Service.

Thus the Royal Flying Corps became, almost from the moment of its inception, a military rather than a joint military/naval formation. The Military Wing's first commander was Captain F. H. Sykes, with Lieutenant B. H. Barrington-Kennett as his adjutant. The War Office had decided that the establishment of the Military Wing should be seven squadrons, each consisting of thirteen aircraft (twelve flown by the ordinary squadron pilots, of which there should be two to each aircraft, and the last by the squadron commander). The Reserve was to be equal in size to the Active strength, and so the Military Wing needed 364 pilots. Naturally enough, the provision of so many pilots was at first impossible, and so the Military Wing grew as the supply of pilots from the Central Flying School allowed. At first the War Office was in favour of having half the pilots commissioned, and the other half non-

commissioned, but for a variety of reasons, not all of them valid, it was later decided that all pilots should be officers. The decision was reversed during World War I.

No 1 Squadron operated the army's airships. No 2 Squadron was commanded by Captain C. J. Burke, Royal Irish Regiment, and had the officers and men stationed at Farnborough as its personnel. No 3 Squadron was commanded by Captain R. Brooke-Popham, and had the officers and men of Larkhill as its personnel. Thus at first there were only two aircraft squadrons: No 4 was formed from a flight of No 2 in September 1912; No 5 out of a flight of No 3 in August 1913; and Nos 6 and 7 were formed in 1914. No 1 became an aircraft squadron in May 1914, when the Royal Flying Corps handed over its airships to the Royal Naval Air Service.

A notable entry into the Royal Flying Corps at this stage, in July 1912, was Captain Hugh Trenchard. At the time Trenchard was working out his last few years of service in a staff job, but then discovered that he could join the Central Flying School if he got a civilian licence. This he managed to do, and after a bit of chicanery involving passing himself for his military 'wings' by using his appointment as Station Staff Officer to set and invigilate his own examinations, Trenchard was appointed Assistant Commandant of the Central Flying School in September 1913. It was a strange start for a man destined to be one of the great formative influences in the service.

The question of aircraft for the Royal Flying Corps

Right Sopwith Camels of the 45 Squadron at an aerodrome. This was Britain's most successful World War I fighter, scoring 1,294 victories. Production totalled 5,490.
Below The de Havilland D.H.9, an unsuccessful development of the D.H.4, was quickly replaced in production by the D.H.9A.

was a pressing one, and in August 1912 there were held at Larkhill the first British Military Aircraft Trials. Because of friction between the Royal Aircraft Factory and the British civilian aircraft industry, the latter claiming that the former was trying to establish a monopoly of aircraft built for the government, none of the Royal Aircraft Factory's designs was allowed to fly in the trials, which were won by the Cody Military Trials Biplane.

Flying *hors concours*, however, the Royal Aircraft Factory's BE 2 had put up such remarkable performances that it was selected for series production, whereas only two of the Cody biplanes were ordered. The BE 2 had been designed by de Havilland, and another designer to make something of a reputation for himself at the military trials if not before was Alliott Verdon Roe, of the Avro company. (The Royal Aircraft Factory had, in its early days, adopted a singular system of nomenclature in order to help disguise the fact that it was developing new types: thus the BE series was of Blériot Experimental aircraft, supposedly rebuilt Blériots, FEs were Farman Experimentals, REs were Reconnaissance Experimentals and SEs were Scouting Experimentals.)

On the whole, in the period up to the beginning of World War I, the Royal Flying Corps opted for aircraft of Royal Aircraft Factory origins, whereas the Royal Naval Air Service went for the designs of private companies such as Short Brothers and Sopwith.

Right from the beginning, the Royal Flying Corps found itself in an experimental situation – there just

were no guidelines for what it was to do, other than act as a reconnaissance force for the army. Thus the way was open for all manner of enterprising men to develop and test out theories of how aircraft could be used, improved and co-ordinated with the conventional ground forces. So diverse were the efforts of individuals, though, that in 1913 it was decided to create an Experimental Branch of the Royal Flying Corps. This was established in March, under the command of Major Herbert Musgrave, with the tasks of investigating kiting, ballooning, radio, photography, meteorology, bombing and artillery spotting. In the fields of radio and photography, in particular, Musgrave and his staff made great strides, but it needed the stimulus of war to create the right type of light radio equipment for aircraft, making spotting for the artillery a reliable, fast and accurate means of bringing down heavy fire on the enemy.

The Army manoeuvres of 1912 and 1913 inevitably produced the greatest opportunities for practical tests on the various ideas devised and worked out in basic form. No 3 Squadron, for example, concentrated on artillery spotting. But without practical radio communication with the artillery on the ground, the squadron had to try other methods of communication – written messages dropped to the ground forces, flags, coloured Véry lights and the like. Progress was made, but all concerned realised that these were only extemporised methods.

Brooke-Popham's No 3 Squadron also excelled in the 1912 manoeuvres in the field of reconnaissance, enabl-

Top R.E.8 reconnaissance and light bomber aircraft. This has been unjustly condemned for its losses, though the type performed well in its intended role, serving with 19 squadrons in 1918.
Above The Martinsyde F.4 Buzzard was Britain's fastest fighter of the war, but only 52 had been delivered by the time of the armistice.

The Sopwith Triplane N500 type

Type: single-seat fighting scout.
Engine: one 130 hp Clerget 9B nine-cyl. rotary
Dimensions: span 26 ft 6 in (8.08 m); length 18 ft
10 in (5.74 m); height 10 ft 6 in (3.20 m).
Weights: empty 1,101 lb (500 kg); max. loaded
1,541 lb (699 kg).
Performance: max. speed 113 mph (182 km/h)
initial climb 1,200 ft (366 m)/min; service ceiling
20,500 ft (6250 m); range 280 miles (450 km).

The Sopwith triplane resembled the Pup, but had
extra wing length and could outclimb every other
plane. As a result of a deal which gave the RFC
urgently-needed Spads, all the Triplanes went to
the RNAS, where they scored notable ascendancy
over practically every German type.
The illustration shows it in the markings of No 8
Squadron, RNAS.

ing his superior, commanding the defence forces, to work with complete information about his attacker's dispositions. Conditions in the 1913 manoeuvres made similar success impossible, but nonetheless the squadrons involved profited greatly, the extended manoeuvres bringing to light numerous instances of inadequate organisation and groundwork, coupled with the inability of most aircraft to stand up to the rigours of sustained operations. But although the implications of these lessons were understood by the airmen, they were not by the high command, and so little of the necessary alterations had taken place before the outbreak of war.

The Royal Naval Air Service was meanwhile having a harder time of it, despite the support of Winston Churchill, the First Lord of the Admiralty, and Captain Murray Sueter, Director of the Air Department. For whereas the Royal Flying Corps' tasks were fairly easy to define, those of the Royal Naval Air Service were not. It was eventually decided in October 1912 that naval aircraft could best be used for coastal reconnaissance, and so a chain of air bases, each one within flying distance of its neighbours on each side, was gradually established. The first was at Eastchurch, the second on the Isle of Grain, and by the middle of 1913 stations had been set up at Calshot, Cromarty, Felixstowe and Yarmouth. By the outbreak of war, similar stations had been established at Dundee, Fort Grange, Westgate, Clacton, Killingholme and Great Yarmouth.

By the end of 1913 the Royal Naval Air Service had about 100 pilots, and was building up considerable experience with landplanes, seaplanes and airships. Yet the rift with the Royal Flying Corps proper was growing all the time, despite the efforts to reconcile the two halves made by a number of people and bodies, the most notable of which was the Air Committee in Whitehall, headed by Colonel the Hon. J. E. B. Seely with Vice-Admiral Sir John Jellicoe as his deputy.

By 1914 the rift had grown so great that it was decided to allow the two halves of the Royal Flying Corps to go their own ways, and on 1 July 1914 the Royal Naval Air Service was divorced from the Royal Flying Corps and became part of the Royal Navy.

Organisation of the Royal Naval Air Service was into flights, squadrons and wings, but none of these had received numbers before the outbreak of war.

The summer of 1914 was destined to see the full strength of the Royal Flying Corps and Royal Naval Air Service mustered for propaganda and display purposes. In June there was a Royal Flying Corps 'camp' at Netheravon. Here gathered Nos 2, 3, 4, 5 and 6 Squadrons, with about 700 personnel. No 1 Squadron was still in the process of converting to heavier-than-air craft, and No 7 Squadron was forming at Farnborough. No 6 Squadron was not up to full strength. The majority of aircraft on show at Netheravon were BE 2s and 2as, Maurice and Henry Farman biplanes, Avro 500 biplanes, Sopwith Tabloid biplanes and Blériot XI monoplanes. Total aircraft strength of the Royal Flying Corps at the time was 179 aircraft, but of these only a relatively small proportion could be considered operationally serviceable.

The Royal Naval Air Service's chance came during the fleet review and manoeuvres held at Spithead between 18 and 22 July 1914. On 20 July the Royal Naval Air Service's full deployable strength, seventeen seaplanes and two flights of landplanes, flew over the fleet.

On the outbreak of war, then, the British air services could muster between them 113 operational aircraft and seaplanes, plus six airships. Although France's operational strength was little greater, she had far greater aeronautical resources in depth.

With the start of hostilities, the Royal Flying Corps was scheduled to send very able man and aircraft to France: 105 officers, sixty-three aircraft and ninety-five motor vehicles. Command in France was entrusted to Brigadier-General Sir David Henderson, who had learned to fly at the age of forty-nine while Director of Military Training, and had long been a staunch advocate of aircraft for military purposes. Henderson's chief-of-staff was Acting Lieutenant-Colonel F. H. Sykes, and the rest of the headquarters staff consisted of Major H. R. M. Brooke-Popham, Deputy-Assistant Quartermaster-General, Lieutenant B. H. Barrington-

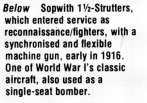

Below Sopwith 1½-Strutters, which entered service as reconnaissance/fighters, with a synchronised and flexible machine gun, early in 1916. One of World War I's classic aircraft, also used as a single-seat bomber.

ennett, Staff Captain, and Major W. G. H. Salmond.
After staging through Dover, the Royal Flying Corps
t off for France, the aircraft by air and the rest by boat
nd train. First to land in France was Lieutenant H. D.
arvey-Kelly of No 2 Squadron, flying a BE 2a, who
nded near Amiens early in the morning of 13 August
914. Soon afterwards the rest of Nos 2, 3 and 4
quadrons, less one flight of the last left at Dover for
atrol duties, had arrived. Nos 2 and 4 Squadrons were
quipped with BE 2 and BE 2a aircraft, No 3 with
lériot XIs, Morane-Saulnier Parasols and Henry
arman F20s. No 5 Squadron, equipped with a mis-
ellany of types (Avro 504s, BE 8s and Farman F20s)
rrived on 15 August. Unfortunately for the Royal
lying Corps there were no spares, although an Aircraft
ark, to supply reserve machines, arrived by rail and

Left Sopwith T.F.2
Salamander ground-attack
aircraft, derived from the
Snipe with 650 lb/295 kg of
armour, two machine guns
and 4,000 rounds of
ammunition. Only 37 reached
France in 1918.
Below B.E. 2, pre-production
version of the B.E. 2a, and
'winner' of the British military
trials in 1912.

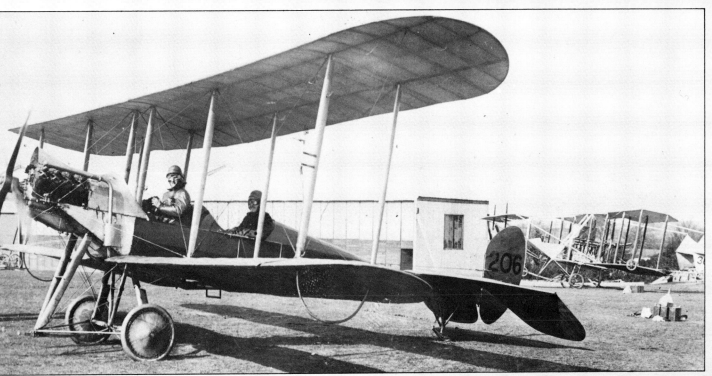

49

road on 18 August with four crated Sopwith Tabloids and some crated BEs.

Left behind in England were forty-one officers and 116 aircraft, of which only about twenty were fit to take to the air. Also left at home was Trenchard, charged with the almost impossible task of building up an organisation to supply the field force with reinforcements and replacements, and also of building up another air service. Thus the Royal Flying Corps went to war.

Henderson was in effect the first real commander of the Royal Flying Corps. When formed, the Royal Flying Corps had been in a somewhat nebulous administrative position. In the summer of 1913, however, there had been established a new section of the War Office, under the aegis of the Director of Military Training, to administer the Royal Flying Corps. This section's head had been Captain W. Sefton-Brancker. Then on 1 September 1913 a Directorate of Military Aeronautics, entirely separate from the other branches of the War Office, had been established under Brigadier-General David Henderson, with Brancker as his deputy. The Directorate contained three sections, responsible for administration and training, for equipment, and for contracts. This last, it should be noted, was a new departure for the War Office, which had hitherto concentrated its 'buying power' in the hands of the Financial Member of the Army Council. For the first time, though, the Royal Flying Corps' budget exceeded £1 million in 1913, as the contracts department of the Directorate soon proved its worth.

But now, by the middle of August 1914, the main strength of the Flying Corps was in France, operating over the British Expeditionary Force. The first two reconnaissance flights were flown on 19 August, by Captain Joubert de la Ferté in a No 3 Squadron Blériot and by Lieutenant G. W. Mappleton in a No 4 Squadron BE 2. The Corps' first casualty came during the course of the twelve flights made on 22 August, when Sergeant-Major D. S. Jillings of No 2 Squadron was wounded in the leg by rifle fire from the ground.

Yet almost immediately such reconnaissance flights began to prove their worth. On 22 August, for example, aerial reconnaissance showed that the British Expeditionary Corps was in danger of being surrounded at Mons by the German 1st Army on its left and the 2nd Army on its right. Accordingly, on 24 August the great retreat from Mons began, in conjunction with the French armies falling back on either side. This tested the Royal Flying Corps to the full: the amount of ground transport available was totally inadequate, as were the number of spares and replacements for aircraft and their components, and yet the corps commanders called for constant reconnaissance.

The deficiencies of the prewar organisation were revealed fully, but somehow or other the Royal Flying Corps managed to keep aircraft in the air and provide the services called for. And it was on the last day of August that Royal Flying Corps reconnaissance aircraft brought in the first news of General von Kluck's turn to the south-east, that would take him to the east of Paris instead of west as planned. The turn was followed by another, and soon the Germans found themselves halted in the 1st Battle of the Marne, and then forced to pull back in the celebrated 'race to the sea' that led to the establishment of a static front from the southern coast of the North Sea to Switzerland.

During the winter pause that followed the 1st Battle of Ypres, Sir John French, commanding the British

Air mechanics fixing bombs under the lower plan of an Armstrong-Whitworth F.K.8. Poperinge Aerodrome.

Expeditionary Force, reported to Lord Kitchener, the Secretary of State for War: 'I wish particularly to bring to your Lordship's notice the admirable work done by the Royal Flying Corps under Sir David Henderson. Their skill, energy, and perseverance have been beyond all praise. They have furnished me with the most complete and accurate information which has been of incalculable value in the conduct of operations. Fired at constantly both by friend and foe, and nor hesitating to fly in every kind of weather, they have remained undaunted throughout.'

High praise indeed, especially considering the scepticism with which aerial reconnaissance had been greeted only a short time before. At the same time, it should be noted, artillery spotting had been improving, and the first operational radio sets had been making their primitive entry into combat in the middle of September. From this time the accuracy of the long-range artillery support available to the Royal Flying Corps began to improve considerably.

The winter lull in operations gave the Royal Flying Corps its first chance to take stock of the lessons of four months of active service. Naturally enough, apart from tactical lessons about the need for armament, homogeneous squadrons and the like, the first priority turned out to be the need for expansion and re-equipment. But the organisation inherited by Trenchard at the beginning of the war had been wholly inadequate – few men, fewer machines, and virtually no immediate hope of receiving more aircraft and engines, so small and ungeared for high production was the British aero industry.

In fact, the Royal Flying Corps in France had been very fortunate in finding that the French aero industry could meet most of the British as well as French requirements. Trenchard was fortunate in that Brancker, now a lieutenant-colonel, had been left at the War Office to help build up the Royal Flying Corps from this centre of army administration. Without real authorisation, Brancker had immediately enlisted every

Designed to bomb Berlin, the Bristol Braemar II was powered by four 400 hp Liberty engines, but arrived too late to see service.

mechanic he could find, as well as civilian pilots, and ordered as many French engines as he could. So far as cooperation with the Admiralty was concerned, Brancker arranged with Sueter that the Army should receive engines of less than 100 hp, and the Navy those developing more than this, seaplanes needing more power than landplanes.

New aircraft were ordered into production before their capabilities had really been worked out, and several older types, past their effective prime, were retained in production. But there was little else that could be done when the Royal Flying Corps in the field needed every aircraft that could be delivered. In the long term this policy was to have severe disadvantages, however. Brancker and Trenchard also took over the civilian airfields at Brooklands, Dover, Gosport, Hounslow and Netheravon, as well as developing new centres at Beaulieu, Castle Bromwich, Catterick, Northolt and Norwich.

Trenchard's main tasks were twofold: first, he had to build up the Royal Flying Corps' training organisation to produce an increased flow of pilots to the front and, second, he was responsible for the formation of new squadrons for field service in France. Both Brancker and Trenchard were fortunate in that Kitchener, a powerful and popular figure, took a keen personal interest in the progress of the Royal Flying Corps, and greatly aided them in pushing forward the idea that one of the Royal Flying Corps' primary needs was homogeneous squadrons – units equipped with the same type of aircraft, that could then fly and fight more efficiently as all the aircraft would have the same performance. Trenchard did not have much time at home, though, for on 18 November he was appointed to the command of the 1st Wing.

Up to October, the squadrons of the Royal Flying Corps in France had been controlled by the Army headquarters in France. Yet most of the work done by the squadrons was for corps headquarters, and so at the end of the month it was decided to allocate squadrons to the various corps on a semi-permanent basis. Thus 'wings', each consisting of two, three or four squadrons, were formed and allocated to the corps. Trenchard's 1st Wing, with Nos 2 and 3 Squadrons, operated under the Indian and IV Corps; Lieutenant-Colonel C. J. Burke's 2nd Wing, with Nos 5 and 6 Squadrons, supported II and III Corps; No 4 Squadron and the radio-equipped unit were controlled by Royal Flying Corps headquarters; and in the spring of 1915 Lieutenant-Colonel H. R. M. Brooke-Popham received command of the 3rd Wing, with Nos 1 and 4 Squadrons, the aircraft of No 9 Squadron, lately the radio unit, being split up between the other squadrons.

By 10 March 1915, the Royal Flying Corps had eight squadrons in France. Unfortunately for both the aircrew and the groundcrew, though, the eighty-five aircraft equipping these squadrons were of twelve different types. Progress was being made towards homogeneous squadrons despite this, and the first such unit, No 11 Squadron equipped with Vickers FB 5 'Gunbus' aircraft, arrived in France on 25 July 1915.

Meanwhile, at the end of 1914 Henderson had been appointed to the command of the 1st Division. On hearing of this, Kitchener immediately cancelled the move on the grounds that Henderson was far better employed where he was, building up the Royal Flying Corps in the field. Shortly afterwards, Brancker was given the task of working out a growth programme for the Royal Flying Corps, based on the need to support the 'New Army' of thirty divisions being trained in Britain. Brancker estimated that fifty squadrons would be needed. Kitchener's answer, despite War Office protests, was a succinct 'Double this'. Accordingly, the Royal Flying Corps in the spring of 1915 found itself with virtual *carte blanche* where finance and powers were concerned.

Tactical developments in the field were numerous, but still largely experimental. Guns had been fitted to aircraft, but the only 'fighting' types, the so-called scouts, were usually armed with small arms rather than machine guns. Nevertheless, the art of air fighting was being gradually developed, and would reach its first flowering with the Morane-Saulnier Type L flown by Roland Garros in April 1915. Communication with advancing troops was also found to be difficult, and so early in 1915 a system of observation by aircraft for GHQ was organised: the advancing troops would lay out strips of cloth when they had reached their objective, and a radio-equipped aircraft would then report to GHQ. The system unfortunately failed in its first test, the Battle of Neuve Chapelle on 10 March 1915, as none of the troops reached their objectives.

This battle, though, saw the first widespread use of the results of aerial photography, accurate maps of the German trench system being available as a result of the development of adequate aerial cameras, largely as a result of the experimental section of the 1st Wing under 2nd Lieutenant J. T. C. Moore-Brabazon. Although great strides had been made in radio equipment for artillery spotting aircraft, the problems were still great, particularly as the set in use early in 1915 weighed something like 34 kg (75 lbs) and took up the observer's cockpit in its entirety. By the autumn, however, the Sterling set had been introduced. This weighed only 9 kg (20 lbs) and was not too bulky. Wireless flights were established in all squadrons, and what had been the radio unit in France, No 9 Squadron, returned to England to become the Wireless School at Brooklands, under the command of Captain H. C. T. Dowding.

Up to the spring of 1915 bombing had been a somewhat slapdash affair, bombs being largely extemporised and sighting a question of judgement by eye. By the time of the Battle of Loos in August 1915, however, the Central Flying School sight, developed by Lieutenant R. B. Bourdillon had reached the front, and bombing accuracy began slowly to improve. Aircraft were still largely inadequate to the tasks they were called upon to perform, unfortunately, and the numbers of even these inadequate aircraft just were not enough to meet the demands of the growing army. As Brooke-Popham pointed out in a memorandum, in the period in which the British Expeditionary Force had grown from four to thirty divisions, the Royal Flying Corps in France had expanded from four to only eleven squadrons, and was being asked constantly to do more.

In August the Royal Flying Corps in France received a new commander: on the 19th Sir David Henderson handed over command to Colonel Trenchard as he set off home to take over command of the Royal Flying Corps at the War Office, with a seat on the Army Council. The position of the Royal Flying Corps in France was strengthened on 19 December 1915, when General Sir Douglas Haig succeeded Field-Marshal Sir John French as C-in-C of the forces in France.

Haig and Trenchard knew each other fairly well from the days in which Trenchard had commanded the 1st Wing in Haig's 1st Army, and this cooperation was to be an ever-strengthening feature of the army and the air service for the rest of the war. Indeed, on 30 March 1916 Trenchard moved his headquarters to St André-aux-Bois, where Haig also had his HQ.

In October 1915 the army in France had the support of only twelve squadrons, all indifferently equipped. But during the winter and spring of 1915, the situation altered considerably: newer types reached the front, homogeneous squadrons were formed, training improved, and morale began to rise as the 'Fokker scourge' receded with the introduction of better French and British aircraft. There was also an organisational

change in the Royal Flying Corps, with the introduction of brigades on 30 January 1916.

The object of the reshuffle was to provide two wings for each army: the Army Wing, under the direct control of the army commander and his staff, was equipped with long-range, high performance aircraft for the basically 'strategic' army tasks; the Corps Wing was concerned with 'tactical' reconnaissance and artillery spotting, and had slightly older aircraft with not quite as good a performance.

To control the two wings with which each army was now to be allocated, the Royal Flying Corps was reorganised into brigades. I Brigade was formed on 30 January, and was commanded by Brigadier-General J. F. A. Higgins; and II Brigade on 10 February, under the command of Brigadier-General J. M. Salmond. Salmond was almost immediately after this posted back to Britain to reorganise flying training, and command of II Brigade was assumed by Brigadier-General T. I. Webb-Bowen. Royal Flying Corps headquarters re-

ained two squadrons, which became the 9th Wing, for pecial purposes.

By the time the 1st Battle of the Somme opened on 1 uly 1916, the Royal Flying Corps had four brigades in 'rance, III Brigade being commanded by Higgins Brigadier-General D. le G. Pitcher having taken over I 3rigade) and IV Brigade by Brigadier-General E. B. Ashmore. The wings of the four brigades were (corps nd army respectively): 1st and 10th, 2nd and 11th, 2th and 13th, and 3rd and 14th. In all there were wenty-seven operational squadrons with 421 aircraft, nd four kite-balloon squadrons with fourteen balloons.)verall commander was Major-General Trenchard, nd the 9th (HQ) Wing was commanded by Lieutenant-Colonel Dowding.

The 'Fokker scourge' was finally ended in May 1916 vith the arrival of the first Allied squadron equipped vith aircraft with interrupted machine guns, No 70 vith Sopwith 1½-Strutters. These aircraft ensured that he Allies obtained air superiority, whereas earlier types the FE 2, DH 2 and Nieuport 11 *Bébé*) had checked ather than overwhelmed the Fokker monoplanes.

The supply organisation had improved sufficiently »y this time for each brigade of the Royal Flying Corps o have its own Aircraft Park, which held available one month's supply of stores, and could undertake minor epairs to aircraft. There were also two Aircraft Depots, vhich held supplies for three months and took delivery »f all new aircraft from England. These two depots held 216 aircraft at the time of the beginning of the 1st Battle »f the Somme. Additionally, there were two Engine Repair Shops.

Trenchard was of the opinion that the French air ervice's main failing during the Battle of Verdun had »een that it had conceded the German air superiority at he beginning, and had thereafter not really been able to lo more than cancel this superiority. The net result of his was that at the beginning of the battle the German tir service had dominated over the battlefield, and that n the closing stages the French had denied this – but tad not been able to dominate the airspace, as it would now be called, over the Germans.

As the war was to be decided on land, in the stimation of most commanders, it was thus important hat one's own armies should operate under cover of air

superiority. The French had held out against attack at Verdun, but Trenchard was now convinced that only offensive air action, at any cost, would suffice to allow the British ground forces to go over to the offensive and so win the war on the ground. Thus Trenchard began to strip the corps wings of their fighters and reallocate them to the army wings. The idea behind this alteration was that the corps wings should operate over the lines to provide support for the ground forces; the army wings, meanwhile, would take the air war to the Germans, with fighters roaming deep into German territory to seek out and destroy the German two seaters and fighters, and so prevent them reaching the lines and attacking the British corps aircraft.

Stripped of any qualifications, Trenchard's edict was that the Royal Flying Corps would take the air war to the Germans, over their own territory, regardless of cost. At the same time, bombers were to cease attacks on small objectives with small numbers of aircraft, and instead concentrate on attacks on important targets with large numbers of aircraft. If the target was within 48 km (30 miles) of the front, the bombers were to be escorted by fighters; if the target was beyond this range, one out of every five bombers was to dispense with bomb-load and carry an extra gunner instead, the defensive fire thus being put up, it was hoped, being enough to deter the German fighters.

All in all, therefore, Trenchard had decided to take the air war to the Germans in the Battle of the Somme. On the whole, moreover, his plans worked well: the land battle was disastrous in human terms, but it had the desired strategic effect of taking pressure off the French and putting it on the Germans; the air war was a classic of Trenchard's offensive policy. General von Below, commanding the German 2nd Army, is quoted: 'With the help of air spotting, the enemy neutralised our artillery and was able to range in his own guns with the utmost accuracy on our infantry trenches; the information for this was provided by uninterrupted front-line reconnaissance and photography ... The enemy aircraft gave our own troops a feeling of helplessness, such was their mastery of the air.'

Quite apart from this, Trenchard had been sufficiently impressed with the concept of aircraft watching for the forward movement of the ground forces and

Below A twin-engine Handley-Page taxiing back to its shed, Hendon Aerodrome, October 1918. This excellent bomber could carry 2,000 lb/907 kg bombs. *Opposite page* Refuelling the Handley-Page 0/400.

reporting this back to headquarters, which had not worked in 1915, to develop the idea further. Elaborate systems of signalling from the ground to the air had been developed, and in the 1st Battle of the Somme the revised 'infantry contact' patrols, normally flown by spotter aircraft, but sometimes by fighters, were very successful if heavy in casualties. Thus the high command was able to keep better track of infantry progress than had been possible before. Casualties to ground fire were, surprisingly, relatively small, the main cause of losses being incoming British artillery fire and the hazards of low-level flight. All types of aircraft operated in support of the ground forces at low level, using machine-guns and light bombs, and flying a large number of sorties whenever possible.

Thus the Royal Flying Corps held sway over the battlefield proper. It also prevented the German air service from playing a more prominent part in the battle by sending its fighters to operate between the German airfields and the front line. However, on 15 September 1916 the first of the new German *Jagdstaffeln* (fighter squadrons) appeared over the Somme battlefield. This was *Jasta* 2, commanded by the redoubtable Hauptmann Oswald Boelcke, perhaps the most important air tactician of World War I, and equipped with Halberstadt and Albatros D-type biplane fighters. Although the Royal Flying Corps outnumbered the German air service by 380 aircraft to 330, the forty-five D-types available to the three *Jagdstaffeln* by October redressed the balance in favour of the Germans.

Royal Flying Corps losses mounted alarmingly in October, and morale fell accordingly, but Trenchard, with his mind firmly fixed on larger objectives, refused to call off the air offensive. Indeed, on 22 September Trenchard signed an historic document entitled *Future Policy in the Air*, outlining his intention of pursuing an uninterrupted air offensive in support of the ground forces no matter what his casualties.

So great was the pace of air operations that many pilots were flying four or more sorties a day. Exhaustion was a major problem, and only partial solutions were found by rotation of Somme squadrons with others from less active sectors of the line, and even by borrowing squadrons from the Royal Naval Air Service's land-based units in the Dunkirk area.

The 1st Battle of the Somme finally petered out in November with the onset of winter. Trenchard, however, felt that air operations should not cease. Clearly the Allies and the Germans had entered a technological race in which the Germans at present had the superiority, and to counter this the Royal Flying Corps would need more fighter squadrons. Thus Haig, with Trenchard's urging, on 16 November 1916 asked the War Office to expand the expansion already planned, and provide an additional twenty fighter squadrons for the spring of 1917.

Part of the problem faced by the Royal Flying Corps in France was that the service had other commitments, in northern Greece, in the Middle East and even over Great Britain, where the activities of airships were causing grave public concern. Thus, the total strength of the Royal Flying Corps could not be deployed in what most considered to be the only theatre worthy of the name, but had to be spread about almost in 'penny packets', although the Western Front enjoyed general priority.

Air fighting continued in a desultory fashion during the winter of 1917–18, but Trenchard now had other worries on his mind. As a result of the artillery spotting

successes during the 1st Battle of the Somme, several senior army officers now recommended that corps squadrons should pass under direct command of the army formations to which they were attached. Trenchard turned down the suggestion on the grounds that it would hamper rather than improve the squadrons' flexibility of response. Fortunately for the Royal Flying Corps, Haig supported Trenchard.

To cope with the extra work now being thrust on such squadrons, though, their establishment of two-seaters was increased from eighteen to twenty-four aircraft. At the same time, more artillery officers were drafted in as observers, and improved radio sets and techniques were introduced. These measures had the effect of doubling the number of spotters able to operate on a given length of front. There was now one aircraft to every 915 metres (1,000 yards).

During this winter the Royal Flying Corps was also being expanded, although only with difficulty because the training organisation was woefully deficient. Early in 1917 a growth to 106 active and ninety-seven reserve squadrons was authorised. The provision of aircraft for this number presented only relatively small problems, for series production of the various types needed was under way. Homogeneous squadrons were now the rule, and even the practice of allocating a few scouts to two-seater squadrons had been abandoned during 1916 after the success of the first true fighter squadron, No 24 equipped with DH 2s, which had arrived in France on 7 February 1916.

Greater problems were common with the question of finding the right types of aircraft: the Royal Flying Corps' 1916 types were definitely outclassed by the German Albatros fighters, and only the Royal Naval Air Service and the French seemed to have aircraft equal to the task in the Sopwith Pup and Triplane, and in the Spad 7. Trenchard realised the problem, but expected that until the arrival of newer Royal Flying Corps types such as the SE 5 and Sopwith Camel in the late spring and early summer, the increased number of Allied types would allow the German air service to be swamped and thus kept in check.

Training was controlled by the Training Brigade commanded by Brigadier-General J. M. Salmond, who worked to produce aircrew to meet War Office figures. This body estimated that the average service life of aircrew in France was four months for two-seater crew, three-and-a-half for fighter-reconnaissance and day bombing crews, and only two-and-a-half months for single-seater fighter pilots. For 1917, therefore, the War Office reckoned on a 230 per cent casualty rate for the year and planned to produce the aircrew to meet such losses.

The decision had been made too early in the year, however, and in the 1st Battle of the Somme the casualty rate had risen to some 300 per cent, and after the arrival of the Germans *Jastas* equipped with Albatros and Halberstadt D types to 400 per cent. During 'Bloody April' 1917 it was to rise to the appalling figure of 600 per cent, this last figure representing an effective front-line life of only two months for aircrew in general.

It is clear from this that the German fighters had been able to cope with Allied numbers with the aid of considerably superior aircraft, and April 1917 was the worst period of the war for the Royal Flying Corps. Despite the losses, Trenchard insisted that the air offensive had to be maintained, and so losses were made up by aircrew only very poorly trained. This in turn

Above Re-assembling planes at No.1 Aircraft Depot at St Omer, December 1917. On the right is a Bristol Fighter presented by the Gold Coast, on the left an S.E. single-seater. The engines of both are being tested.

Building B.E.2 aircraft in the aeroplane department of Messrs Denny's Works, Clyde. Note the relatively large number of women employed.

establishment of the special school at Gosport under Major R. R. Smith Barry.

Smith Barry had long been of the opinion that the major failing of most pilots was that they did not understand their aircraft and were thus chary of them and their handling characteristics, and so failed to make the best use of their manoeuvrability. This was a trait inherited from indifferent flying instructors, who tended to be inferior pilots sent home by squadron commanders who wished to be rid of them, or good pilots eager to return to the front and so indifferent to their pupils' progress. Smith Barry recognised the need for competent, full-time instructors completely at home in their aircraft, and from 1917 he produced such instructors at his special school. Aerobatics, hitherto regarded with extreme caution and even official condemnation, were now encouraged as a means of air fighting and also as a way of getting to know the aircraft and its characteristics. The Smith Barry system is now the one in general use throughout the world, *mutatis mutandis*.

At the same time, gunners who had previously had to learn their trade the hard way, in the rear cockpit of a combat aircraft, were now sent home for proper training. Groundcrew were also better trained at the central school at Halton than they had been previously at polytechnic schools. Thus the majority of the 17,000 pilots and the aircrew and groundcrew necessary to support them, which the War Office reckoned necessary for 1917 and 1918, were produced. The programme was greatly aided by the setting up of a three-squadron Training Wing in Egypt in April 1916, and by the establishment of flying training facilities in Canada.

But the main beneficial effects of this programme were to be in the future, and meanwhile the Royal Flying Corps in France continued to suffer. In August 1916 the average flying life of an officer before he was killed or injured had been 295 hours. By April 1917 this figure had dropped to an alarming ninety-two. The Royal Flying Corps' most testing hours had started with the opening of the Battle of Arras on 4 April 1917.

British air strength was 365, German 195, but the latter were in most respects technically far superior. Thus 'Bloody April' marked a period of complete German ascendancy, highlighted by the loss of seventy-five Royal Flying Corps aircraft in combat and another fifty-six in accidents in the first five days of the battle, and by the large scores built up during the month by German aces such as Manfred von Richthofen.

The desperate losses of April had been largely made up by June, but a month later fighter squadrons had to be returned from France to Great Britain for the defence of London against daylight raids by Gotha bombers on the capital, and by the retention of the first of the excellent Sopwith Camel fighters for metropolitan defence. Nonetheless, when the 3rd Battle of Ypres began on 31 July 1917, the Allied air forces could muster some 840 aircraft, including 360 fighters, against the Germans' 600, including 200 fighters.

The Allies generally held the advantage, and it was noticeable that there was a slight decline in the standard of the German pilots, the result of training failing to keep up with front-line demands. All in all, therefore, the Royal Flying Corps was able to furnish the Army with the support it needed, especially where artillery spotting, reconnaissance and infantry contact and support were concerned. The bombers also ranged over the Germans defences, and the fighters were able to prevent the German air service from interfering in a major way

further contributed to losses as the newer pilots stood little chance against the superior German fighters.

In April pilots reaching the front often had as little as seventeen-and-a-half hours flying training. This was only about enough time to teach them the very rudiments of how to fly, but not how to fly in a combat situation or what to do when attacked. Without adequate reserves, though, there was little else Trenchard could do. He did realise the appalling nature of the situation, however, and did his best to ameliorate it. New training methods and organisation helped considerably, moreover, and by September 1917 pilots reaching the front had an average of forty-eight-and-a-half hours of flying instruction.

The training situation had been greatly improved by a reorganisation of the training command. The brigade had been elevated to divisional status and decentralised into the London, Salisbury and York Groups. Six Cadet Wings were set up. And the specialised nature of air operations was recognised by the establishment of schools for aerial gunnery, artillery and infantry cooperation, bombing and equipment. Such a reorganisation was bound to improve the quality of the aircrew reaching France, but just as important, and perhaps more important in the long run, was the

with the progress of British operations.

At the end of the year, four fighter squadrons were temporarily engaged in special low-level attacks on German troops and artillery positions with light bombs and machine-guns. Although losses were heavy, in the order of thirty per cent, successes were achieved, and the Royal Flying Corps decided that such attacks and tactics were worth persevering with, but only with specially armoured ground-attack aircraft.

Specifications were thus drawn up, and in 1918 produced types such as the Sopwith Salamander. Crisis on the Italian Front after the Battle of Caporetto meant that British and French forces had to be diverted to this theatre. Amongst the British formations was Webb-Bowen's VII Brigade of five squadrons. The easing of the crisis early in 1918 meant that the scale of the air effort could be reduced, and so only Lieutenant-Colonel de la Ferté's 14th Wing was left in Italy.

Meanwhile high command alterations had been taking place. On 11 May 1916 the first Air Board had been formed under Lord Curzon; a second had been set up under Lord Cowdray on 6 February 1917. Then on 13 June 1917 there occurred the first major daylight raid against London by German bombers.

Consternation, already high because of the Zeppelin raids, was increased, and only eight days after the War Office recommended that the active strength of the Royal Flying Corps be expanded from 108 squadrons (the 106 squadrons of the 12 December 1916 programme plus two extra night-flying squadrons) to 200. This vast increase in size, with the Royal Naval Air Service also receiving a large number of new squadrons, prompted questions on the status and organisation of the flying services, and on 11 July Lieutenant-General Jan Smuts, a distinguished South African, was appointed head of a Cabinet Committee on Air Defence and Air Organisation.

Smuts' committee reported on air defence on 19 July, and on air organisation on 17 August. The latter report recommended that an independent air force, under a separate Air Ministry, should be established, and should comprise the Royal Flying Corps and Royal Naval Air Service under a unified command. The report was accepted by the cabinet.

Major-General Salmond had been replaced as head of the Training Division by Major-General C. A. H. Longcroft, and had in turn taken over from Lieutenant-General Sir David Henderson as the Royal Flying Corps' representative on the Army Council. With the cabinet's approval of the Smuts Committee's suggestions for an independent air force on 24 August 1917, Henderson was appointed to the committee to advise on the organisation of the air force, whose establishment was made certain by the royal assent to the Air Force Bill on 29 November 1917. The Smuts Committee had recommended that the new force should be headed by an Air Ministry, with under it an Air Council and Air Staff. This last had been lacked by the earlier Air Councils, which also lacked executive authority to arbitrate between the differing requirements of the Royal Flying Corps and the Royal Naval Air Service, whose competition for engines, airframes and personnel was hampering the front-line efforts of both.

The Air Ministry came into being on 3 January 1918 with Lord Rothermere as Secretary of State and Sir David Henderson as Vice-President. An Air Staff was quickly set up, with Major-General Sir Hugh Trenchard as its first Chief of Air Staff. On 18 January Trenchard left France after commanding the Royal Flying Corps in the field for two-and-a-half years, and was succeeded as General Officer Commanding-in-Chief by Major-General Sir John Salmond.

Under Trenchard, the Air Staff immediately set about co-ordinating the amalgamation of the Royal Naval Air Service and Royal Flying Corps into the Royal Air Force. In this joint effort the Deputy Chief of Air Staff, Rear-Admiral Mark Kerr, played a great part. The Royal Air Force was finally born on 1 April 1918, although at first there were few signs of the new formation's existence in front-line units, for on 26 March the Germans had launched their last major offensives on the Western Front, designed to eliminate the British and French before the full weight of American manpower and industry could make itself felt on the Western Front.

Mention has been made of the German air raids that were the final stimulus towards the establishment of the Smuts Committee and the Royal Air Force, the world's

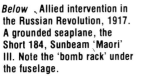

Below Allied intervention in the Russian Revolution, 1917. A grounded seaplane, the Short 184, Sunbeam 'Maori' III. Note the 'bomb rack' under the fuselage.

first independent air service. These air raids were part of a German effort to persuade the British people to leave the war by attacks on them and their property, although the first intention had been to attack only military targets.

The first air raid on England was launched by a seaplane which dropped a bomb near Dover Castle on 24 December 1914, and the first Zeppelin raid took place on 19 January 1915. The air defence of Great Britain had, by arrangement, become an Admiralty responsibility from 3 September 1914, but aircraft could not reach the Zeppelins in time after they had been spotted. The first Zeppelin raid to reach London did so on 31 May 1915, and the year of 1915 saw more damage in the capital than any other year.

On 16 February 1916 the air defence of Great Britain was restored to the War office, coming under Sir John French, Commander-in-Chief Home Forces. To meet the air defence requirements, a seven-squadron Home Defence Wing was formed, all the aircraft being of the BE type. Incendiary ammunition was in widespread use for these machines by July. Gradually successes against the Zeppelins mounted, and the raids became less effective until the advent of the Gotha bombers on 13 June 1917.As a result the Smuts Committee was set up, and on 19 July this reported its findings: an anti-aircraft gun barrage should be set up, and three special squadrons should be raised for the defence of the capital. On 5 August the air defence of London became the responsibility of a special headquarters under Brigadier-General E. B. Ashmore. The fighters proved something of a deterrent, and the Germans went over to a night offensive, causing considerable damage at times. Once again Smuts was called in to head the Aerial Operations Committee (later renamed the War Priorities Committee) from 21 September 1917. Amongst other things, the committee recommended more searchlights and balloons, but more importantly that the air war should be taken to German cities by a bomber force to be based near Nancy in France. The German raids gradually petered out from May 1918 onwards, but had achieved the result of draining large numbers of aircraft and skilled pilots from France for about a year in a particular period of the war.

By the time the Royal Air Force came into being on 1 April 1918, the British aircraft industry had undergone a complete transformation. The right aircraft were pouring from the production lines at the prodigious monthly rate of 2,668 during 1918, and by the middle of the year the Royal Air Force could muster 1,736 front-line aircraft in France, 104 in Italy, forty-one in Greece, 269 in the Middle East, 144 in the Mediterranean and 336 for home defence. Of these some 920 were corps two-seaters, 1,120 single-seat fighters, 422 bombers and only ten heavy bombers of the Handley Page O/100 and O/400 variety.

During 1916 the Royal Naval Air Service had planned to raid into Germany with the fifty-five aircraft of No 3 Wing, based near Nancy. But constant demands for help from the Royal Flying Corps meant that No 3 Wing could operate only desultorily before it was disbanded in the dire days of spring 1917. Then as a result of the Smuts Committee recommendation that the air war should be taken to Germany, VIII Brigade was formed for the independent bombing of Germany of 1 February 1918. This took over a number of Royal Naval Air Service squadrons in the 41st Wing at Ochey near Nancy, which had launched several raids on Germany since October 1917.

A pilot of a British seaplane releasing a carrier pigeon. The plane is a Sopwith Baby derivative of the Schneider floatplane, itself basically a Tabloid. Used for coastal patrol and light bombing.

Meanwhile in London Trenchard had found himself unable to work with Rothermere, and had thus resigned as Chief of Air Staff, being replaced by Major-General Sir Frederick Sykes. Rothermere lasted only a little longer, being replaced on 27 April by Sir William Weir.

So successful had early raids by VIII Brigade been, however, that in May the cabinet decided that it should be expanded into the Independent Force, Royal Air Force. Trenchard took command of this first independent bomber force on 5 June. The Independent Force had four squadrons of O/100 and O/400s, two of DH 9s, one of DH 9as, one of FE 2bs, one of DH 4s and one of Sopwith Camels. Primary targets included poison gas factories, airframe and aero engine factories, blast furnaces and railways. In the last five months of the war, the Independent Force dropped some 550 tons of bombs, and proved a great thorn in the side of the Germans. The success of this force was great enough, moreover, to prompt Great Britain's allies into joining it, and on 26 October 1918 Trenchard became head of the Inter-Allied Independent Air Force. Little had been done to make this a combat formation by the time of the Armistice on 11 November 1918, however.

During 1918, despite the great German spring offensives, the Royal Air Force had gone from strength to strength, and by the time of the Allied summer offensives had total command of the air. Great support for the ground forces was furnished, and at the time of the armistice was an immensely powerful tactical force: 188 operational squadrons and fifteen flights, with 291,170 men and 22,647 aircraft.

The Allied superiority in the closing stages of the war is in no way better exemplified than by the growth of the Royal Flying Corps and Royal Air Force in France between 21 March and 11 November 1918. On the former date the Royal Flying Corps and Royal Naval Air Service mustered some 1,232 aircraft in sixty-three squadrons and one flight; on the latter date, the Royal Air Force mustered some 1,799 aircraft (747 of them single-seat fighters) in one GHQ squadron, seven brigades and the Fifth Group. This last, consisting of one Sopwith Camel and two DH 4 squadrons and one Camel flight, was designed for use with naval forces. Yet this was only part of the Royal Air Force's strength for, apart from France, there were several other countries and theatres in which Royal Air Force units were to be found.

The Palestine Brigade consisted of the 5th (Corps) Wing with three squadrons and the 40th (Army) Wing with four squadrons, as well as No 21 Balloon Company. In Mesopotamia there was the 31st Wing with Nos 30, 63 and 72 Squadrons, plus No 23 Balloon Company. The 16th Wing was located in Macedonia, its three squadrons being Nos 17, 47 and 150, plus No 22 Balloon Company. Italy was the location of the 14th Wing's Nos 28, 34, 42, 66 and 139 Squadrons. And in the Eastern Mediterranean were the 62nd, 63, 66th and 67th Wings, all composed of previous Royal Naval Air Service units.

To a very great extent, the Royal Naval Air Service has received short shrift for its part in the air fighting of World War I. Contrary to the wishes of the founders of the Royal Flying Corps before World War I, the Naval Wing had gone its own way, sufficiently so, indeed, for the Royal Naval Air Service to become an independent entity in 1914.

Under Admiralty control, the Royal Naval Air Service's ill-defined purposes were to help the fleet in its work and to defend the shores of Great Britain. The latter responsibility was removed by the agreement of 3 September 1914, and so the Royal Naval Air Service's task became fleet support, a task so little explored that it eventually became a multiple one: reconnaissance against enemy surface activities called for seaplanes and flying-boats; hunting and destroying U-boats called for the use of specialist landplane and seaplane types; the threat of the Imperial German Navy's Zeppelin airships required high-flying fighter aircraft; German reconnaissance and bomber aircraft operating from Belgium and northern Germany required the location of fighters in the Calais and Dunkirk areas; and the existence of the airships and bombers of the German air services called for bombing aircraft that could take the war to these most dangerous adversaries of the British fleet.

There were, in addition, other duties such as anti-submarine patrol with small non-rigid airships; fighter patrol with aircraft launched from platforms laid over the guns of capital ships' turrets; and attack on German ships and shipping with torpedoes and bombs. Inspired by men such as Commodore Murray Sueter, Commander C. R. Samson and Commander Raymond Collishaw, however, the Royal Naval Air Service was always aggressive in the extreme.

Royal Naval Air Service unit nomenclature is difficult, for in June 1915 the Admiralty ordered that the basic unit was to be known as a wing (or squadron) made up of six-aircraft squadrons (more accurately described as flights). Fortunately this system lasted only until the end of 1915 and was then replaced by the more conventional system.

Throughout the war, defence of the ports on either side of the English Channel, through which passed the great majority of the men and *matériel* for the British Expeditionary Force, was an Admiralty responsibility, and the fighter squadrons of the Royal Naval Air Service acquired for themselves an enviable reputation. They introduced, moreover, some of the best fighting

Below Torpedo being launched from a Short 184. One of these achieved the first aerial torpedo sinking of a ship on 12 August 1915.

aircraft used by the British in World War I, such as the Sopwith 1½-Strutter, Sopwith Pup, Sopwith Triplane and Sopwith Camel. Especially notable amongst the Royal Naval Air Service fighter squadrons were Nos 1, 3, 4, 6, 9 and 10. With the amalgamation of the Royal Flying Corps and Royal Naval Air Service, the squadrons of the latter service were renumbered in the 200 series, No 1 Squadron becoming No 201, and so on. The size of the Royal Naval Air Service on 1 April 1918 was 2,949 aircraft, with some 5,000 officers and 55,000 ratings at forty stations in Great Britain, two in France and ten in the Mediterranean.

At the end of the war, what had been the Royal Naval Air Service was deployed as follows: in East Anglia and northern Kent were the two wings (70th and 73rd) of the Fourth Group, with ten squadrons and one flight; in southern Kent and the southern side of the Channel were the four squadrons of the Fifth Group; although a Royal Air Force formation, the Eighth Group at Gosport held sway over the Torpedo Development Squadron; in the west of England was the Ninth Group with nine squadrons; in southern England and on detachment in Northern France, the four squadrons of the Tenth Group's 74th and 75th Wings covered the English Channel; in Wales was the Fourteenth Group's three squadrons; in the north-east of England was the Eighteenth Group with five squadrons; and in Scotland was the Twenty-second Group operating airships and three aircraft squadrons. Apart from these there were other squadrons abroad or on board ships.

The main strength of the Royal Air Force on 11 November 1918, though, was deployed in France. This considerable force was deployed as follows:

IX (HQ) Brigade had the 9th, 51st, 54th and 82nd Wings, totalling 295 aircraft in seventeen squadrons

I Brigade had the 1st (Corps), 10th (Army) and 91st Wings, totalling 215 aircraft in eleven squadrons and two flights

II Brigade had the 2nd (Corps), 11th (Army) and

65th Wings, totalling 334 aircraft in nineteen squadrons and one flight

III Brigade had the 12th (Corps), 13th (Army) and 90th Wings, totalling 248 aircraft in thirteen squadrons and one flight

V Brigade had the 15th (Corps) and 22nd (Army) wings, totalling 285 aircraft in fifteen squadrons and one flight

X Brigade had the 81st (Corps) and 80th (Army) Wings, totalling 201 aircraft in ten squadrons and one flight

VIII Brigade had the 41st, 83rd and 88th Wings, totalling 140 aircraft in ten squadrons

Fifth Group had sixty-three aircraft in three squadrons and one flight

General Headquarters had one squadron with eighteen aircraft

In all, therefore, on the Western Front the Royal Air Force deployed seven brigades and one group, with twenty wings, ninety-nine squadrons (three of them belonging to the Australian Flying Corps), seven independent flights, 1,576 serviceable aircraft and 223 unserviceable aircraft.

Peace brought immediate reductions, and by the middle of 1919 the Royal Air Force had shrunk to thirty-three squadrons. But on 11 January 1919 Trenchard was reappointed Chief of Air Staff, with Sykes as Controller-General of Civil Aviation; and on 12 February Winston Churchill became Secretary of State for War and Air. With such men at the head of air affairs, financial restrictions might bite hard, but would not destroy the fledgling Royal Air Force.

Royal Flying Corps, Royal Naval Air Service and Royal Air Force casualties during World War I had been 6,166 killed and died, 7,245 wounded and injured, and 3,212 missing, captured and interned. Production in the United Kingdom had amounted to 55,093 aircraft and 41,034 engines; 3,051 aircraft and 16,897 engines were bought from abroad, most of them from France.

Below The British seaplane tender H.M.S. *Engadine*, one of the first 'aircraft-carriers'.

CHAPTER FOUR

THE MINOR AIR FORCES 1900-18

Although it was Germany, France and Great Britain which dominated air warfare in World War I, naturally enough there were other countries involved in the air war. The most important of these were Italy, Imperial Russia and Austria-Hungary. Close behind these came the United States, which would undoubtedly have risen to the first rank had the war continued into 1919. And following some way behind were the other combatants, such as Belgium, Greece, Japan, Portugal and Romania on the side of the Allies, and Bulgaria and Turkey on the side of the Central Powers.

A Bristol Scout D, one of the underestimated aircraft of the early war years. Pictured here are men of the US Air Service, which trained personnel in Britain and France.

ITALY

Heavier-than-air flight came to Italy in 1908, when the French pioneer Léon Delagrange made a series of demonstration flights at Milan, Rome and Turin. This fuelled the aeronautical fires simmering in Italy, and soon the number of persons involved in aviation began to increase considerably. Amongst this number were several military personnel, although their involvement was on a purely private basis. One of the early leading lights of this group of military men was *Tenente* Mario Calderara, who was taught to fly in some twenty-three lessons by Wilbur Wright during the latter's visit to Italy in the spring of 1909.

At this stage the interest in military aviation expressed by the authorities was purely academic, but they had no objections to officers learning to fly, so long as they did it in their own time and with their own money. Thus, when the first Italian flying school was established at Centocelle just outside Rome in 1910, several military personnel enrolled for the course. Enthusiasm for flight was considerable at the time, evidenced by the setting up of other schools at Bovolenta, Cameri, Cortile, Malpensa, Pordenone and Salussola during the next few months.

Another leading military light at this stage was *Tenente* Savoia, who created something of a sensation by flying a new Henry Farman from Mourmelon all the way to Centocelle. Here he took the Italian Minister of War, *Generale* Spingardi, for a flight on 2 August. Only eighteen days later, however, the Italians suffered their first military flying casualty, when *Tenente* Vivaldi was killed in a crash during a cross-country flight from Rome to Civitavecchia. Nevertheless good progress was made in 1910, by the end of which some thirty-one military men had qualified as pilots, sixteen of them in Italy and the rest in France and Germany.

Although there was as yet no formal military aviation establishment, during 1911 two military flying schools were opened, joining the military-civilian school at Centocelle in the teaching of army personnel. Both the schools were located in the north of Italy, at Aviano, near Udine, and at Somma Lombardo. Aviano came into existence during April 1911, and had several aircraft types: five Blériot monoplanes, one Etrich monoplane, one Nieuport monoplane and three Henry Farman biplanes.

The first time aircraft were used for military purposes in Italy was during the manoeuvres of 22–29 August 1911, under the command of *Tenente Generale* Pollio. On the 'Red' side were *Capitano* Carlo Piazza in a Blériot, *Capitano* Riccardo Moizo with a Nieuport, *Tenente* Costantino Quaglia with a Savay biplane and *Sottotenente* Guilio Gavotti with an Etrich monoplane; on the 'Blue' side were *Tenente Vasc.* Manlio Ginocchio and *Tenente Vasc.* Francesco Roberti with Blériot monoplanes, *Sottotente Vasc.* Ugo de Rossi with a Nieuport and *Tenente* Leopoldo da Rada with a Henry Farman biplane. While the manoeuvres were based on Monferrato, the aircraft were flown each day from Novi, and proved their use as reconnaissance vehicles time and time again. Following the manoeuvres, several of the military pilots took part in the *Circuito d'Italia* air race during September, Piazza and Gavotti being awarded the *Medaglia d'Oro* for their efforts by the king.

War with Turkey broke out on 29 September 1911 for the possession of Libya, and soon military aircraft were on their way to the theatre by sea. The 1st Aeroplane Flotilla, with aircraft from the Aviano flying school, was based at Tripoli and the 2nd Aeroplane Squadron at Benghazi. The first Italian use of aircraft in war was on 23 October 1911, when Piazza flew a reconnaissance of the Turkish lines in a Blériot. Other military firsts followed: aerial bombing by Gavotti on 1 November; artillery spotting by Moizo on 24 November; photographic reconnaissance by Piazza on 23 February 1912; and night bombing by Piazza and Gavotti on 4 March 1912. All in all, the Italian use of aircraft in Libya proved very useful for the ground forces, and the Italian authorities planned to raise formal military aviation units. Meanwhile a public subscription between April and October 1912 raised the sum of 3,250,000 *lire* for the purchase of aircraft for the armed forces.

Caproni Ca 33 bomber of the Italian Air Service at Pordernone base, October 1915. The Ca 33 could carry 1,000 lb/454 kg of bombs.

Aviation was by now so well established in the Italian army that it was decided to organise aircraft units on a formal basis. Thus on 27 June 1912 the *Battaglione Aviatori* (Air Battalion) was formed under the auspices of the *Ufficio d'Ispezione Servizi Aeronautici* (Aeronautical Services' Inspection Office). By the end of the year, though, this organisation had proved itself inadequate, and had been replaced as of 28 November 1912 by the *Servizi Aeronautici Militare* (Military Aeronautical Services). This took over responsibility for both heavier- and lighter-than-air aviation from the *Brigata Specialisti del Genio* (Special Engineer Brigade), part of the Engineering Corps, which had been formed in 1894 to look after the army's balloons. The *Brigata Specialisti* had run the *Battaglione Specialisti* which had operated in Libya.

At about the same time that the army formed the *Battaglione Aviatori*, the navy set up the *Sezioni Idrovolanti* (Seaplane Sections) which would patrol Italy's long coastline with seaplanes. It should be noted, moreover, that Italy had one of the pioneers of aerial torpedo bombing, *Capitano* Alessandro Guidoni, amongst its airmen. As early as 1911 Guidoni had started experiments with the launching of torpedoes from aircraft. Another innovation during 1912 was the introduction of the *Servizio d'Aviazione Coloniale* (Colonial Aviation Service).

By the beginning of 1913 the *Servizi Aeronautici* had some fifty miscellaneous aircraft, and the *Sezioni Idrovolanti* had fourteen flying-boats. Several flying schools were in operation, including a naval one at Venice. The army had thirteen airfields: Aviano, where there was a flying school with Blériots; Bologna, the VIII *Squadriglia*; Busto Arsizio, the V *Squadriglia*; Centocelle, the IV and XI *Squadriglie*; Cuneo, the III *Squadriglia*; Mirafiori, the I *Squadriglia*; Padua, the VII *Squadriglia*; Piacenza, the XVI *Squadriglia*; Pordenone, the XII *Squadriglia* and a flying school; San Francesco, the IX and X *Squadriglie*; Somma Lombardo, a flying school; Taliedo, the VI *Squadriglia*; and Venaria Reale, the II *Squadriglia*. During the course of 1913 the designation numbers of the squadrons were changed from Roman to Arabic numerals. The evolving theories of air reconnaissance were tested satisfactorily during the manoeuvres held in September 1913, the 'Red' side having the services of two squadrons, one equipped with Blériot-SIT parasols and the other with Savoia-Farmans, and the 'Blue' side also enjoying the benefits of two reconnaissance squadrons, one with Savoia-Farmans and the other with Nieuport-Macchis. The 'Red' side had eleven aircraft, the 'Blue' ten.

By 1914 the service had grown to fourteen airfields, housing thirteen squadrons and two flying schools. Italy declared her neutrality at the beginning of World War I, despite her treaty obligations to the Central Powers, and an intensive training plan for the armed forces started. The air service concentrated on developing the ability to fly long reconnaissance flights, and began making great progress in the development of the theory of strategic bombing, using the large aircraft built by Gianni Caproni.

Seeing how the air services of the combatants were increasing in size and in importance during the first months of war, the Italians upgraded their air services, and on 7 January 1915 there came into existence the *Corpo Aeronautico Militare* (Military Aeronautical Corps). Under this overall title were the *Direzione Generale di Aeronautica* (General Headquarters for Aeronautics), the *Comando Dirigibili* (Airship Command), the *Comando Aerostieri e Aviatori* (Balloon and Aviation Command), *Battaglione dirigibilisti* (Airship Battalions), *Battaglione Squadriglie aviatori* (Flying Squadron Battalions), *Battaglione Scuole aviatori* (Flying School Battalions), *Stabilimento costruzioni aeronautiche* (Establishment for Aviation Construction), the *Direzione Tecnica dell'Aviazione Militare* (Military Aviation Technical Headquarters), and the *Istituto Centrale Aeronautico* (Central Aeronautical Institute).

Italy entered the war on the side of the Allies on 24 May 1915, and by this time the *Corpo Aeronautico Militare* had fifteen squadrons with seventy-two pilots and eighty-six aircraft. The navy had twelve serviceable floatplanes and flying-boats, fifteen seaplane trainers and one seaplane carrier.

One of Italy's first requirements was for more modern combat aircraft, and soon after her squadrons had gone to war, a major re-equipment programme was instituted, most of the newer types being licence-built copies of French types, and copies of the better Austro-Hungarian seaplanes. Some thought had been given to the development of fighting aircraft, but combat experience soon showed that the ground forces could profit most from an air service that concentrated on reconnaissance and long-range bombing. In this latter role the Italians launched their first Caproni raid, on Ljubljana, on 18 February 1916. During 1915 the only true fighter unit was the 8ª *Squadriglia* defending Udine, although some fighters were also allocated to the defence of Aviano flying school.

During 1916 the *Corpo Aeronautico Militare* was reorganised and expanded, and many squadrons were renumbered. Expansion raised the number of squadrons to thirty-five, but combat showed that the co-operation of squadrons with the ground forces was still too haphazard. Thus early in 1917 another reorganisation was launched, the object being to simplify the air service command structure. From this time on, each army had one or more Air Group attached to it, each of the groups containing a variable number of squadrons. There was also an independent formation under the direct control of GHQ, with its headquarters at Udine, for long-range bombing and reconnaissance. Detach-

The Caproni Ca 5 was a variant of the Ca 35, shown here, converted to carry eight passengers.

Italian pilots with locally built Nieuport 11s. Note the gun mount on the upper wing which allowed the pilot to pull the gun down to reload in flight.

ments were allocated to the Italian forces in Albania and northern Greece.

A typical section of the revised command structure now gave the 1st Army, in the Vicenza sector, the support of the III and IX Air Groups. III Air Group had seven squadrons: 5^a and 9^a with Capronis, 31^a with Savoia-Pomilio SP2 reconnaissance aircraft, 46^a and 50^a with Caudron G4 reconnaissance aircraft, 72^a with SAML reconnaissance biplanes, and 1^a with FBA flying-boats on Lake Garda. IX Air Group had six squadrons and a flight: 37^a with SPs, 71^a and 75^a with Nieuport fighters, 73^a, 74^a and 112^a with SAMLs, and the flight of Spad 7 fighters at Verona.

Expansion had raised the strength of the *Corpo Aeronautico Militare* to sixty-five squadrons, twelve of which were equipped with Macchi-built Nieuport fighters. These were *Squadriglie* 70^a, 78^a and 82^a of X *Gruppo*, 71^a and 75^a of IX *Gruppo*, 76^a and 81^a of II *Gruppo*, 77^a and 80^a of I *Gruppo*, 79^a of XII *Gruppo*, and flights from 83^a and 85^a in Albania and northern Greece. Other fighters units had the excellent Spad 7: the elite 91^a *Squadriglia* at Santa Caterina, and flights serving with the 1st and 3rd Armies at Verona and Santa Maria la Longa. By the middle of August 1917 many squadrons were in the process of re-equipping, and rather than withdraw them from the front the air service sent new aircraft up to the squadrons in batches, so that most squadrons for a time had a mixture of machines. By November 1917 the *Corpo Aeronautico Militare* numbered fifteen fighter squadrons (eight with

Hanriot HD1s, four with Spads, and three with Nieuports), eight heavy bomber squadrons with Capronis (the independent force based round Padua) and thirty artillery spotting and reconnaissance squadrons.

Strength once again increased during 1918, and many of the foreign-designed types were supplanted or supplemented by indigenous designs. Thus by the time of the armistice with Austria-Hungary on 4 November 1918, the *Corpo Aeronautica Militare* totalled sixty-eight *squadriglie*, including eighteen of fighters (sixteen with Hanriots and two with Spad 13s). Strength was 1,758 aircraft of front-line types. Whereas production had been 382 aircraft and 606 engines in 1915, in 1918 it was 6,488 aircraft and 14,840 engines. Some 5,100 pilots had been trained, and enemy aircraft shot down totalled 763, most of them Austro-Hungarian. *Corpo Aeronautico Militare* losses, combined with those of the *Aeronautica della Regia Marina* (Naval Air Service), were 1,784.

The *Aeronautica della Regia Marina*, which controlled the *Sezione Aviazione Marina* had also grown considerably during the war. In 1915 the strength of this force was thirty-nine aircraft of all types, but by 1916 it had grown to 172, and by 1917 to 467, including seaplanes and landplanes. The main naval air stations (with numbers of seaplanes based there) were: Ancona (13), Brindisi (78), Grado (46), Pescara (17), Porto Corsini (21), Santa Maria di Leuca (9), Taranto (21), Valona (42), Varano (51) and Venice (87). Losses totalled 114 aircraft in action.

IMPERIAL RUSSIA

Before setting about the institution of heavier-than-air forces, Imperial Russia had had a long association with lighter-than-air craft, dating back as far as the Napoleonic wars at the beginning of the nineteenth century. During 1904, the Russians were the first people to use kite-balloons in war, when several were deployed as part of the defence against the Japanese attacking Port Arthur. The possibilities of airships for military purposes also seemed considerable, and in the period immediately after the Russo-Japanese War the Russians bought a number of airships from France and Germany, as well as building indigenous designs.

Official interest in heavier-than-air flight began in 1910, with the establishment of the Army Central Flying School at Gatchina, near Saint Petersburg, the Russian capital. A year later the Naval Flying School at Sevastopol was opened. Located at the northern and southern ends of 'civilised' Russia, these two schools trained both army and navy personnel. It should be noted, though, that in 1909 military funds had been used for the purchase of five Wright biplanes and a few Bristol Boxkite biplanes. At the time there were about ten private pilots in the country, and these formed a special military reserve. After the formation of the Gatchina flying school, the surviving aircraft were allocated to it in 1910.

Although not much success was enjoyed by Russian pioneers in their efforts to produce workable aircraft, the Russians even at this early date showed great flair in the designs, and were extremely forward looking, especially in military aircraft. As early as 1909, for example, A. A. Porokhovshchikov produced an aircraft with an armoured cockpit for ground-attack work. Considerable work was also done on the problems of helicopter design, especially by Igor Sikorsky and B. N. Yuriev. Two aircraft factories were opened in St. Petersburg in 1907 and 1909, with the full support of the Imperial Russian Technical Society, which formed an aviation section in 1910.

Aviation was also fortunate in enjoying royal and military patronage from men such as the Tsar, the Grand Duke Aleksandr Mikhailovich and General Baron A. Kaulbars. The most important of these was the Grand Duke Aleksandr, who used the sum of 2,000,000 roubles, raised by public subscription during the Russo-Japanese War to buy torpedo boats, instead to secure from France a number of Blériot monoplanes and Voisin biplanes, and to have Russian officers trained by French pilots. Much additional support, in the way of finance, came from enterprising private citizens, the Russian authorities being cautious about the expenditure of large public sums on aviation until it had proved itself.

Overall control of military aviation was the prerogative of the Grand Duke Aleksandr, in his capacity as Inspector-General of Aeronautics and Aviation in the Field. But real control, up to the middle of 1912, was exercised by the Aviation Division in the Electrical Service Section of the Department of Engineers, a branch of the War Office. Thereafter control was by the Council of Defence set up in the summer to control all Russia's military preparations. On 30 July an Aviation Division, commanded by a major-general, was formed within the Chief Administration of the General Staff.

Second-in-command was a chief engineer of field rank. Organisation was on the French pattern, with one department responsible for flying training and aviation in the field, and another for technical and supply matters.

In 1913 this organisation was altered again, with two General Staff agencies taking over from the erstwhile Aviation Division. These agencies were the Technical Division of the Chief Military Technical Administration, and the Organisation and Troop Service Division of the Chief Administration of the General Staff. The navy had its own air organisation, set up in 1910, which will be discussed separately.

Russian internal military organisation is into military districts, each containing two or more corps. To each of these corps was allocated one six-aircraft squadron (*otryad*), while other squadrons were attached to fortresses and higher commands for special reconnaissance duties, the only function as yet envisaged for military aircraft. The object of this organisation was to provide each corps and fortress with one six-aircraft squadron, with two to six aircraft in reserve, by April 1914. The programme proved hopelessly ambitious in the event.

Although a Russian-designed Gakkel biplane won the first Military Aviation Meeting, held in 1911 at Gatchina, the authorities preferred foreign aircraft, especially French ones, although the army also bought British, German and American aircraft, and the Imperial Russian Navy displayed a penchant for Curtiss seaplanes. Russian builders produced mostly foreign types under licence, although Sikorsky delivered some of his own types. Strength was increased by a factor of about seven up to the outbreak of World War I (with airships in brackets): by the end of 1910 forty (three); by the end of 1911 100 (nine); by 1 April 1913 150 modern and 100 obsolescent (thirteen); and in August 1914 263 (fifteen–twenty-two), although some estimates put Russian strength at this time at 224 aircraft, twelve airships and forty-six kite-balloons. Unfortunately, the air service had aircraft of sixteen types in service at the beginning of World War I, this making supply, already a difficult problem, virtually impossible. At the same time, although Russia boasted several aircraft factories, their output was low and inconsistent in quality, and

Voisin Type 3 (LA) bomber armed with Maxim machine gun. The type was also built in Russia as the Anatra VI.

The Sikorsky Ilya Muromets was the world's first 4-engined bomber. Only three were lost in the war: one crash-landed, one lost in an accident, and one shot down after disposing of four attacking fighters.

many of these factories relied heavily on German technicians, all removed by the outbreak of war.

As government allocations for the purchase of new aircraft were so low, in 1911 the Tsar granted the All-Russia Aero Club permission to raise funds to supplement the public allocations. Other bodies were granted similar rights. In April 1914 the War Office at last realised how niggardly it had been, and increased its purchases considerably: ten Sikorsky *Ilya Muromets* bombers, three airships and 326 aircraft were ordered, too late for delivery in quantity before the war.

Flying training was well provided for in terms of schools. In 1910 a naval school had been established at Kronstadt in the Gulf of Finland, and by 1912 the Gatchina, Sevastopol and Kronstadt schools had been joined by others at Kiev, Moscow and another two at St. Petersburg and Sevastopol. The next year other schools were opened or planned at Odessa, Omsk, Tashkent and Tauride. The trouble lay in the courses, which were wholly inadequate. Although in March 1913 there were only seventy-two military and forty civilian pilots, and this figure had risen to several hundreds by the outbreak of war, perhaps only 15 per cent of the latter were competent. In real terms, therefore, the position was no better than it had been eighteen months before. The situation with aircraft was similar: although in August 1914 Russia had the largest military fleet in Europe, only a small percentage of her aircraft were of any real military use.

By the end of 1915 the number of aircraft available had risen to 553, by the end of 1916 to 724, and by the time the Kerensky government took power in February 1917 to 1,039. The outbreak of war revealed the many technical and tactical deficiencies in Russia's air fleet, and a major effort was made in the spring of 1915 to

rectify this, mostly with the purchase of newer French types. To a certain extent the Russians had failed to appreciate the value of homogeneous squadrons, especially from the logistical point of view, and so right up to the time of the Bolshevik revolution of November 1917, which finally took a faltering Russia out of World War I, mixed equipment was to be found in the squadrons.

Operations revealed the need for better equipment, especially if the ground forces were to receive the support they so desperately needed, and a partial reorganisation to produce the necessary units was achieved by the beginning of 1916. Thereafter the squadrons were reorganised into specialist bomber, fighter and reconnaissance units, which allowed them to play a more effective part in the war on the Eastern Front. At the same time the number of aircraft in squadrons was increased from six to ten, with two more machines kept in reserve as replacements.

Although foreign designs continued to feature in the Russian inventory after the spring of 1916, the need for specialised types such as fighters and bombers led the adoption of more Russian designs. A good example of this is the world's first four-engined bomber, the *Ilya Muromets*, which had been adopted before the war, but was built in increasing numbers, as engine supplies allowed, to equip the 'Squadron of Flying Ships' and its sister unit in 1916. The specialised nature of air combat led to the formation of the first Russian fighter units in the spring of 1916. During the course of the year these squadrons were sometimes grouped together into fighter wings (*istrebitelnyi divisyon*) and allocated to armies.

Late in 1916 an even larger fighter formation, the group, was introduced, and there were four of these

groups by the spring of 1917: the 1st commanded by Captain A. A. Kazakov; the 2nd commanded by Captain E. N. Kruten, who had been sent to inspect British and French tactics and organisation on the Western Front during the winter of 1916–17, and was the architect of the Russian fighter forces; the 3rd commanded by Captain I. J. Zemitan; and the 4th commanded by Captain Kulvinski. There were also twelve independent fighter units, but it must be noted that most Russian fighters were probably allocated in penny packets to other units, and so the real effect of the Russian fighters on so great a front was small.

Further tactical thinking led to the attachment of a reconnaissance flight or squadron to each corps, reconnaissance and fighter flights or squadrons to each army headquarters, and the heavy bombers, together with their associated fighter and reconnaissance elements, to front headquarters (the Russian 'front' being equivalent to a western 'army group'). Aviation groups were also formed by many armies and fortresses, and a start was made on providing each brigade of artillery with flights of artillery spotting aircraft.

Complications in the administration and command of the flying services were exacerbated by the fact that the tactical control of the units involved was exercised by the relevant ground force chief-of-staff via the air unit commander, whereas logistics remained entirely separate, in the hands of air service rear-echelon personnel. The complications of the supply service, which had to deal with numerous foreign types in addition to the 4,700 aircraft built by the Russians during the war, were enormous, and combined with insufficient high command interest in the air service and with poor aircrew quality to negate the strenuous efforts of forward-thinking junior officers.

The net result was that the Russian air service played a relatively small part in deciding Russia's destiny on the Eastern Front. Moreover, the training schools just could not keep up with demands, despite the opening of extra schools during the war at Baku (for naval aircrew), Belbek, in the Caucasus, Evpatoriya, Kiev (for observers), Kacha and Tbilisi. These schools turned out 100 pilots per year, and by the middle of 1917 there were 500 pilots at the front. But as early as December 1915 the casualty rate had risen to 25 to 30 per cent — a large part of this attributable to crashes resulting from poor training, and Russia could not meet her pilot needs. The Germans and Austro-Hungarians were thus able to maintain total air superiority with small air forces, and the fighting over the Eastern Front never reached the proportions it did over the Western and Italian Fronts.

Naval aviation was a poor relative of military aviation in Russia during World War I. At the beginning of hostilities the Imperial navy had only one flying-boat base, at Libau on the Baltic, with flying schools at Revel and Sevastopol. Naval aviation in the Baltic was under the control of the Coastal Communication Service (Department North), under the overall command of the Chief of the Fleet. Naval Aviation in the Black Sea was similarly controlled, by the Department South.

With the exception of some landplanes for the defence of naval bases, the Imperial Navy's aircraft were all seaplanes. In 1917, the strength of the two halves of the naval air service were as follows: the Baltic Fleet had forty seaplanes and eight landplanes, and the Black Sea Fleet had ninety-seven flying-boats and two landplanes. Flying personnel in the Baltic Fleet totalled sixty-six. In all, the efforts of the naval air service were little, although several daring bombing raids against Turkey and Romania were tried without success.

UNITED STATES

Both the Federal and Confederate states used balloons for observation purposes in the American Civil War (1861–65), the principal unit being the Balloon Corps of the Army of the Potomac, on the Federal side, which had some seven balloons and was commanded by Thaddeus S. C. Lowe from September 1961. But with the departure of Lowe, a civilian, after a year, the Balloon Corps declined and was formally disbanded in June 1863.

Thereafter, although some officers maintained an interest in ballooning on a purely private basis, ballooning for military purposes remained in decline until Brigadier-General Adolphus W. Greely, the US Army's Chief Signal Officer and an avid balloonist, received permission to set up a Balloon Section within the Signal Corps. This operated one French balloon, which was used to some effect in Cuba during the Spanish-American War of 1898 to direct artillery fire.

During this same year the US Army, in a burst of unaccustomed enthusiasm, funded the secretary of the Smithsonian Institute, Samuel Pierpoint Langley, to the tune of $50,000 for the development of a man-carrying aircraft. The failure of Langley's 'Aerodrome', as the machine was called, in two tests in the last quarter of 1903 brought some ridicule and disapproval on the army that it subsequently shied away from heavier-than-air flight for some time. The United States were thus left with no active military interest in aviation, the Balloon Section having been disbanded towards the end of the Spanish-American War when its one balloon was severely damaged by Spanish fire.

Despite general scepticism of the Wright brothers' claim to have flown successfully just after the failure of the Langley 'Aerodrome', by 1907 there were a number of enthusiastic bodies investigating the possibilities of flight and these, coupled with public pressure, persuaded the army once again to court the possibility of flight for military purposes. Thus on 1 August 1907 the Aeronautical Division, under the overall command of the Chief Signal Officer, was established to control 'all matters pertaining to military ballooning, air machines, and all kindred subjects'. The first commander of this 'division' was Charles de Forrest Chandler, and his personnel comprised two enlisted men. The Aeronautical Division's first equipment was a Baldwin airship, designated Army Dirigible No 1 on its acceptance on August 1908.

Meanwhile the Aero Club of America had succeeded in interesting President Theodore Roosevelt in heavier-than-air craft, and so on 10 February 1908 the army accepted a tender from the Wright brothers to build such a machine. The sum of $25,000 was offered, with bonuses should certain parts of the specification be exceeded, but stringent acceptance tests were specified. Forty-one bids had been received, three had been accepted, but only the Wrights' machine came anywhere near meeting the specifications. Despite a crash during the tests at Fort Myer just outside Washington, DC, in which the pilot, Orville Wright, was severely injured and the passenger/observer, Lieutenant Thomas E. Selfridge, killed, the performance of the Wright biplane had been so impressive during August 1908 that the Wrights were given permission to rebuild the machine. New tests were flown in 1909, and the aircraft was accepted as Aeroplane No 1 on 2 August 1909.

This aircraft became the army's sole heavier-than-air

craft for the next two years. As part of their contract the Wrights had to teach two army officers to fly, and this they did at College Park, Maryland. The two officers were Lieutenants Frank P. Lahm and Frederick E. Humphreys, although Lieutenant B. D. Foulois was later added to the list. Although they were the only qualified pilots, Lahm and Humphreys were soon returned to their parent arm, the cavalry.

In March 1911 the Congress finally voted more funds to the Aeronautical Division, which was thus able to order five new aircraft. Manpower also grew, and the Aeronautical Division was able to experiment with cross-country flights, aerial bombing and machine-gunning, photography and other facets of what the aircraft might be able to do in war.

By November 1912 the division had grown to nine aircraft (Wright, Curtiss and Burgess machines), with fourteen officer pilots and thirty-nine enlisted men. Inclement weather had meant in previous years that the Aeronautical Division had moved its base of operations south during the winter months, and in the winter of 1912–13 the Wright aircraft and their personnel moved to Augusta, Georgia, while the Curtiss aircraft and crews moved to North Island, San Diego, where

Curtiss operated a private flying school. The site later became army property, and the location of the army's first permanent flying school.

The Mexican Civil War, which had been going on since 1911, began to concern the United States from February 1913, and the Aeronautical Division was ordered from Augusta to Texas City to cooperate with the 2nd Division. The better to do this, the men and machines sent south to Texas were organised as the 1st Aero Squadron in March 1913. Although this little squadron was fortunately not called upon to fly in combat, as no military hostilities broke out, much experience in cross-country operations in hostile terrain was gained. In June most of the unit moved to San Diego, leaving only two aircraft, three pilots and twenty-six men at Texas City. The centre of the Aeronautical Division thus became San Diego, with detachments at Texas City, and also at Fort William McKinley just outside Manila in the Philippines, set up in March 1912, and at Fort Kamehameha in the Hawaiian Islands, set up in 1913. At the end of the year College Park was abandoned, and the Aeronautical Division's headquarters moved to North Island, home of the Signal Corps Aviation School.

At this time the aviation record of the army came under close inspection, for of the twenty aircraft bought to date, nine had been written off in crashes, and eleven of forty pilots had also been killed. Early in 1914, therefore, after inspection the eleven surviving Wright and Curtiss pushers were condemned, leaving the army with only five aircraft, all of them in dire need of reconstruction. Thus virtually all flying came to a halt. Fortunately, though, a new Curtiss type was available, and seventeen of this tractor biplane design, the J, were ordered.

Legislation now made aviation a permanent aspect of army organisation: on 18 July 1914 an Aviation Section of the Signal Corps was formed, with a strength of sixty unmarried lieutenants for flying duties, and 260 enlisted men. Overall command was exercised by General Scriven, the Chief Signal Officer, who at the end of the year recommended that the Aviation Section should have a strength of eighteen squadrons, each with twelve aircraft. It was not until the United States entered the war, that anything like this number were formed.

Trouble along the border with Mexico had been considerable during 1914 and 1915, and so the 1st Aero Squadron had been posted to Galveston in Texas in

General Mitchell who flew frequent reconnaissance flights in the Spad XI two-seater, a generally unsuccessful type of plane used by two US and three Belgian squadrons.

When the United States entered the war they had no significant combat aircraft and had to rely on British and French aircraft like the Nieuport 28C.1 (above), however they built an excellent trainer in the Curtiss JN-4 (above right).

1914 and to Brownsville, also in Texas, in 1915. Then in March 1916 Pancho Villa, the Mexican bandit-cum-revolutionary, raided Columbus, New Mexico, and killed seventeen Americans in the process. Immediately a punitive expedition was organised under the command of Brigadier-General John J. Pershing. The 1st Aero Squadron, with eight aircraft, ten pilots and eighty-four enlisted men, was ordered from Fort Sam Houston, Texas, to Columbus as an artillery spotter force. But conditions over Mexico were vile, and by April only two aircraft were left, both of them soon condemned as unairworthy.

In a backhanded fashion, the failure of the army's aircraft over Mexico proved useful, for reports of the failure spurred the Congress to action. In August 1916, when major air battles were raging over the 1st Battle of the Somme, $13 million were voted for the development of military aviation. In the same year the National Defense Act provided for the manpower expansion of the Aviation Section, and also set up a reserve. The immediate effect of these two measures was the establishment of a number of army flying schools. This was a move in the right direction, but as the United States entered World War I on 6 April 1917 this modest programme was soon overtaken by vastly more ambitious schemes. At the time of the American entry into the war, the Aviation Section's strength was about 250 aircraft deployed into several flying schools and seven squadrons: the 1st, 3rd, 4th and 5th in the metropolitan United States, the 2nd in the Philippines and the 6th and 7th in the Panama Canal region; manpower consisted of only 131 officers and 1,087 men. None of the aircraft could in any way be considered fit for combat, and no real plans for the conversion of the Aviation Section into a combat force existed.

Initial American mobilisation plans called for a large army, numbering some 1,000,000 men, but only a relatively small air service to support them. Yet within a few weeks of the announcement of this scheme, public pressure was forcing the authorities to reconsider, and the arrival of British and French missions completed the process. Both the United States' allies called on her to increase her air effort, and ambitious plans were drawn up. Some '22,625 aeroplanes plus 80 per cent spares and 44,000 engines' were to be produced by American industrial methods, and on 24 July the Congress voted $640,000,000 million for the implementation of the scheme, urged on by Secretary of War Newton D. Baker. The Aviation Section itself was to be expanded to 345 combat squadrons, forty-five construction companies, eight-one supply squadrons, eleven repair squadrons and twenty-six balloon companies. It was planned that 263 squadrons would be deployed to Europe by June 1918.

American industry not surpisingly failed to meet the

vastly over-ambitious production dates set for American equipment, and rather than supply the other Allies with aircraft and engines, the Americans found themselves in the embarrassing position of having to call on them for aircraft. Allied practical knowledge of combat methods and tactics was also widely used. This failure to meet their own, let alone Allied, needs was in retrospect not surprising. It had been hoped that American mass production methods would allow aircraft and their engines to be produced as easily as cars, but the problems proved to be considerably more than expected, and so the overseas deployment had to be curtailed considerably to 202 squadrons in France by July 1919. In fact there were only forty-five combat squadrons in France by the time of the armistice of 11 November 1918, although by this time expansion was increasing so rapidly that the target figure of 202 squadrons might well have been met by July 1919.

The chief stumbling block on the road to expansion was the provision of adequate training aircraft, and so in May 1917 the Council of National Defense set up the Aircraft Production Board, whose name was changed to the Aircraft Board in October. Failure of all production programmes, whose target figures had been widely spread in the press, was a national scandal, and an investigation was held in the spring of 1918.

In May, as a result of this investigation, several departments to control aviation were set up, with direct responsibility to the Secretary of War. These authorities were part of the new Air Service, and consisted of the Division of Military Aeronautics, which controlled operations and training, and the Bureau of Aircraft Production (lately the Equipment Division of the Signal Corps), which administered all supply requirements of the service. In August John D. Ryan was appointed Director of the Air Service and Second Assistant Secretary of War.

Training was in three phases: ground school, primary training and advanced training. Right from the outset, the Air Service decided that advanced training should take place only in Great Britain, France and Italy, where there were modern combat aircraft and instructors fully up to date with the air war requirements in Europe. Ground schools were established at eight universities, and primary training was carried out at American and Canadian flying schools. In April 1917 the United States had possessed only three training schools, but during the war this figure grew to twenty-seven in the United States and another sixteen in Europe.

Typical of the American training centres in Europe was the 3rd Aviation Instruction Center at Issoudun in France, one of seven such centres in Europe. This had a main base with modern aircraft and complete repair facilities, plus eleven satellite flying fields. Of the 14,835 cadets who started primary training, 8,688 received commissions, and some 2,500 received advanced training in Europe. Great efforts were made, both in the United States and in Europe, to produce skilled groundcrew to support the flying units in combat.

Control of the Air Service in France was exercised by General John J. Pershing, commander-in-chief of the American Expeditionary Force. Although the Allies wished the Americans to be integrated with their own forces, Pershing adamantly refused to allow this, and instead demanded that the Americans fight as a national body with their own sector of the line. Pending the arrival of enough forces to make this possible, though, Pershing allowed the first ground and air units to arrive

General Mason M. Patrick, the Chief of the Air Service in France.

to be deployed under British and French command to gain combat experience. The American national force was eventually realised only in August 1918.

Although there had been Americans serving in Europe for some time, notably in the Lafayette *Escadrille* of the French air service and several British squadrons, these had been volunteers, most of whom transferred to the Air Service after America's entry into the war. Thus the first truly American unit to arrive in Europe was the 1st Aero Squadron, which landed in France on 3 September 1917. It received French aircraft and underwent a period of strenuous training before making its first operational flight on 15 April 1918. Meanwhile other American air units had arrived in France and Great Britain in the winter of 1917–18.

The first sector allocated to the Americans was the relatively quiet Toul area, and here the American squadrons began to gather: in February 1918 the 94th Pursuit Squadron arrived, followed by the 95th Pursuit Squadron in March. The 94th made the Americans' first combat sortie on 3 April, and opened the American score on 14 April, when two German aircraft were shot down. The 94th and 95th Squadrons were later amalgamated into the 1st Pursuit Group.

By the end of May the 1st Corps Observation Group, consisting of three squadrons, had been formed, and operated under French control. The first bomber unit, the 96th Bombardment Squadron, then entered combat in June, and at last the Americans had the makings of a fully comprehensive combat air service in France. Yet even in late June the Americans could not field a fully comprehensive force, for when the 1st Brigade was formed under Colonel William Mitchell at Château Thierry, several French squadrons had to be added to the American units provided by the 1st Pursuit Group and the 1st Corps Observation Group. The 1st Brigade, which was allocated its own sector of front line, had a hard time of it right from the start, for its units were opposed by larger, experienced German forces.

The Chief of the Air Service, General Mason M. Patrick, reorganised the Air Service in France in August, to conform with the allocation of an entire sector to the newly formed American 1st Army. Mitchell, promoted to brigadier-general, was given command of the Air Service, 1st Army, which comprised three wings and included some French elements: pursuit (fighter), observation and bombardment (bombing). Under Mitchell's immediate command were thus some forty-nine squadrons, about half of them French. He also controlled a French air division of forty more squadrons, and could call on the support and cooperation of the British Independent Force. All in all, therefore, Mitchell controlled some 1,500 aircraft for the American offensive around Saint Mihiel, the largest concentration of aircraft yet seen in war. The air battle during the offensive was severe, but Mitchell's forces kept the Germans on the permanent defensive, and the bombardment wing, in particular, proved its worth several times over. While about one-third of the aircraft available supported the ground forces, two-thirds took the air war deep into German territory.

At the armistice there were forty-five American combat squadrons in France. These had some 800 pilots and 500 observers, and a strength of 740 aircraft. Losses were 289 aircraft and forty-eight balloons, while victories were 781 aircraft and seventy-three balloons.

The equipment of the Air Service in France was basically French: by the time of the armistice, the Americans had received 4,881 French aircraft, 258 British machines and nineteen Italian types. In the absence of suitable American combat designs, in August 1917 it had been decided to adopt Allied designs: the de Havilland DH 4, Handley Page O/400 and Caproni bombers. By early 1919 some 4,868 DH 4s had been built but had not seen combat. Thus the American effort remained a relatively small one, despite the great hopes and plans entertained for it in the spring of 1917. But had the war continued into 1919 the American role would have been a greater one by far.

The interest of the US Navy in aviation dates back to 1898, with the contract to Langley, and naval officers observed the failure of the 'Aerodrome' in its two tests. Thereafter interest languished until 26 September 1910, when Captain W. I. Chambers was designated the officer to whom all correspondence concerning aviation should be directed. In 1911 the Congress voted funds for naval aircraft, and Chambers selected Curtiss to build the navy's first aircraft, the A-1 Triad.

The centre of naval operations so far as aviation was concerned was flexible in the first few years: Annapolis, Maryland; San Diego; Pensacola, Florida; and even Guantanamo Bay, Cuba. In 1914, though, naval aircraft cooperated with surface forces in operations in Mexico, notably Vera Cruz.

On 1 July 1915 the Office of Naval Aeronautics was established, at last putting naval aviation on a formal footing. In August 1916 a Naval Flying Corps was authorised, with a strength of 150 officers and 350 enlisted men. At the same time, US Marine Corps and Coast Guard officers began learning to fly in naval flying schools, their services also having been authorised to raise flying units.

On 6 April 1917, the day on which the United States declared war on Germany, the Naval Flying Corps numbered fifty-four aircraft, forty-eight pilots (including those under instruction) and one base. In the next nineteen months the corps expanded enormously, there being twelve bases in the United States and twenty-seven in Europe. Strength totalled 2,107 aircraft and fifteen airships, manned and serviced by 6,716 officers and 30,693 enlisted men, plus 282 officers and 2,180 men of the US Marine Corps. The first combat sortie by a US Navy aircraft during World War I had been on 18 November 1917, when a Tellier flying-boat took off on a patrol from Le Croisic at the mouth of the Loire river. The main effort was devoted to anti-submarine patrol in European waters.

General Mitchell's staff. Among Mitchell's far-sighted ideas was a plan for the parachuting of one division of infantry to take Metz, the operation to take place in 1919.

AUSTRIA· HUNGARY

In the first decade of the twentieth century the Austro-Hungarian Empire was in some disarray, and although still rated a great power, was already showing the distinct signs of dissolution associated with backward-looking to the days of greatness. Nowhere was this more apparent than in the empire's approach to modern military matters, which was at best lukewarm. In aviation, for example, the authorities were content to buy a few Etrich *Taube* monoplanes of indigenous design, and otherwise leave aviation to the enterprise of individual officers.

By 1912, however, the growth of the French and German air arms, and the lessons of Italian air operations in Libya, could no longer be ignored, and Oberst Emil Uzelac was appointed to the command of the new *Luftfahrtruppen* (Aviation Troops). At forty-four, Uzelac immediately learned to fly, and in the next few years acquired a great reputation for himself as a test pilot who insisted on flying every new type considered for service with the *Luftfahrtruppen*. Uzelac's task was an immensely difficult one, for apathy so far as the flying services were concerned was rife, and funds were always in very short supply.

Early operations in Galicia against the Russians revealed the shortcomings and numerical inadequacies of the air service, and Germany had reluctantly to supply her ally with quantities of Aviatik and Rumpler B-type reconnaissance biplanes. Meanwhile at home the Austro-Hungarian authorities began a belated attempt to build up the air service and the manufacturing industries upon which they depended.

Austria-Hungary's problems were exacerbated in May 1915 by the entry into the war of Italy on the side of the Allies, forcing the Austro-Hungarians to deploy some of their already overstretched forces against the new enemy in some of the most inhospitable flying country in the world.

In 1917, typical *Luftfahrtruppen* organisation was into *Fliegerkompagnien* (Flying Companies). These were divided into three types in a common numerical series irrespective of type: *Aufklärungskompagnien* (Re-

connaissance Companies) with eight or more C types and four escort fighters; *Jagdkompagnien* (Fighter Companies) with sixteen to twenty single-seat fighters; and *Geschwader* or *Fliegerkompagnien-G* (Wings or Bomber Companies) with ten bombers and four escort fighters. *Fliegerkompagnien* were usually abbreviated to *Flik*, with fighter units being denoted by a J suffix to the unit's number.

The increase in the pace of air operations during 1917 led Uzelac to try to form larger fighter formations, but the official army policy was to use fighters basically as escorts for the artillery spotting and reconnaissance two-seaters. This policy combined with a general shortage of combat types to defeat Uzelac's efforts to form homogeneous fighters formations capable of taking the air war to Italy. But although there had been only seven *Jagdkompagnien* in 1917, Uzelac managed to raise this number to thirteen in 1918, although many of them had only reduced scales of equipment. During the year, though, the growing strength of the Italian air force finally took the air war completely to the Austro-Hungarians, and despite the introduction of limited numbers of new aircraft, there was nothing Uzelac could do to stem the Allied tide. With the armistice of 4 November 1918 the *Luftfahrtruppen* finally dissolved.

The Austro-Hungarian naval air arm got off to a hesitant start in 1909, when some naval officers were sent to France and Great Britain to learn to fly. One of these men was Lieutenant-Commander Viktor Klobucar Rukavina de Bunic, who became head of the naval air arm in 1910.

While the indigenous aircraft industry was being built up, the naval air arm decided to develop its ideas and pilots with French seaplanes, several types of which were bought. But by the time of the outbreak of war, several Austro-Hungarian designs had entered service, the most notable being of Lohner construction.

By the end of the war, the Austro-Hungarian navy had naval air stations in the following places (with the number of aircraft in brackets): Cattaro (45), Cosada Training station near Pola (30), Santa Catarina arsenal (18), Santa Catarina central flying station near Pola (53) and Trieste (27). Losses had amounted to ninety aircraft and six airships. After the armistice, all surviving flying-boats but two (taken to the United States) were destroyed.

A three-bay version of the Lohner L.47 flying boat of the Austro-Hungarian Navy.

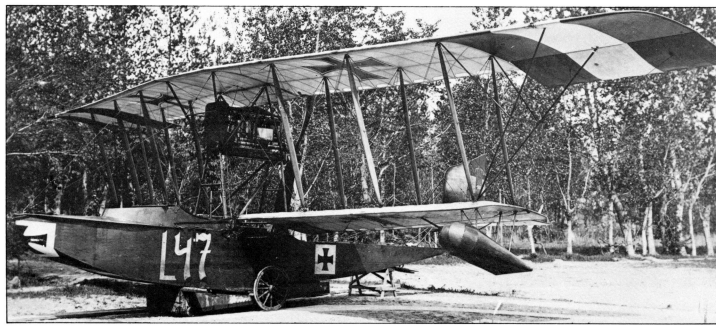

BELGIUM

The first heavier-than-air flight in Belgium was made on 26 May 1908 by Léon Delagrange, who thus electrified a number of young Belgians into trying to emulate the feat. Yet in 1909 only two Belgians, Professor Emile Allard and the Baron Pierre de Caters, managed to fly, although a number of enterprising men had succeeded in getting into the air, one of the most prominent being *Chevalier* Jules de Laminne, who learned to fly in France at the Farman school at Mourmelon.

By 1910 there were two airfields in Belgium, the one at Saint Job 't Goor near Antwerp being owned by de Caters, and the other, at Kiewit, being the home of the Farman III bought by de Laminne. It was at this latter airfield that *Général* Hellebaut, the War Minister, made his first flight on 7 July 1910, with de Laminne at the controls of the Farman. So impressed was Hellebaut that he immediately decided to develop the cadre of an aviation service within the Belgian army. Laminne, in a fit of enthusiasm, told the War Minister that he would train any officers the army sent to him, entirely free of charge. *Commandant* Le Clément de Saint Marcq, commander of the *Compagnie des Ouvriers et Aérostiers* (Mechanics' and Balloonists' Company) at Wilryck, was placed in charge of the training programme, but his ideas on pilot instruction received almost total disapproval, and the high command recommended that the Belgian pilots be trained in the French manner before joining the *Compagnie des Ouvriers et Aérostiers*. As the company was part of the Engineer Corps, it was decided, all future military pilots should be volunteers from this corps.

Two artillery officers, *Sous-Lieutenants* Baudouin de Montens d'Oostenryck and Alfred Sarteel, had already taken up flying at the de Caters school, however, and their efforts, becoming known to other junior officers throughout the army, resulted in a flood of letters requesting flying training on the desks of the War Ministry. Hellebaut therefore instructed Le Clément de Saint Marcq on 9 September 1910 to speed up arrangements with de Laminne for the purchase of a Farman biplane and the start of flying lessons.

Impatient of delay, however, two cavalry officers, *Lieutenants* Emmanuel Bronne and Robert Dhanis, started a course of private tuition with de Laminne. De Montens d'Oostenryck qualified at the end of September 1910, and Sarteel a month later, and the news of these successes prompted a further flood of applications.

Meanwhile *Lieutenant* Georges Nelis of the *Compagnie des Ouvriers et Aérostiers* was on 3 October 1910 sent off on the first official training course with de Laminne. After a short period of tuition at Kiewit, Nelis and three mechanics were sent off for more advanced training in France, where the pilot received his brevet on 21 December 1910.

Back in Belgium, a committee had been established on 31 October to examine the future organisation of the Belgian air service. In its report, the committee recommended that a military flying school should be set up, that personnel should be recruited from all branches of the army, that a Farman biplane, a hangar, spares and tools should be bought from France, and that an airfield should be built on the artillery range at Brasschaet near Antwerp. The report was accepted *in toto*, and had been fully implemented by spring 1911, with the exception of the aircraft. However, de Laminne with his usual generosity offered a 50-hp Aviator aircraft to King Albert, who in turn passed it on to the military. The

Officers at the Belgian Aviation School at Estampes, June 1915. The aircraft in the background are Maurice Farmans.

Commandant Tournay of the Belgian Aviation School at Estampes.

Belgian air service now had five pilots (de Montens d'Oostenryck, Dhanis, Bronne, Sarteel and a new entry to the field, Lebon), one aircraft, two mechanics and one carpenter.

The Military Aviation School was officially opened on 5 May 1911, although not without tragedy, as Bronne crashed during the inaugural display and was badly burned, the Farman delivered that day being totally destroyed. The Aviator proved impossible, and pending the arrival of another Farman flying was suspended and the school was put on a sounder administrative footing. The second machine arrived on 24 May, but this too was written off on 25 July when Dhanis, with *Lieutenant* Soumoy as observer, crashed. Both aircrew were unharmed. Two more machines arrived during August, one on the 7th and the other on the 31st.

Commandant Mathieu was now in command of flying, and he persuaded the authorities to allow him to alter the basic Farman layout by abandoning the forward elevator and adding a nacelle for the crew. The actual alterations were carried out by the Antwerp firm of Bollekens.

In September 1911 aircraft, all two of them, were used in the army manoeuvres held near Antwerp. Several useful reconnaissance flights were made, and the importance attached to reconnaissance had been attested at the end of August by the issue of a directive entitled *Cours d'observation et de renseignements par aeroplanes* (Course of observation and intelligence by means of aircraft). To be fully qualified, pilots had to pass this course as well as have a pilot's brevet. By the end of November, all the pilots had also qualified as observers. Some thirteen Belgians had qualified as military pilots, but as yet the air arm was untested in any real sense, and was too small to be considered of any importance to the army in general.

In 1912, therefore, the Belgian general staff began to develop the theories of air war which the air arm would be expected to fulfil. At the same time *Général* Michel had replaced *Général* Hellebaut as War Minister, and the new man decided that the Military Aviation School should be reorganised into three sections catering for basic, advanced and operational training, with a view to the eventual expansion of the air service. At this time, it may be noted, the Belgians air tested the remarkable air-cooled light machine-gun designed by an American Colonel Isaac Lewis, who had come to Europe as his invention had been spurned by his compatriots. Although the gun had many teething problems, it was in essence an exemplary weapon, and was destined for great use in both ground and air roles in World War I. The first of four Jero-built Farman F20 biplanes was delivered on 9 July 1912, and it was on one of these machines that the Lewis gun was air tested on 12 September, with great success.

On 29 March 1913 Monsieur de Brocqueville, the new War Minister, turned Kiewit into a military airfield, at which all primary training was now to take place. The growing size of the heavier-than-air force, together with the number of pilots, also prompted de Brocqueville to institute a reorganisation in which lighter- and heavier-than-air craft were put into separate commands, and the control of training and operations for heavier-than-air craft became functions of different bodies. On 16 April, by royal decree, there was established a *Compagnie des Aviateurs* (Aviators' Company) under Mathieu, and a *Compagnie des Aéro-stiers* (Balloonists' Company), the two bodies becoming effective on 26 April. The Belgian army of the time consisted of four divisions, and it was hoped to form four aircraft squadrons, rising to six as the army expanded to six divisions.

Manoeuvres were held near Beverloo during May 1913, and several aircraft took part, astonishing all with the speed and accuracy with which they could bring

Below FBA Type H flying-boats for anti-submarine and coastal patrol. The type was widely used by France, Britain and Italy.

back information about the enemy's dispositions and strength. At this time the main strength of the *Compagnie des Aviateurs* lay in Farman HF20 biplanes, and further deliveries of this type during July 1913 brought total aircraft strength up to twenty. At last this allowed the four squadrons planned in April to be formed. Each squadron had four aircraft, with eight pilots and fairly lavish amounts of mechanical transport for both men and equipment, this making the squadrons as mobile, if not more so, than the divisions they were intended to support.

The new organisation was tested in further manoeuvres, held in August 1913 between the Meuse and Sambre rivers. The 1*ère Escadrille* (1st Squadron) under *Lieutenant* Demanet operated with the 3rd Division (red side), the 2*me Escadrille* under *Lieutenant* Wahis with the 2nd Division (blue side). Despite some grave misgivings about the safety problem posed by aircraft, exemplified by warnings to local residents about what to do in the event of a forced landing, all went well, and the aircraft of both sides performed creditably, confirming the general staff's belief in the utility of air reconnaissance.

Further progress was made with the development of the *Compagnie des Aviateurs* in the last year before the start of World War I, especially in the development of radio communication for artillery spotting, and in reconnaissance work, but the size of the air service did not increase significantly. Thus, on the outbreak of war, the strength of the *Compagnie des Aviateurs* comprised the main depot and base at Brasschaet, the 1*ère Escadrille* with Henry Farmans operational with the 2nd Division, the 2*me Escadrille* with Henry Farmans operational with the 4th Division and the 3*me* and 4*me Escadrilles* formed but not yet operational with their divisions.

All thirty-eight available military pilots had been mobilised by 2 August, and in addition strength had been swelled by the arrival of eight civilian pilots, some of whom brought their own aircraft: Jan Olieslagers, for example, turned up with his Blériot, and Henri Crombez with his Deperdussin. On the next day the two operational squadrons were sent off to their war stations the 1*ère* to Liège to fly reconnaissance for the great ring of forts surrounding the city, and the 2*me* to the outskirts of Namur. The other units remained in reserve at Brasschaet, and these were the dispositions when the Germans invaded Belgium on 4 August 1914.

Within three days, however, the *Compagnie des Aviateurs* had suffered heavy losses: two Farmans had crashed, another Farman had come down behind the German lines, and Crombez' Deperdussin had had to be abandoned. On the 11th, though, eight Maurice Farman MF14s were delivered from France to Berchem-Sainte-Agathe, where a flying school was set up. On the 12th the 3*me Escadrille* was declared operational as the GHQ reconnaissance unit with the four Blériot monoplanes delivered from France on that day. But one day later only two of the Blériots were left.

Namur was soon so threatened by the German advance that the 2*me Escadrille* was pulled back to Buc near Paris for reorganisation. In September it returned to Belgium to operate from the racecourse in Ostende. During the month a great storm destroyed three of the *Compagnie des Aviateurs*' aircraft. With the exception of two artillery spotting Blériots, it was then decided to pull all Belgian aircraft back to Saint Pol for a reorganisation. Unfortunately the French could supply no new aircraft, and the workshops at Calais were so

At the time of the great Allied offensive in Flanders in September 1918, part of the final drives that caused the Germans to sue for an armistice, the *Aviation Militaire* was deployed as follows:

1*ère Escadrille* at Houthem, under *Commandant* Michaux, had aircraft of several types, and was a maintenance unit

2*me Escadrille* at Les Moeres, under *Commandant* Issenrentent, had Breguet 14s in the observation role

3*me Escadrille* at Les Moeres, under *Capitaine* Dhanis, had Breguet 14s in the observation role

4*me Escadrille* at Hondschote, under *Commandant* Richard, had Spad 11s in the observation role

5*me Escadrille* at Houthem, under *Commandant* Hugon, had Breguet 14s in the observation role

6*me Escadrille* at Houthem, under *Commandant* Desmet, had Spad 11s in the observation role

7*me Escadrille* at Houthem, under *Commandant* Jaumotte, had Henry Farmans in the observation role

8*me Escadrille* at Hondschote, under an unknown commander, had Farman F40s in the night bombing role

9*me Escadrille* at Les Moeres, under *Capitaine* Gallez, had Hanriot HD 1s in the fighter role

10*me Escadrille* at Les Moeres, under *Capitaine* Dony, had Spad 13s in the fighter role

11*me Escadrille* at Les Moeres, under *Commandant* Hiernaux, had Sopwith Camels in the fighter role.

Belgian naval aviation was on a very small scale, some Schreck-built FBA flying-boats being operated from Calais during 1916 and 1917, where they were joined by four Short 827s which had been used previously in the Belgian Congo.

much overburdened that the effort of the Belgian air service was severely curtailed. Following a raid on Saint Pol on 24 December by two German aircraft, the Belgians at last decided to start fitting machine-gun armament to some of their aircraft.

Early in 1915 the *Compagnie des Aviateurs* was renamed the *Aviation Militaire* to recognise the reorganisation and expansion of the air arm. Then in April the new force moved up to airfields in the Coxyde and Houthem areas, where its five squadrons operated with the five Belgian field divisions. A sixth Belgian division, held in reserve, had no air unit attached, and it was not until 1916, when the Belgians received some BE 2c aircraft from Great Britain, that a 6*me Escadrille* was formed. The five squadrons in service during 1915 were equipped with Voisins, Henry Farmans and Maurice Farmans.

In 1916 the 1*ère Escadrille*, previously equipped with six Maurice Farmans and one Nieuport, was equipped throughout with Nieuport 11 *Bébé* aircraft to become Belgium's first fighter unit. Later in 1916 the 5*me Escadrille* was also turned into a fighter unit, and both squadrons operated from an airfield at Les Moeres. Expansion continued during 1916 and 1917, Belgium becoming a leading exponent of the agile Hanriot HD 1 fighter. Equipment was predominantly French, most of it fairly modern.

No major alterations in the organisation or tactics of the Belgian *Aviation Militaire* were carried out in 1917, but in February 1918 the first fighter group was formed, with three squadrons: the 1*ère* and 5*me Escadrilles*, renumbered 9*me* and 10*me*, were joined by the new 11*me Escadrille*, which received the Hanriots which the 9*me* was replacing with Sopwith Camels. These eleven squadrons formed the main strength of the *Aviation Militaire* for the rest of the war. By mid-year the numerical strength of the *Aviation Militaire* was sixty-nine single-seat fighters and fifty-eight two-seaters.

AUSTRALIA

An Australian Flying Corps was raised in 1913, with one squadron. This was equipped with two BE 2a and two Deperdussin aircraft, some Farmans being bought later. A BE 2a and a Farman were used in the 1914 campaign to take German New Guinea. In 1915 Australian elements were used alongside the Royal Flying Corps in Mesopotamia. By 1916 there were four Australian Flying Corps squadrons in Egypt and Great Britain, all equipped with British aircraft.

BULGARIA

A Bulgarian Flying Corps was formed during the Balkan Wars of 1912–13, and operated about twelve Blériot and Bristol monoplanes, all flown by foreign pilots. Disbanded after the Balkan Wars, the corps was re-formed in 1915 after Bulgaria had allied herself to the Central Powers. Nominally Bulgarian, the corps' aircraft and pilots were in fact supplied by Germany and Austria-Hungary. After the end of the war, the Bulgarian Army Flying Corps was disbanded again on the orders of the Allies.

CANADA

The Dominion of Canada formed a Canadian Aviation Corps in 1914, with a strength of one aircraft. This accompanied the Canadian forces to Europe on the outbreak of war, and was scrapped the following year. Thereafter many Canadians served with great distinction in the Royal Flying Corps, Royal Naval Air Service and Royal Air Force. Two Canadian squadrons, one equipped with SE 5a fighters and the other with DH 9a bombers, were formed in 1918.
A Royal Canadian Air Service was formed in 1918 with eight Sopwith Baby floatplanes.

GREECE

The Greek War Ministry began to investigate the possibilities of aircraft as a means of reconnaissance in 1911, and sent one lieutenant from each of the artillery, cavalry, engineers and infantry to receive pilot training in France. The first to qualify was Lieutenant D. Kamberos, who returned to Greece in May 1912 with a Farman two-seater. This took part in the summer manoeuvres, as did the Nieuport owned by Emanuel Argyropoulos, a civilian.

After the start of the Balkan Wars in October 1912, the *Proti Mira Aeroplanon* (1st Aircraft Squadron) of the *Lochos Aeroplanon* (Aircraft Company) was formed in Larissa under Kamberos, its equipment being two Farmans. By this time there was also an *Apospasma Aeroploias Ipirou* (Epiros Aviation Detachment) with two Farmans operating under a Frenchman, Lieutenant Barès, from Nikopolis near Preveza. Both these units proved their worth in the war, and even harassed Turkish ground forces with hand grenades dropped from the air.

The end of the war in 1913 found the army reduced to two aircraft, which then became the equipment of a somewhat peripatetic *Aeroporiki Sholi* (Aviation School). The general staff saw little future use for aircraft, and so nothing was done about putting the flying service on a more permanent and stable footing, or buying new aircraft.

The Royal Hellenic Navy, though, was more ambitious. In 1912 two Astra seaplanes had been bought and based on Mudros. Then in 1913, urged on by a British mission, a Sopwith two-seat seaplane was bought, with the object of training pilots for the planned *Naftiki Aeroporiki Ypiressia* (Naval Air Service). Six more Sopwith seaplanes were ordered in March 1914, but these were later commandeered in Great Britain by the Admiralty. With the entire staff of the school laid low by malaria, no flying was done until all moved to the more healthy air of Phaleron and delivery had been accepted of four Henry Farman F22 seaplanes which formed the equipment of the *Naftiko Smynos* (Naval Flight) under Lieutenant Moraitines, the navy's first pilot.

Thereafter Greek service flying stagnated until 1916, when the provisional government of Eleftherios Venizelos assumed power. Then all aviation elements came under joint control. What had been the naval element moved once again to Mudros, where it operated under British control, and an army-navy flying school, the *Sholi Ekpedefseos Moudrou*, was set up on Mudros, Greek pilots going on to Royal Flying Corps' schools in the Middle East for further training.

In June 1917 Greece formally joined the Allies, and with French assistance a *Stratiotiki Aeroporia* (Army Air Force) was gradually built up. Training was undertaken by the French, who opened the *Centre d'Entrainements des Armées Alliées en Orient* (Training Centre for the Allied Armies in the East) at Sedes, near Salonika.

In November 1917 the first Greek squadron, the 532 *Mira Vomvarthismou ke Anagnorisseos* (532nd Bombing and Reconnaissance Squadron) was commissioned. Operating in Macedonia, the squadron was joined in 1918 by the 531 *Mira Dioxeos* (531st Fighter Squadron). All flying equipment was French. On 1 June 1918, the third Greek unit, 533 *Mira Dioxeos*, was formed. Despite its fighter designation, the squadron was a bomber and reconnaissance unit. A final squadron, the 534th, had been formed on 20 September 1918, but the war in this theatre had ended on 4 September, and so the unit saw no action in World War I. The Army Air Force's strength at the end of the war was twelve Breguet 14, twenty-two Dorand AR 1, fourteen Nieuport 24bis, sixteen Spad 7 and eight Spad 13 aircraft. Overall command was exercised by a French officer, *Commandant* de Thezy.

May 1918 had seen the reorganisation of the naval air service into four independent flights (*Anexartita Elleniki Naftika Smyni*), H1 at Thasos, H2 at Mudros, H3 at Stavros and H4 at Mitilini. Equipment consisted of Sopwith Pup and Camel fighters, and Sopwith Baby and Short 184 seaplanes, plus a few de Havilland 4 bombers. Command was exercised by the Royal Naval Air Service up to the end of the war.

JAPAN

Both the Imperial Japanese Army and Navy established air services in 1912, but their interest in aviation had started earlier than this. The army had acquired balloons in 1877 and used them successfully in the Russo-Japanese War of 1904. Then in 1910 Captain Yoshitoshi Tokugawa had been sent to France to learn to fly, and Captain Kumazo Hino to Germany for the same purpose. During 1911 several foreign aircraft were bought, further officers were sent abroad for training, and finally a batch of officers was trained in Japan. Most aircraft were imported, or built in Japan as modified versions of Western aircraft. Considerable effort was devoted to the building up of the number of trained personnel, but no army aircrews fought in World War I except a few seconded to France. In December 1915 the army air service was reorganised as the Air Battalion of the Army Transport Command, and as such achieved a small measure of independence.

In June 1912 the Imperial Navy had set up the Naval Aeronautical Research Committee. Shortly afterwards six officers were sent to France and the United States with orders to learn to fly, and to buy some suitable seaplanes. Two of these officers made the first naval flights in Japan, in a Farman and a Curtiss seaplane, on 2 November 1912 from the new naval air station outside Yokosuka. Other naval pilots were soon in training, and the navy commissioned its first seaplane tender, the *Wakamiyu Maru*, in 1913.

Japanese naval aircraft played an important part in the reduction of the German concession at Tsingtao in China in September and October 1914, making several useful reconnaissance flights and sinking a small mine-layer with bombs. Thereafter operational activity was non-existent, although organisation improvements took place with the formation of the Yokosuka Naval Air Corps in April 1916, the Sasebo Naval Air Corps in March 1918 and manufacture of indigenously designed aircraft at Yokosuka Naval Arsenal from 1917 onwards.

and the *Serviço de Aviação do Corpo Expedicionário Português* (Portuguese Expeditionary Corps Air Service) had no aircraft, which were to be obtained in France when the service's *Esqualdrilha Inicial* (1st Squadron) arrived there. No aircraft were available, however, and the squadron's twelve pilots were deployed in French squadrons.

The navy also had its air arm, the *Serviço de Aeronáutica Naval* (Naval Flying Service). Although the first personnel had been trained at the army school, in September 1917 the *Escola de Aviação Naval* was formed at Bom Sucesso naval base near Lisbon, with three FBA flying-boats. These boats were used for coastal patrols from November onwards, although greater use was made of Portuguese facilities in Portugal and in the Azores by the other Allies, notably the French.

The Expeditionary Corps air service was recalled from France before the end of the war, and some of its more experienced pilots were transferred to the new *Esquadrilha Expedicionária a Angola* (Expeditionary Squadron to Angola), which had nine Caudron G4s. The war ended before the squadron could be used operationally, however.

ROMANIA

The Romanian army set up a Flying Corps in 1910. By the end of the next year this had four Blériots and four Henry Farmans, to which were added some Bristols and two Morane-Saulnier Type Fs in 1912. During World War I some Nieuport 12s and 17s were delivered, but the Romanian Army Flying Corps was overwhelmed by the air force of Germany and Austria-Hungary soon after Romania's entry into the war.

PORTUGAL

Although the Portuguese National Assembly had agreed in 1912 to the formation of an army air service (*Serviço de Aeronáutica Militar*) no funds for the purpose were forthcoming, and nothing was done to implement the decision. The same thing happened to the *Escola de Aeronáutica Militar* (Army Flying School) it was decided to establish at Vila Nova da Rainha in May 1914. With the entry into the war of Portugal on 23 November 1914, following German incursion into Moçambique from German East Africa, twelve pilots, all volunteers from the army and navy, were sent abroad for training – four each to France, Great Britain and the United States. On their return these officers became the instructors at the flying school which had at last been formed. Unfortunately, the school's only aircraft was an elderly Deperdussin owned by Colonel Albino Costa, a Brazilian. The first course began on 17 July 1916, but matters were eased when two Maurice Farman MF 11 trainers were delivered in August, with another seven aircraft, five Farman F41s and two Caudron G3s following in October and a Morane-Saulnier Type H later still.

Finally, in July 1917, the army was able to establish its first operational units. The *Esquadrilha Expedicionária a Moçambique* (Expeditionary Squadron to Mozambique) had three Farman F40s and nine personnel, and flew its first operational sortie in August;

SOUTH AFRICA

The South African Aviation Corps was set up in 1915, using the services of South African officers who had learned to fly from 1913 onwards. Intended for operations against the Germans in South-West Africa, the corps' first equipment consisted of Henry Farmans and BE2as. Although there was little for the corps to do in the South-West African campaign, it did serve with some distinction in the prolonged war against von Lettow-Vorbeck in East Africa.

TURKEY

As with many other nations in the area, Turkey's interest in military aviation began with the Balkan Wars in 1912. In that year the Ottoman Empire ordered a number of foreign aircraft, notably of Bristol, Deperdussin, DFW, Mars, Nieuport and REP design, to serve with its ground forces. Lacking her own pilots, Turkey had to rely heavily on foreign aircrew.

With her military matters heavily influenced and even controlled by Germans, Turkey in 1915, under pressure, established a Flying Corps on German lines. A number of German aircraft were operated, all with German pilots, but often with Turkish observers.

CHAPTER FIVE

AIR TACTICS
1914·18

Painting of a typical air battle over the Western Front in 1916. The aircraft in the foreground is a British Royal Aircraft Factory F.E.2 two-seater, under attack by German biplanes, with a Fokker monoplane heading towards the lines in the background. Combats involving numerous aircraft became increasingly common during 1916.

Given the fact that air fighting was non-existent before the beginning of World War I, it was natural that the first steps in the direction of air fighting should have been hesitant, crude and experimental, and then evolved with some speed towards a fair measure of sophistication, limited only by the performance of the aircraft and the production rate of the aircraft factories.

But although the air fighting itself was a new feature of World War I, some thought had been given to the problem in the years beforehand. During 1911, for example, at a hearing of a sub-committee of the Committee of Imperial Defence, charged with the investigation of 'measures which might be taken to secure to (Great Britain) an efficient aerial service', Captain Bertram Dickson submitted that: 'In the case of a European war between two countries, both sides would be equipped with large corps of aeroplanes, each trying to obtain information of the other, and to hide its own movements. The efforts which each would exert in order to hinder or prevent the enemy from obtaining information ... would lead to the inevitable result of a war in the air, for the supremacy of the air, by armed aeroplanes against each other. This fight for the supremacy of the air in future wars will be of the first and greatest importance.'

In other countries, too, similar visionaries were foreseeing the inevitability of war in the air, should aerial reconnaissance prove of as great a benefit as most thought it would be. And while such officers tried to explain to their superiors that there would be war in the air, other men were experimenting with the actual means of taking war up into the air. In June 1910 the pioneer Glenn Curtiss had dropped dummy bombs on the outline of a battleship marked with buoys on the surface of Lake Keuka in New York state, and the practice of such dummy bombing became a popular feature and competition in prewar flying displays.

The first trials with live bombs were also carried out by two Americans, Lieutenant Myron S. Crissy and Philip O. Parmalee, in a Wright biplane on 7 January 1911 at San Francisco. In the same year *Capitano* Guidoni, an Italian, made the first air launching of a torpedo, weighing 160 kg (352 lbs), from an aircraft of his own design.

In air-to-air combat, though, the early pioneers realised that rifle-calibre armament was essential, although experiments with a wonderful assortment of other weapons were tried in the period before the war, and even during the opening phase of that conflict. These ranged from fairly sensible weapons such as shotguns and pistols, to more fanciful attempts with grenades, grappling irons and darts to be dropped from above the aircraft to be attacked. On a more practical level, though, the first trials with an air-fired rifle were made in August 1910 by an American, Jacob Fickel. It was apparent, however, that the sustained fire of a machine-gun would be necessary to pour sufficient weight of fire into a hostile machine, in the short time it would be in the sights, to damage it crucially. In June 1912, therefore, Captain Charles de Forest Chandler, first air-fired a Lewis light machine-gun from the rudder bar of a Wright Model B of the US Aeronautical Division.

Experiments then continued with some success before World War I, but the main use foreseen for such armament was defensive, except in pusher types with the propeller behind the nacelle occupied by the crew. For in tractor aircraft, which had the better performance that would be needed for fighting aircraft, the

propeller located at the front of the fuselage was in the machine gun's line of fire.

Clearly a gun fixed to fire along the pilot's line of sight was the optimum solution to offensive machine gun armament, for then the pilot merely had to point the aircraft at the enemy and fire, and so several inventors tried to devise methods of halting the fire of the machine gun while a propeller blade was in line with the muzzle. Raymond Saulnier in France, and Franz Schneider in Germany, both devised simple 'interrupter gears'. but their prewar efforts were hampered by lack of government cooperation and the temperamental nature of much machine gun ammunition, which sometimes 'hung fire' just long enough to allow the blade to move in line with the muzzle as the round fired. To ward off these stray rounds, Saulnier devised wedge-shaped deflector plates to be fitted to the rear of the blades, and it was with these that Roland Garros became on 1 April 1915 the first pilot to shoot down an enemy aircraft with a fixed forward-firing machine gun. To save weight and complexity, Garros had dispensed with the actual interrupter gear, relying on the deflectors to ward off the few bullets that would otherwise have hit the propeller. This method was at best a stopgap, however, for the vibrations of the occasional bullet striking the deflectors was enough to cause the engine eventually to fail, bringing Garros

Opposite page top Morane-Saulnier Type N, with a Hotchkiss 8-mm machine gun and deflector plates. *Opposite page centre* Nieuport 11 with a Lewis gun on an overwing mount. *Opposite page bottom* Spad S.XIII with twin synchronised Vickers machine guns. *Below* Voisin Type 4 (LA) with 47-mm Hotchkiss gun.

down behind the German lines. Realising the implications of this simple device, the Germans instructed Anthony Fokker, a Dutch designer working in Germany, to copy the system on his latest aircraft; Fokker's designers went one better, however, and quickly developed an efficient mechanical synchroniser gear which was fitted to the Fokker M5k, which thus became the world's first true fighter, the Fokker E I.

Before this, however, there had been some successes with more primitive fighting methods. On 5 October 1914, for example, Caporal Quénault, gunner in a Voisin pusher flown by Sergeant Joseph Frantz, shot down with his flexible Hotchkiss machine gun an Aviatik reconnaissance aircraft, this being the first time in which an aircraft had been shot down by a machine gun in the air. Other aircrews had already been taking pot shots at each other with rifles and pistols, but the chances of success were slight, although men such as the British Captain Lanoe G. Hawker proved quite adept at deflection shooting with a rifle fixed to fire at $45°$ to the aircraft's line of flight, so as to clear the disc swept by the propeller.

In the period before the introduction of the Fokker E I and true air fighting, considerable progress had been made with the development of bombing, the British and French to the fore with heavier-than-air craft, and the Germans with lighter-than-air craft. The Germans, firm believers in the offensive power of their considerable Zeppelin fleet, launched the first of many airship raids against Great Britain on 19 January 1915, when two Zeppelins raided Great Yarmouth and other East Anglian towns, killing two people and injuring thirteen more.

These raids were to prove of great nuisance value, and in efforts to frustrate them the British severely hampered their efforts in France. Eventually, however, the growing efficiency of the British defences began to inflict heavier losses on the Zeppelins, which then began to fly higher in an effort to stay out of reach of the defending fighters. At these high altitudes, however, accurate navigation and bombing were all but impossible, and the efficiency of the crew fell off markedly. In an effort to maintain a worthwhile bombing offensive against Great Britain, therefore, bomber aircraft were used, but these too suffered heavy losses in daylight raids and had to operate with less impact at night.

The Royal Naval Air Service was an early proponent of strategic bombing, especially against Zeppelins. The first, but unsuccessful, raid was launched on 22 September 1914; on 8 October 1914, however, the Zeppelin Z IX was destroyed by a bomb hit. The basic problem with all these early bombing attempts, apart from the largely extemporised nature of the bombs themselves, and the small bomb load that could be carried by early aircraft, was the difficulty of accurate dropping.

In an effort to overcome this problem, most of the first raids were carried out at very low level, where the variables (altitude, speed, cross wind) would have little effect. But with the increasing number and quality of the anti-aircraft guns deployed on both sides, bombers had to operate at higher altitudes, in the order of 1,800 m (6,000 ft), above the accurate ceiling of the anti-aircraft guns. Here accurate bomb-aiming by eye was impossible, and so a number of moderately sophisticated bomb-sights were introduced in 1915 onwards: the German Görz, the French Dorand and Lafay, the British CFS and the American gyroscopically-stabilised Sperry.

In many respects, however, bombing was a sideshow

in the early stages of the war, the two most important functions of aircraft at this and later stages of the conflict being artillery spotting and reconnaissance, the tasks of what the British described as corps aircraft. It was these aircraft, usually two-seaters of only moderate performance, that carried out the tasks essential to the progress of the ground forces by whom the war would be won or lost, or so it was supposed. Therefore, if it was more than useful for one's own side to have the services of such aircraft, it was, as Dickson had prophesied, more than necessary that the other side be prevented from enjoying the same benefits.

Thus was born the need for fighter aircraft, to protect their own side's two-seaters, and to prevent the other

side's two-seaters from working effectively. Although some pilots had realised this early in the war, and had thus tried to equip their machines with machine guns and other weapons, it was only after the success of aircraft in the first month of the war that the higher command staffs were fully persuaded of the fact, and started to press for the introduction of armed types. At first these were conversions of standard two-seaters, the observer being provided with a flexible gun, but soon custom-built types such as the Vickers FB 5 'Gunbus' began to enter service.

With the introduction of the Fokker E I in the summer months of 1915, the Germans had the first true fighter aircraft. But how was the new machine to be

Demonstration of air fighting manoeuvres by the Bristol Fighters of 48th Squadron.

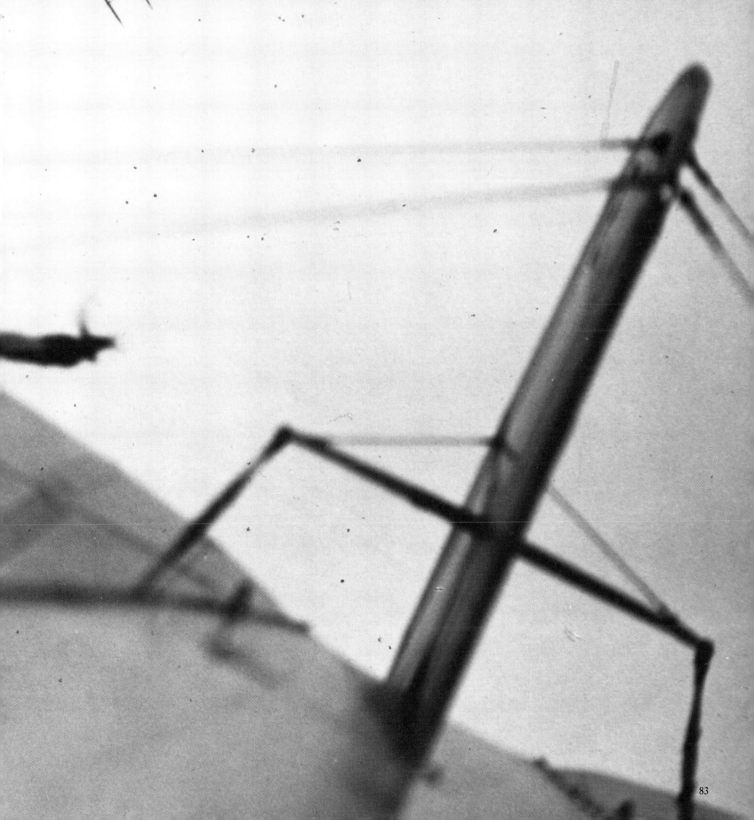

used? At first the E types, at first only of Fokker design, but later of Pfalz and Siemens design also, were allocated to the *Flieger Abteilungen* at the scale of two per unit, as escort machines for the two-seaters. Two of the earliest E-type pilots, Oswald Boelcke and Max Immelmann, realised that this was not the best way to employ the rather limited advantages of the E types, which did not excel particularly as aircraft but relied rather on the tactical superiority inherent in the fixed forward-firing armament: far better, Boelcke and Immelmann thought, if the E types were used offensively, to take the war to the enemy.

The notions of these two pioneer air fighters were entirely correct, but there was no way in which the authorities should listen to the ideas of two unknown pilots. So Boelcke and Immelmann set about proving the new air weapon, and in the process developed a sound background of tactical skill and ability, and started to build great reputations for themselves. Although they had to fly escort missions, both men also flew 'free' sorties on their own, stalking and despatching Allied two-seaters.

The two favourite tactics evolved by Boelcke and Immelmann made clever use of the weak spots in the two-seaters' defence, and the tactical advantages of height and surprise. Thus they would try to close up underneath the tail of the two-seater, in the gunner's blind spot, then pull up the nose of the E-type and fire into the exposed belly of the two-seater at close range, or dive out of the sun to make one fast, close-range firing-pass at the hostile aircraft before diving out of range. Immelmann added a refinement that bears his name to this day – the Immelmann turn: after the diving pass had carried the attacker past the enemy, a zoom climb put the attacker once again above the enemy, and also in front of him; here a turn over the vertical, or a half roll at the top of a loop, would put the attacker in position for another firing pass as he dived. Although Immelmann has acquired the reputation for the invention of this and other manoeuvres and tactical innovations, it was only his contemporary reputation that led to this.

Boelcke is far more important in aviation history, though, for it was he who thought out tactics involving several fighter aircraft, and possessed the ability to pass on his own knowledge and enthusiasm to others. Thus while Immelmann was essentially a 'doer', Boelcke was both a 'doer' and a 'thinker', and the real father of aerial fighter tactics. Despite the equality of their fame at the time, the superiority of Boelcke over Immelmann is exemplified by their respective victory scores: forty to fifteen.

In November 1915 Boelcke was called to supreme headquarters, together with representatives of other elements of Germany's air service, to discuss with *Major* Thomsen the future air policy of Germany. Here Boelcke expounded his ideas: fighters should be grouped together in homogeneous units, with three main tasks: the prevention of enemy air activity, the pro-tection of German air activity, and harassment of enemy ground forces with machine gun fire.

With the partial implementation of Boelcke's theories, the period which the Allies called the 'Fokker scourge' reached its height in the spring of 1916. But it was not until the dire days of the 1st Battle of the Somme, in the summer and autumn of 1918, that German losses at last compelled the authorities to start introducing homogeneous fighter units on a large scale, the first of which was formed by Boelcke, although he was killed in a combat accident shortly afterwards. It should be noted, though, that in the Battle of Verdun, *Hauptmann* Haehnelt, *Stofl* of the 5th Army, had formed fighter units; and Immelmann and Boelcke themselves had belonged to pioneer fighter units, *Kampfeinsitzerkommandos*, three of which had been set up by *Major* Stempel of the 6th Army earlier in the summer of 1916.

The Allied answer to the German use of fighters first came in August 1915, when *Capitaine* Felix Happe introduced the Vee or Vic formation. In this unarmed aircraft were escorted by three or four armed machines, the rear gunners of which could put up a 'box' of fire sufficient to deter all but the most daring of German pilots.

This introduction of close formation flying, soon adopted almost universally by the Allies, severely hampered the activities of small groups of single-seat fighters, and was in itself instrumental in formulating the idea of mass fighter attacks in Boelcke's mind, for it was only by the distraction of the enemy gunners by

Opposite page top and centre Two views of the German Parabellum machine gun showing swivel mounting and ammo belt on bobbin.
Opposite page bottom Lewis gun and mounting. Note the carrier pigeon.
Below Twin Lewis machine guns mounted on a Scarff ring in a Breguet 14A.2.

attacks right round their defensive perimeter that some fighters could get through to their two-seater targets. At the same time, it became clear that in order to fulfil their role successfully, future fighters would have to have better performance and agility than their opponents.

During the second half of 1915 and the beginning of 1916, though, the factor that most limited the development of large-scale air fighting was the production of suitable aircraft: by the end of 1915, for example, only eighty-six of the definitive Fokker monoplane, the E III, had been built; and the only two Allied fighters capable of taking it on, the Nieuport 11 and de Havilland 2, numbered only 210 and about twenty by the end of February 1916.

Meanwhile, the sophistication of the tactics used by 'corps aircraft' had been increasing, largely as a result of British efforts. In the Battle of Neuve Chapelle in March 1915, four new approaches had been tried: improved artillery spotting and correction techniques, based on the 'clock system', a celluloid disc inscribed with concentric circles and many radii, the target being located at the centre of the disc, and the fall of shot being plotted in the segments of the disc formed by the radii and circles; improved maps of the German trenches, using better cameras and the interpretation techniques pioneered by the French; methodical patrolling of the German side of the lines by reconnaissance aircraft at medium and long ranges to detect the arrival of German reinforcements; and an overall bombing plan to ensure concentration in time and space, especially against railway junctions and ground force headquarters. The British also tried contact patrols in the Battles of Neuve Chapelle and Aubers Ridge (May 1915). Although these early developments were not very successful, they were soon built up into useful adjuncts to conventional communications.

By the time of the 1st Battle of the Somme, the Allies had a decided numerical superiority, which they were not to lose for the rest of the war, and to a certain extent this played into German hands: the new *Jagdstaffeln*, patrolling on their own side of the lines at high altitude, could see the swarms of Allied aircraft heading east across the front. Then, under the inspired leadership of men such as Boelcke and Martin Zander, the first two *Jasta* commanders, each pilot picked his target and, on a hand signal from his commander, dived down into the attack, trying to get through the fighter screen to the two-seaters without getting engaged in a dogfight with the fighters, definitely a secondary target compared with the two-seaters.

All the Germans now had to do was wait on their own side of the lines, and the British in particular would send 'trade' their way. And British losses were higher than they might have been because the prevailing wind over the Western Front was a westerly: this meant that a crippled German aircraft had a helping wind as it tried to get home, but any Allied aircraft on the German side of the lines had a difficult time of it, especially if it were the engine that had been damaged.

The Germans had developed the concept of an aerial barrage of fighters during the Battle of Verdun, through which French offensive aircraft would have to fight their way in order to achieve their objectives, and this system was further expanded during the 1st Battle of the Somme. The first German attempts to use contact patrols during this time were a failure, however.

The French, not as offensively minded as the British, were more content to stay on their own side of the lines: whereas the British sought to ensure the security of

their corps machines over the front by placing an aerial barrier of fighters between the German fighters and the front line, the French relied more on escort over the battlefield combined with large-scale fighter sweeps to deter the Germans. Thus the French were well placed in 1916 to develop air photography to a fine art, and thus produce excellent trench maps. Up to 5,000 photographs per day were taken.

Allied air successes in the 1st Battle of the Somme prompted a thorough reorganisation of the German air arm, which was greatly expanded and received a new commander, von Hoeppner, on 8 October 1916. At the same time as this organisation reshuffle, which did much to clarify the objectives of the air service and

provide the right tactical units for the task, new aircraft such as the Albatros and Halberstadt D-type biplane fighters arrived on the scene, swinging the technological balance entirely Germany's way by the spring of 1917, a period which culminated in the Royal Flying Corps ghastly 'Bloody April'.

The keynotes of Germany's new air policy were three: priority was to be given to artillery spotting aircraft, for which more efficient radio equipment was essential; contact patrols, hitherto universally a disaster for the Germans, were to be improved in theory and practice with new ideas and aircraft, and expanded organisationally; and airship operations were to be curtailed in favour of multi-engined aircraft operations

RAF Gunnery School at Rang-du-Flers-Verton. A Pilot Officer firing at fixed targets representing German aircraft from a 'cockpit' moving along curving rails.

against 'strategic' targets, especially in Great Britain. In this last factor the Germans were heavily influenced by the increasing successes of the French and Royal Naval Air Service attacks on targets deep in Germany, and the threat posed by newer types, such as the Admiralty's 'blood paralyser', the Handley Page O/100. In an effort to emulate the Allied bombing successes, *General* Erich Ludendorff, the First Quartermaster-General, ordered the formation of the 'England *Geschwader*' or *Bombengeschwader* 3 of thirty twin-engined Gothas for the campaign against Great Britain that was to be started in January 1917.

Tactically, for the fighters, the year 1917 held few surprises. More and more aircraft were available at the front, and so larger formations of fighters became the norm: whereas during 1916 flights and sometimes squadrons had been the standard operational formation, during 1917 the standard became the squadron, and quite frequently groups of squadrons operated together. This spelled the end of the day, with a few exceptions, for lone operators, a special breed of air fighter that had been exemplified by men such as the great British and French aces Albert Ball (forty-four victories) and Georges Guynemer (fifty-four victories), killed on 7 May 1917 and 11 September 1917 respectively. From this time on, aerial battles involving up to 100 aircraft became increasingly frequent.

The most notable features of 1917 were the growing

strength of the air effort in support of ground operations, and the growth of 'deep penetration' bombing, the first pioneered by the British, and the second tried with varying success by all the major combatants.

On 11 May 1917 the Royal Flying Corps launched the first low level air attacks coordinated with infantry assault. Previously aircraft cooperating with the ground forces had enjoyed a free hand, and had delivered their attacks where and when possible. In the effort of 11 May, time attacks were made by waves of aircraft just beyond the extent of the artillery barrage; when this had lifted and the infantry assault went in, the aircraft stayed over the battlefield to deal with any pockets of German resistance encountered on the ground. So impressed were the Germans that they immediately started to develop similar tactics, and the first use of a whole *Staffel* in such a role, on 10 July, proved so successful that the Germans set about the organisation of a number of special squadrons (*Schlachtsaffeln*) to support their infantry.

While the British and French continued bombing raids in Germany as before, both the Germans and the Italians were making great strides in the field of 'strategic' bombing of distant targets. Although results in physical terms were not especially devastating, the effect on civilian morale was considerable. The effect of the German effort may be gauged from the raid of 25 May 1917, the first time that the Gothas of *Bombengeschwader* 3 attacked Great Britain. Led by *Haupt-*

mann Ernst Brandenburg, twenty-three bombers set out to attack London. Of these twenty-one got to Gravesend, where they were turned back by heavy cloud. Some bombs fell on Folkestone as the bombers returned home, and the Germans lost two aircraft, only one possibly to a British fighter. Yet the British had sent up seventy-four aircraft to intercept, although none did so as the British home defence fighters were wholly obsolete. The result was that on 13 June the Royal Flying Corps in France had to send two good squadrons back to England for home defence. From this time onwards, moreover, the strength of the German raids increased. The redeployment of better British fighters had the desired effect, though, and German daylight losses worsened to the extent that after August the daylight effort against England was discontinued.

On 7 June 1917 the British went a step further with their development of ground-support tactics with carefully planned air attacks coordinated with the initial infantry assault in the Battle of Messines, which started with the explosion of nineteen huge mines beneath the German lines rather than the normal great artillery barrage lasting for several days. Considerable initial tactical successes were achieved before the attack petered out.

The Germans also persevered with mass ground-attack tactics, a notable example occurring on 30 November, during the Battle of Cambrai. Here the British had made a great dent in the German lines with

Below Twin Lewis guns on a Scarff ring for the gunner of an R.E.8.

Above Wrecked Handley-Page bomber showing twin Lewis guns and mounting.
Right 13 pdr 9 cwt anti-aircraft gun on Thornycroft lorry in action.

Opposite page F.E.2d aircraft of 20th Squadron, RFC at St Marie Capelle, France 1916–17. One fixed Lewis for the pilot, and 2 flexible Lewis guns for the observer. To fire the rear gun he had to stand on his seat.

the first mass use of tanks, and in a surprise counter-attack the Germans threw in all their *Schlachtstaffeln* together, under the experienced cover of *Jagdgeschwader* 1. Success was total, the British were thrown back.

There were few tactical innovations during 1918, with the Germans gradually being pressed into the ground, despite the initial successes of their spring offensives. By the summer these had been halted, and then the exhausted Germans were driven back by the Allies, revitalised by the arrival of significant American forces. The only 'new' factors of the year were continuations of trends apparent in 1917: the increase in the bombing effort, although its real effects were still relatively small; ever more aircraft involved in the air fighting over the Western Front, the war's main theatre; and the continued development and use of ground-support tactics. Other differences in the air fighting of 1918 compared with previous years were mostly reflections of the superior performance of the latest aircraft compared with earlier types: speeds were higher, although not greatly so; ceilings and range were superior, the former particularly so; armament was the standard two guns, improved in reliability slightly; and manoeuvrability combined with adequate handling enabled pilots to fly with more aerodynamic safety and get better combat efficiency out of their machines.

A typical scene over the Western Front in 1918 might be seen as follows. The same type of operations would be seen over the Italian Front and, on far smaller scale, on the Macedonian and Palestinian fronts.

Over the front line, and operating at low level, would be ground-attack aircraft and infantry contact patrol machines, reporting progress back to headquarters and harrying the enemy with machine gun fire and light bombs. Perhaps 2,000 m behind each front line would be the balloons which carried on much of the donkey work of artillery observation. Each of these balloons could be hauled down quickly at the approach of an enemy fighter, and was also ringed with light anti-aircraft guns for local defence. Despite this, balloons were still a favourite target for some fighter pilots, and the occupants of these contraptions on each side of the lines wore static-line parachutes. (Of the airmen, only the Germans were equipped with parachutes.)

Some 4,000 m behind each front were the main artillery positions, both conventional and anti-aircraft, with the corps aircraft on station above them and between them and the front line, operating at about 1,200 m (4,000 ft) or lower. The British corps aircraft were covered by fighters such as the Sopwith Camel flying at about 2,300 m (7,500 ft). This was also the altitude at which the majority of German fighters operated. On the Allied side there was also a medium altitude cover of fighters, usually Spad 13s or SE 5as, flying at about 4,250 m (14,000 ft), and high-altitude cover provided by types such as the Bristol F2B at 5,400 m (18,000 ft), where the Germans also kept strong patrols much of the time.

At this high altitude also operated the German reconnaissance and bomber aircraft trying to cross the lines to operate deep behind them, whereas the Allied reconnaissance and bomber aircraft (medium bombers probing some 160 km/100 miles, and heavy night bombers some 480 km/300 miles into German territory) normally operated at between 3,000 m (10,000 ft) and 4,250 m (14,000 ft). Thus at most altitudes there was some air activity, with the ubiquitous but largely ineffective anti-aircraft fire following the route of hostile aircraft.

CHAPTER SIX

THE ACES
1914-18

Spad fighter of a *Cicognes* squadron.

The word *as*, meaning 'ace', was in current French usage before World War I to denote sportsmen who excelled above others in their field. Then, because of the odd reputation enjoyed by the early airmen, the term came to be used of these men too. But during World War I, 'ace' came to have a completely different connotation: one who had proved his aerial superiority by downing a number of enemy aircraft. The word was first used by the French for men who had shot down more than five enemy aircraft.

At this stage the pilot's name was mentioned in official communiqués, and his career could thus be followed by a public avid for tales of success to balance against the grim news from the trenches. At the time of the word's 'acquisition' of this military sense, the shooting down of five aircraft was sufficiently difficult for the fact to be notable, which was why the French adopted the figure of five aircraft shot down to qualify an ace. Later in the war, with the improvement in aircraft armament, the high abilities of pilots and the larger number of aircraft in the air, five did not seem so impressive a figure, but by then the qualifications for the accolade were so firmly fixed that they could not be altered. The world's first ace, naturally enough, was a Frenchman, Eugène Gilbert, who shot down five German aircraft before his death on an unknown date in the summer of 1915.

The British deprecated the system right from the start, particularly under the influence of Trenchard. This influential figure in the development of British military aviation, and all the attitudes to it, was of the firm opinion that the introduction of an ace system into the Royal Flying Corps would *ipso facto* lead to invidious comparisons between fighter pilots, and to bad blood between fighter pilots and the crews of other aircraft. And as Trenchard rightly pointed out, it was the crews of the two-seater corps aircraft who were the *raison d'être* of the air war, and thus deserved as much praise, if not more so, than the pilots of the 'glamorous' single-seaters. Thus the British never adopted an ace system, and although rigorous tests were applied to all victory claims, this was for War Office purposes, not so that an ace's status might be established. Despite this official frowning on the system, though, the names and deeds of the better pilots soon became known throughout the flying service, and then in civilian life.

The Americans came into the war late, and this factor combined with the French influence on their air service to persuade them to adopt the five-victory qualification.

The Germans, on the other hand, realised quite early on that the exploits of their ablest pilots could be turned to good propaganda use, at home as well as abroad, and so formalised their system from an early date. Contrary to the practice of the other major powers, however, to qualify as an *Oberkanone* (top gun), a German had to have achieved ten confirmed victories. This higher number as a basic qualification seems to have had a twofold origin: a desire to go one better than the French in the apparent calibre of their aces, and a realisation that air fighting was in the summer of 1915 a new thing, and that in the future the scale of these aerial battles would increase, making ten a reasonable lower figure. In the latter reasoning they were absolutely correct, as events in both World Wars I and II were to prove.

The term ace therefore has a number of meanings, especially as the confirmation needed to establish the validity of a victory claim varied enormously from country to country. In general, however, five reasonable claims have served to establish a pilot as an ace, and this criterion was adopted by Italy and Belgium during World War I.

French rules for the confirmation of victories were fairly strict – the aircraft had to crash on the Allied side of the lines, or otherwise be seen to crash by an independent witness either in the air or on the ground. It thus happened that a number of fairly conclusive victories were not confirmed because the wreckage fell far on the German side of the lines, and was not seen to come down by an independent witness. This factor has led to the victory scores of several notable aces, who liked to operate alone and deep in German territory, being smaller than they otherwise might have been. Examples of this are René Fonck and Georges Guynemer. A peculiarity of the French system not liked, and therefore, not copied, by the British was the practice of grouping together the greatest aces in élite units. This, the British felt, removed the beneficial influence of the abler pilots, lowering morale in general and denying average pilots the personal contact with better pilots which could only serve to improve standards throughout the squadron.

The unit to which most of the great French aces

Opposite page
Jagdstaffel 12 of Jagdegeschwader 2 at Toulis, in 1918.
Below Manfred von Richthofen while recuperating from a wound when shot down on 6 July 1917. Richthofen was the most famous of the World War I aces, owing his eighty victories to superlative marksmanship and great stalking ability.

belonged was *Groupe de Combat No 12 'Les Cigognes'*, which at its peak had five *escadrilles*, numbers 3, 26, 73, 103 and 167. For most of the time, though, it consisted of only the first four *escadrilles*. Most of the great men served in *Escadrille No 3*, making this squadron an élite within an élite. Other celebrated French squadrons were *No 77 'Les Sportifs'*, which had a number of famous sporting stars amongst its ranks, *No 90 'Les Coqs'*, which had a number of lesser aces, and the *Lafayette Escadrille*, which contained Americans who had volunteered to serve against the Germans before the entry of the United States into the war in April 1917. It was standard French practice to post up and coming fighter pilots to one of the élite units as soon as he had started to make his name in an 'ordinary' fighter squadron.

One effect of this practice was that the French élite units were particularly strong, and thus came to be regarded as 'fire brigade' units – if a crisis occurred anywhere along the front, one of these specially mobile units would be dispatched to the area to supplement the ordinary squadrons in coping with the problem. Another effect was that on the whole the pilots of the ordinary squadrons, without the influence of the better pilots, tended to be slightly less mettlesome than their British counterparts, and so not take the air war so aggressively to the Germans as their commanders would have liked.

Perhaps the most rigorous system of victory confirmation in World War I was the German one, which asked for tangible evidence of the crash as well as eyewitness confirmation. This was in general relatively easy for the Germans, whose air policy dictated that the fighters should on the whole wait on their own side of the lines, with 'trade' coming to them from the Allied side. This meant that the great majority of German victims fell on the German side of the lines, where tangible confirmation was thus possible.

The Germans, like the French, tended to group aces together in élite units such as those commanded by Manfred von Richthofen, Oswald Boelcke and Rudolf Berthold. Unlike the French, the Germans did not carry the practice to the extreme, so the ordinary *Jagdstaffeln* were not left totally devoid of good pilots.

To a certain extent, the efficiency of the air services of World War I may be gauged by the number and quality of the aces each produced. One must here be careful, though, for the process of confirmation varied very considerably from country to country, and of course the size of the air services was also wildly disparate, from the great size of the Royal Air Force down to the relatively small size of the Belgian air service.

By the standard mentioned above, the most successful air service of World War I was that of Great Britain: 784 aces with five or more victories. Of these fourteen scored forty or more victories, eleven between thirty and thirty-nine victories, fifty-seven between twenty and twenty-nine victories, 226 between ten and nineteen victories, and 476 between five and nine victories. Quite apart from the sheer number of British and Empire pilots who became aces, the most remarkable factor noticeable amongst the British aces is the large number at the top of the list with very high scores: Major Edward Mannock, VC, DSO and Bar, MC and Bar, with seventy-three victories; Major W. A. Bishop, VC, DSO and Bar, MC, DFC, *Légion d'Honneur* and *Croix de Guerre* (a Canadian), with seventy-two victories; Major R. Collishaw, DSO and Bar, DFC and *Croix de Guerre*, with sixty victories; Major J. T. B.

Above Major Lanoe G. Hawker was Richthofen's 11th victory on 23 November 1916. He had scored 9 'kills', and received the VC for shooting down 2 German aircraft with a machine gun from a Bristol Scout, and routing a third. He was flying a D.H.2 when killed by Richthofen.

McCudden, VC, DSO and Bar, DSO and Bar, MC and Bar, MM and *Croix de Guerre*, with fifty-seven victories; Captain A. W. Beauchamp-Proctor, VC, DSO, MC and Bar and DFC, with fifty-four victories; Captain D. R. MacLaren, DSO, MC and Bar, DFC, *Légion d'Honneur* and *Croix de Guerre* (a Canadian), also with fifty-four victories; Major W. G. Barker, VC, DSO, MC and two Bars, CC, *Légion d'Honneur*, *Croix de Guerre* and *Valore Militare* (a Canadian), with fifty-two victories; and Captain P. F. Fullard, DSO, MC and Bar, AFC, also with fifty-two victories. Between them, the top ten British and Empire aces scored 570 victories, an average of fifty-seven each.

Next in the list of successful air services would be the German one: 363 aces with five or more victories. Of these twelve scored forty or more victories, twenty-one between thirty and thirty-nine victories, thirty-eight between twenty and twenty-nine victories, ninety-six between ten and nineteen victories, and 196 between five and nine victories. Compared with the eight British and Empire aces who scored fifty or more victories, there were only three Germans to achieve this: *Rittmeister* Manfred, *Freiherr* von Richthofen, with eighty victories; *Oberleutnant* Ernst Udet, with sixty-two victories, and *Oberleutnant* Erich Loewenhardt, with fifty-three victories. Between them, the top ten German aces (the tenth equal were *Hauptmann* Oswald Boelcke, *Leutnant* Franz Büchner and *Oberleutnant* Lothar, *Freiherr* von Richthofen, brother of the great Manfred, all with 40 victories) averaged 49.7 victories each.

Next down on the list would be the French air service: 158 aces with five or more victories. Of these four scored more than forty victories, two between thirty and thirty-nine victories, eight between twenty and twenty-nine victories, thirty-nine between ten and nineteen victories, and 105 between five and nine victories. Only two Frenchmen scored more than fifty victories: *Capitaine* René Fonck with seventy-five victories and *Capitaine* Georges Guynemer with fifty-four victories. The ninth-ranked French aces were three in number, all with twenty-three victories: *Sous-Lieutenant* René Dorme, *Lieutenant* Gabriel Guérin and *Sous-Lieutenant* Claude Marcel Haegelen. The top ten men averaged 38.5 victories each.

The United States came next: eighty-eight aces with five or more victories. Of these, none scored more than thirty victories, two more than twenty victories, eight between ten and nineteen victories, and seventy-eight between five and nine victories. The two highest scoring American aces were Captain Edward V. Rickenbacker, Medal of Honor, Distinguished Service Cross, *Légion d'Honneur* and *Croix de Guerre*, with twenty-six victories; and Second Lieutenant Frank Luke Jr, Medal of Honor, Distinguished Service Cross and *Croix de Guerre*, with twenty-one victories. Between them, the top ten American aces averaged 13.3 victories.

Fifth on the list would be Italy: forty-three aces with five or more victories. Of these, none scored more than forty victories, one between thirty and thirty-nine victories, four between twenty and twenty-nine victories, five between ten and nineteen victories, and thirty-three between five and ten victories. Top scorer was *Maggiore* Francesco Baracca with thirty-four victories, followed by *Tenente* Silvio Scaroni with twenty-six victories, *Tenente* -Colonnello Pier Ruggierro Piccio with twenty-four victories, *Tenente* Flavio Torello Baracchini with twenty-one victories and *Capitano* Fulco Ruffo di Calabria with twenty victories. The

tenth-ranked Italian ace was *Sergente* Antonio Real with eleven victories, and the top ten Italians averaged 19.3 victories each.

Austria-Hungary followed Italy: something between twenty-five and thirty aces with five or more victories (Ten or more victories were required in Austria-Hungary to qualify as an ace, and the situation is also made more difficult by a conflict between Austrian and Italian sources as to the exact victory scores of the Austro-Hungarian aces.) Of these, none scored more than forty victories, four scored between twenty and forty victories, and eleven between ten and nineteen victories. Top scorer was *Hauptmann* Godwin Brumowski, with thirty-five to forty victories, followed by *Offizierstellevertreter* Julius Arigi with twenty-six to thirty-two victories, *Oberleutnant* Frank Linke-Crawford with twenty-seven to thirty victories, and *Oberleutnant* Benno Fiala, Ritter von Fernbrugg with twenty-seven to twenty-nine victories. The tenth-ranked Austro-Hungarian ace was *Oberleutnant* Ernst Strohschneider, with fourteen victories, and the top ten Austro-Hungarian aces averaged between 20.2 and 22.4 victories each.

Last but one of the major powers came Imperial Russia: eighteen or nineteen known aces with five or more victories. Of these none scored more than twenty victories, seven scored between ten and nineteen victories, and eleven or twelve between five and nine victories. Top of the Russian list was Staff-Captain Aleksandr Aleksandrovich Kazakov, with seventeen victories, followed by Captain Paul V. d'Argueev with fifteen victories. The aces ranked tenth equal, all on six victories, were Ensign Ivan Aleksandrovich Orlov, Ensign Olgerd J. Teter and Ensign Vasili I. Yanchenko, and the average score of the top ten Russian aces was 12.2 victories.

Last of the important combatants of World War I was Belgium: five aces with five or more victories. Of these one, Second Lieutenant Willy Coppens, DSO, scored thirty-seven victories, two scored between ten and nineteen victories, and two between five and nine victories. The average score of the Belgian aces was 14.2.

Even allowing for the disparity of the air forces deployed by the various combatants, it is clear that the British system produced the best results by spreading the available ability evenly through the squadrons. This meant that as the quality of new pilots improved during 1917 and 1918, experienced and successful pilots in each squadron could shepherd them in combat at the beginning, and also help them along with encouragement and advice. It should be noted, though, that some squadrons did receive slightly preferential treatment so far as personnel was concerned. This was usually the result of a celebrated commander, who could ask for special pilots from other squadrons if he were forming the unit. Most notable of the British squadrons in World War I, therefore, were Nos 40, 56, 60, 74 and 85.

Although the French system could yield very useful results at one time on one sector of the front, a factor very useful in emergencies, and one also appreciated by the Germans, it had the corollary result that in general the fighter arm of the air service was not as aggressive or efficient as it might be, keeping up pressure on the enemy and causing a fair rate of attrition, weakening him against the day of the major offensive.

Most of the aces were unusual men, especially those with high scores, but several of them are particularly worthy of note both as air fighters and as examples of

Above **Hauptmann** Oswald Boelcke, one of the greatest tactical thinkers of air warfare, initiated the new *Jagdstaffeln* or *Jastas* (fighter squadrons). He led *Jasta 2*, the first pure fighter unit, made up of pilots hand-picked by himself. He remained the top-scoring ace, with forty victories, until surpassed in 1917 by his protégé von Richthofen.

the factors that were needed to make up the best pilots and leaders of World War I in the air.

The 'ace of aces' of World War I was *Rittmeister* Manfred, *Freiherr* von Richthofen, who had amassed eighty victories by the time of his death on 21 April 1918. The eldest son of a landed Silesian family, Richthofen started the war as an *Uhlan* cavalry officer. He then transferred to the flying service and served without distinction on the Eastern Front in two-seaters until spotted by Oswald Boelcke, who had him transferred to the new *Jasta* 2 in September 1916. Von Richthofen started his fighter career relatively slowly, but then quickly emerged as an air fighter of outstanding ability, his most important attribute being a superlative shooting 'eye' and stalking ability. Richthofen rose rapidly in importance, aided by the German propaganda machine, and received command of the new *Jagdgeschwader Nr* 1 in June 1917. Well known in Allied flying circles for the 'circus' colours of his unit's aircraft, von Richthofen was personally known for his predominantly red aircraft, usually an Albatros or a Fokker triplane. A cold and somewhat aloof man, von Richthofen proved a successful leader by his example rather than personal qualities, and in no important way can he be considered a tactical innovator.

Perhaps the only major ace who exceeded von Richthofen in marksmanship was the Allied ace of aces, *Capitaine* René Fonck, who had an official total of seventy-five victories. Like von Richthofen, an aloof man, Fonck was not well liked by most of his companions in *Escadrille* SPA 103 of *Les Cicognes*, a fact which seemed to worry him little. He spent much time practising with any weapon he could lay his hands on, and personally supervised the harmonisation and maintenance of the guns of his Spad fighter. The results speak for themselves: Fonck returned to his airfield on numerous occasions having expended only five or six rounds of ammunition, and then waited for the confirmation of his 'kill' to come in. Fonck was an analytical tactician and a superb deflection shot, but also a lone operator by preference, and there seems little reason to doubt his own estimate of 127 victories, making him the most successful fighter pilot of World War I.

Two other 'loners' are also worthy of mention: *Capitaine* Georges Guynemer, second on the list of French aces with fifty-four victories, and Captain Albert Ball, tenth on the list of British aces with forty-seven victories. Both men were loners, and both very sensitive. They were also impetuous, aggressive pilots to a degree, and were very popular at home with the public.

Guynemer was apparently frail, and was twice turned down for military service before being accepted for the air force. But once a pilot he was quickly noted for the total aggression he showed, without regard for his own safety. Given the way he flew, his death in combat was all but inevitable: he was in fact shot down seven times before being killed. Yet his death on 11 September 1917 was a great blow to the French air service and public alike.

Ball was Great Britain's first great ace, but only slowly came to the public's attention as a result of the British dislike of lionisation, especially in the Royal Flying Corps. Considering that his favourite tactic was a headlong charge at large numbers of German aircraft, Ball seemed to bear a charmed life. Flying both Nieuports and SE 5s, Ball made great use of the quadrant-mounted machine gun on the upper wing centre-section, flying underneath his prey, hauling the

gun back and firing a no-deflection shot up into the belly at 45° at pointblank range. On 7 May 1917 Ball flew into a cloud; his unwounded body was later found in his crashed SE 5, and no explanation for his death has even been found.

Germany and Great Britain also produced great leaders, of entirely different characters. *Hauptmann* Oswald Boelcke may be considered the true father of air fighting, and the most important operational airman of World War I. A visionary fighter pilot, Boelcke thought as well as fought, and managed to secure the ear of the high command, which had the sense to listen. Boelcke had the gift of leadership, which he exploited to the full, but also had the gift of teaching, and was thus able to impart his ideas and enthusiasms to his subordinate pilots. By the time of his death on 28 October 1916, following a mid-air collision with an Albatros fighter flown by *Leutnant* Boehme in which his upper wing was badly damaged by Boehme's undercarriage, Boelcke had amassed the sum of forty victories, for the time a quite staggering number. Had he survived longer, there seems every reason to suppose that his victory tally might have rivalled those of von Richthofen, Fonck and Mannock.

Probably the greatest leader produced by Great Britain was Major Edward Mannock, who remained almost unknown until some time after his death on 26 July 1918, when a bullet from the ground pierced his petrol tank. Repatriated from Turkey in April 1915 on the grounds of his poor health, Mannock eventually managed to get into the Royal Flying Corps despite being astigmatic in his left eye, and then embarked on an unspectacular but magnificent career. Quite remarkably for the time, he was possessed by an absolute hatred of all things German, and pursued his vocation with total dedication. Despite this aspect of his character, which might have isolated him from his squadron companions, Mannock was in fact the best squadron leader and patrol tactician of the war. He took immense pains to analyse situations and prepare his missions accordingly, so as to minimise risks by obviating German tactics and thus maximise the chances of his patrol's success in shooting down as many German aircraft as possible. He was especially concerned for his new pilots, and took great care to guard them on their first missions, at the same time setting up their first 'kills' by damaging the German aircraft or drawing the fire of the gunner. Indeed, there seems every reason to suppose that Mannock's real score was far higher than seventy-three, possibly over 100.

Perhaps the strangest breed of fighter airmen in World War I were the balloon specialists. Floating over the battlefield, balloons were tempting and important targets, and were accordingly very heavily protected by anti-aircraft guns. They were also difficult to shoot down, for despite the fact that they were filled with highly inflammable hydrogen, bullet holes let in relatively little air, and thus oxygen, and so ordinary ball ammunition was comparatively ineffective. Rockets and incendiary ammunition were, however, and it was the latter that was used by the great balloon-busters, Second Lieutenant Willy Coppens of Belgium, who shot down twenty-eight balloons as part of his score of thirty-seven; Second Lieutenant Frank Luke of the United States, who shot down fifteen balloons in a score of twenty-one; *Sergeant* Marius Ambrogi of France, who had ten balloons in a score of fourteen; and *Leutnant* Heinrich Gontermann of Germany, whose score of thirty-nine included eighteen balloons.

HEROES IN THEIR OWN TIME

Above Clockwise from left: Major J. T. B. McCudden, Major E. C. Mannock, Major W. A. Bishop, Captain A. Ball, *Oberleutnant* Lothar von Richthofen, *Oberleutnant* Ernst Udet, *Rittmeister* Manfred von Richthofen, *Hauptmann* Eduard Schleich.

The leading German aces

Rittmeister Manfred von Richthofen	80
Oberleutnant Ernst Udet	62
Oberleutnant Erich Loewenhardt	53
Leutnant Werner Voss	48
Hauptmann Bruno Loerzer	45
Leutnant Fritz Rumey	45
Hauptmann Rudolph Berthold	44
Leutnant Paul Baümer	43
Leutnant Josef Jacobs	41
Hauptmann Oswald Boelcke	40
Leutnant Franz Büchner	40
Oberleutnant Lothar von Richthofen	40
Leutnant Karl Menckhoff	39
Leutnant Heinrich Gontermann	39

The leading British aces

Major E. C. Mannock	73
Major W. A. Bishop	72
Major R. Collishaw	62
Major J. T. B. McCudden	57
Captain A. W. Beauchamp-Proctor	5•
Captain D. M. MacLaren	5•
Major W. G. Barker	5:
Captain P. F. Fullard	5.
Major R. S. Dallas	5'
Captain G. E. H. McElroy	49
Captain A. Ball	4:
Captain R. A. Little	4:
Major T. F. Hazell	4:
Major J. Gilmour	40

The leading French aces

Capitaine René P. Fonck	75
Capitaine Georges M. L. J. Guynemer	54
Lieutenant Charles E. J. M. Nungesser	45
Capitaine Georges F. Madon	41
Lieutenant Maurice Boyau	35
Capitaine Armand Pinsard	27
Sous-Lieutenant René Dorme	23
Lieutenant Gabriel Guérin	23
Sous-Lieutenant Claude M. Haegelen	23

Sous-Lieutenant Pierre Marinovitch	22	**The leading Austro-Hungarian aces**	
Capitaine Alfred Heurtaux	21	Hauptmann Godwin Brumowski	40
Capitaine Albert Deullin	20	Offizierstellvertreter Julius Arigi	32
		Oberleutnant Franke Linke-Crawford	30
The leading Italian aces		Oberleutnant Benno Fiala,	
Maggiore Francesco Baracca	34	Ritter von Fernbrugg	29
Tenente Silvio Scaroni	26		
Tenente-Colonello Pier Ruggiero Piccio	24		
Tenente Flavio Torello Baracchini	21	**The leading Belgian aces**	
Capitanio Fulco Ruffo di Calabria	20	2/Lieutenant Willy Coppens de Houthulst	37
Sergente Marziale Cerutti	17	Adjutant Andre de Meulemeester	11
Tenente Ferruccio Ranza	17	2/Lieutenant Edmond Thieffry	10
Tenente Luigi Olivari	12	Capitaine Fernand Jacquet	7
The leading American aces			
Captain Edward V. Rickenbacker	26		
Captain William C. Lambert	22	**The leading Russian aces**	
Captain August T. Iaccaci	18	Major A. A. Kazakov	17
Second Lieutenant Frank Luke Jr	18	Captain P. V. d'Argeyev	15
Captain Frederick W. Gillet	17	Lieutenant Commander A. P. de Seversky	13
Major Raoul Lufbery	17	Lieutenant I. W. Smirnoff	12

Above Clockwise from left: Captain A. W. Beauchamp-Proctor, *Maggiore* Francesca Baracca, *Tenente* Silvio Scaroni, *Capitaine* Georges M. L. J. Guynemer, *Capitaine* René P. Fonck, *Lieutenant* Charles E. J. M. Nungesser, Second-Lieutenant Frank Luke Jr, Captain Edward V. Rickenbacker.

CHAPTER SEVEN

INTERWAR TECHNICAL ADVANCES

Despite an almost universal financial retrenchment in the years immediately after World War I, the period between the two World Wars (1919–39) was marked by a steady improvement in the performance and capabilities of aircraft. The rather cumbersome, fabric-covered, wooden biplanes of World War I gradually gave way, not altogether gracefully, to the sleeker, metal monoplanes of World War II.

What, then, were the typical aircraft of World War I? Although there were exceptions, which anticipated the developments of the 1920s and 1930s by some considerable period, the aircraft of World War I were basically wooden biplanes covered with fabric, with a fixed undercarriage and an engine developing something in the region of 200 hp at the end of the war. The whole structure was based on a box-like fuselage (body): four wooden longerons (main longitudinal members) running fore and aft, separated by bulkheads and spacers, both horizontal and vertical, the whole being braced diagonally into a rigid structure by wires.

In the tractor types which became the norm from 1916 onwards, the engine was located at the front of this fuselage, with the fuel tanks, ammunition magazines, guns and oil tanks behind it and in front of the pilot. In two-seaters the gunner was normally located immediately aft of the pilot, with his gun mounted on a circular track allowing all-round traverse. Elevation of his flexible gun was by means of quadrants on each side of the gun mounting. Located under the fuel tanks etc. was the fixed undercarriage, normally two steel-tube vees with their upper ends attached fore and aft to the lower left and right longerons. Across the apices of the two vees, separated by the spreader bar, ran the axle of the undercarriage, held down by rubber shock cord ('bungee') to provide a measure of springing. At each end of the axle, outside the apices, were the wheels.

Attached to the fuselage between the engine and the pilot was the biplane wing cellule. Located above the fuselage on cabane struts was the upper wing centre section, which often contained the radiator for inline-engined aircraft, or the gravity-feed fuel tank for the engine, the fuel being pumped up into it by a slipstream-powered pump on the cabane structure. From the centre section extended the port and starboard upper wings, with the lower wings stretching out underneath and usually slightly to the rear of them from the region of the lower longerons. The upper and lower sets of wings were connected towards their outboard ends by interplane struts, running between the front and rear spars (the main spanwise structural members of the wings) of the upper and lower wings, and braced fore and aft by diagonal wires. The cellule on each side of the aircraft was also braced in the vertical plane by flying and landing wires: the flying wires ran up from the undercarriage vees and the lower-wing centre section towards the outer ends of the lower and upper wings respectively, to brace these wings against the lifting force developed by their aerofoil sections in flight; the landing wires ran from the upper-wing centre section down towards the points where the interplane struts met the lower wing, to hold up the weight of these wings when the aircraft was on the ground. The weight of the upper wings was taken by the interplane struts.

The wings themselves normally consisted of a pair of main spars running spanwise. Across these ran the aerofoil-shaped ribs of the wing, usually composite structures or single pieces of plywood fretted out for lightness. The whole was braced fore and aft with the usual diagonal wires and compression struts, and then covered with fabric sewn to the ribs and then doped with a cellulose preparation to taughten and airproof it. The structure of the empennage (fin, rudder, tailplane and elevators) at the tail was basically similar.

Refinements consisted of aerofoil-shaped struts and external wires, the suppression of too many protuberances, and a measure of streamlining afforded by fairing the fuselage into a more circular shape with formers and stringers over which went the plywood or fabric covering.

Such then was the basic airframe of most World War I aircraft. Though there were very large aircraft, such as the Zeppelin (Staaken) R VI giant bomber, which was larger than most World War II aircraft, the basic structure was still used, with a proliferation of scantlings and wires to maintain the strength of the whole contraption. Monoplanes were also used to a certain extent, but suspicion was attached to their structural integrity, and so they were comparatively rare.

Towards the end of the war, however, Hugo Junkers in Germany began to develop a number of combat aircraft with metal structures, including monoplanes such as the J 10 of 1918. Although only a metal ground-attack biplane saw combat service, the Junkers metal aircraft pointed the way forward, despite the fact that in

Beardmore (Rohrbach) Inflexible all-metal cantilever monoplane experimental bomber of 1928.

structural concept they adhered to the older wooden practices, reworked in metal. But the Junkers aircraft pioneered the way forward towards cantilever wings, which could do without bracing wires or struts, towards all-metal structures and towards low-wing monoplane design.

Other designers, notably the gifted Reinhold Platz of the Fokker concern, were evolving similar ideas, but were as yet content to stick with wooden structures. Reluctance about metal aircraft was not confined to designers only, however, for the German authorities, to take but one example, were unwilling to turn to such structures which, they thought, were too heavy and would lead to production difficulties for lack of trained metal workers. The first objection had some validity in Junkers' early aircraft, which were of steel, but the use of duralumin from the J4 ground-attack aircraft onwards removed this problem; the second problem was also to some extent a real one, but considering the shortages of properly seasoned wood, adhesives and the like, an early realisation of the advantages of metal structures would have paid handsome dividends.

Part of the legacy of World War I was an abhorrence of all things military, reflected by the rapid way in which the armed forces of the victors were run down, and funds denied them for major re-equipment programmes. Thus the air forces of the world were mostly starved of truly modern aircraft, the authorities being largely content to use the little money they had to keep abreast of developments in the aerodynamic field with experimental and racing aircraft; combat aircraft gradually came to incorporate a bigger proportion of metal in their structures, mainly to obviate the problems caused by wood shortages in World War I, and some of the more modern aerodynamic concepts introduced on

racing, record-breaking and commercial aircraft. Th process was, however, a slow one, and in the 192c military aircraft most decidedly lost their performanc edge over the increasing number of relatively sophist cated commercial types, for which great hopes wer entertained by the public, the aircraft industry and th government alike.

Although Junkers and Platz had shown the wa forward with their ideas about metal structures an cleaner design, what was needed was an advance structural concept to make the best use possible c metal.

Here there enters a remarkable and little know figure, Dr. Adolph Rohrbach, also a German. In 191 having realised that the Junkers' construction, makin use of corrugated skinning over a fairly tradition: structure, was inefficient in terms of drag, complexit and weight, Rohrbach started to build smooth wing covered in metal. The longitudinal corrugations of th Junkers' wing had made the structure longitudinall stiff, but had made the whole structure fairly heavy, a the internal structure could not be lightened to an great extent.

The beauty of the Rohrbach concept of what was t be called 'stressed skin' construction from 1924 on wards, lay in the fact that the metal skinning ha considerable strength in two dimensions, enabling th internal structure to be lightened as the aerodynami covering could itself now bear part of the structura load. The 'cleaner' skinning, compared with that of th Junkers aircraft, also permitted a higher performanc by reducing drag by a considerable degree. Rohrbac produced some interesting designs in Germany befor moving to Britain, where his ideas found full expressio in the Beardmore Inflexible, and then to the Unite

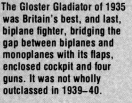

The Gloster Gladiator of 1935 was Britain's best, and last, biplane fighter, bridging the gap between biplanes and monoplanes with its flaps, enclosed cockpit and four guns. It was not wholly outclassed in 1939–40.

States, where he and his associate H. A. Wagner were instrumental in inspiring American designers of the 1930s to make full use of stressed skin construction.

Stressed skin construction was the answer to progress in the design of flying surfaces, the corresponding answer to the problems of the fuselage lying in monocoque construction, which is similar in concept to stressed skin construction and was pioneered before World War I by the French designer L. Bechereau in his remarkable Deperdussin *Monocoque* racer. The idea here was that the conventional box structure should be replaced by a single (mono) shell (coque) skinning of wood, stiffened and strengthened inside by ring-like formers and stringers. The skin was thus made to bear part of the structural load, making the concept akin to the later stressed skin one. Semi-monocoque structure, with bulkheads and internal bracing, was used to good effect in World War I in Albatros D-type fighters and a number of French aircraft. The notion was taken a step further after the war by a British firm, Short Brothers, which produced the all-metal Swallow (later Silver Streak) in 1920. This had a duralumin monocoque fuselage. It was to be some time, however, before metal monocoque fuselages became the norm for civil, let alone military, aircraft.

Throughout the early 1920s, therefore, the biplane layout continued to predominate for military aircraft. The advantages of this layout were considerable: a large wing area (resulting in low landing and take-off speeds) could be contained in a cellule of small overall dimensions (resulting in a high order of manoeuvrability), which was also very strong as a result of its interplane struts and cross-bracing. The disadvantages were apparent, but not as yet important because of the low speeds attainable on the engines of the time: high drag resulting from wires, struts and fixed undercarriage, which kept down performance marginally and reduced range considerably.

By 1927, however, aircraft such as the Lockheed Vega light transport had showed what could be achieved by the combination of careful detail design, a spatted undercarriage, monoplane layout and a monocoque fuselage: range and speed shot up as a result of lower drag and weight, while usable volume in the fuselage remained unaltered despite the reduction in 'wetted area' by about 40 per cent. Although a fixed undercarriage produced great drag, designers were on the whole content to use such a landing gear arrangement as it saved on weight and mechanical complexities.

M. B. Sellers in the United States had experimented with a retractable undercarriage before World War I, and several racing aircraft, notably the Dayton-Wright RB of 1920 and the Bristol Racer of 1922, had featured rudimentary retractable undercarriages, but it was not until the advent of more powerful engines and a fuller understanding of streamlining in the 1930s that the need for retractable landing gears, especially on monoplanes, was comprehensively understood and implemented.

Typical of the development of British high performance aircraft during the 1920s were fighters such as the Fairey Firefly, the Gloster Grebe and Gamecock, the Armstrong Whitworth Siskin, the Bristol Bulldog and the Hawker Fury, the last appearing in 1929 and being the first British fighter capable of more than 320 km/h (200mph). Notable American fighters of the decade were the Boeing PW-9, F2B, F3B, F4B and P-12, and the Curtiss PW-8, P-1, F6C, F7C and P-6.

Other significant aircraft were the French Dewoitine D 9, D 21 and D 27, Loire-Gourdou-Leseurre 32, Nieuport-Delage 42, 52 and 62, and Spad 61; the Italian Fiat CR 20; the Polish PWS 10; and the Russian Polikarpov I-3. Bombers tended to be light, the British in particular opting for multi-purpose aircraft combining the functions of light bomber, reconnaissance aircraft and army co-operation machine. Such creations were desirable financially, and operationally viable in the 'imperial policing' role British aircraft were called upon to perform in the 1920s and 1930s. A few heavy bombers were built, but these were mostly for experimental purposes. Notable examples were the Curtiss B-2 and Martin NBS-1, both American machines. Many World War I light bombers, such as the ubiquitous de Havilland 4 and 9 family, remained in service well into the 1920s, newer light bombers being exemplified by the British Fairey Fox and Hawker Hart.

Thus although the 1920s were notable for the almost completely conservative policies of the world's air forces, a factor imposed on them by public opinion and lack of resources, it should not be supposed that the air forces were entirely backward-looking. Considerable effort went into the development of advanced aerodynamics, more powerful and reliable engines, better materials, and more efficient equipment. These factors were not often represented on major service aircraft, but rather on the large number of machines that appeared only in small numbers or even as single examples. A number of great flights were made by these types, but it was the development of civil aviation, and the record-breaking flights of a number of courageous pioneers that occupied the aeronautical limelight to the virtual exclusion of military aircraft and airmen.

One feature of aerodynamic research to be adopted in a widespread way, however, was the slotted wing, in which a slot in the leading edge of the wing controlled the airflow at high angles of attack and so helped obviate the worst effects of the stall. Pioneered by Handley Page

The Ford Trimotor pioneered clean, metal cantilever construction in the US.

and Lachmann in the early 1920s, such slots were made mandatory on all British service aircraft from 1928 onwards, and were universally accepted in the early 1930s, with a consequent decline in the accident rate.

Yet the foundations for the rapid developments of the 1930s were laid in this period: stressed skin construction, monocoque fuselages, slots, flaps, retractable undercarriages, better instruments and safer aerodynamics were thought about and tested, and racing aircraft such as the British, Italian and American floatplanes involved in the Schneider Trophy races pushed forward the boundaries of the aeronautical science yet further, at the same time offering scope for the development of more powerful aero engines which by the end of the decade were capable, in the most advanced models, of developing power in excess of 1,750 hp. Civilian use in airliners, and service use in areas all over the world, had made both inline water-cooled and radial air-cooled engines developing up to 550 hp quite reliable in general use.

Progress in both the power and power-to-weight factors of aero engines continued in the 1930s, and was instrumental in raising the performance of military aircraft well above that of civilian types by the outbreak of World War II in 1939. Power outputs doubled, both inline and radial engines developing over 1,000 hp in service use. Classic examples are the Rolls-Royce Merlin and Daimler-Benz DB 601 inlines, and the Bristol Hercules, Pratt & Whitney R-1830 Twin Wasp and Wright R-1820 Cyclone radials.

This power output would have been next to useless, especially at the high engine revolutions required in the 1920s, for the propellers of the time were incapable of using so much energy. By the end of the 1920s, however, well designed and made metal propellers were the norm, and in the 1930s multi-blade propellers gradually came to be accepted. Combined with the introduction of the variable-pitch propeller in 1932 and the constant-speed propeller in 1935, this allowed high outputs to be used, and cruising outputs to be used most economically.

Above Napier Cub of 1,000 hp used in the Avro Aldershot II bomber, test-flown by Bert Hinkler.
Opposite page A page from the propaganda magazine 'Signal'. The Junkers J.13 (F.13) also made the first east-west crossing of the North Atlantic on 12–13 April 1928.
Below The Heyford night bomber served 1933–9, when other air forces were adopting monoplanes. The type's most unusual feature was the attachment of the fuselage to the upper wing, and the accommodation of most of the bombload in the thickened lower centre section.

The stolen invention

The Junkers F 13 "Annelise," which had a 120 H.P. engine, established an altitude record of 6,750 metres on 13th September 1919 when carrying eight passengers. This new world record, however, did not receive international recognition because the vanquished Germany of 1919 had not been allowed to join the "Fédération Aéronautique Internationale"

A new name for "Annelise." The United States Government's expert on aviation, John Larsen, purchased the wonderful new machine constructed at Dessau on behalf of U.S. transport services. He established himself as a shareholder. According to the agreement, J-L stood for Junkers-Larsen. Then, however...

In the summer of 1920 an aeroplane was flown in the United States which created a sensation, for the whole body, wings and rudder were made of metal. The all-metal plane became the symbol of technical progress, of American technical progress, of course. Its wings were marked—and this is very important —with large white circles proudly bearing the initials of the plane's constructor: J.L.

What American in those days did not know who J.L. was? It was John Larsen, the American Government's aviation expert. That this quiet man was already thinking of the employment of his wonderful construction for war purposes was proved by an advertisement published by his firm containing the assurance that the Larsen plane, which was equipped with thirty machine-guns, could fire 3,000 bullets in four seconds.

But what did J.L. actually stand for? The letter J stood for Junkers and L for Larsen. Junkers-Larsen, because it had been Larsen who, as the representative of the American Government, had inspected the first all-metal transport plane, the F 13, made at the German Junkers Works in Dessau, and recommended its immediate adoption for American air transport. Of course, he did not do this without making profits for himself on the transaction in his capacity as the middle-man. We need not do more than mention the fact that he did not fulfil his financial engagements towards the Junkers Works and that his drafts were not honoured.

In a statement issued by the Entente Commission of 19th June 1920 the plane

MID-WEEK PICTORIAL

Airplane That Made Remarkable Non-Stop Flight

2019

THE JL-6 IN FLIGHT OVER POTOMAC RIVER, RACING A BIPLANE, WHICH IT EASILY OUTDISTANCED, SHOWING EXTRAORDINARY SPEED AND POWER.

← **... the little hyphen was dropped.** The J suddenly lost its original significance and it no longer stood for "Junkers" but for "John" which was Larsen's Christian name!

→ **John Larsen pretended to be an inventor.** He was always ready with a friendly smile to explain to anybody the technical details and advantages of "his" construction

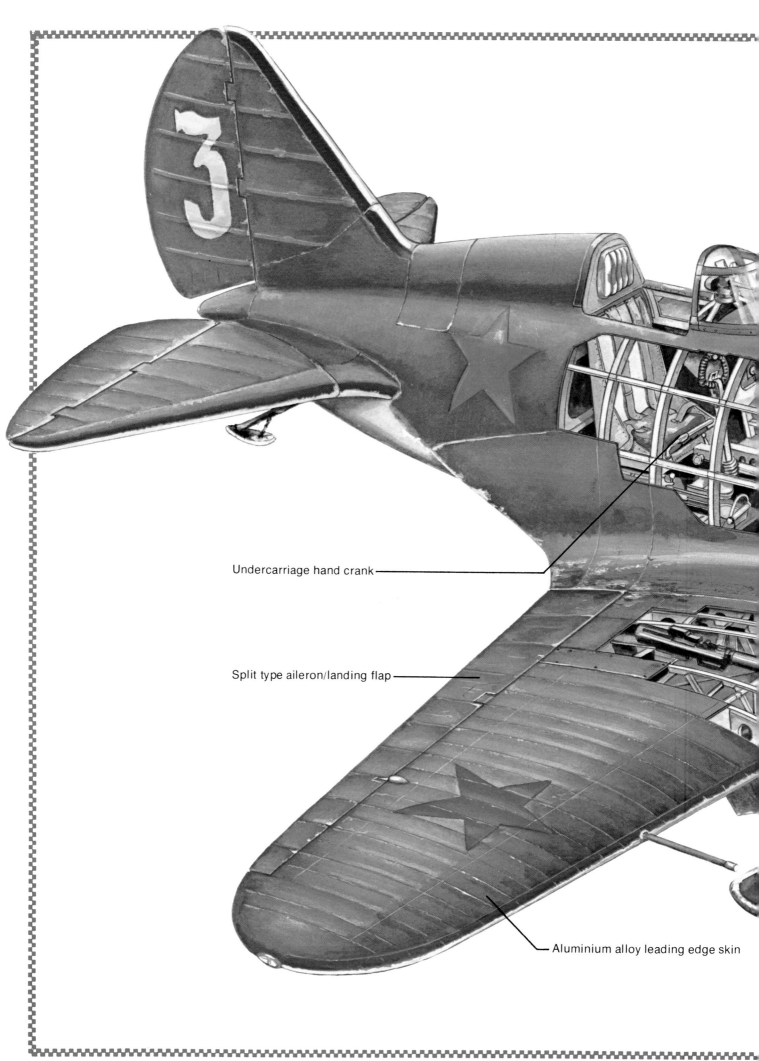

Undercarriage hand crank

Split type aileron/landing flap

Aluminium alloy leading edge skin

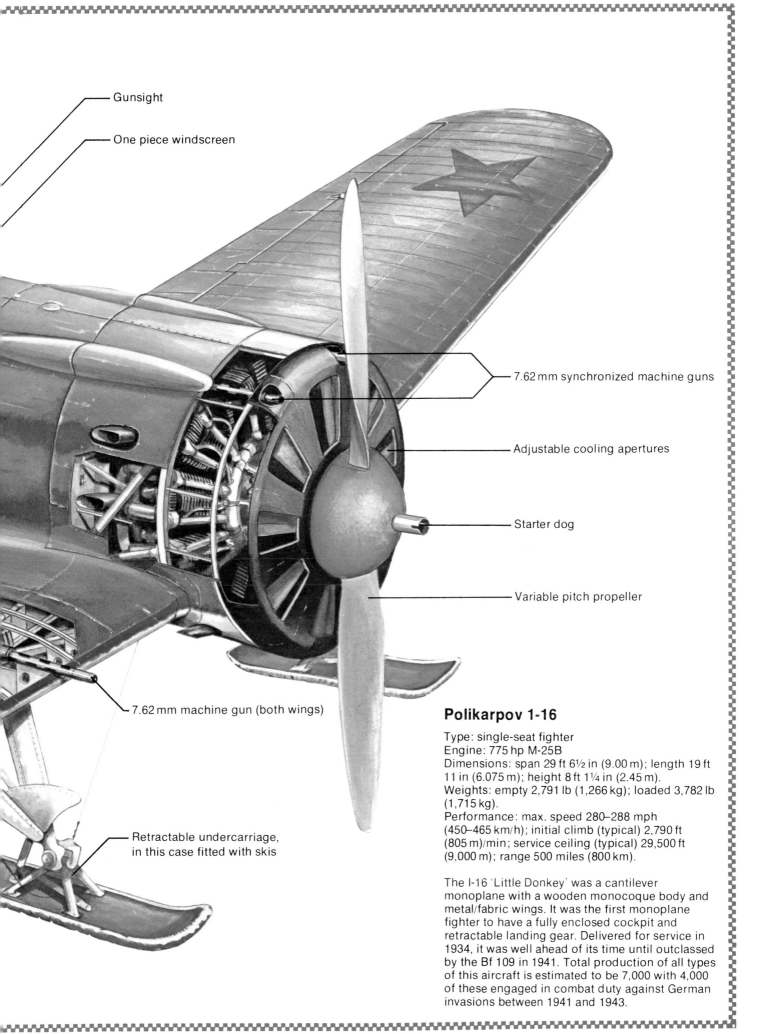

Gunsight

One piece windscreen

7.62 mm synchronized machine guns

Adjustable cooling apertures

Starter dog

Variable pitch propeller

7.62 mm machine gun (both wings)

Retractable undercarriage, in this case fitted with skis

Polikarpov 1-16

Type: single-seat fighter
Engine: 775 hp M-25B
Dimensions: span 29 ft 6½ in (9.00 m); length 19 ft 11 in (6.075 m); height 8 ft 1¼ in (2.45 m).
Weights: empty 2,791 lb (1,266 kg); loaded 3,782 lb (1,715 kg).
Performance: max. speed 280–288 mph (450–465 km/h); initial climb (typical) 2,790 ft (805 m)/min; service ceiling (typical) 29,500 ft (9,000 m); range 500 miles (800 km).

The I-16 'Little Donkey' was a cantilever monoplane with a wooden monocoque body and metal/fabric wings. It was the first monoplane fighter to have a fully enclosed cockpit and retractable landing gear. Delivered for service in 1934, it was well ahead of its time until outclassed by the Bf 109 in 1941. Total production of all types of this aircraft is estimated to be 7,000 with 4,000 of these engaged in combat duty against German invasions between 1941 and 1943.

The greater speeds and other performance factors attainable by the application of this brute force were also increased by the universal adoption of metal stressed skin construction, and the final realisation that the biplane had outlived its usefulness as a combat type. Thus the monoplane finally became the definitive layout, with refinements such as retractable undercarriages, enclosed cockpits and fully cowled engines. Thus the brute of engine power was aided by the beauty of aerodynamic cleanliness. And the renewed threat of major wars once again gave the air forces of the world the finance to re-equip, worldwide rearmament programmes giving the air forces of the European nations the chance at last to turn the dreams of the 1920s into hardware. The lessons of the 1920s and early 1930s had been studied, but operations were to show that often they had been incorrectly appreciated.

Yet although combat was to show that some tactical lessons had been misapprehended, there can be no doubt that the military aircraft that emerged from the middle of the 1930s onwards marked a new step in aeronautical design and construction. The new generation of monoplane fighters and bombers had indeed been presaged by the introduction earlier in the decade of a number of interim types, ranging from advanced biplanes with flaps and enclosed cockpits, such as the Gloster Gladiator, and intermediate monoplanes, such as the Boeing P-26 Peashooter, the Mitsubishi A5M, the Nakajima Ki-27 and a number of French and Polish 'gull-wing' braced monoplanes. But it was only with the introduction of the Polikarpov I-16 in 1934 that the world's first low-wing monoplane fighter with a retractable undercarriage entered service. Other nations, proceeding more cautiously, did not rush to produce competitive first-generation rivals to the I-16, but instead went ahead with second-generation machines such as the Messerschmitt Bf 109, Hawker Hurricane, Supermarine Spitfire, Bloch 151 and Curtiss P-40.

Bomber design had also improved markedly, and by the outbreak of World War II most of the major combatants had considerable numbers of light bombers, capable of carrying bomb loads in the order of 500 kg (1,100 lbs), medium bombers carrying 2,000 kg (4,400 lbs), and heavy bombers carrying more than this. Examples of the three categories can be found in the Fairey Battle and Bloch 175; the Dornier Do 17, Heinkel He 111, Junkers Ju 88, Handley Page Hampden, Tupolev SB-2, Mitsubishi G4M, Lioré et Olivier LeO 451 and various American aircraft under development; and the Armstrong Whitworth Whitley, Vickers Wellington and Boeing B-17 Flying Fortress. Although flexible machine guns were still the rule on lighter bombers and all German bombers, the other nations had on the whole turned to multiple gun turrets.

Forward-looking defence planners had also appreciated the need for defensive armour, self-sealing fuel tanks and armoured windscreens, but these were only being introduced as the war began. Fighter armament had also increased, with multiple machine guns and cannon the norm, and the earlier ring-and-bead sights replaced by reflector gunsights. The two rifle-calibre guns of World War I had given way to eight rifle-calibre guns, or a smaller number of heavy machine guns, or a mixture of 20-mm cannon and machine guns.

Opposite page The Messerschmitt Bf 108 was the design predecessor of the Bf 109, and many similarities may be seen, though the 108 was a touring, sport and liaison aircraft.
Below The Bristol 142M Blenheim prototype.

CHAPTER EIGHT

INTERWAR COMBAT EXPERIENCE

air combat in World War I had, quite naturally, produced a number of lessons, both technical and tactical, on the vices and virtues of combat aircraft and on the needs and nature of air combat itself. As with all such matters, however, the lessons were open to a variety of interpretations depending on the open-mindedness or bias of the country in question. This, combined with financial constrictions after the war and in the late 1920s running into the middle 1930s, meant that although new aircraft types were produced, they were built only in limited numbers, and experience in the use of them in 'modern' war was restricted to exercises or 'policing' operations in the Middle East and North Africa, for the most part.

To prove more conclusively whether the world's air forces had drawn the right conclusions from World War I air operations, therefore, air war against comparable opposition was essential, and this came about only in the 1930s, as the world had appreciated that World War I was not the 'war to end all wars', but rather the precursor of a greater conflict made inevitable by the expansionist ideals of Germany and Japan, aided and abetted by Italy. The similarity in these countries' aims and ethics was signalised in September 1940 by the signature of the Tripartite Pact, whose principal objective was prevention of American interference.

These three countries were all directly or indirectly involved in the 'interwar' wars in which the tactics of early World War II were evolved and tested: The

(c. 1931–45) and the 'border clashes' between Japan and Soviet Russia in Mongolia in 1938–39. The Italians also used aircraft widely in their conquest of Abyssinia (now known as Ethiopia) during 1935–36, but there was no air opposition, so although the Italians themselves adduced a number of conclusions from the performance of the *Regia Aeronautica* in this campaign, the conclusions had little to do with air combat as such. Other occasions on which air fighting of greater or lesser intensity had taken place during the period were during the Russian Civil War (1917–22), where air fighting of a relatively intense nature sometimes occurred in the south, and the Russo-Polish War (1920), in which both sides made fair use of aircraft in the ground support role. Both these wars were so close to World War I, however, that their air operations are best dignified by being linked both conceptually and materially with the Great War. There were also some occasions during the Gran Chaco War (1932–35) between Bolivia and Paraguay in which air fighting played a part, but as the air units involved were small, poorly equipped and operating almost completely out of the limelight, few conclusions could be or were drawn.

Manchuria, controlled by the Japanese Army's Kanto Command almost as a separate and expansionist state, and independent in all but name from the Japanese civilian government, was the scene for the world's first major air fighting after World War I. Here, after an 'incident' typical of the military politics of the

Air power played only a minimal part in the internecine Chinese civil wars during the 1920s and 1930s. Note the machine gun and magazine for the pilot.

area in September 1931, the Japanese and Chinese air forces met in large-scale air operations. All the aircraft were of European design: on the Japanese side Nieuport 29 fighters and Salmson A2 reconnaissance-bombers (reflecting the French influence on the Japanese Army Air Corps as a result of the French mission that had aided that formation after World War I); and on the Chinese side Potez 25 reconnaissance machines. The time-scale of the air war was short, however, for after quick initial successes both in the air and on the ground, the forces of the Kanto Command overran the Chinese base areas and captured most of their surviving aircraft. In October, the French aircraft in the theatre were joined by examples of the first successful Japanese designed and built army aircraft, the Kawasaki Type 88 reconnaissance bomber. The immediate result of Japan's success in this 'incident' was the formation of the puppet state of Manchukuo in Manchuria.

Further conflict between China and Japan flared up again in January 1932 with the 'Shanghai Incident'. By this time the army deployed several Japanese-designed types in addition to the Type 88: these included the Mitsubishi Type 87 light bomber and the Nakajima Type 91 fighter. The Imperial Japanese Navy was also involved, supplying some 76 fighters and torpedo-bombers from the aircraft-carriers *Hosho* and *Kaga*, and seaplane reconnaissance aircraft from the carrier *Notoro*. The brunt was borne by the army, though, for navy aircraft were involved only on 5 February 1932, when nine Chinese aircraft were encountered, one of them being damaged by an aircraft from *Hosho*. In other naval operations no air opposition was encountered, but three aircraft were lost to ground fire. The army quickly established itself as vastly superior to the Chinese forces, who employed a number of western 'mercenary' pilots. It was a westerner, moreover, who was the first victim of a Japanese fighter pilot: on 22 February Robert Short, demonstrating the Boeing 218 fighter, attacked one of *Kaga*'s torpedo-bombers; he was quickly engaged by part of the escort, one of which, a Nakajima A1N naval fighter, shot him down and killed him.

Despite their successes in the Shanghai Incident, though, the Japanese realised that their air forces were superior only to the distinctly second-rate forces of China, and set about a considerable modernisation and expansion programme designed to raise their air services to a level on which they could engage western air forces on qualitative and quantitative parity, if not superiority. It was while this programme was being pushed through that the major war between China and Japan started in 1937.

The Italians, meanwhile, had launched their conquest of Abyssinia in 1935, and despite the extreme backwardness of the opposing armed forces, which had few aircraft, took eight months to conquer the country, and another year in which to pacify it tolerably. Some 320 aircraft were used, most of them trimotor Caproni Ca 101 reconnaissance-bombers and transports, with smaller quantities of the Ca 111, Ca 133 and Savoia-Marchetti SM 81. Eight fighter *squadriglie* were also used, five of them flying IMAM Ro 37 two-seater biplanes and the other three Fiat CR 20 single-seater biplanes.

The few obsolete Abyssinian aircraft were soon eliminated, and the Italians could thereafter use their aircraft, fighters and bombers alike, for ground-support work. The Italians incurred the virtually useless wrath of the 'civilised' world for their indiscriminate use of mustard gas dropped from the air. Perhaps the mos successful and valuable task undertaken by the *Regi Aeronautica*, however, was the mapping of the country and the transport of men and supplies, both tasks bein carried out by the ubiquitous trimotors, which perfor med with great credit throughout the campaign.

The limited air war over China and Manchuria ha not received much attention in western air circles, bu the Spanish Civil War, which broke out in July 1936 soon received very great attention as the air fightin flared up to considerable intensity, especially after th intervention of German and Italian forces. At the star of the war, most of the aircraft deployed by the Spanis air force (*Aeronáutica Militar Española*), under arm control, were in Spain: some 200 aircraft against th Nationalists' sixty in Morocco at the disposal of th rebel Nationalist leader, General Francisco Franco.

These aircraft were fairly old: Breguet Br.19 recon naissance bombers, Nieuport-Delage 52 sesquiplan fighters and Vickers Vildebeest bombers. Fortunatel for the rebels, however, most of the available pilots soo showed their allegiance to lie not with the government or Republican, side. The air ranks of each side wer soon swollen by newer aircraft, however, as a number o nations supplied extra *matériel*. The Republicans, es pecially, received aircraft from several sources: De woitine D.373, D.500 and D.510, Lioré-Nieupor LN.46 and Spad S.510C fighters; Potez 56 and Bloc MB.200 bombers from France; Letov S-231 fighter and Aero 100 general-purpose aircraft from Czecho slovakia; Polikarpov I-15 and I-16 fighters, anc Tupolev SB-2 bombers from Russia; and a number o other types from the United States. The Nationalists on the other hand, received great assistance fron Germany and Italy, both eager to help their fellow fascists, and at the same time test their latest comba aircraft in an operational medium.

The Nationalists, based in Morocco, had to get thei numerically inferior, but qualitatively superior forces t the Spanish mainland quickly if victory were to b secured, and appealed to Germany. Hitler responde by sending twenty Junkers Ju 52/3m bomber transport to Morocco on 27 July 1936, and on the next day thes aircraft started an airlift of troops and *matériel* acros the Straits of Gibraltar. Eventually, some 13,500 troop and 570,000 lbs (253,785 kg) of supplies were carrie across.

This marked only the start of German and Italia intervention, however, for on 9 August the Italian started using Savoia-Marchetti SM 81s for maritim patrol, while earlier in the same week the first si Heinkel He 51 biplane fighters and eighty-six *Luftwaff* advisers had arrived from Germany. At first th Nationalists profited little from the advice of th Germans and the use of German aircraft, so th Germans requested permission to fly their own aircraf in combat. This permission was readily granted, and or 14 August the Germans flew their first combat sortie, successful bombing attack on the Republican battleshi *Jaime I*, which was incapacitated. On this same date th first Italian Fiat CR 32 biplane fighters appeared ir Spain. At this stage the Republicans asked for Russia and Western aid, the former starting to arrive in ar ever increasing stream from September 1936.

Realising the importance of flying their own aircraf in combat so that they could themselves assess perfor mance, the Germans and Italians set up their own expeditionary forces in Spain, the *Legion Condor* anc the *Aviacione Legionaria*. The German force had bom-

A few Junkers Ju 87A dive-bombers were used in 1937 in the Spanish Civil War. The model illustrated is a Ju 87 R-2 long-range version of the Ju 87B series. The Germans inherited the early American enthusiasm for the dive-bombing concept, but, unlike the Americans, they did not lose it.

...er, fighter, reconnaissance, seaplane and anti-aircraft units, all of which soon began to play an important part in the Nationalists' initial successes. During 1937, however, the numerically superior Republicans held a Nationalist offensive towards Madrid, and static fighting ensued as both sides sought and received massive foreign assistance.

The large-scale arrival of foreign aircraft and aircrew immediately revived bitter air fighting, in which the Russians proved superior with their SB-2 bombers and I-15 and I-16 fighters. The Germans, indeed, had to relegate the He 51 to ground-attack work. The pendulum then swung back to the Nationalist side with the arrival of Messerschmitt Bf 109 monoplane fighters, Dornier Do 17 and Heinkel He 111 monoplane bombers, and Savoia-Marchetti SM 79 and Fiat BR 20 monoplane bombers from Germany and Italy. All these proved more than a match for the Republican defence.

The superiority of the Nationalist forces was amply demonstrated in April 1937 by the most infamous air raid of the war, and perhaps of all time, when Guernica in the Basque country was heavily damaged by German He 111 and Ju 52/3m bombers. So great was the moral defeat of the defenders, moreover, that two days later Nationalist ground forces were able to take the town relatively easily. More importantly, the Germans were able to gauge the effect of concentrated bombing on a 'soft' target, and public opinion throughout the western world received a highly exaggerated fear of the efficacy of air bombardment, to the extent that air attack became one of the great bogeys before World War II showed that although the damage that could be caused by moderate numbers of aircraft against undefended targets could be severe, decisive damage was extremely difficult to inflict, especially against a determined opposition. Only with the development of the atom bomb in 1945 would these fears really have any ground in reality.

By the end of 1938 the air position of the Nationalists was impregnable, with 146 Spanish, 134 Italian and 106 German aircraft at the front, to virtually nothing on the Republican side. The air war came to an end in March 1939 with the elimination of the Republican air force. During the war it had received some 2,000 aircraft, nearly 1,400 of them from Russia: of the 2,200 aircraft available, however, some 1,500 had been shot down or destroyed on the ground by the Nationalist air forces.

The Nationalists, on the other hand, had received only about 1,200 aircraft, 730 of them from Italy and 400 from Germany. Of the Republican aircraft shot down, the Italians claimed 703, the Nationalist 294, the German fighters 277, and the German *Flak* (AA) arm another 108.

The most successful fighter pilot of the war was a Nationalist, Major Joaquin Garcia-Morato, with forty victories. Italy's highest scoring pilot was *Colonello* Mario Bonzano with fifteen 'kills', and Germany's was *Leutnant* Werner Mölders with fourteen victories. On the Republican side the highest honours went to a Russian, A. K. Serov, with fifteen victories. The highest scoring Republican Spanish pilot was *Capitano* Andres Garcia Lacalle. Other notable foreign pilots on each side were a Belgian, *Compte* Rodolphe de Hemricourt de Grunne, with ten victories for the Nationalists, and an American, Frank Tinker, with eight victories for the Republicans.

Most important, in the long run, were the lessons of the modern air war in Spain, the first time that western pilots and aircraft of the very latest types had flown against each other in combat. Of the parties directly involved, and who were later to play important parts in World War II, Germany and Italy on one side, and Russia on the other, were best placed to assess the air war in Spain. Firstly, it was clear that although speeds had risen considerably since World War I, fighter aircraft could still be used in their 'traditional manner', with speed, rate of climb and rate of turn still paramount; secondly, there appeared to be very useful dividends to be obtained from the use of fighters, fitted to carry light bombs in addition to their gun armament, in a secondary ground-attack role; thirdly, air superiority over the battlefield was seen to have decisive results, allowing all types of attack aircraft to play a crucial role in the land battle; and fourthly, loose fighter tactics seemed to be clearly superior to the rigid mass-tactics that had been evolved in the 1920s and early 1930s.

For the Germans and Italians, however, the air war over Spain had some unfortunate results as well, for it led them both into a number of errors whose results were to have dire results in World War II. On the German side, for example, the success of their fast medium bombers against limited fighter defence persuaded the *Luftwaffe* that bombers could rely on speed and light defensive armament, in an air of general superiority, to go about their tasks relatively unmolested. The success of the medium bombers in a tactical role, moreover, persuaded them that the use of air power tactically would bring superior results to the use of strategic air power, especially in the swift, decisive campaigns that were being considered.

Thus the development of advanced medium bombers was slowed down, and that of heavy bombers virtually abandoned, while the development of ground-attack aircraft and tactical dive-bombers was speeded up. So convinced were they of the complete superiority of the *Luftwaffe* and its machines, moreover, that the

Germans failed to look ahead further than the next generation of combat aircraft, whereas their combat experience in World War II from 1941 onward convinced the more perspicacious of them that they should have been looking at least a generation after that in 1938.

The Italians made the same type of mistake, and also another one concerning fighter developments. The Italians' fully developed CR 32 biplanes had held their own against the Russians' first generation monoplane, the I-16, and so the Italians assumed that the CR 32 was a match for the latest British and French monoplane fighters. World War II was to disabuse them of the

concept of the biplane's superiority, based on manoeuvrability and adequate performance compared with the monoplanes superior performance but reduced agility. In short, therefore, the Germans and Italians failed to take into account the fact that, compared with the wars in which they were likely to be involved in the next few years, the Spanish Civil War had lacked the intensity of air operations necessary for the making of fully adequate assessments.

Although the Germans had found that their He 51 biplane fighter and Ju 52/3m fixed undercarriage monoplane bomber were soon outclassed by the Russian I-15 and I-16 biplane and retractable undercarriage mono-

plane fighters, and that the retractable undercarriage monoplane SB-2 bomber was difficult to catch, they thought that the imbalance had been more than redressed by the introduction of the Bf 109 fighter and Do 17 and He 111 bombers, which normal updating would keep in the forefront of warplane development for at least five years.

The trouble lay in the fact that the I-16 was already obsolescent by western standards, and Germany's potential enemies were looking to far superior aircraft, in both bomber and fighter categories. Thus although the Bf 109, Do 17, He 111 and Ju 87 'Stuka' prevailed in the opening campaigns of the war, when the audacity of

The Junkers Ju 52/3m trimotor transport was developed from the single-engined Ju 52 in 1932. It served as a bomber as well as a general-purpose transport, and was vitally important to Germany's effort in World War II. This is a montage of Ju 52/3m aircraft over Burgos in Spain.

Left Heavy bomb being loaded by 'White' Army soldiers in China, 1927.
Right A Cantonese seaplane supplied to the Red Chinese Army by the Soviet Government, during the war in China in 1927. The plane is a copy of the German Junkers machine.

the German offensives combined with the tactical skill of the German aircrews against inferior opposition to ensure German air superiority and therefore tactical success, from the time of the invasion of France in May 1940 onwards the writing was on the wall for the *Luftwaffe*.

The turn of the tide against it in 1938 had led to the withdrawal of the Russian air contingent by Stalin, and the Soviet Union then started a careful examination of what had gone wrong. The aircraft themselves, both current and on the drawing boards, seemed to be more than adequate; but the production abilities of the Russian aircraft industry, and the skill of the majority of its aircrew were found to be deficient. Realising this, the Russians set in motion plans to remedy the situation, but were hampered by the political purges of the time and by the monolithic nature of the state and its administrative processes in peacetime.

While these 'interventionist' forces were making their combat debuts over Spain, the smouldering conflict between China and Japan once again flared up in July 1937. At the time, the strength of the Imperial Japanese Army air force was about 500 aircraft in forty-nine first-line squadrons, and that of the Imperial Japanese Navy air force some 400 aircraft in twenty-nine squadrons. The Chinese air force, which had been largely trained by Italian and American air missions, was much smaller and less well equipped.

In the opening stages of this conflict, which was to turn into a full-scale war involving vast Japanese forces until the defeat of Japan in 1945, the army at first committed only six squadrons from Manchukuo, to patrol along the border with northern China while the ground forces pushed south. The army's main effort was thus utilised to build up new units for a revised organisational structure.

The brunt of early operations thus fell on the Japanese navy, which operated over central China from bases in western Japan and Formosa. But once their aircraft had covered the arrival of troop transports in the area, the carriers *Hosho*, *Ryujo* and *Kaga* were able to use their combat machines against the Chinese mainland. Quick victories were soon scored, and the Chinese withdrew most of their aircraft from areas likely to be raided by the Japanese.

Although their successes were considerable, the air units of the Japanese navy also suffered some losses, at times severe: on 14 August 1937, Mitsubishi G3M 'Nell' bombers attacked Hanchow after crossing the South China Sea, and several were shot down by Curtiss Hawk fighters of the Chinese air force; in a later raid over Hanking eight out of the eighteen attacking 'Nells' were shot down; and on 17 August eleven of twelve torpedo-bombers from *Kaga* were shot down over Shanghai. Successes there were, but the cost was high, perhaps too high. Only with the arrival of newer aircraft, such as the elegant Nakajima A5M 'Claude' carrier-based fighter on 22 August 1937, were the Japanese able to shrug off Chinese fighter defences.

But on 29 August the Chinese signed a non-aggression pact with the Russians, who sent in some 400 aircraft, mostly I-15 and I-16 fighters and SB-2 bombers. This had the immediate effect of increasing the scope of the air war, much to the liking of the Japanese pilots, who quickly got the measure of the Russian aircrew. By the late autumn most of the fighter force defending China had been destroyed, leaving the Japanese navy with a free hand to tackle targets in central China. Up to the end of October 1937 sixty-one major attacks were made on Chinese cities before the Japanese attention was switched to southern China. In the following year 170 targets in central China were engaged, as well as sixty in the south.

Only in the middle of 1938 did the Japanese again begin to suffer heavy losses to their bombers, which were attacking the Chinese airfields remote from the combat zone in an effort to eliminate the last vestiges of Chinese air power. Operating beyond the range of even the long-legged naval fighters, the bombers received some rough handling from Chinese fighters. Only with the arrival of the superb Mitsubishi A6M Zero fighter, with its prodigious range, excellent performance and powerful armament, in late 1938 did the Japanese losses decline as raids were escorted right through their long flights. In general, however, the Japanese had things much their own way in the air, although they were at times given nasty shocks when they overextended themselves or got careless, as when some 200 aircraft were caught in neat lines on an airfield by a Chinese sneak raid and nearly all destroyed.

From 1939 onwards, therefore, the Japanese had things much their own way in China, although their losses were still considerable, especially when the American Volunteer Group under Colonel Claire Chennault started operations late in 1940. Chennault's success was quite remarkable, thanks to the skills of his pilots and the early warning network he had established in previous years, but this could be little more than a difficult thorn in the side of the Japanese, who in general were able to do as they wished in the air.

From the tactical point of view, the effects of the Sino-Japanese War on the Japanese air forces was to convince them of the value of tactical air power with fast, manoeuvrable but only lightly built and armoured aircraft. These operational requirements were featured in the design of Japanese aircraft from 1936 onwards, with the result that although Japanese fighters could fly circles round their Allied counterparts in the first stages of the Pacific War, once the Allied pilots had mastered the Japanese tactics, they avoided getting into turning dogfights, in which the Japanese aircraft were always superior, and instead concentrated on diving attacks, using the superior firepower, speed and weight of their own aircraft to make one firing pass before escaping.

By 1943, therefore, as the Allies introduced a whole new breed of high-performance aircraft, the Japanese found themselves equipped largely with obsolescent types lacking the protection and sturdy structures necessary to absorb considerable combat damage. The one really positive performance factor in the favour of the Japanese, or at least of the naval air force, was excellent range: operations over China from bases in Japan or Formosa, or from carriers in the South China Sea, had given the navy a keen appreciation of engine reliability and long range, and naval aircraft used by Japan throughout most of World War II were notable for their magnificent fuel economy and range.

The aircraft of the army air force, however, were designed principally for operations in the chilly climate of Manchuria and northern China, and at short ranges. Therefore their aircraft were of little use in the Pacific, where range and the ability to perform reliably in hot, damp conditions was of paramount importance.

The most severe air fighting of the period between the two world wars, though, took place between May and September 1939, and remains to this day very little known. The protagonists were Soviet Russia and the Japanese Kanto Command, and the location the border area between Manchukuo and Mongolia, the scene of trouble between Manchurian nomads and Mongolian (Russian) border guards. The Kanto Command, ever keen for action, decided to protect its interests with aircraft operations, despite the fact that the Russian air forces were far superior, at least numerically, with 1,500 aircraft. The Japanese air units, on the other hand, were well trained, well equipped and combat experienced.

Despite the fact that Imperial Headquarters in Tokyo had expressly forbidden any such activity, the Kanto Command almost immediately committed its aircraft, and on 27 May there occurred the first major air battle of this border war: nine I-16s were shot down, seven of them by Captain Shimada and Warrant Officer Hiromichi Shinohara. The very next day the intensity of operations was again stepped up, the Japanese claiming forty-two victories; Shinohara and Shimada claimed six and five of these victories respectively.

Highly worried by these Japanese successes, betokening the complete superiority of the opposition in the air, the Russians maintained a defensive posture while awaiting reinforcements, which had arrived by the middle of June, when the Russian and Mongolian ground forces launched a major armoured offensive across the Khalkin Gol river with five armoured brigades supplementing the three divisions under the command of General Georgi Zhukov. Although suffering some 20,000 casualties, the Russians drove the Japanese back from their gains of May. The Japanese air formation in the area was II Joint Air Corps, which had 120 serviceable aircraft.

This was quickly in action, and outshone the rest of the Japanese forces involved, gaining general air superiority thanks to the agile Nakajima Ki-27 'Nate' fighter. On 22 June, in two major air battles, the Japanese shot down forty-nine Russian aircraft for the loss of only five of their own machines. Then, on 27 June, air reconnaissance revealed the arrival of Russian air reinforcements. An immediate strike was ordered, and ninety-nine Russian aircraft were shot down, with another 111 being destroyed on the ground. Japanese losses were again only five aircraft. This was really Shinohara's day, for he claimed eleven victories, the highest score claimed in a single day so far in the history of air warfare.

July saw further Japanese air successes, with some 560 victories against thirty-one losses. But despite this, the Japanese ground forces were driven steadily back, and then in August the nature of the air war also began to change, with the Russians gradually gaining the ascendancy. The Japanese were exhausted, and the Russians were introducing new units, armour protection for their aircraft and novel tactics – the diving pass which allowed them to use the greater speed and weight of their aircraft without entering a turning fight. Such was the western preoccupation with the imminence of World War II in Europe, however, that this campaign went almost unnoticed, and Allied fighter pilots had to rediscover these tactics for themselves in the Pacific campaign.

A Japanese counteroffensive planned for 24 August was forestalled by a large-scale Russian and Mongolian offensive on 20 August, which raised the intensity of air combat to a new height. For six aircraft lost, the Japanese claimed sixty-one aircraft shot down and another forty-five destroyed on the ground. Air battles continued unabated, with over twenty battles occurring within a fortnight. On 27 August over 100 fighters from each side engaged each other, and during the course of this clash Shinohara was shot down and killed. With fifty-eight victories he was the highest scoring ace of the interwar period.

During September the air clashes continued, though the Russians switched their main effort to support of the ground forces. The Japanese continued to strike at the Russian air bases in preparation for another offensive, but on 16 September a negotiated peace settlement was reached.

From this point onwards, however, the major preoccupation of the Imperial Japanese Army was the security of Manchukuo, which they felt was threatened by an expansionist Russia. Accordingly, therefore, during World War II the army located many of its best air units in Manchukuo, where they remained idle until called south to try to stem the American advance towards Japan. Then finally, when the Russians did strike, only second-rate units were left to oppose them right at the end of the war.

The main weight of the air war in the Pacific, therefore, descended on the shoulders of the Imperial Japanese Navy's air force, which had discovered in the Sino-Japanese War that operations over land were tasks that could be fulfilled by naval aircraft so long as their performance was high enough. The performance of Japanese naval aircraft, especially in the first stages of World War II, was certainly high enough, as the Allies were to find out to their cost. Convinced of the basic inferiority of Japanese pilots and aircraft, despite the warnings of men such as Chennault, they had for the most part deployed obsolescent types in the Far East.

CHAPTER NINE

THE LUFTWAFFE 1919·45

At the end of World War I, Germany's front-line squadrons mustered some 2,500 bomber, fighter and reconnaissance aircraft, total German aircraft strength being in the order of 20,000 machines. The whole German air effort, however, was rendered impotent by acute shortage of fuel.

The war with Germany was technically ended by the Treaty of Versailles in June 1919: by this the Germans were forbidden to possess or develop a military air force, or to produce military aircraft even for export. And for the very limited period of six months she was forbidden to manufacture or import aircraft, aero engines or their components. In accordance with the terms of the treaty, the Allied Control Commission in late 1919 and early 1920 accepted the surrender of 15,000 aircraft and 27,000 aircraft engines. Thus by the end of 1920 Germany's air force had ceased to exist, except for a few police air units.

Laudable as the Allied intentions may have been, in that the possession of an air force was considered an inducement for aggression by Germany, the Treaty of Versailles could not prevent the Germans from laying, both materially and organisationally, the foundations

for another air force, to be unveiled when the conditions were right for the military terms of the Treaty of Versailles to be abrogated. The foundations were laid by flouting both the letter and the spirit of the treaty in a number of enterprising ways.

The way was opened by the Treaty of Versailles itself, which forbade the building of military aircraft in Germany, but did not impose similar restrictions upon the construction and possession of civil aircraft. And although in 1922 the Allies placed a limit on the size and numbers of civil aircraft which the Germans could build, and also on the number of people who could be employed in the aircraft industry, the Paris Air Agreement of 1926, however, lifted these restrictions just at the time that the German civil aircraft industry was beginning to expand production.

Germany thus had total freedom in the field of civil aviation by 1926. The government quickly spurred on private and commercial aviation with the establishment of flying clubs, airlines, and widespread training facilities for both private and commercial air and ground crews. The object of the whole exercise was to build up 'air-mindedness' in Germany, and to provide the

nther Rall, Germany's third ghest-scoring ace with 275 ctories, in his Messerschmitt 109F, perhaps the st-handling version of this eat fighter. Rall served with 52, 11 and 300.

trained nucleus of the air force once this latter was judged possible.

It is often supposed that the *Luftwaffe*, when finally revealed in 1935, was the exclusive child of the Nazi government which had come to power in January 1933. But Adolf Hitler and Hermann Göring, the latter being the new arm's commander, had in fact only speeded up a process that had been under way since 1920, when *Colonel-General* Hans von Seeckt, the army chief of the *Reichswehr Ministerium* (Defence Ministry), sanctioned the organisational activities of a small group of ex-*Luftstreitkräfte* and army officers. Thus von Seeckt may be regarded as the real father of the future *Luftwaffe*, for it was he who had foreseen the need for an air force and taken appropriate steps. With hindsight, it is easy to see that the Allies made a grave mistake in allowing the existence of the *Reichswehr Ministerium*, which gave the banned German Great General Staff a chance of perpetuating itself under another guise.

It is interesting to note that von Seeckt not only appreciated that an air force would be essential in the creation of balanced armed forces in the future, but also saw the type of officers who would be needed to command the *Luftwaffe*. Although the officers allocated to the air force cadre at this early stage of the game were few in number, it is interesting to note that most of them became not only senior commanders, which could be regarded as inevitable, but also very able air commanders. The names include men such as Hellmuth Felmy, Albrecht Kesselring, Hugo Sperrle, Hans-Jürgen Stumpff and Walther Wever. Another illuminating factor is that these men were drawn from a slightly different class from the ex-*Junker* class which provided so high a proportion of the German Army's officers. These men were more middle class in their upbringing, most of them with more catholic educations than was the norm in the army, and most of them with service in one of the army's more technical branches behind them.

Although the army and the navy had guarded the subordinate position of the air services almost jealously during World War I, as early as 1923 von Seeckt had decided that for future military operations the air force would have to be totally independent of the army and the navy. It was a piece of considerable foresight.

Any major air force is of course dependent on indigenous aircraft production for prolonged wars, and here the *Luftwaffe* was to be well served, principally because of the Allies' laxity in prohibiting any aircraft industry in Germany after World War I, and partially because of the Germans' subterfuges in establishing military aircraft design and production facilities outside Germany, notably in Sweden and the Soviet Union. As noted above, Germany had in June 1919 been banned from aircraft production for six months only.

Thus by 1920 governmental and commercial pressures were prompting the establishments of a number of major production facilities: Junkers at Dessau in early 1920 (and soon afterwards in Russia, Sweden and Turkey); Heinkel at Warnemunde in 1922 (and in Sweden); Dornier in Switzerland and Italy, as well as at Friedrichshafen, also in 1922; Focke-Wulf at Bremen in 1924; and Willi Messerschmitt took over the *Bayerische Flugzeugwerke* (Bavarian Aircraft Company) in 1925.

By 1926, when the Paris Air Agreement removed the building restrictions from Germany, there were already in existence five of the companies whose future military aircraft would serve Germany so well in the 1930s and early 1940s. And thanks to the government's far-

sighted air policy, German aircraft production even at this early stage of the game matched or even excelled that of any other European country.

With the development of purely military aviation, perforce clandestine, von Seeckt quickly realised that only astute manipulation of civil aviation could provide the practical experience and development that would be needed. Therefore, as early as 1924, von Seeckt ensured the appointment of an ex-*Luftstreitkräfte* officer, *Hauptmann* Ernst Brandenburg, to head the Ministry of Transport's *Abteilung Luftfahrt* or Civil Aviation Department. This appointment meant that the civil aviation administration would treat military needs sympathetically. Brandenburg was finally removed after a row with Göring in 1934, having served the needs of his country ably and well.

Germany had in the 1920s been the breeding ground for a number of small airlines. Lacking capital and government backing, though, they had not been able to expand to any great extent. But then in 1926, largely as a result of the efforts of Erhard Milch, initially an employee of Lloyd Ost airline and then of Junkers, the government with military backing decided to establish a national airline, *Deutsche Lufthansa*, with Milch as chairman. Milch ensured that *Deutsche Lufthansa* had the best aircraft, extensive airfields all over Germany, very lavish numbers of personnel, and more than

adequate training in all types of flying, including navigation and blind flying by both day and night.

It is remarkable that no one at the time seems to have remarked on the military uses, especially bombing, that such training would give to *Deutsche Lufthansa*'s over-abundant flying personnel. But just as things seemed to be going well, in 1928 the German government halved the lavish grants made to *Deutsche Lufthansa*. It was only because Milch at this time met Hermann Göring, a member of the *Reichstag* (German parliament), and persuaded him to support *Deutsche Lufthansa* in the assembly, that matters were partially rectified.

By 1926, then, Germany was well placed for the future development of an air force. To increase all-important air-mindedness, in 1920 the *Deutscher Luftsportverband* (German Air Sport Association) had been founded, and by the end of the decade numbered some 50,000 members, most of whom had some flying experience in gliders and light aircraft, and were devoted to the concept of air power. The influence of the *Reichswehr Ministerium* in the *Deutscher Luftsport-verband* may be seen in the appointment of men such as *Hauptmann* Kurt Student, then head of the Air Techni-cal Department and later commander of the *Luftwaffe*'s airborne arm, to organise the glider instruction courses.

But what of the covert air force structure within the *Reichswehr Ministerium*? On 1 March 1920 the follow-

ing departments had been established: the Air Organ-isation and Training Department, under the command of *Major* Helmut Wilberg, was directly subordinate to the *Truppenamt* or Troop Department (the cover name for the rump of the Great General Staff) and was the central office for all military aviation matters; the Foreign Air Department, subordinate to the Foreign Armies Department, evaluated foreign air forces; the Air Technical Department, subordinate to the Wea-pons and Equipment Office of the *Heereswaffenamt* (Army Ordnance Department), was the compiler of information on technical matters; the Air Armaments Economics Office or *Fliegerrüstungswirtschaftliches Referat* (WaWiL), under *Hauptmann* Wilhelm Vogt, compiled economic dossiers on foreign air power fac-tors; and a Procurement Office was planned but never realised.

At the same time Air Consultant Officers, each with two assistants, were allocated to each of the seven military districts headquarters (*Wehrkreiskommandos*) under the cover title of Special Duty Consultants, for aerial reconnaissance purposes. In 1929 another three Air Consultant Officers were found for the three cavalry divisions.

The 3rd Company of the 2nd (Prussian) Motor Transport Battalion and the 1st Company of the 7th (Bavarian) Motor Transport Battalion were made re-

German infantry emplane in a Junkers Ju 52/3m for the invasion of Norway. This aircraft served as a trainer, transport, liaison, paratrooping and glider tug aircraft throughout the war.

sponsible for the continuance of air traditions in the Prussian and Bavarian units of the army respectively. These latter semi-overt developments were made easier by the fact that in 1926 the Allies permitted the *Reichswehr* an air defence branch, although this was limited to anti-aircraft artillery. Thus the Air Organisation and Training Department, which had operated under the cover title Air Defence Department, could at least admit to its cover!

The air staff was thus very small, and its efforts mainly devoted to planning and the collection of information. There were technically no aircraft allowed within the German armed forces, although on the occasion of the French seizure of the Ruhr in 1923 President Friedrich Ebert had been persuaded to disgorge enough funds for the purchase of 100 Fokker D XIII reconnaissance aircraft from neutral Holland. But the aircraft were delivered so late that fifty were immediately sold to Romania and the other fifty sent off to Russia for use in the German training school at Lipetsk.

The school at Lipetsk was the result of Russia's urgent need for advanced technology, which had been almost totally missing in World War I. In April and May 1921 a Russian 'trade delegation', led by Leonid Krassin, had come to Germany, and under cover of this military negotiations had been opened between the *Reichswehr Ministerium* (with officers such as von Seeckt, *Oberst* Herman von der Lieth-Thomsen, *Generalleutnant* Johann Hasse and *General* Kurt von Schleicher among those primarily involved) and Karl Radek as the Russians' chief negotiator. These talks paved the way for the secret military protocols agreed at the end of 1922, although the Allies suspected that such accords had been part of the Treaty of Rapallo of 16

April 1922, by which Russia waived her right t demand reparations from Germany.

Under the terms of the late 1922 agreements, th Germans were given access to Russian airfields and labour for the testing of German aircraft and equip ment, in return for the supply to the Russians of th technical results of the tests. In February 1923 the hea of the *Truppenamt*, Hasse, travelled to Moscow t finalise arrangements. The importance attached by th Germans to the agreement may be gauged from th seniority of the officer sent to Moscow. A liaison office the Moscow Centre, was immediately set up unde Thomsen, working under the pseudonym von Litz. H was later replaced by *Major* Oscar, *Ritter* vor Niedermayer.

Soon German pilots and technical experts were ir Russia, and when the Russians offered the use o Lipetsk airfield, some 300 miles (480 km) south-east o Moscow, the Germans accepted and soon established flying school. Here proper military training was immediately instituted. Facts are still uncertain, but i seems that instructors probably started on training courses in 1925, and that it was not until April 1927 tha ordinary aircrew started on courses at Lipetsk.

Another part of the Russo-German accord provided for the building of a Junkers aircraft factory at Fili halfway between Moscow and Mozhaisk, with German government subsidies. This plant operated between 1924 and 1927 under German control, and was instrumental in training large numbers of Russian personnel to high technical standards.

By 1925, as a result of an easing of Allied pressure on Germany, the armed forces were able to shrug off a little of the great secrecy under which they had been operating for the last six years. This was to have

Messerschmitt Me 323D-1, the first production variant of the powered version of the Me 321 glider, an adaptation made necessary by the *Luftwaffe's* lack of heavy transports before the war.

mportant results for the fledgling air force. Before discussing this, it may be useful to examine the overall workings of the *Reichswehr Ministerium*, which naturally enough had a civilian at its head. Under this minister were the service chiefs, heading the Army Command (*Heeresleitung*) and Naval Command (*Marineleitung*).

These two commands each had various subordinate departments under the control of Department Chiefs (*Amtschefs*) with the authority of divisional commanders; at the same level, but responsible to the minister, was the Armed Forces Branch. Under the departments were the branches, each headed by a Branch Chief with the authority of a regimental commander. In large departments a number of branches might be formed into a department group under a Department Group Chief with the authority of a brigade commander. At the lower levels, in descending order below the branch, were the group, section and finally consultant.

In 1925 the Air Organisation and Training Department was renamed Group T2 III (L), and placed under the control of the chief of the *Heeresleitung* with responsibility for organisation. Wilberg had been replaced by *Oberstleutnant* Wilhelm Wimmer, and successive heads of Group T2 III (L) were *Major* Hugo Sperrle (who had been involved in the setting up of the Lipetsk school) and *Major* Hellmuth Felmy.

Army air agencies in existence in 1926 were as follows: Group T2 III (L), which had absorbed the Foreign Air Department; Group V of the Weapons and Equipment Department of the Army Ordnance Department, dealing with questions of aircraft and equipment manufacture; and Groups Wa 1 and WaB 6, dealing with air armament procurement. On 1 February, however, Groups WaB 6 and Wa Pruf 6 (techni-

cal development and testing) were amalgamated as Group Wa L under the command of *Hauptmann* Helmuth Volkmann in an effort to centralise weapons development and procurement procedures.

At the same time Group T2 III (L) was redesignated Group T2 V (L). Despite its ancestry as a department, Group T2 V (L) was commanded in 1929 by *Major* Felmy, who was thus very low in the priorities pecking order with departments commanded by more senior officers. Felmy had the ear of *Generalmajor* Werner von Blomberg, chief of the *Truppenamt*, but Blomberg resigned shortly after this, and it was not until 1931, when Group T2 V (L) was raised in status to branch level, that matters improved.

In 1928 *Major* Kesselring had suggested, in his capacity as *Vereinfachungskommissar* or rationalisation expert, the formation of a *Flieger-Inspektion* or air inspectorate, but this was vetoed by *Major* Wilhelm Keitel, head of the Army Organisation Department, on political grounds.

But in 1931 further easing of the international political scene allowed another slight step into the open for the Germans. Thus there was formed the Training Inspectorate (In 1), under whose aegis the whole German military air effort operated. Group T2 V (L) became Inspectorate 1 (L), while the real Training Inspectorate became Inspectorate 1 (W). The head of the Training Inspectorate, *Generalmajor* Hilmar, *Ritter* von Mittelberger, took over Inspectorate 1 (L), with Felmy as chief-of-staff. Thus military aviation finally had a commander of general rank, responsible only to the head of the *Heeresleitung*. But the *Truppenamt*, as the general staff, continued to control basic planning.

Although the German Navy had an equivalent organisation running its naval air power development,

the two branches did little more than liaise with each other, and no real efforts to co-ordinate army and navy air policy were ever made, to the final detriment of both parties.

Training Inspectorate 1 (L) was divided into a number of *Referate* or sections with the following responsibilities: *Referat* I strategy and tactics; *Referat* II officer personnel; *Referat* III air technology; *Referat* IV foreign air forces and economic planning; *Referat* VII air defence; *Referat* VIII flying training; and *Referat* IX meteorology. *Referate* I, V and VII were headed by general staff officers, and all *Referate* personnel had to be able to fly. Despite the easing of the general international political situation, the continued existence of the Treaty of Versailles and its restrictions meant that all the work of Inspectorate 1 (L) had to be carried out in conditions of the utmost secrecy, especially where the Lipetsk facility was concerned, the dispatch of military missions to other powers being strictly prohibited by the Treaty.

The priorities of the army's air service in the late 1920s is revealed by its choice of aircraft, all for clandestine use and all built by Heinkel: the HD-17 tactical reconnaissance aircraft, the HD-32 trainer and the HD-33 strategic reconnaissance aircraft. By 1929, moreover, there were eight aircraft and four engine manufacturers available in Germany: Albatros, Arado, *Bayerische Flugzeugwerke* (an amalgamation of the earlier Messerschmitt and Udet), Dornier, Focke-Wulf, Heinkel, Junkers and Rohrbach for aircraft; and Argus, BMW, Junkers and Siemens for aircraft engines.

By 1926, Germany's secret mobilisation plans called for an air force of some 1,000 aircraft. Unfortunately, even had the aircraft themselves been available, the number of pilots available was only about 180, many of whom were World War I veterans, considered unsuit-

able for operations by the second half of the 1920 Thus it was essential to boost the number of younge pilots in the armed forces, principally by using th facilities at Lipetsk after a period of intensive groun and air training in Germany.

It was decided at this time to train 60 new officers year for the air service: 30 *Reichsheer* officers, known a *Altmärker*, and 30 other young men, known as *Jung märker*, who must be prepared to join the *Reichsheer* These candidates were to train for one year in German and six months at Lipetsk (only the best 10 *Jungmärke* were to go on to Lipetsk for fighter training).

By 1929 there were enough well trained instructor to form a fighter training squadron, whose primar responsibility was the production of a comprehensiv manual on air fighting, including bombing. Two prac tice squadrons were formed, with camera guns as the weapons. This device proved very successful, an between 1925 and 1933 some 125 fighter pilots wer trained at Lipetsk. About 100 reconnaissance aircre were also trained, in the period between 1928 and 193

Although the Russians at times caused trouble, th programme was on the whole smooth-running, and th success of the *Jagdfliegervorschrift* or Fighter Manual eloquent testimony for this. General Yakov Ivanovic Alksnis and Colonel S.A. Mezheninov, commander-in chief and operations officer respectively of the Red Ai Force, were frequent visitors to Lipetsk and to con ferences organised in Germany. And there can be littl doubt of the value to the Russians of the informatio they received after the testing of Germany's lates military aircraft.

By 1932, however, the Germans had cut back th amount of work being carried out at Lipetsk quit considerably, most testing now taking place at Rechlir and the majority of reconnaissance training at Braun schweig. *Generaloberst* Wilhelm Groener, the defenc

Below The Junkers Ju 88 was perhaps World War II's most versatile aircraft, having good payload and performance in a number of roles, and being very durable.

minister, had criticised the air component's lack of reality in the 1931 autumn manoeuvres in Silesia, and as a result the instructors' squadron at Lipetsk had been disbanded, re-forming in Germany as three four-aircraft *Reklamestaffeln* or Propaganda Squadrons, based at Königsberg, Berlin-Staaken and Fürth. Ready by 1932, the three new units were used for film work, and for army manoeuvres when appropriate. Lipetsk was finally closed down by the Germans in the late summer of 1933, much of the flying equipment there being handed over to the Russians.

Plans for long-term procurement of aircraft and munitions for the air force, which would only come into official existence with the declaration of mobilisation were Germany invaded, were the responsibility of Keitel, promoted to lieutenant-colonel on 1 February 1929. The *Reichstag* was chary of allowing the stockpiling of aviation necessities for the air force, which was planned as a body complementing a 21-division army

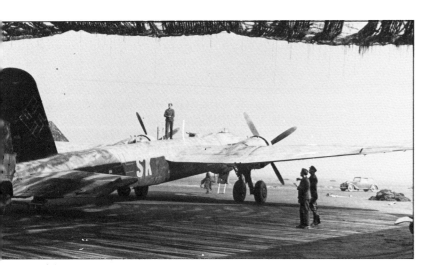

until 29 November 1930. But secrecy meant that large-scale stockpiling would be impossible even had the air force's small budget allowed the purchase of the necessary aircraft and munitions. So even by the time of the earliest practicable mobilisation, in 1934, there were plans for only eight squadrons. Although the number of *Reklamestaffeln* was soon increased to seven, and later to ten, most of the air force's flying personnel would have to come from *Deutsche Lufthansa*.

During this period the German Navy had also dabbled in the field of clandestine air organisation, but only on a very limited scale. The main effort went into a firm named Severa, which supposedly towed air targets for naval AA gunnery practice, but in fact undertook the training of naval personnel from its bases at the former naval air stations at Warnemünde and Stettin-Alt Damm. In 1928 another navy front, the Commercial Flying School, began training observers at Warnemünde and at List on the island of Sylt. Technical matters were the province of the *Entwicklungsreferat* or Development Section, and finished articles were tested by the *Erprobungsstelle des Reichsverbandes der deutschen Luftfahrtindustrie* or Testing Station of the Reich Association of German Aviation Industries. In general, however, the efforts of the navy were negligible, especially where development of an air-dropped torpedo were concerned.

Planning for the future *Luftwaffe* had been constantly bedevilled by lack of unified thought and a proliferation of interested parties, all on about the same level of seniority. In 1932 the *Truppenamt* realised that the planners needed a vertical rather than horizontal command structure, and ordered Inspectorate 1 (L) to investigate the matter. Inspectorate 1 (L) at length suggested the following reorganisation: an air group in the *Truppenamt*; an *Abteilung für Fliegertruppen* or Air Force Branch in the Defence Department; an *Inspizient der Fliegertruppen* or Air Force Inspectorate in the Defence Department; a *Wehrmachtluftabteilung* or Armed Forces Air Branch in the *Wehrmacht-Rüstungsamt* or Armed Forces Armaments Department to deal with the army and navy air armament; and a *Fliegerreferat* or Air Section in the T1 Branch and another in the *Wehrmacht-Nachschubamt* or Armed Forces Supply Department.

Little had been done about these proposals before the advent to power of the Nazi Party in January 1933, however. But immediately Hermann Göring was appointed head of the *Reichskommissariat für die Luftfahrt* with effect from 30 January, and from this time on, change came rapidly. Fearing that Göring would not restrict himself merely to the civil aviation matters in his brief, the army and navy decided to meet his plans for extended power with a united front. The first move to meet the Nazi 'threat' was the transfer of the navy's Development Section to the army as part of Wa Prüf 8.

On 1 April 1933 there was established a *Luftschutzamt* or Air Defence Department, comprising the following: Inspectorate 1 (L), Wa Prüf 8 and Wa NL, both previously part of the Ordnance Department, the Air Defence sections of the Defence Department, and various small naval departments. Head of the new department was *Oberst* Eberhardt Bohnstedt, with a naval officer, *Commandant* Rudolf Wenninger, as his chief-of-staff. The tasks of the *Luftschutzamt* were widespread, including technological developments, organisation, mobilisation planning, training, *matériel* development, finance and all matters pertaining to air defence not assigned to other *Wehrmacht* agencies.

To meet these requirements, the *Luftschutzamt*'s organisation provided for: its head to be directly responsible to the *Reich* defence minister, the department to represent both the army and the navy in all matters within its sphere of responsibility, its head to have the authority of a *Waffeninspekteur* or Inspector of a service branch to deal with all air units, and a selection from different *Wehrmacht* branches for the department's head and chief-of-staff.

Abbreviated LA, the *Luftschutzamt* was organised as follows: Branch 1 (LA-1), the precursor of the *Luftwaffe* general staff, controlled the whole apparatus, and was subdivided into LA-1 (Army) and LA-1 (Navy), each in turn being divided into three groups, Group I dealing with tactics, Group II dealing with organisation and Group III dealing with training.

This was the final development of the planning that had been going on under the Defence Ministry of the Weimar Republic since 1919, and was only short-lived. Göring's brief in aviation was soon expanded by the establishment of the *Reichsluftfahrtministerium* or Reich Air Ministry on 1 May 1933, and under this senior Nazi's initially dynamic leadership, the *Luftwaffe* was to flower into a major force in European politics. It should be noted, though, that this flowering was only made possible by the careful work undertaken by the secret planners of the Weimar Republic, allied with the expansionist ambitions of the Nazi Party.

Although an independent *Luftwaffe* had been strongly advocated by von Seeckt, after his dismissal in 1926 the independence of the future force was not so strongly stressed. But the appointment of the ambitious Göring first to the rank of *Reichskommissar* and then to *Reichsminister* ensured that the *Luftwaffe* would be a force separate from the army and the navy. Thus on 1 May 1933 the new *Reichsluftfahrtministerium* absorbed the month-old *Luftschutzamt*. Supposedly a civilian ministry, the RLM as it was normally abbreviated now directly controlled the still illegal activities to build up an air force, and so officers seconded to the ministry had to be discharged from the army and wear civilian clothing.

Göring's deputy at the RLM was the able Erhard Milch, who held the post of *Staatssekretär der Luftfahrt* or State Secretary of Aviation. It is impossible to overrate the importance of Milch in the establishment of the new *Luftwaffe*: energetic, strong-willed and clear-headed, yet genial, Milch did most of the hard work of organising the large new force from ex-army officers and civilians, and spurred on the great aircraft building programmes that gave the *Luftwaffe* its aircraft.

Under Göring and Milch, the RLM was organised as follows: the Central Branch, the Air Command Department (LA), the General Air Department (LB), the Technical Department (LC), the *Luftwaffe* Administrative Department (LD) and the *Luftwaffe* Personnel Department (LP).

The most important of these departments was the Air Command Department, subdivided into the Operations Branch (LA-I), Organisation Branch (LA-II), Training Branch (LA-III), Anti-Aircraft Artillery Branch (LA-IV), Supply Branch (LA-V), plus signals and medical branches. Most of the personnel were general staff officers, and the Air Command Department may properly be regarded as the *Luftwaffe*'s general staff in embryo.

Although the military departments of the RLM were the heirs to Inspectorate 1 (L) and *Luftschutzamt*, its

Above   The Junkers Ju 87B. The bombload was one 1,100 lb bomb and four 110 lb bombs. The Stuka proved a potent weapon in the Polish and French campaigns.

Right   A Messerschmitt Bf 110C-3 twin-engined fighter. Designed as a long-range fighter, the Bf 110 proved ineffective until later marks became radar equipped night fighters. The engine and machine guns are being serviced.

considerably greater size meant that the necessary officers had to be obtained from the army, and although these were men of some seniority, they were all obliged to learn to fly. Among the early arrivals were *Oberst* Hans-Jürgen Stumpff, head of LP, *Oberst* Walther Wever, soon to be head of the Air Command Department, and *Obersten* Albrecht Kesselring, Karl Kitzinger and Wilhelm Wimmer. As head of the Air Command Department, Wever was in effect *Luftwaffe* chief-of-staff, the post to which he was appointed when the *Luftwaffe* was finally unveiled in 1935. On Wever's untimely death in an accident in 1936, he was replaced by Kesselring, who was in turn succeeded by Stumpff as a stop-gap before the appointment of Wever's nominee, Hans Jeschonnek, on 1 February 1939. Most of his contemporaries at the RLM agreed that Wever showed distinct qualities of genius, and from Germany's point of view, perhaps the saddest fact about his death was that with him effectively died the plans for the development of a strategic bomber force, the lack of which was so keenly felt in World War II. Part of Wever's genius, moreover, lay in his marvellous ability to get on with all parties, and so ensure the smooth running of the *Luftwaffe*.

Before discussing in detail the growth of the *Luftwaffe* after its official birth on 10 March 1935 (at which time its strength stood at 1,888 aircraft of all types and some 20,000 men), three points need to be made about the factors affecting the force's development up to the beginning of World War II on 1 September 1939.

Firstly, there were the differing personalities of the two top men, Göring and Milch, the former seeing matters in a generally personal way and the latter in a more logical, constructive way; secondly, there was the novelty of the whole force, which meant that there were no precedents on which the basic running of the *Luftwaffe* could depend; and thirdly, there was no proper general staff, and even after the institution of this body on 1 August 1936, lack of tradition and clear-cut objectives combined with lack of proper training at the highest levels to defeat the objects of the body in many instances.

The problems facing the *Luftwaffe* high command can perhaps best be illustrated by a typical instance: the clash between Milch and Kesselring about command of the *Luftwaffe* during late 1936 and early 1937. Göring finally decided on 2 June that the *Luftwaffe* chief-of-staff would be responsible to him alone, but must inform the state secretary of all policy decisions. This meant that Kesselring (soon to be replaced at his own request by Stumpff) and Milch were on a par – hardly the best command structure! Quite apart from this, Göring's decision meant that the whole *Luftwaffe* chain of command was thrown into turmoil, with officers wondering if they were now responsible to the chief-of-staff or to the state secretary.

Göring's decision also led to a conflict between Milch and Stumpff about the need to reorganise the *Luftwaffe* high command to obviate this problem. Milch suggested that two offices equal to the general staff should be established: a *Luftwehramt* or Air Defence Department (basically a war ministry) and a *Generalinspekteur* or Inspector General, with authority over the chief-of-staff, the chief of the *Luftwehramt* and the head of LP. This latter position, as Göring's deputy, Milch clearly wanted for himself, as it would leave its holder in supreme power in the increasingly long periods during which Göring was absent with his many other interests.

Stumpff offered to subordinate himself to Milch if Göring would only decide that actual command of the *Luftwaffe* was a general staff responsibility, but at the same time laid down other conditions that would have diminished Milch's powers.

Göring finally adjudicated on 18 January 1938, reducing Milch's powers very considerably: no longer was the *Staatssekretär* to be *de jure* permanent deputy of the *Reichsminister und Oberbefehlshaber der Luftwaffe* (Reich Minister and Commander-in-Chief of the *Luftwaffe*), but only to act in this capacity on the explicit orders of Göring. At the same time the *Luftwaffe* general staff was made part of the RLM's planning staff, with responsibility for all military preparations.

Another reorganisation, though, on 23 January 1938 made Milch *Generalinspekteur* and once more appointed him Göring's deputy. Stumpff resigned on 1 February 1939 as a lieutenant-general, and became head of the Air Defence Department and Milch's deputy! *Oberst* Hans Jeschonnek became *Luftwaffe* chief-of-staff.

Jeschonnek had right of direct access to Göring, and had to inform Milch of the meetings he had with Göring only if command and leadership were discussed. In other matters he was expected first to consult Milch. The *Luftwaffe* Quartermaster General also had direct access to Göring, which meant that Milch was excluded from many of the supply decisions he later had to implement.

General Ernst Udet, a World War I associate of Göring, was head of the new Department of Procure-

Luftwaffe senior commanders at Le Bourget airfield outside Paris. On the left is *Generaloberst* Erhard Milch, the State Secretary of Aviation in the *Reichsluftministerium*, who was one of the key figures in the growth of the *Luftwaffe* before the beginning of World War II. He finally fell from grace with Hitler in 1944 over the question of how best to use the Messerschmitt Me 262 jet fighter. Next to Milch is *Generalleutnant* Bodenschatz, *Generalleutnant* Ernst Udet, wearing the *Pour le Mérite* decoration at his throat, was the Chief of the Technical Office of the *Luftwaffe* and the Chief of the Office of Special Supply and Procurement until his suicide in 1941.

ment and Supply, with the title of *Generalluftzeug-meister* or GL for short. As such, Udet was responsible for all armament, and controlled six staff branches, the Technical Department, the Supply Department, the Economics Department, and the Anti-Aircraft Artillery Development Department. Udet had direct access to Göring, and so Milch, whom Göring always suspected of over-ambition, was neatly frozen out of all technical matters.

This, then, was the *Luftwaffe*'s high command structure, such as it was. It says much for the ability of the more senior officers involved that they managed to make a war machine, initially so effective, in the circumstances. Göring distrusted everyone with the possible exception of Udet, and had successfully snarled up the high level chain of command so that no one officer could rival himself.

Below this level, an intermediate stage of command had been developing since 1934. On 1 April 1934, six *Gehobene Luftämter* or Senior Air Departments were established under five retired generals and one retired admiral. Disguised as civilian enterprises, these *Luftämter* were the air equivalents to the army's *Wehrkreise*, and were officially revealed as such after 10 March 1935, as *Luftkreise* or Air Service Commands. On 1 April 1937 a seventh *Luftkreis* was formed. The headquarters of these bodies were located as follows: *Luftkreis* I in Königsberg, *Luftkreis* II in Berlin, *Luftkreis* III in Dresden, *Luftkreis* IV in Münster, *Luftkreis* V in Munich, *Luftkreis* VI (Sea) in Kiel and *Luftkreis* VII in Braunschweig. Commanded by generals, the *Luftkreise* were responsible only to the *Luftwaffe* high command, and the local high commands and field command agencies.

Under each of these *Luftkreise* were a *Höherer Fliegerkommandeur* or Senior Air Commander, commanding all the air units in the area; a *Höherer Flakkommandeur* or Senior Anti-Aircraft Artillery Commander (after 1 October 1935), commanding all the AA units in the area; two or three *Luftgaukommandos* or Air Administrative Area Commands; a

Nachrichtenführer or Signals Communication Commander with his Air Service Area Signals Communication Battalion; a *Luftzeuggruppe* or Procurement and Supply Group with its apparatus of dumps and depots; an Air Service Area Medical Battalion; a Personnel Replacement Battalion (after 1 April 1935); a *Fliegerersatzregiment* or Personnel Replacement Regiment (after 1936) and a Pilot Training School; and a variety of local agencies, schools etc.

Thus each *Luftkreis* was supposedly an independent entity, containing all the elements necessary for it to raise and supply air units in war. The *Luftkreis* commanders were given extensive powers, with the right to commandeer civilian airfields and take all necessary steps for air defence.

Organised on traditional army lines, the *Luftkreise* were not the right answer to the *Luftwaffe*'s needs, and this was realised after the annexation of Austria on 11 March 1938, when the *Luftkreis* organisation had not functioned smoothly. Göring ordered an immediate reorganisation, which came into effect on 1 April 1938. *Luftkreise* II, III, IV, V and VII were reallocated to a new organisational feature, the *Gruppenkommandos* or Group Commands. *Gruppenkommando* I, with HQ in Berlin, comprised *Luftkreise* II and III; *Gruppenkommando* II, in Braunschweig, had *Luftkreise* IV and VI; *Gruppenkommando* III, in Munich, had *Luftkreis* V. *Luftkreis* I in Königsberg became *Luftwaffekommando* East Prussia, and *Luftkreis* VI became *Luftwaffekommando* (*See*) IV, with its HQ at Kiel. Austria became *Luftwaffekommando Österreich*, with its HQ in Vienna. The object of these new formations was to separate the command and administrative functions of the old *Luftkreise*, and make the *Gruppenkommandos*' operational headquarters more mobile.

Under the *Gruppenkommandos* were the primary operational formations, the *Fliegerdivisionen* or Air Divisions, command of which for operational purposes was assumed by the three new *Luftflotten* established on 1 April 1939. *Luftflotte* I was commanded by Kesselring, had its HQ in Berlin, covered northern and eastern Germany, and comprised the 1st and 2nd *Fliegerdivisionen*; *Luftflotte* II was commanded by Felmy, had its HQ in Braunschweig, covered north west Germany, and comprised the 3rd and 4th *Fliegerdivisionen*; and *Luftflotte* III was commanded by Sperrle, had its HQ in Munich, covered south-west Germany, and comprised the 5th and 6th *Fliegerdivisionen*. The *Luftwaffekommandos* and *Gruppenkommandos* controlled only reconnaissance and signal units.

Administrative backing for the *Luftwaffekommandos* and *Gruppenkommandos* was now provided by the ten *Luftgaue* or Air Administrative Area Commands: III (Berlin), IV (Dresden) and VIII (Breslau) to *Gruppenkommando* VIII; VI (Münster) and XI (Hannover, but transferred to Hamburg on 1 April 1939) to *Gruppenkommando* II; VII (Munich), XII (Wiesbaden) and XIII (Nuremberg) to *Gruppenkommando* III; XVI (Vienna) to *Luftwaffekommando Österreich* (Austria) and *Luftwaffegau* I (Königsberg) to *Luftwaffekommando Ostpreussen* (East Prussia).

It was the *Gruppenkommandos* that were transmogrified into *Luftflotten* on 1 April 1939. At the same time *Luftwaffekommando Österreich* became *Luftflotte* IV, receiving *Luftgau* VIII for extra logistical backing, and *Luftwaffekommando Ostpreussen* was absorbed into *Luftflotte* I. *Luftwaffekommando* (*See*) was done away with, being replaced by a new grouping under the

General der Luftwaffe beim Oberbefehlshaber der Marine und Befehlshaber der Marinefliegerverbände or Luftwaffe General with the Commander-in-Chief of the Navy and Commander of Naval Air Units.

From 1 August 1938, all Luftwaffe air units had been organised into five Fliegerdivisionen, which thus became the organisational cornerstone of Luftwaffe field structure. Allocated to each Fliegerdivision were several Geschwader or Wings, their number and type depending on the task the Fliegerdivision had to undertake. The average Fliegerdivision usually had one Jagdgeschwader or Fighter Wing and two or three Kampfgeschwader or Bomber Wings, and some also had a Sturzkampfgeschwader (usually abbreviated to Stukageschwader) or Dive-Bomber Wing. As soon as was possible, each Fliegerdivision was given a Fernaufklärungsstaffel or Strategic Reconnaissance Squadron and a signals battalion. Each Gruppenkommando (later Luftflotte) had two Fliegerdivisionen under command.

The next two divisions did not fall into the same category as the first five Fliegerdivisionen: the Lehrdivision or Training Division (formed on 1 August 1938 from two antecedents, II Gruppe, Kampfgeschwader 152 in 1936 and the office of the Höherer Kommandeur der Lehrtruppen or Senior Commander of Training Troops, set up on 1 October 1937) for the operational testing of new aircraft and weapons; and the 7th Fliegerdivision, established on 1 June 1938, as the Luftwaffe airborne arm. General Kurt Student was the commander of the 7th Fliegerdivision, and was in January 1939 given the job of Inspekteur der Fallschirm- und Luftlandetruppen or Inspector of Parachute and Air-Landed Troops.

Shortly before the outbreak of war, the lessons of the Spanish Civil War so far as ground-attack and support aircraft were concerned saw concrete expression in the formation of the first Schlachtgruppe or Battle Group under Generalmajor Wolfram, Freiherr von Richthofen, the officer who had been responsible, as a colonel, for the development of the necessary tactics in Spain. Despite its small size, this group was to play a decisive part in the Polish campaign, and lead to the formation of far larger ground-support formations as the war went on.

Since the death of Wever, the Luftwaffe had been considered as a tactical force, and so cooperation with the other two branches of the Wehrmacht (das Heer or Army and die Kriegsmarine or Navy) was essential. For this purpose, a Luftwaffe general was appointed to the office of the army commander-in-chief. After 1 March 1939, this officer was known as Befehlshaber der Heeresfliegerverbände und General der Luftwaffe beim Oberbefehlshaber des Heeres or Commander of the Army Air Units and Luftwaffe General with the Commander-in-Chief of the Army. Under the strategic command of this officer, and thus of the army high command, were three reconnaissance Geschwader with ten Gruppen. It was also decided that in the event of hostilities, a

Below Hermann Göring started his career as a fighter pilot in World War I, serving in von Richthofen's famous squadron. Said to be the father of the Luftwaffe, he was made Reichmarschall in 1940.

Opposite page The Focke-Wulf Fw 190 was Germany's best 'conventional' fighter of World War II. *Left* Stuka pilots comparing notes on tactics during the Polish campaign.

Kommandeur der Luftwaffe, usually abbreviated to *Koluft*, or *Luftwaffe* Commander was to be assigned to each army group and army command, the appointee being a staff officer of the high command reconnaissance *Geschwader*. These wings, it should be noted, were not formed until 1 August 1939.

The *Luftwaffekommando* (*See*) had been closed down on 1 March 1939, and the naval air commander was then subordinated to the *Luftwaffe* General with the Commander-in-Chief of the Navy.

At the lower end of the *Luftwaffe*'s organisation were the operational sub-units of the *Fliegerdivisionen*: the *Geschwader*, made up of two or more *Gruppen* or Groups, each in turn comprising two or more *Staffeln* or Squadrons.

The activation of the bomber force after the public admission of the *Luftwaffe*'s existence on 10 March 1935 at first went smoothly, and by 1936 there were five twin-engined *Kampfgeschwader* (the 152nd, 153rd, 154th, 155th and 253rd) with 16 *Gruppen* between them. By the end of 1937 the total of *Geschwader* had reached 10, with the making of a few more in Spain. By September 1939 the total had again increased, this time to 13. The trouble lay in the fact that although the number of *Geschwader* had increased fairly rapidly, the number of *Gruppen* in them had not: by 1939 there were only 24 twin-engined *Gruppen*, and it had earlier been decided that for war, which was not expected before 1942 according to Hitler, 54 *Gruppen* in 18 *Geschwader* would be essential.

Although relatively slow off the mark with the idea of dive-bombing, the *Luftwaffe* accepted the idea totally during 1937, and eight Stuka *Gruppen* were raised during the year, plus another $1\frac{1}{3}$ in the *Lehrdivision*.

The *Luftwaffe* had always recognised the need for fighters, and three single-seat interceptor *Gruppen* were formed in 1935. By the beginning of April 1936 four more *Gruppen* had been established, as had two *Jagd-geschwader* headquarters. In the next 12 months a further eight *Gruppen* were raised, so that by April 1936 there were 15 *Gruppen* in three *Jagdgeschwader*. 1938 saw another increase in single-seat fighter strength, to $19\frac{1}{3}$ *Gruppen* in four *Jagdgeschwader*, *Lehrgeschwader* II and the *Legion Condor*. At the same time twin-engined fighter production had started, and conversion to this type had got under way. Thus by September 1939 the fighter arm had five single-seat *Jagdgeschwader* with $18\frac{1}{3}$ *Gruppen*, plus three independent fighter *Staffeln*, one of them trained for night-fighting; and ten twin-engined fighter *Gruppen*.

Great importance was attached to long-range, or strategic, reconnaissance by all three German armed services, especially the *Luftwaffe* and the army. Five long-range reconnaissance *Staffeln* were formed in 1935, all of them under *Luftwaffe* command until 1937, although they would have been used for army purposes should war have broken out. By September 1939 there were 25 long-range reconnaissance *Staffeln*, ten of them allocated to the army, and the remaining 15 to the *Luftwaffe*, three of the latter being reserved for *Luftwaffe* high command use.

Tactical reconnaissance was also high on the list of *Luftwaffe* priorities, and two such *Staffeln* were formed in 1934, another five *Staffeln* being raised in 1935 from the output of the reconnaissance schools at Braunschweig and Hildesheim. By 1936 the number of tactical reconnaissance *Staffeln* available to the army had risen to 14, controlled by six *Gruppe* staffs. These six *Gruppen* each had their full complement of three *Staffeln* by 1 July 1937. Exactly one year later, control of these units was officially given to the army, which continued the expansion and so had 30 *Staffeln* by September 1939, with another six being found on mobilisation.

All important in a tactical air force such as the *Luftwaffe* had become was communications, and here the Germans were fortunate to find a man of the calibre of *Oberstleutnant* Wolfgang Martini, on 12 July 1933 appointed to command the new air force's signals command. Over him were two *Inspekteurn*, *Generalmajor* Günther-Hans von Kluge and *Oberst* Erich Fellgiebel. Under these three, the *Luftwaffe*'s tactical signals equipment and techniques became first class.

Up to March 1935, anti-aircraft artillery (*Fliegerabwehr Kanone* or *Flak*) had been the responsibility of the army, with the most important person in the early stages of its development being *Oberst* Günther Rüdel, head of the Air Defence Branch. Then in March 1935 the Air Defence Branch was transferred to the new RLM, which thus became responsible for all Germany's AA defences through the Air Defence Branch's Inspectorate for *Flak* Artillery.

While still under army control, the *Flak* arm had standardised the 2-, 3.7- and 8.8-cm weapons for low-, medium- and high-altitude AA defence respectively, and on the arm's transfer to the *Luftwaffe* in 1935 this was not altered, although the main agent in the design and adoption of these weapons had been the army's Training Staff 3 at Berlin-Döberitz. There were many valid reasons for the transfer, not least of which was the fact that the *Luftwaffe* could provide the *Flak* arm with all necessary information about likely enemy air tactics

and other factors, and that the *Flak* arm could now be integrated more closely with the home defence organisation. At this early stage of the game, it must be remembered, Germany was thinking in terms of a defensive war, and so the protection of Germany's cities and industries against enemy bombing was of prime importance. And with the 'pull' that Göring had thanks to his political position, the *Luftwaffe*'s procurement finances were far greater than the army's.

By the autumn of 1935, there were *Flak* commands attached to five of the *Luftkreise* in existence, with 1 heavy and 3 light *Flak* battalions, all of them motorised. There was also a *Flak* School at Rerik, under the control of the *Flak* Inspectorate. In 1937 the training battalion at this school was redesignated the *Flak* Training and Experimental Battalion, and on 1 April of the same year, one *Flak* regiment, with one heavy *Flak* battalion, one light *Flak* battalion and one searchlight battalion, was assigned to the *Lehrdivision*.

Under *Luftwaffe* command, the expansion of the *Flak* arm was rapid, the number of battalions (the basic tactical unit) almost doubling by the end of 1936: 26 mixed and 8 light *Flak* battalions with 87 heavy batteries, 53 medium and light batteries and 29 searchlight batteries.

In October 1937 the *Luftwaffe* entered the third

Below Messerschmitt Bf 109F fighters of 8./JG51. *Inset* The bulge in front of the cockpit covers the breach of a machine gun (same on the other side), and there is a drop tank under the fuselage.

phase of its *Flak* arm expansion, establishing one senior *Flak* command (air), five regimental *Flak* staffs, six mixed battalions and nine light battalions. Thus the total force available was 6 senior *Flak* commands, 11 regimental staffs, 1 *Flak* Command (Sea), 35 mixed battalions, 17 light battalions and 1 searchlight battalion, with 115 heavy batteries, 14 cadre batteries, 69 medium and light batteries and 37 searchlight batteries.

The fourth phase of expansion was initiated in October 1938, providing each of the ten *Luftgaue* with a senior *Flak* command controlled by an officer with the rank of *Oberst* or *Generalmajor*. At the same time strength was increased locally by between 25% and 50%. To meet this expansion, nine new regimental staffs, ten mixed battalions (three light battalions having been broken up), five fortress battalions and fifteen searchlight battalions were set up. Special Air Defence Commands to protect important industrial areas were also formed at Berlin, Düsseldorf, Hamburg, Leipzig and Stettin.

The main land threat to Germany seemed to come from France in the west, and to meet it great efforts had been made to build up the *Westwall* line of static defences. As part of this formidable obstacle, there was established the Command Headquarters of the Western Air Defence Zone, under the control of the Senior Commander, Fortress *Flak* III. The command had five fortress *Flak* battalions, and two *Flak* reconnaissance units, one in the Black Forest and the other in the Eifel.

The *Luftwaffe*'s ground organisation was the responsibility of the *Leithorstkommandanturen* or Airfield Commands, which controlled all airfields and ensured that they were supplied with all necessary fuel, supplies and personnel.

This, then, was the basic structure of the *Luftwaffe* at the time of the invasion of Poland, which triggered off World War II. Overall command of the force was exercised by Hermann Göring and Erhard Milch, the command apparatus being the *Oberkommando der Luftwaffe* (OKL) or *Luftwaffe* High Command. This high command had come into operation late, thanks largely to the obstruction of Göring and Milch, who distrusted the conventional high command structure. Nevertheless the *Luftwaffe*'s general staff had come into existence on 1 August 1936, initially comprising the forty general staff officers who had come into the *Luftwaffe* on its formation. During 1936 and 1937 they were supplemented by other officers from the *Kriegsakademie* or Army War Academy, and in 1938 by officers from the *Luftkriegsakademie* or Air War Academy. But it was only just before the invasion of Poland that OKL had sufficient general staff officers.

Left to right **General** Sperrle, **General** Wever, **General** Kreipe, **GeneralFeldmarschall** Göring, **General-Major** Martini, **General** Udet.

The most significant of the *Luftwaffe*'s senior personnel were *Feldmarschall* Hermann Göring, *Oberbefehlshaber der Luftwaffe* or Commander-in-Chief of the *Luftwaffe*; *General* Erhard Milch, *Generalinspekteur der Luftwaffe* or Inspector-General of the *Luftwaffe*; *General* Ernst Udet, *Generalluftzeugmeister* or Director-General of *Luftwaffe* Equipment; and *General* Hans Jeschonnek, *Chef des Generalstabes der Luftwaffe* or *Luftwaffe* Chief-of-Staff. Other notable commanders, in alphabetical order, were: *Oberst* Walter von Axthelm, Inspector of *Flak*; *General* Hellmuth Felmy, Commander-in-Chief of *Luftflotte* II; *General* Albrecht Kesselring, commander of *Luftflotte* I; *Generalleutnant* Karl Kitzinger, Supreme Commander of Air Defence; *Generalmajor* Fritz Loeb, Chief of the *Luftwaffe* Administration Department; *General* Alexander Löhr, commander of *Luftflotte* IV; *Fliegerchefingenieur* Rudolf Lucht, Chief Engineer in the Department of the Director-General of *Luftwaffe* Equipment; *Generalmajor* Wolfgang Martini, head of the Air Signals Branch; *Generalmajor* Hermann Plocher, Chief of Plans and Mobilisation, *Luftwaffe* General Staff; *General* Günther Rüdel, Chief of Air Defence; *General* Hugo Sperrle, commander of *Luftflotte* III; *Generalleutnant* Kurt Student, *Inspekteur der Fallschirm- und Luftlandetruppen* or Inspector of Parachute and Air-Landed Troops; and *General* Hans-Jürgen Stumpff, commander of *Luftflotte* I after Kesselring's removal to *Luftflotte* II.

From top to bottom, the Luftwaffe's chain of command ran as follows, with Hermann Göring (promoted to *Reichsmarschall* on 19 July 1940), at its head: *Oberkommando der Luftwaffe*, commanded by a *Generaloberst* or *General der Flieger*; *Luftflotte*, commanded by a *Generalfeldmarschall* or *General der Flieger*; *Fliegerkorps* or Air Corps, commanded by a *General*

der Flieger or *Generalleutnant*; *Fliegerdivision*, commanded by a *General der Flieger*, *Generalleutnant* or *Generalmajor*; *Geschwader* (in Allied terms a Group of about 100–120 aircraft), commanded by a *Generalmajor*, *Oberst*, *Oberstleutnant* or Major; *Gruppe* (in Allied terms a Wing of about 30–36 aircraft), commanded by an *Oberstleutnant*, Major or *Hauptmann*; *Staffel* (in Allied terms a Squadron of about 9–12 aircraft), commanded by a *Hauptmann* or *Oberleutnant*; *Schwarm* (in Allied terms a Flight of four aircraft, used by the Germans only for fighter forces), commanded by an *Oberleutnant*, *Leutnant* or *Unteroffizier*; *Kette* (in Allied terms a Flight of about three or four aircraft, used mostly for the bomber forces), also commanded by an *Oberleutnant*, *Leutnant* or *Unteroffizier*; and the *Rotte* of two aircraft, used only by the fighter forces.

The *Staffel* was the lowest organic flying unit in the *Luftwaffe* and its commander had the title *Staffelkapitän*. Flying personnel were at first about ten in fighter units and more than forty in bomber units, with some 150 and eighty ground personnel respectively. The bomber *Staffel*'s small number of ground personnel is explained by the fact that much maintenance was done at *Luftgau* level. In the course of the war, *Staffel* strength gradually rose from nine aircraft to sixteen.

The *Gruppe*, one step up from the *Staffel*, was the *Luftwaffe*'s smallest operational and administrative unit, and its commander bore the title *Gruppenkommandeur*. Initial complement of a *Gruppe* was three *Staffeln* and a *Stabskette* or *Stabsschwarm* of three aircraft, making thirty aircraft in all. By the middle of the war most fighter *Gruppen* had a fourth *Staffel*, bringing aircraft strength up to sixty-seven aircraft. Personnel strength was 35–150 aircrew and 300–515 ground personnel. Among these were an adjutant,

technical specialists and medical personnel.

Above the *Gruppe* was the *Geschwader*, the largest *Luftwaffe* unit with a fixed establishment: three *Gruppen* and a *Stabskette* or *Stabsschwarm* with four aircraft, for a total of ninety-four. During the war, most *Kampgeschwader* added a fourth *Gruppe*, the *Ergänzungsgruppe* or Replacement *Gruppe* for operational training. At the end of the war some *Kampfgeschwader* even had a fifth *Gruppe*. The commander of a *Geschwader* usually bore the title *Geschwaderkommodore*.

All *Geschwader* and independent *Gruppen* were given arabic numeral designations, such as *Jagdgeschwader 26* and *Aufklarüngsgruppe 124*. *Gruppen* forming part of a *Geschwader* were given roman numeral designations, II./JG26 being IInd *Gruppe* of *Jagdgeschwader 26*. *Staffeln* were given consecutive arabic numeral designations, the 1st, 2nd and 3rd *Staffeln* being part of I. *Gruppe*, the 4th, 5th and 6th *Staffeln* part of II. *Gruppe* etc. Thus 4./JG26 was the 4th *Staffel* of *Jagdgeschwader*, and the first of II./JG26's three *Staffeln*.

Command of the various branches of the *Luftwaffe* was exercised from the top by *Abteilungen* or Directorates of the OKL: *Abteilung* 1 for Operations, 2 for Organisation, 3 for Training, 4 for Movements, 5 for Intelligence, 6 for Equipment, 8 for History and 9 for Personnel. *Abteilungen* 1, 3 and 5 were directly responsible to the Chief of the Operations Staff; and the others, with the exception of *Abteilung* 8 which reported directly to the *Chef des Generalstabes*, were part of the empire of the *Generalquartiermeister* or Quartermaster-General. Under the *Chef des Generalstabes* there were also numerous Inspectorates dealing with specific matters such as fighters, bombers, navigation etc.

OKL was itself split into two parts, a forward echelon and a rear echelon. The forward echelon was made up of the *Chef des Generalstabes*, Operations Staff,

Director-General of Signals, Director of Training and part of the Intelligence Department, and was code-named '*Robinson*', operating close to Hitler's headquarters for most of the war; the rear echelon, made up of the rest of OKL and codenamed '*Kurfürst*', was located in Berlin. The two echelons kept in touch with the aid of large numbers of liaison officers. It is worth noting here that the *Fliegerkorps*, introduced at the beginning of the war, was the operational counterpart of the *Luftgau*, and controlled between 300 and 750 aircraft. In many respects it assumed many of the original functions of the *Fliegerdivision*.

To cope with the problems of air administration once Germany had expanded all round her boundaries, during the war the operational areas of the original four *Luftflotten* were greatly extended: *Luftflotte* I into the Baltic states and towards Leningrad; *Luftflotte* II into Italy, North Africa and the Aegean; *Luftflotte* III into France and the Low Countries; and *Luftflotte* IV into southern Russia and the Balkans. Further requirements in this field led to the formation of another three *Luftflotten*: *Luftflotte* V for Norway and northern Russia; *Luftflotte* VI for central Russia; and *Luftflotte Reich* to assume the functions of the original four *Luftflotten* for the defence of Germany proper.

Naturally enough, the *Luftwaffe* grew very considerably during the war, but the basic structure remained largely unaltered, with the exception of the fighter arm and the large-scale expansion of the ground-attack arm. Expecting a quick victory against all their enemy's, Germany's political leadership had refused to allow work on a new generation of weapons to proceed with any real priority, and so in the later stages of the war, from 1943 onwards, the *Luftwaffe* had to fight on with weapons gradually becoming obsolete, the later weapons, which might have produced structural chan-

Above **Oberstleutnant** Adolf Galland.

ges in the *Luftwaffe*, appearing only right at the end of the war, in numbers too small to affect the outcome of the conflict.

So long as the war was running in their favour, the Germans found little need to alter the organisation of their fighter forces. But once the Allies had held their own, and then started to take the war back to Germany, the British and American night and day bomber efforts against Germany's cities and key industries showed the *Luftwaffe* that newer methods were essential. Nearest the fighter arm's original tactics were those devised for use against the American bomber boxes that struck so devastatingly against Germany's prime military industries and fuel production facilities. Operating by day, and in tight cohesive boxes, the bombers were able to cover each other quite well, and with the advent of the P-51 escort fighter, the task of the German fighter defences was made even more difficult.

The basic fighter tactics of the *Luftwaffe* had been devised during the Spanish Civil War, and perfected by *Oberst* Werner Mölders, the Inspector of Fighters, shortly before the start of World War II. These tactics, based on a loose formation of two *Rotten* or Cells, had proved very effective in the opening campaigns of the war, during the Battle of Britain and in the first half of the Russian war.

Mölders was killed in a flying accident in November 1941, and his successor as Inspector of Fighters was another celebrated ace, *Oberst* Adolf Galland. A year later, at the age of 30, Galland was promoted to *Generalmajor*, thus becoming the youngest general in the German armed forces.

The growth of the American bombing raids on Germany became a real menace during Galland's inspectorate, however, and it was Galland who supervised the introduction of new battle formations to meet this threat. The earlier attacks from the beam or from the stern by *Rotten* or *Schwärme* were supplemented by head-on attacks, in the hope that some bombers could be crippled, to be finished off after they had fallen behind the rest of their box. The tactics proved quite effective, although attacking strength was gradually raised to *Gruppe* level by the size of the American raids.

But from the spring of 1944 onwards, however, the Americans were able to escort their bombers to most European targets and back by the use of the superlative North American P-51 Mustang fighter. This meant that the Germans had to come up with new tactics so that they could get through the escort to get to the bombers themselves. Galland thus instituted a novel tactical organisation known as the *Gefechtsverband* or Battle Formation. This was made up of one heavy *Sturmgruppe* or Assault Group of rocket- and heavy cannon-armed single- and twin-engined fighters, and two light *Jagdgruppen* of conventionally armed fighters, comprising in all more than one hundred fighters. The tactic was posited on the ability of the *Jagdgruppen* to engage the escorting P-51s sufficiently closely for the *Sturmgruppe* to get through and so engage the bombers which were the real threat to Germany.

In theory the *Gefechtsverbände* were excellent solutions to the problem, and sometimes caused very considerable losses. But in fact the formations were unwieldy and slow to form up, and often provided the free-roving American escort fighters with excellent targets long before they came within range of the bomber force.

The real solution to the daylight bombers was found only late in the war – jet fighters too fast for the escort to engage. But the fact that development of such aircraft had had only low priority meant that they were late entering service, and then delayed yet further by Hitler's wish to turn them into fast bombers. So magnificent types such as the Messerschmitt Me 262 were too late to affect the course of the war. Galland, for some time a severe critic of the way Göring and OKL was running the German air effort, especially with the late delivery of new types and the poor quality of replacement pilots, was finally relieved as Inspector of Fighters in January 1945, whereupon he appointed himself commander of *Jagdverband* 44, an Me 262 unit which he led for the last months of the war.

Night-fighting had been virtually unknown in Germany until May 1940, when the first British night raids brought about by earlier losses to the German *Flak* and day-fighter arm, revealed the total inadequacy of *Flak* and single-seat fighters by night. *Oberst* Josef Kammhuber was ordered to form an efficient night-fighter force, and it was thanks to his efforts that the *Nachtjagddivision*, later *Fliegerkorps* XII, became such a potent force against RAF Bomber Command. Starting with two understrength *Gruppen* with no radar, Kammhuber started the process that raised the night-fighter arm to some six *Nachtjagdgeschwader* with 700 aircraft, plus six searchlight regiments and about 1,500 radar stations. Kammhuber was promoted to *Generalmajor* and Inspector of Night-Fighters on 16 October 1940, with two missions: to protect the Third *Reich* with a belt of defensive night-fighters along Germany's western frontiers, and to take the night-fighter war to the British bombers with intruder missions.

Kammhuber had been promoted to *Generalleutnant* by the end of 1941, and to *General der Flieger* in January 1943, by which time *Fliegerkorps* XII was perhaps the *Luftwaffe*'s single most important formation. But in July 1943 the close-control radar interception technique pioneered by Kammhuber was ruined by the British introduction of 'Window' chaff, or *Düppel* as it was known to the Germans, and Kammhuber fell from favour, commanding *Luftflotte* V in the relative backwater of Norway from November 1943 to February 1945. Then finally his past services to Germany were remembered, and he was appointed Göring's Special Plenipotentiary for Jet and Rocket Aircraft, in a last desperate effort to step up production and introduction of the all-important types with which Germany hoped finally to stem the Allied tide. With the dismissal of Kammhuber, who had started the war in the OKL as head of the Organisation *Abteilung*, the new Inspector of Night-Fighters and commander of *Fliegerkorps* XII became *Generalmajor* Josef 'Beppo' Schmid, until then head of the OKL Intelligence *Abteilung*.

The tactics and successes of the night-fighter arm are discussed more fully in Chapter 16. The night-fighter arm's companion in the fight against Bomber Command was the *Flak* arm, which during the war became one of the largest and most important forces in the German armed services. The roles of the *Flak* arm were twofold: the protection of the *Reich*, and air defence for the armies in the field. The importance the *Luftwaffe* gave to these two tasks right from its formation may be gauged from the fact that at the beginning of World War II nearly one million men, almost two-thirds of the *Luftwaffe*'s personnel strength, was in the *Flak* arm, and that in the autumn of 1944 this strength had risen to about $1\frac{1}{4}$ million, or about half the *Luftwaffe*'s personnel. The production effort needed to supply the guns and ammunition, and the logistics exercise to feed, ouse and otherwise supply these forces played a major part in German planning.

During the war, the *Flakkorps* or *Flak* Corps was the highest command echelon; it was mobile and attached to field armies, controlling two, three or four *Flakdivisionen*. *Flakdivisionen* could be either static or mobile, the former usually located within Germany for some defence under the control of a *Luftgau* and the latter controlled by a *Flakkorps*.

A static *Flakdivision* comprised two or more *Flakbrigaden* or *Flak* Brigades, each made up of two, three or four *Flakregimenter*, each in turn controlling four, five or six *Flakabteilungen* or *Flak* Battalions. A mobile *Flakdivision* comprised two, three or four *Flakregimenter*, each of these having about four *Flakabteilungen*. By the beginning of 1945, the *Luftwaffe* had seven *Flakkorps*, twenty-nine *Flakdivisionen*, thirteen *Flakbrigaden* and 160 *Flakregimenter* staffs.

The basic *Flak* unit was the *Flakabteilung*, which came in four varieties: *schwere* or heavy, *leichte* or light, *gemischte* or mixed (having both heavy and light guns) and *Scheinwerfer* (searchlight). *Flakabteilungen* were also divided into motorised, semi-motorised and static.

The *schwere Flakabteilung* usually comprised four *Batterien* or Troops (with guns over 7.5-cm in calibre); *leichte Flakabteilungen* comprised three or four *Batterien* (with 2- and 3.7-cm weapons); *gemischte Flakabteilungen* comprised three heavy and two light *Batterien*; and *Scheinwerfer Flakabteilungen* comprised three or four *Batterien*. Static *Flakabteilungen* generally had more and larger *Batterien* than semi-motorised *Flakabteilungen*, and this had more and larger *Batterien* than motorised *Flakabteilungen*.

'*Flakdivision*' may produce an erroneous impression of the formation's size, for compared with other divisions the *Flakdivision* was very large. The 14th *Flakdivision*, for example, was defending the Leuna synthetic oil refinery in the closing stages of 1944, and had 62,550 personnel: 28,000 *Luftwaffe* troops, 18,000 *Reichsarbeitdienst* or *Reich* Labour Service, 6,000 *Luftwaffehelfern* (teenage schoolboys called out during raids), 3,600 Russian prisoners-of-war, 3,050 *Flakhelferinnen* (female auxiliaries), 3,000 miscellaneous support elements, and 900 Hungarian and Italian volunteers.

On 1 September 1939, the first-line strength of the *Luftwaffe* comprised 1,170 medium bombers, 335 dive-bombers, 1,125 single-engined fighters, 195 twin-engined fighters, 280 long-range reconnaissance aircraft, 340 tactical reconnaissance aircraft and 205 coastal aircraft, for a total of 3,750 first-line aircraft. Of these, 648 medium bombers, 219 dive-bombers, thirty ground-attack aircraft, 210 single- and twin-engined fighters, and 474 reconnaissance and transport aircraft (1,581 in all) were used in the Polish campaign.

For the beginning of the war with Russia, Germany deployed a nominal 1,945 aircraft from *Luftflotten* II, IV and V. Of these, however, only 1,400 were serviceable: 510 medium bombers, 290 dive-bombers, 440 single-engined fighters, forty twin-engined fighters and 120 reconnaissance aircraft. The nominal strength was some 61% of the *Luftwaffe's* total strength on 22 June 1941.

At the end of 1942, despite considerable production increases, *Luftwaffe* first-line strength had risen little from September 1939: 1,135 medium bombers, 270 dive-bombers, 1,240 single-engined fighters, 515 twin-engined fighters, 395 long-range reconnaissance aircraft, 275 tactical reconnaissance aircraft and 135 coastal aircraft, for a total of 3,960 aircraft. This denotes an increase in strength of only 210 aircraft, despite Germany's far greater commitments, and it is notable that most offensive types had fallen in number, and that defensive types (single- and twin-engined fighters) and long-range reconnaissance aircraft had swelled in number.

Thus there are clear indications that by the end of 1942 the *Luftwaffe* was on the defensive, and this trend is confirmed by the production figures for various categories of aircraft in 1943 and 1944, the last two full years of the war:

	1943	1944
bombers	4,649	2,287
fighters	10,898	25,285
ground-attack aircraft	3,266	5,496
reconnaissance aircraft	1,117	1,686
seaplanes	259	141
transport aircraft	1,028	443
gliders	442	111
liaison aircraft	874	410
trainers	2,274	3,693
jets	0	1,041

Production was 24,807 in 1943, and 40,593 in 1944, eloquent testimony of the effectiveness of the dispersed factory concept adopted in the face of Allied heavy bombing. Aircraft production in 1939 had been 2,518 aircraft, in 1940 10,247, in 1941 12,410, in 1942 15,409 and in 1945 7,539, bringing the war total to 113,514 aircraft of all types. The aircraft built in largest numbers were the Messerschmitt Bf 109 fighter (30,480), the Focke-Wulf Fw 190 fighter (20,001), Junkers Ju 88 multi-role aircraft (15,000), the Messerschmitt Bf 110 fighter (5,762), the Heinkel He 111 bomber (5,656), the Junkers Ju 87 dive-bomber (4,881), the Junkers Ju 52 transport (2,804), the Fieseler Fi 156 liaison aircraft (2,549), the Dornier Do 217 bomber (1,730), the Heinkel He 177 bomber (1,446), the Messerschmitt Me 262 jet (1,294), the Junkers Ju 188 bomber (1,036) and the Messerschmitt Me 410 fighter-bomber (1,013).

The inevitability of Germany's final defeat became clear to all except the most stubborn after the failure of her final effort to wrest the strategic initiative from Russia in the disastrous Battle of Kursk in July 1943, and was signalled in the *Luftwaffe* by the suicide of the *Chef des Generalstabes*, Jeschonnek, on 19 August 1943, after Göring informed him that he was personally responsible for the eclipse of the *Luftwaffe*. Jeschonnek was replaced by *Generaloberst* Günther Korten, who had been chief-of-staff with *Luftflotten* IV, III and then back to III in the Polish, Belgian and Balkan campaigns respectively. In August 1942 he commanded *Luftwaffekommando* Don in Russia, from which he moved to command *Luftflotte* I in June 1943. Severely wounded in the bomb attempt on Hitler's life on 20 July 1944, Korten died a few days later.

His replacement as *Chef des Generalstabes* was *General* Werner Kreipe, latterly in charge of the *Luftwaffe* training programme, which had been greatly hindered by the need to send off replacements before their training was finished, by shortages of fuel, and by the loss of training aircraft when they had to be used for operational purposes. Kreipe held the post for only a few months, from August to November 1944, when he was replaced by *General* Karl Koller. This officer had started the war as head of the operations staff of *Luftflotte* III, becoming its chief-of-staff in January 1941. Koller had been appointed head of the *Luftwaffe* operations staff in September 1944, and held this post until his appointment as *Chef des Generalstabes*, a position he then held right to the end of the war.

Right at the top of the command structure there were also changes. Milch was dismissed from all his positions after a row with Hitler in May 1944: the latter wished to see the Messerschmitt Me 262 produced as a bomber, while the former supported the parent company in its contention that the plane had been designed as a fighter and should be placed in production as such.

Finally, Hermann Göring fell from favour. Even before the suicide of Jeschonnek, the decline in the *Luftwaffe*'s power had become all too apparent to Hitler, who blamed Göring for the problem. Thereafter Göring's importance declined steadily, and after an abortive effort to topple Hitler in April 1945, Göring was stripped of all his powers and saved from a worse fate only by the protection offered to him by loyal *Luftwaffe* ground troop elements. The second and last *Oberbefehlshaber der Luftwaffe* thus became *Generalfeldmarschall* Robert, *Ritter* von Greim. Von

Greim had started the war as commander of the 5th *Fliegerdivision*, later *Fliegerkorps* V. He held this position right through to the first stages of the Russian war, when *Fliegerkorps* V was redesignated *Luftwaffe kommando Öst* (East) in April 1942, later becoming *Luftflotte* VI in July 1943. Von Greim committed suicide after being taken prisoner at the end of the war.

By 1945 Germany was on her last legs, and the *Luftwaffe*'s last few efforts were devoted to the defence of what was left. Manpower was short, many thousands of men having been released to industry, the army and the SS; aircraft were in relatively plentiful supply thanks to the sterling efforts of the Minister for Production, Albert Speer, but trained aircrew and fuel were in desperately short supply.

Up until February 1945 the *Luftwaffe*'s chain of command had been little different from that with which it started the war, with the exception of two special fighter commands, *Jagdkorps* I for strategic defence over Germany herself, and *Jagdkorps* II for tactical operations over North-Western Europe. These two corps had been disbanded in February 1944, their functions being assumed by the 14th and 15th *Flieger-divisionen*, and by *Fliegerkorps* IX(J) respectively.

Inset The Messerschmitt Bf 109 E-3. This aircraft was better than the Spitfire in some respects, but its deficiencies were made even more apparent by the disastrous tactics employed by the Luftwaffe. This machine was flown by 11./JG77.

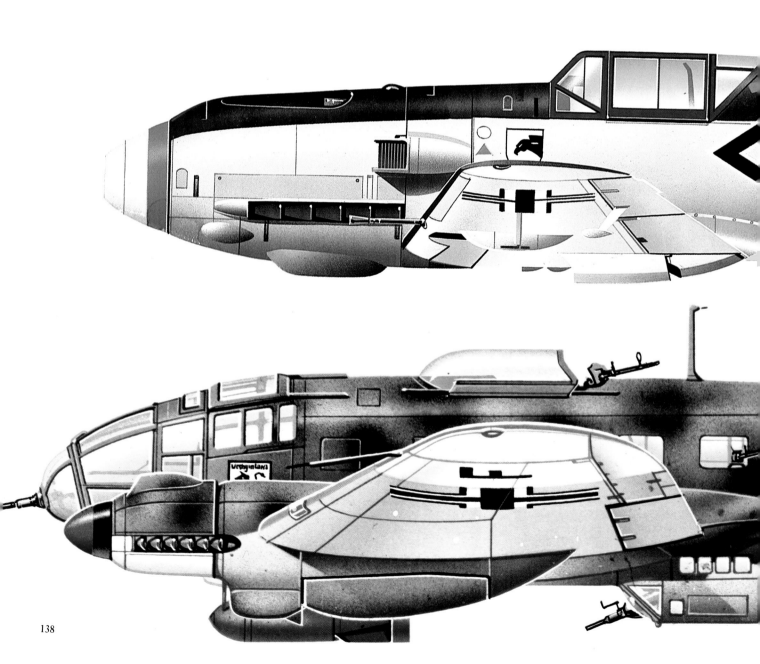

The dispositions of the *Luftwaffe* at the beginning of March 1945 were thus as follows: operating against the Western Allies in North-West Europe was *Luftwaffekommando West* under *Generalleutnant* Schmid with the 4th, 15th and 16th *Fliegerdivisionen*; controlling the air forces in Germany was *Luftflotte Reich* under *Generaloberst* Stumpff with *Fliegerkorps* IX(J) and the 1st, 2nd, 3rd, 7th and 8th *Jagddivisionen*, the latter commanded by *Generalmajor* Dieter Peltz, latterly Inspector of Bombers and *Angriffsführer England* ('Attack Leader for England') for the bombing of England from March 1943; and operating against the Russians on the Eastern Front were *Luftwaffekommando Kurland* (lately *Luftflotte I*), cut off in Latvia, *Luftflotte VI* under *Generaloberst* von Greim with *Fliegerkorps* II and VIII, and *Luftflotte IV* under *Generaloberst* Dessloch with *Fliegerkorps* I and the 17th *Fliegerdivision*.

Another reorganisation took place on 7 April, when the 14th *Fliegerdivision* was given to *Generalfeldmarschall* Busch, the army's Commander-in-Chief North-West, and *Luftwaffekommando* West came under the command of *Generalfeldmarschall* Kesselring's High Command West. *Fliegerkorps* IX(J), with Peltz desperately trying to keep it separate as a strategic defence force, moved from Weimar to Prague and thence to Munich. On 14 April von Greim's *Luftflotte VI* assumed command in south-eastern and southern Germany, with *Luftwaffekommando West* and the 7th *Jagddivision* in south-west Germany, *Luftwaffekommando* IV (ex-*Luftflotte* IV) with its earlier commands and the 8th *Jagddivision* in south-east Germany, and *Fliegerkorps* VIII in eastern Germany. Northern Germany came under Stumpff, who had *Fliegerkorps* II (redesignated *Luftwaffekommando* North-East on 11 April) operating against the Russians, what was left of the 1st and 2nd *Jagddivisionen* in the centre and the 14th *Fliegerdivision* operating against the British in the west.

Further change came on 25 April, when *Grossadmiral* Karl Dönitz, commander-in-chief of the German Navy, took overall command in the north, with *Luftflotte Reich* directly subordinate to him, together with the rump of *Luftflottekommando Kurland* and the air units controlled by *Generalleutnant* Roth in Norway and by *Generalleutnant* Holle in Denmark. There was further turmoil from other command changes, and although all this reorganisation sounded fine, it should be remembered that the *Luftwaffe* had only about 1,500 aircraft and precious little fuel even for these.

A Heinkel He 111 H-6 of 11 *Staffel* of *Kampfgeschwader* 26 This operated from Sardinia, against British shipping.

CHAPTER TEN

THE ROYAL AIR FORCE
AND FLEET AIR ARM
1919·45

The Hawker Typhoon IB with rockets. The Typhoon was one of the most successful fighter-bombers of World War II, some 3,330 being built between 1941 and 1945.

Despite its new-found position as an autonomous member of the British armed forces, the Royal Air Force was, like the army and navy, pruned right back in the political and economic retrenchment that followed World War I. Try as he might, there was virtually nothing that Sir Hugh Trenchard could do about it when he returned to the post of Chief of the Air Staff in February 1919. He saw clearly that his most important task in the years ahead would be to maintain the autonomy of the RAF against the encroachments of the army and the navy, and to turn the peacetime RAF into a sturdy sapling from which a great RAF tree could grow in the event of threatened hostilities. Therefore the relatively *ad hoc* structure of the RAF, formed hastily during World War I, must be rationalised to allow efficient cadres for a more efficient RAF to be set up. For this, Trenchard reasoned, it was not so much the 'tooth' elements (the fighting squadrons) but the 'tail' services (maintenance, training, equipment and other support elements) that were important. So he set his considerable energies to putting the RAF on a firm logistical footing within the United Kingdom. As Trenchard himself put it, the main task was therefore 'to reduce the Service squadrons to the minimum considered essential for our garrisons overseas, with a very small number in the United Kingdom as a reserve, and to concentrate the whole of the remainder of our resources on the perfecting of the training of officers and men'. For the training of men, a Cadet College was established at Cranwell, Apprentice Wings were formed at Halton, and an RAF Staff College was set up in Andover. Clearly technological advances were of the utmost importance to the RAF, and so experimental stations were established for the evaluation of landplanes, seaplanes, torpedo aircraft and radio. To make the best possible use of the large number of officer-calibre men who would like to join the RAF, a short-service commission was introduced for half the officer strength of the RAF: suitable candidates served for five years on the active list, followed by four years on the reserve. Thus the RAF would be able to train a relatively high number of suitable flying officers.

A more ambitious plan had been suggested by Sir Frederick Sykes, the previous Chief of the Air Staff, and its rejection had been instrumental in his resignation, and in that of his chief, Lord Weir, the Secretary of State for Air, to be replaced by Trenchard and Winston Churchill respectively in February 1919. Sykes had been an advocate of an Imperial Air Force, to which all the members of the British Empire would contribute.

In March 1920, when the Air Estimates were introduced, the RAF had 25 squadrons in service, with another eight in the process of formation. Great Britain was divided into two main areas, the Coastal and Inland Areas, the latter being subdivided into the Southern and Northern Commands. The Coastal Area included all units intended to cooperate with the Royal Navy. Total manpower strength of the force was 3,280 officers and 25,000 other ranks.

Nevertheless, by 1921 the RAF was in poor shape, with useful strength sufficient only to meet the requirements of the army alone. But in March of that year the RAF was given a considerable fillip, not least against the wish of the army and navy to absorb those parts of the RAF that most concerned them, in the conference held in Cairo: this decided that the RAF's peacetime functions should be at least as important as those of its two sister services. This was the result of representations to delegates attending the conference made by Trenchard and Churchill, the latter being in his capacity as Secretary of State for the Colonies the chairman of the conference, which had been called to consider the question of how best to defend the mandated territories Britain had been given by the Treaty of Versailles.

Trenchard and Churchill argued that by far the most effective method of protecting these mandates, such as Iraq, and of keeping them peaceful, was 'air policing' by the RAF. If trouble were detected, air units could deal with the problem quickly and efficiently. To look after Iraq, it was decided, would need twelve battalions of infantry, one cavalry regiment, one pack battery of artillery and a contingent of engineers, if a conventional

Fairey Swordfish

Type: two-seat torpedo carrier and three-seat spotter reconnaissance.
Dimensions: span 45 ft 6 in (13.87 m); length 35 ft 8 in (10.87 m); height 12 ft 4 in (3.76 m).
Weights: empty 4,700 lb (2,134 kg); loaded 7,510 lb (3,410 kg).
Performance: max. speed 138 mph (222 km/h); initial climb 1,220 ft (372 m)/min.; service ceiling 19,250 ft (5,867 m); range with full ordnance load 546 miles (879 kmh).

The Fairey Swordfish, one of the greatest combat aircraft ever built, was delivered for service in 1936, and served valiantly and successfully throughout World War II, in a variety of roles. Pre-war Swordfish were often twin-float seaplanes, but most were used in land-plane torpedo squadrons by the Fleet Air Arm. This aircraft played a major part in the sinking of the *Bismarck*, disabled several of Italy's capital ships at Taranto in November 1940, and sank many submarines during operations from escort carriers.

efence posture were adopted; the RAF, on the other and, could achieve the same results with only four quadrons of twin-seat general purpose aircraft, one quadron of fighters, one squadron of reconnaissance ircraft, two squadrons of bombers converted into roop-carriers, and some armoured cars. To reinforce he local ground forces the army would have to provide nly one brigade of infantry and a pack battery of rtillery. The saving to Britain in terms of manpower nd money would be immense, and the Cairo conerence immediately opted for the RAF scheme of nperial 'air policing'. It was a masterly stroke by renchard, finally making the RAF fully the equal of he army and navy during the troubled interwar period.

There remained, however, the vital problem of netropolitan defence of the United Kingdom, which vas still basically an army responsibility. The chief ody examining the question was the Standing Comiittee of the Committee of Imperial Defence, chaired y A. J. Balfour. In an atmosphere that was rapidly oming to accept the axiom that 'the bomber will always et through', Balfour was much impressed by the fact hat France had a striking force of 300 fighters and 300 ombers, and that Britain's equivalent totalled a maxnum of forty aircraft. In the spring of 1922, therefore, he RAF received primary responsibility for the deence of the United Kingdom, and in the autumn the orce for this purpose was fixed at fourteen bomber and ine fighter squadrons, the former to consist of nine egular and five auxiliary squadrons, with a total of only 58 aircraft. It was considered that attack was the best neans of defence, hence the relatively larger size of the omber force over the fighter force, but the scheme's npracticality is shown by the fact that only 158 ombers were allocated to defend the country against ossible attack from a force almost twice the size.

In 1923, though, Sir Samuel Hoare had been appoined Secretary of State for Air. Hoare found on taking ffice that the RAF had grown by only two squadrons ince 1920, to a total of thirty-five squadrons at home nd overseas. Soon matters were to be improved, for the Conservative administration that had succeeded the Coalition Government in late 1922 had appointed a ub-Committee of the Committee of Imperial Deence, under Lord Salisbury, to examine the whole uestion of metropolitan and imperial defence, with hree main topics to be looked at: firstly, the relations of he RAF and Royal Navy insofar as air work for the fleet vas concerned; secondly, the relations of the RAF and he army insofar as air work for the army was conerned; and thirdly, how best to define the standards by vhich RAF strength for home and overseas defence hould be assessed.

Though there were certain elements in the army and navy who hoped that deliberations about the first and econd topics might lead to the dissolution of the RAF nd the return to the army and navy of the portions of he RAF concerned with land and sea cooperation, the eality was that by 1923 the RAF was too well estabished for this to be the case. Nevertheless, the Salisury Committee decided that the army and navy should ave full operational control of the RAF units working vith them, and moreover that RAF units on board hips of the Royal Navy should be subject to naval iscipline. Within these strictures, the design of airraft, and the initial training of aircrew remained an RAF responsibility, with the rider that the army and avy should be consulted at every level so that their eeds could be met as fully as possible.

It was also decided that the navy should provide the majority of the pilots needed for carrierborne aircraft, these pilots being attached to the RAF for the purpose. Naval spotting and reconnaisance was also to be undertaken by naval officers.

With so many naval personnel directly involved in air activities, it was logical that in 1924 there should be formed a Fleet Air Arm, controlled by the RAF and comprising the RAF units allocated to carriers and other naval vessels. Initial organisation was into flights of six aircraft. In 1933, however, squadrons were formed for carrier deployment. These new squadrons had between nine and twelve aircraft, and were numbered from 800 upwards. Six-aircraft flights were maintained for use on battleships and cruisers. The 1933 establishment was fixed at twelve squadrons and six flights, an establishment that was maintained until control of the Fleet Air Arm passed to the Royal Navy in 1937.

The third, and most important, topic to be investigated by the Salisbury Committee was 'the standard to be aimed at for defining the strength of the Air Force for purposes of Home and Imperial Defence'. The results of the committee's deliberations were revealed on 20 June 1923 to the House of Commons: 'In addition to meeting the essential air power requirements of the Navy, Army, Indian and Overseas Commitments, British air power must include a Home Defence Air Force of sufficient strength adequately to protect us against air attack by the strongest air force within striking distance of this country … In the first instance the Home Defence Force should consist of 52 squadrons, to be created with as little delay as possible, and the Secretary of State for Air has been instructed forthwith to take preliminary steps for carrying this decision into effect. The result of this proposal will be to add thirty-four squadrons to the authorised strength of the Royal Air Force. The details of the organisation will be arranged with a view to the possibility of subsequent expansion.'

The last sentence was of particular importance, revealing that the plan was at best an interim measure. The authorised strength of this 52-squadron force was 394 bombers and 204 fighters. The enemy force envisaged in the announcement was the French air force, but although the figures were basically those submitted

Below The Bristol Beaufighter, a two-seat torpedo strike fighter saw service in many roles, among them night-fighting and anti-shipping strikes with rockets. Nicknamed the 'Whispering Death' by the Japanese, it carried four 20mm cannon and six .303 machine guns.

Above The Westland Whirlwind was originally designed as a heavy or advanced fighter. Some successes were achieved with this aircraft, but engine problems and trouble with the four 20mm cannon led to its early retirement. Only 114 were built.

Air Chief Marshal Sir Robert Brooke-Popham

to the committee by Air Chief Marshal Trenchard, Sir Samuel Hoare said in November 1923 that at least five years would be needed to implement the plan, which would give the RAF parity with the French air force's 1923 strength. No allowance was made for an increase in French strength. Nevertheless, good initial progress with the implementation of the plan was made, and by the autumn of 1925 twenty-five of the fifty-two squadrons were in service.

The origins of this plan lay with the scheme devised in February 1923 by Air Commodore J. M. Steel and Colonel W. H. Bartholemew, for a combined RAF and army metropolitan defence area: anti-aircraft guns defended central London; eight fighter squadrons defended a belt from Duxford, south of Cambridge, round the south-east of London, to a point just south-east of Andover; an outer ring of AA guns operated beyond the RAF's loop round east, south-east and south London; a belt of observer corps positions surrounded this belt; and there were special defence areas for Harwich, Shoeburyness and Sheerness, Dover and Portsmouth. This Steel-Bartholemew Plan must, in fact, be considered the precursor of all the south-east England defence plans right into World War II.

The Steel-Bartholemew Plan was combined with the fifty-two squadron scheme during 1924 by a committee chaired by Major General C. F. Romer and including Major General E. B. Ashmore, who had commanded the air defences of London and south-east England during World War I and later moved to the command of 1st Air Defence Brigade. The Romer Committee's final plan called for the formation of three main bomber base areas (Oxfordshire or Gloucestershire, with five or six stations for fourteen squadrons; Wiltshire with four stations for eleven squadrons; and northern East Anglia, with three or four stations for eight squadrons) for the thirty-five bomber squadrons, and ten fighter sectors running south from Cambridge, round the south-east of London, to a point on the Bristol Channel south-west of Bristol. These ten sectors would be manned by fourteen of the fighter squadrons allowed for in the fifty-two squadron scheme, the remaining three squadrons operating from forward bases at Hawkinge near Dover, Tangmere between Eastbourne and Portsmouth, and one of the two bases on each side of Southampton Water.

The whole organisation was called the Air Defence of Great Britain (ADGB), and was formed in the early part of 1925 under the command of Air Marshal Sir John Salmond, who thus controlled a comprehensive force of bombers, fighters, AA guns and searchlights. For operational purposes, Salmond controlled the bomber force directly, the control of the other elements

of ADGB being in the hands of the Fighting Area command. AA units and searchlights received their orders through the army chain of command. The port which the Steel-Bartholemew Plan had considered ought to be defended received no allocation in the ADGB plan. With the formation of ADGB, a new Observer Corps also came into being, and recruitment quickly became impressive. As may readily be imagined, the main failings of the ADGB scheme were lack of squadrons, and the divided army/air force command structure.

The plan called for thirteen of the fifty-two squadrons to be raised from sources other than the regular RAF: six by the Auxiliary Air Force and seven from the Special Reserve. The Auxiliary Air Force squadrons would be raised by County Associations.

The idea was impressive, and admittedly on the right lines, but many years of work were still needed to complete the deployment of the Observer Corps, the direct landline communications that would allow it to report to the appropriate headquarters, the raising of squadrons, the building of airfields, and the working-up of the whole organisation into a valuable and effective defence system.

With the establishment of better relations with France during 1924, the Labour administration of that year set up a committee under Lord Birkenhead to examine whether or not to press ahead with the fifty-two squadron scheme within the five-year schedule originally envisaged. In November 1925 the Birkenhead Committee reported that although the scheme should not be abandoned, its completion could with safety be delayed for several years. This was a decision subsequently accepted by the Conservative government that replaced the Labour one at the end of 1924, final completion of the scheme being fixed for 1935 instead of 1928. The results were very nearly disastrous for Britain. Between 1925 and 1928, therefore, only six home defence squadrons were raised, bringing the total to thirty-one in 1928. No new squadrons were raised in 1928–29, but in the following year six were formed, with another two in 1930–31 and a further three in 1931–32, bringing the total in 1932 to forty-two. Thus ten years after the decision to raise the home defence total to fifty-two squadrons as quickly as possible, the RAF was still ten squadrons short of the total. The only thing that can be said in support of this delay is that lack of quantity turned the minds of the Air Ministry's planners more and more to quality as a partial remedy. This was, in fact, in the long run to prove decisive in the eventual survival of the RAF in wartime conditions.

In the middle of 1926, the ADGB was organised as follows: the Wessex Bombing Area with regular bomber forces, and the Fighting Area with the fighter squadrons. Over the next few years these were joined by No 1 Air Defence Group, comprising the Auxiliary Air Force and Special Reserve squadrons. Then in 1931 came a further reorganisation to make use of the total of forty-two squadrons available. In this the Wessex Bombing Area and No 1 Air Defence Group squadrons were reshuffled to form a Western Area, with its headquarters at Andover; a Central Area, with its headquarters at Abingdon; and No 1 Air Defence Group controlling the Auxiliary Air Force squadrons. The Wessex Bombing Area disappeared, and the Fighting Area remained unaltered.

In 1933 the other metropolitan commands in the RAF were the Inland Area Command with five army cooperation squadrons, and the Coastal Area Com-

and with one bomber and four flying-boat squadrons. The latter also administered the Fleet Air Arm.

Abroad, the RAF had the Royal Air Force, Middle East, whose one transport-bomber, one army cooperation and three bomber squadrons were controlled from Cairo; the Transjordan and Palestine Command, whose one armoured car company and two bomber squadrons were controlled from Jerusalem; the British Forces in Iraq, whose one armoured car company, one flying-boat squadron, one transport-bomber squadron and three bomber squadrons were controlled from Hinaidi; the Royal Air Force, India, whose one transport-bomber flight, four army cooperation squadrons and four bomber squadrons were controlled from New Delhi; the Royal Air Force, Mediterranean, whose one flying-boat squadron was controlled from Malta; Aden Command, whose one armoured car section and one bomber squadron were controlled from Aden; and the Royal Air Force, Far East, whose one bomber, one torpedo-bomber and one flying-boat squadrons were controlled from Singapore.

In 1932 the service heads of the three fighting forces warned the government of the poor state of their commands. This combined with a serious deterioration in international relations to persuade the government formally to abandon the 'ten-year rule' (first announced by the Lloyd George Coalition government in 1919, and meaning that the British Empire would not be involved in a war with a major power for at least ten years, and reiterated annually and religiously since that date) and consider moves to strengthen the British armed forces.

Thoughts in this direction were given added impetus in 1934 when the Air Ministry revealed intelligence on the revived, but still clandestine German air force, to be known as the *Luftwaffe*. According to these early reports, the *Luftwaffe* aimed to have, in October 1935, a front-line strength of 576 aircraft, rising to 900 by the end of the year, and ultimately three or four air divisions, each possessing between 500 and 600 aircraft. Further intelligence, in October 1934, suggested that the German expansion had already started, and that the target figure for October 1936 was now 1,368 aircraft (this was posited on an assessment of a squadron strength of twelve aircraft, so when it became known that the squadrons would have only nine aircraft each for immediate use, the figure for the 114 squadrons was reduced to 1,026 aircraft).

By the end of 1934 the Germans had in fact formed twenty-two of the forty-two squadrons called for in the first stage of their expansion, with 146 aircraft from an establishment of 246. Although a nominal 565 aircraft were available, many of these lacked essential components such as engines and instruments.

In July 1934, however, the British government decided on a new expansion scheme, to replace the 1923 plan. This was designated Scheme A, and called for a metropolitan air force of five army cooperation, forty-three bomber, twenty-eight fighter, four flying-boat and four general-purpose squadrons by the beginning of 1939. Amongst the equipment for these squadrons would be 500 bombers and 336 fighters, compared with the 1923 scheme's 394 bombers and 204 fighters. Thus the establishment offensive strength of the RAF was to be raised from 598 to 836 aircraft. There were also to be 124 army cooperation, flying-boat and general-purpose aircraft, giving the metropolitan air force a strength of 960 aircraft in all. Overseas commands were to have twenty-seven squadrons with 292 aircraft, giving the RAF 111 squadrons and 1,252 front-line aircraft.

The object of the exercise was to persuade the Germans to desist from their expansion, but the

Below A row of Bristol Blenheim IVs with a Percival Q-6 in the foreground. An all-metal, cantilever low-wing monoplane, the Bristol Blenheim was moderately successful during 1939–40. From 1942, it was replaced in Europe by Douglas Bostons and de Havilland Mosquitos, although they continued to serve in the Middle and Far East until the end of 1943.

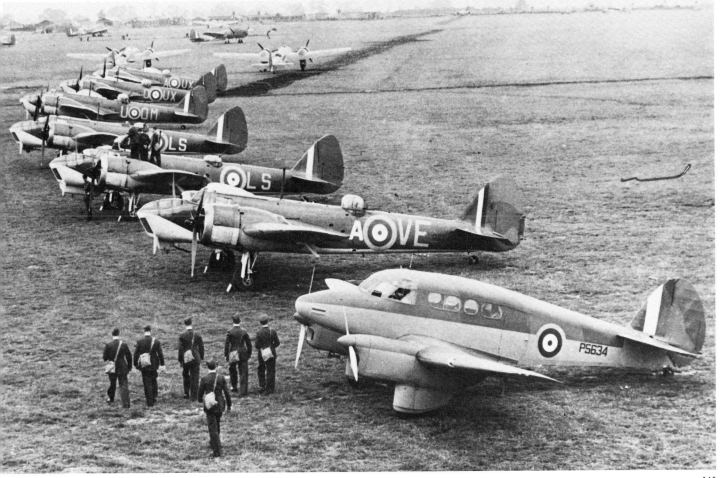

immediate flaw of the whole scheme was that the Germans could work out quite simply that if the RAF actually had this front-line strength, the output of the British aircraft industry just could not have provided ample reserves. Therefore the new scheme would merely be an inducement rather than a deterrent to the Germans.

In Parliament, though, Scheme A was attacked principally for its limited front-line scale, Churchill amongst others claiming that the *Luftwaffe* was almost as strong as the RAF, and that by 1937 it would be nearly twice as strong. The prime minister, Stanley Baldwin, was able to show that the RAF had 880 front-line aircraft, 560 of them at home, whereas the *Luftwaffe* had only between 600 and 1,000 aircraft of all types, nothing like a match for the RAF.

Believing that an agreement to limit air armaments might be possible, Baldwin sent Sir John Simon and Anthony Eden, Foreign Secretary and Minister for League of Nations Affairs respectively, to Berlin for talks with the Germans. In March the two British statesmen reported back to the cabinet that the Germans had told them that the *Luftwaffe* was already as strong as the RAF. Although this was flatly contradicted by the RAF, coming so soon after Churchill's attack in the House of Commons it made the government suspicious of the RAF's sources. The cabinet

thereupon asked for confirmation from the Germans and Erhard Milch, the State Secretary for Aviation replied that the German air strength was between 800 and 850 aircraft. Later Hermann Göring, *Reich* Minister for Aviation, claimed that Germany was aiming to have some 2,000 aircraft, and thus parity with the French air force, by the end of 1935. The British government thus came to the conclusion that although the *Luftwaffe* might have 2,000 aircraft of all types by the end of 1935, this would certainly not rival the RAF's front-line strength.

It was clear, though, that a German front-line strength of 1,500 in the spring of 1937 was reasonable from both the production and military points of view. For it was at this date that it was expected that French first-line strength in metropolitan France and her North African territories would reach that figure, and Germany's avowed aim was parity with France. All interested British parties then agreed that Germany's air strength was likely to reach 1,532 first-line aircraft in April 1937. Thus it became clear that the British Scheme A had singularly failed in its object of making the Germans reduce the scale of their air rearmament.

So the British abandoned Scheme A in favour of a new Scheme C in the middle of 1935, the completion date for the new scheme being the spring of 1937. Scheme C called for seventy bomber and thirty-five

fighter squadrons, with greater emphasis being placed on heavy and medium bombers squadrons at the expense of light bomber units. This was in fact the only real advance of the scheme over its predecessor, although aircraft numbers were increased by about half:

	Scheme A		Scheme C	
	squadrons	aircraft	squadrons	aircraft
Metropolitan AF				
heavy bomber	8	80	20	240
medium bomber	8	96	18	216
light bomber	25	300	30	360
torpedo-bomber	2	24	2	24
fighter	28	336	35	420
reconnaissance	13	124	18	252
Fleet Air Arm	$16\frac{1}{2}$	213	$16\frac{1}{2}$	213
Overseas commands	27	292	27	292
	$127\frac{1}{2}$	1,465	$166\frac{1}{2}$	2,017

The Fleet Air Arm and overseas commands were to get nothing extra, and the Air Staff's thinking, that only offensive action would avail in any future air war, is reflected in the fact that two-thirds of the metropolitan air force's aircraft would be bombers (with a higher percentage now of the heavy and medium categories), and only about one-third fighters. Also notable, in the financial aspects of the plan, were limited provisions for reserve aircraft, clearly showing that the government was more interested in deterring Germany with a brave show of first-line aircraft than in laying in the stocks necessary for a real shooting war. The production of so many bombers at the expense of the fighter force was also a mistake, as it would have left the country very vulnerable in the short term to heavy bomber attacks.

The Air Staff in the ministry did realise part of this, though, and some effort was devoted during 1934 and 1935 to an updating of the Steel-Bartholemew and Romer plans for metropolitan defence. The potential enemy had altered from France to Germany, and so the defence from London to Bristol was shortened, while that north of London was lengthened almost up to the Tees estuary. The plan was the result of the work carried out since 1933 by the Reorientation Committee headed by Air Chief Marshal Sir Robert Brooke Popham, commander since that date of ADGB. London itself was to be covered by an Inner Artillery Zone, while the whole of the defensive belt was to consist of an Aircraft Fighting Zone with an Outer Artillery Zone in front of it. Twenty-five fighter squadrons and 456 guns would be required. The ports of Newcastle, the Tees estuary, the Humber estuary, Harwich, Dover and Portsmouth were also to be defended.

Below Fairey Battle light bombers on patrol in France. This type was a great failure, lacking the performance and armament needed to cope with the German fighters. 1,000 were in service when the war began, but within six months of the Blitzkrieg, they were withdrawn from front-line service.

In 1935 the government decided that only the first stage of the plan should be implemented by 1940: this envisaged the establishment of the Aircraft Fighting Zone between Huntingdon and the Solent, 136 guns and 1,008 searchlights, plus the formation of Observer Groups and extra army AA forces. The second and third stages, for the extension north and the defence of Birmingham, Sheffield, Manchester and Leeds, were impossible for financial reasons.

With the seventy bomber and thirty-five fighter squadrons ordained under Scheme C, the RAF decided that a more flexible command structure was desirable, and in July 1936 ADGB was disbanded, its place being taken by four new commands. Bomber Command assumed control of all metropolitan bomber squadrons (its commanders being Air Chief Marshal Sir John Steel from 14 July 1936, Air Chief Marshal Sir Edgar Ludlow-Hewitt from 12 September 1937, Air Marshal Sir Charles Portal from 3 April 1940, Air Marshal Sir Richard Peirse from 5 October 1940 and Air Chief Marshal Sir Arthur Harris from 22 February 1942). Fighter Command had command of all fighter and army cooperation squadrons, as well as the Observer Corps (its commander was Air Chief Marshal Sir Hugh Dowding from 14 July 1936). Coastal Command had all flying-boat and general reconnaissance squadrons, as well as some training units (its commanders were Air Marshal Sir Arthur Longmore from 14 July 1936 and Air Marshal Philip Joubert de la Ferté from 1 September 1936). Finally there was Training Command, established on 1 May 1936 under the command of Air Marshal Sir Charles Burnett, controlling all the other training units in the United Kingdom.

Overall control of the four home commands was the responsibility of the Air Staff, whose chiefs had been Trenchard until his retirement on 31 December 1929,

Marshal of the Royal Air Force Sir John Salmond from 1 January 1930 to 28 February 1933, Air Chief Marshal Sir Geoffrey Salmond from 1–27 April 1933, and Marshal of the Royal Air Force Sir Edward Ellington from 22 May 1933. Ellington was succeeded by Air Chief Marshal Sir Cyril Newall on 1 September 1938, and Newall by Marshal of the Royal Air Force Sir Charles Portal on 25 October 1940.

During 1936 the RAF was authorised to build another twenty-six operational airfields, nine of them for Fighter Command. Operational training was at the time done within the operational squadron framework, so Training Command, the successor to the previous Inland Area Command, was restricted to basic and advanced flying training and technical instruction. The earlier Coastal Area Command was the formation, of course, which became Coastal Command. Training Command was later split into Flying Training and Technical Training Commands, and other commands were added: Balloon, Maintenance, Reserve, Transport and, in 1943, Army Cooperation. Reserve Command was established in 1937 to look after the Royal Air Force Volunteer Reserve, announced on 30 July 1936. Originally designed to produce 800 volunteer pilots for the RAF each year, by 1939 the RAFVR had trained or had under training some 5,000 NCO pilots and aircrew, as well as numbers of technical personnel.

Before 1935 the RAF had run six Flying Training Schools. Now with the growing expansion of the force, during 1935 and 1936 another five such schools were opened, and thirteen civilian flying schools were permitted to undertake the elementary training of service pilots (four of these had already been granted permission to train RAFVR trainees). The expansion schemes of the period called for an additional 2,500 pilots, and these were found by adding 1,700 short-service com-

Research, and Squadron Leader Ralph Sorley, a keen protagonist of multiple machine gun armament for fighter aircraft. The result of the two men's efforts, so far as aircraft were concerned, were the Hawker Hurricane and Supermarine Spitfire.

Some notion of the state of Great Britain's defences against air attack at the time of Dowding's appointment to Fighter Command may be gauged from the forces at his disposal: the 1st AA Division (Major General R. H. D. Tompson), newly formed and not yet operational, but evidence of the army's decision to give up tactical control of its AA forces to the RAF; No 11 (Fighter) Group, under Air Vice-Marshal P. B. Joubert de la Ferté, with eight airfields and eleven squadrons in south-east England; the Observer Corps, under Air Commodore A. D. Waddington-Morris, with nine Observer Groups south of the Wash, and another two in Lincolnshire and Yorkshire; and No 22 (Army Co-Operation) Group, for administrative purposes only. In addition, Dowding had a Regular fighter squadron forming in Cambridgeshire, three Auxiliary squadrons converting from bombers to fighters, and five Regular squadrons in Egypt and Malta, which came under his command when they returned to Great Britain in September 1936. Shortly after this, No 12 Group was formed to cover the Midlands and North. Later No 13 Group was formed and took over the North, and in 1940 No 10 Group was formed to cover the south-west of England.

Each of these groups controlled a number of major bases, known as Sector Stations, which had operations centres and repair facilities. The sector stations were all well established airfields, and had semi-permanent fighter squadrons. Each sector also had a number of smaller, less well prepared satellite airfields closer to the enemy, from which the squadrons could operate on a temporary basis for operational or survival reasons.

At first dependent on sound locators and the Observer Corps for information about oncoming enemy raids, the Fighter Command tactical control organisation was greatly aided by the introduction of radar in the last years of peace. Known by the cover name of Chain Home, radar (called radio direction-finding at the time) allowed speedier and more accurate reactions from the defence. On spotting a raid, the NCO operator in the CH station immediately contacted his Group Filter Room by direct landline. Here the raid was plotted on a large mapboard, and the information passed to the Fighter Command Operations Room, the Group Operations Room and Sector Operations Rooms immediately. Thereupon, Group and Sector Controllers could direct their forces to intercept in the right place and with the right numbers of aircraft. Comprehensive communications equipment kept all interested parties up to date with the state of various squadrons' readiness for combat.

War clouds were still gathering during 1935 and 1936, and tension was heightened by Italy's invasion of Ethiopia in the autumn of 1935. Therefore in February 1936 the government decided on a further expansion, designated Scheme F. Although the home defence force was strengthened only by making the light bomber provisions of Scheme C into medium bombers in Scheme F, the real value of the plan lay in its adequate provision of funds for reserves, showing at last that the government had appreciated that war was only just round the corner, and that the war would demand reserves as well as first-line aircraft. Scheduled for completion on 31 March 1939, compared with Scheme

Above The Bristol Beaufighter TF.X was a great strike fighter, armed with cannon, rockets, bombs and torpedos.
Left A gunner boards a Westland Lysander. Originally designed as an army co-operation aircraft, this type won fame for its clandestine spy-ferrying operations to the Low Countries and France.
Right General Eisenhower, Air Chief Marshal Tedder and Air Vice Marshal Broadhurst.

missions to the RAF, and recruiting 700 NCO pilots.

New equipment and ideas were also much in evidence at this time, as witnessed by the development of new eight-gun monoplane fighters, with retractable undercarriages, enclosed cockpits and refinements such as flaps, and experimentation with radar, both technically and operationally as an aid to the fighter defences. Key figures in this technical revolution were Air Marshal Sir Hugh Dowding, appointed to the Air Staff on 1 September 1930 as Air Member for Supply and

C's 31 March 1937, Scheme F allowed for 225%
reserves, for which £50 million were allocated. For the
Scheme C reserves only £1.2 million had been allowed.
A comparison of Schemes C and F reveals the
following:

	Scheme C		Scheme F	
	squadrons	aircraft	squadrons	aircraft
Metropolitan AF				
heavy bomber	20	240	20	240
medium bomber	18	216	48	750
light bomber	30	360	0	0
torpedo-bomber	2	24	2	32
fighter	35	420	30	420
reconnaissance	18	252	24	294
Fleet Air Arm	16½	213	26*	312*
Overseas	27	292	37	468
	166½	2,017	187	2,516

*by 1942 there were to be forty squadrons with 504 aircraft.

At the same time the government made the eminently
sensible decision not to await the start of hostilities
before undertaking the construction of 'shadow' aircraft factories, but to begin at once. These 'shadow'
factories, run by the major car manufacturing companies, and built by government finance, were to ensure the
production of proven types should the parent factory be
destroyed. By building the factories from 1937, the
government allowed the mass production of certain

A flight formation of Handley Page Hampdens. Fast and manoeuvrable, Hampdens had a successful career in the early years of the war. They operated first as heavy day bombers, raiding German naval installations and ships in 1939. Later, inadequate defensive armament caused them to be transferred to night operations, where they were used as mine-layers and torpedo bombers.
Above Air Chief Marshal Sir Arthur Tedder, right, with Air Marshal Sir John Slessor on his arrival in North Africa.
Below Air Vice Marshall R. S. Sorley, OBE DSC DFC, Assistant Chief of the Air Staff (Operational Requirements).

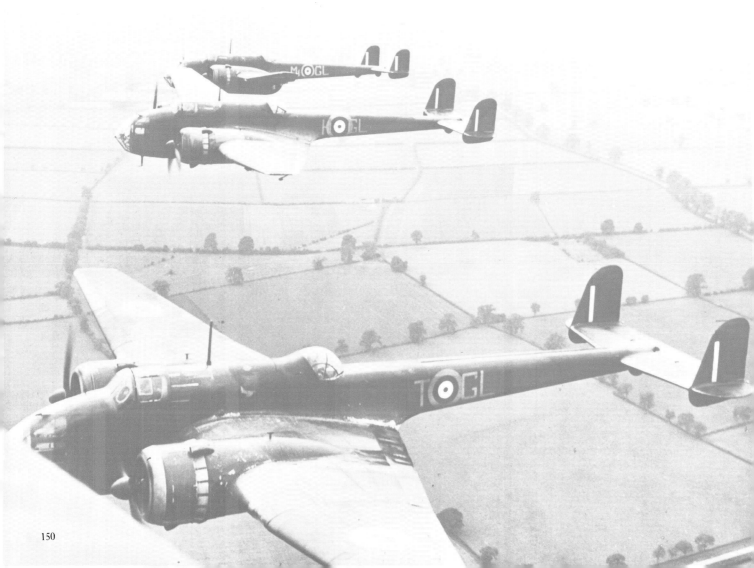

types of aircraft and engine to begin that much sooner.

In 1933 the establishment strength of the RAF stood at 29,400 officers and men of the Regular force, plus 10,600 Reservists and 1,480 men of the Auxiliary Air Force. By 1937, the Regular establishment of the RAF had risen to 55,000 officers and men, plus the personnel of the Auxiliary Air Force and the RAFVR.

The growing scale of the air threat against the metropolitan United Kingdom was recognised by new thinking about defence. The Reorientation Committee, which had remained in existence, was invited by Sir Thomas Inskip, Minister for the Coordination of Defence, to draw up an ideal plan for national air defence. This must be seen in the context of a German announcement in October 1936 that the second stage of their air rearmament plan was almost finished, giving the *Luftwaffe* 114 squadrons with some 1,100 aircraft, it was believed in London, with the threat of 1,500 by the spring of the next year. At the time British strength was 696 first-line aircraft, due to rise to 1,736 by the spring of 1939.

The Reorientation Committee submitted its new plan in February 1937: this called for the defended zone to be extended north of Newcastle, and widened to include the West Riding of Yorkshire and the Midlands; defended zones were to be created for the Clyde and the Forth in Scotland, and Bristol in south-west England; and needed would be forty-five fighter squadrons, 1,264 guns and 4,700 searchlights, plus pom-poms against low-flying aircraft, and extra Observer Corps groups. But there just were not the guns or the

fighter squadrons. Nevertheless, the Committee of Imperial Defence realised the gravity of the situation, and in the summer of 1937 authorised a start on the new plan.

On 12 March 1938 Hitler annexed Austria, and the British government at last realised that war could no longer be avoided. Finally the ruling that normal trade should not suffer because of rearmament was lifted, and the Air Ministry was informed that it could order 12,000 aircraft for delivery by the spring of 1940. The result was Scheme L, in which the RAF at last found itself in a position to prepare for war against a formidable enemy rather than just make defensive preparations intended by the government to act as a deterrent.

Scheme L was based on the assessment that the British aircraft factories could produce a maximum of 4,000 aircraft between the spring of 1938 and April 1939, with another 8,000 between the latter date and April 1940. Scheme L thus called for:

	squadrons	aircraft
Metropolitan AF		
heavy bomber	47	752
medium bomber	26	600
fighter	38	608
reconnaissance	30	413
Overseas	39	490
	180	2,863

Below The Armstrong Whitworth A.W.41 Albermarle was an RAF glider tug, used in the Sicily and Arnhem landings. *Inset* The Airspeed AS.51 Horsa assault glider, of which great numbers were built. By 1943 the usual tug for these was the Albermarle. The Horsa was widely used, hundreds taking nearly a quarter of the air-supplied loads in the Normandy invasion.

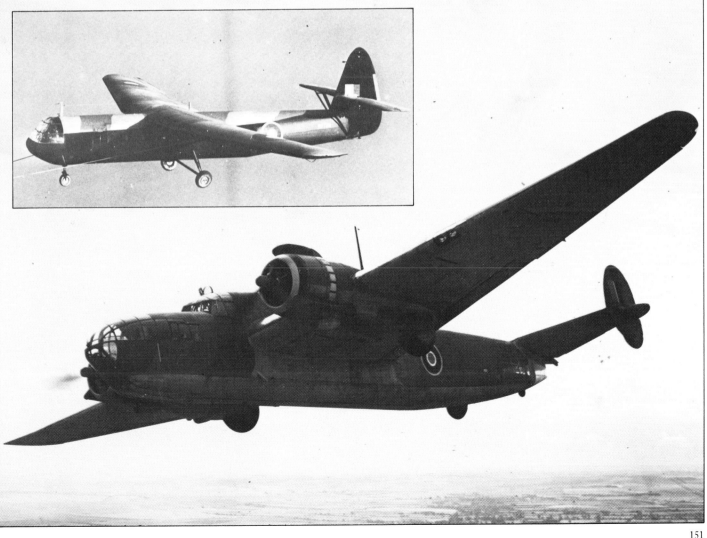

Left The Hawker Typhoon survived an unsuccessful beginning to become one of the fastest fighter bombers of World War II, forming the backbone of the 2nd Tactical Air Force Attack strength.
Below Air Marshal Barrat, right, checking maps with an army officer.
Bottom Air Chief Marshal Sir Cyril Newall with Air Commodore Lord Londonderry and Air Vice Marshal Playfair, furthest on right, inspecting an aircraft in France.

For the fighter and reconnaissance squadrons, reserves for sixteen weeks of war wastage were to be built up, and nine weeks for other types. Also, the establishment strength of the bomber, fighter and general reconnaissance squadrons was increased from the twelve of Scheme F to sixteen in Scheme L (average figures). On the credit side, Scheme L made fairly good use of the available industrial capacity; on the debit side, there was still too much emphasis on the bomber over the fighter, providing in two years only about three-quarters of the fighter strength recommended in the 'ideal' plan of the Reorientation Committee.

With the fearful crisis of Munich gone in late September 1938, and peace bought for a few months more at the cost of a potentially decisive ally, Czechoslovakia, the new Secretary of State for Air, Sir Kingsley Wood, who had succeeded Lord Swinton on 16 May 1938, announced a new Scheme M, in which priority was at last given to fighters:

	squadrons	aircraft
Metropolitan AF		
heavy bomber	85	1,360
medium bomber	0	0
fighter	50	800
reconnaissance	28	389
Overseas	49	636
	212	3,185

With war very much in mind, there were also organisational changes: the establishment of an organisation to salvage and restore damaged aircraft, and the establishment of Group Pools (later redesignated Operational Training Units) to undertake the combat training of new pilots, and to supply replacements for front-line squadrons. Six main repair depots were set up in he United Kingdom, each of them capable of undertaking the reconstruction or major overhaul work that would otherwise have had to have gone back to the manufacturer, so slowing production. The first Group Pool appeared in the spring of 1939, in Fighter Command.

In 1939 the 'ideal' plan was again modified, largely as a result of the Royal Navy's requirements:

	'ideal' plan	*1939 modification*
fighter squadrons	45	53
heavy guns	1,264	2,232
light guns (barrels)	0	2,000
searchlights	4,700	4,128
barrage balloons	0	1,450

The trouble lay in the fact that the loss of Czechoslovakia as a potential ally left only France as a major land force, and she was weak in the air. So it was eventually decided that the British would have to remedy some of her aerial deficiencies, by the dispatch to France in the event of war of an Advanced Air Striking Force, to be made up of ten Fairey Battle light bomber squadrons, in addition to the Air Component of the British Expeditionary Force. The Air Component was to consist of eight army cooperation squadrons and four Hawker Hurricane fighter squadrons, much to the chagrin of Dowding.

Thus, at the outbreak of war in September 1939, of the fifty-seven fighter squadrons available to the British, only forty-six were available to the air defence of metropolitan Great Britain. The others were disbursed

as follows: four to the Air Component, four to trade protection, two to the defence of Scapa Flow and one to the defence of Northern Ireland. But this was only a plan, prepared in peacetime, and in reality only 35 fighter squadrons were available for metropolitan defence when war actually broke out in September 1939.

Soon after the beginning of hostilities, the organisation of the Royal Air Force was as follows, under the overall control of Nevile Chamberlain's National government: the political and service heads were Sir Kingsley Wood and Air Chief Marshal Sir Cyril Newall. Under his control Newall had seven Commands and part of the semi-independent forces in France; and seven overseas Commands. The Home Commands were Bomber Command under Ludlow-Hewitt, Fighter Command under Dowding, Coastal Command under Air Chief Marshal Sir Frederick

Below The magnificent de Havilland Mosquito FB.VI fighter-bomber shown here was only one version of this versatile aircraft.
Bottom The de Havilland Sea Hornet, a naval version of the Hornet fighter bomber, used the same design principles as the Mosquito. This aircraft was delivered just too late for World War II service.

Bowhill, Training Command under Air Chief Marshal Sir Arthur Longmore, Maintenance Command under Air Marshal J. S. T. Bradley, Reserve Command, Balloon Command, and the combined Air Component of the British Expeditionary Force and No 22 Army Co-Operation Group. (On 15 January 1940 the Advanced Air Striking Force and Air Component were amalgamated as the British Air Forces in France, under the command of Air Marshal A. S. Barratt.)

Overseas Commands were the RAF, Middle East under Air Chief Marshal Sir William Mitchell; the RAF in Palestine and Transjordan; the British Forces in Iraq; the British Forces in Aden; the RAF, Mediterranean; the Air Forces in India under Air Marshal Sir John Higgins from 6 October 1939; and the RAF, Far East, under Air Vice-Marshal J. T. Babington, with Air Chief Marshal Sir Robert Brooke-Popham as Commander-in-Chief, Far East.

Training Command was split into Flying Training and Technical Training Commands on 27 May 1940, under the commands of Air Marshal L. A. Pattinson and Air Marshal Sir William Welsh respectively; and when Ferry Command was formed on 18 July 1941 its commander was Air Chief Marshal Sir Frederick Bowhill.

Bomber Command had six subordinate Groups: the Advanced Air Striking Force (ex-No 1 Group), with ten squadrons; No 2 Group, with seven squadrons; No 3 Group, with eight squadrons; No 4 Group, with six squadrons; No 5 Group, with eight squadrons; and No 6 Training Group, with sixteen squadrons and the New Zealand Flight.

Fighter Command had three subordinate Groups: No 11 Group, with nineteen squadrons; No 12 Group, with ten squadrons; and No 13 Group, with seven squadrons.

Coastal Command had four subordinate Groups: No 15 General Reconnaissance Group, with five squadrons; No 16 General Reconnaissance Group, with five squadrons; No 17 Training Group; and No 18 General Reconnaissance Group, with nine squadrons.

Training Command had Nos 21, 23, 24 and 25 Training Groups; Maintenance Command Nos 40, 41, 42 and 43 Maintenance Groups; Reserve Command Nos 50, 51, and 54 Training Groups; and Balloon Command Nos 30, 31, 32 and 33 Balloon Barrage Groups.

The RAF, Middle East had the Egypt Group of ten squadrons, No 252 Fighter Wing of two squadrons and the Sudan Wing of two squadrons. The RAF in Palestine and Transjordan had one squadron. The British Forces in Iraq also had only one squadron. The

Below A line of Hawker Siddeley Gloster Meteors being refuelled. This type was the Allies' only operational jet aircraft of World War II, and the world's first operational jet fighter. The Gloster Meteor entered service a few days before the Messerschmitt Me 262, a potentially war-winning aircraft whose development was hindered by official lack of interest.

British Forces in Aden had three squadrons. The RAF, Mediterranean had only one squadron. The Air Forces in India had the Indian Air Force, with one squadron, No 1 (India) Group with four squadrons and two independent squadrons. And the RAF, Far East had nine squadrons.

During the war, the organisation of the Royal Air Force did not alter significantly, although there was an enormous increase in size. This is indicated by the organisation of the RAF in March 1943, when the political and military chiefs were Sir Archibald Sinclair and Marshal of the Royal Air Force Sir Charles Portal, under the overall control of Winston Churchill's Coalition Government:

Bomber Command (Air Chief Marshal Sir Arthur Harris) had Nos 1, 2, 3, 4, 5, 6 (Royal Canadian Air Force), 8 (Pathfinder Force), 26 Signals, and 91, 92 and 93 Operational Training Unit Groups. Fighter Command (Air Marshal Sir Trafford Leigh-Mallory) had Nos 9, 10, 11, 12, 13, 14, 60 Signals and 81 Operational Training Unit Groups. Coastal Command (Air Marshal Sir John Slessor) had Nos 15 General Reconnaissance, 16 General Reconnaissance, 17 Training, 18 General Reconnaissance, and 19 General Reconnaissance Groups, plus Headquarters, RAF, Gibraltar, and Headquarters, RAF, Iceland. Army Co-Operation Command (Air Marshal Sir Arthur Barratt) had Nos 72 Army Co-Operation and 70 Army Co-Operation Training Groups. Flying Training Command (Air Marshal Sir Philip Babington) had Nos 21, 23, 29, 50, 51 and 54 Training and 25 Armament Groups. Technical Training Command (Air Marshal Sir John Babington) had Nos 20, 24, 27 and 28 Training Groups. Maintenance Command (Air Marshal D. G. Donald) had Nos 40, 41, 42 and 43 Maintenance Groups. Balloon Command had Nos 30, 32, 33 and 34 Balloon Barrage Groups. And RAF Ferry Command (Air Chief Marshal Sir Frederick Bowhill) had Ferry Command and No 44 Ferry Group.

Overseas there were Headquarters, Mediterranean Air Command (Air Chief Marshal Sir Arthur Tedder) with a number of subordinate commands including five fighter groups and a number of miscellaneous other groups; Air Forces in India (Air Chief Marshal Sir Richard Peirse) with seven groups; and other area commands.

The RAF continued to grow right up to the end of the war, by which time the 1,911 first-line aircraft with which it had started on 3 September 1939 had grown to 9,200 aircraft. Personnel amounted to 1,079,835, of whom 193,313 were aircrew. To this must be added the 181,909 women of the Women's Auxiliary Air Force.

CHAPTER ELEVEN

THE MINOR AIR FORCES
1919·45

Apart from the major powers (Germany, Great Britain, Japan, the Union of Soviet Socialist Republics and the United States of America), a number of lesser powers played a part in World War II. From the air aspect, the most significant of these were France and Italy, followed by the Dominions of the British Empire, Poland and then the smaller nations. The air forces of these countries are discussed in alphabetical order of their parent countries.

Italian Fiat CR.42 fighter abandoned in Western Desert. One of the best biplane fighters of all time, the CR.42 was introduced only in 1940, when the biplane had been made wholly obsolescent as a fighter type by monoplanes.

AUSTRALIA

Australia formed a flying corps during World War I, but this was disbanded in 1919. In 1920, however, the Australian Flying Corps was re-formed, becoming the Australian Air Force in 1920, and receiving its 'Royal' prefix shortly after this. Initial equipment was British, war surplus aircraft handed over as part of the 'imperial gift'. This allowed two army cooperation squadrons and the Fleet Co-Operation Flight to be formed in 1925. New equipment was obtained in 1929, but financial restrictions prevented more equipment until 1934. In 1937 an expansion scheme was inaugurated, intended to provide thirty-two operational squadrons. But by September 1939 the RAAF had only twelve squadrons, 165 aircraft and some 3,500 personnel. Notwithstanding, six squadrons were offered to the RAF, but logistical reasons kept the offer from being accepted, though Australians did join the RAF and there were eventually thirteen Australian-manned squadrons in the RAF. Australia's main contribution to the Allied war effort, though, was the inauguration and operation of the Empire Air Training Scheme, under which the RAAF trained 280 pilots, 184 navigators and 320 radio operators/air gunners per month. Other aircrew received basic training in Australia before moving on to Canada for final training. Australian squadrons fought in most theatres of the war, and suffered some 10,000 casualties out of a total personnel of 200,000. The RAAF as such fought with particular distinction in the Malayan campaign, over Australia and under American command in the New Guinea campaign.

BELGIUM

Belgium had only a small air force, the *Aéronautique Militaire*. After World War I, the *Aviation Militaire* had been reorganised and cut back: there were twenty-six *escadrilles* (squadrons) in eight *groupes* (groups). The 1ère *Groupe* operated balloons; the 2ème observation aircraft; the 3ème army cooperation aircraft; the 4ème and 5ème fighters; the 6ème reconnaissance aircraft; the 7ème a variety of aircraft for technical evaluations; and the 8ème trainer aircraft. Further reorganisation in 1925 led to the adoption of three *escadres* (wings) in place of the eight *groupes*, and in 1927 these *escadres* became

regiments. By the time of the German invasion in May 1940 there were the 1er *Régiment d'aéronautique* of six army cooperation *escadrilles* with sixty-two aircraft; the 2er *Régiment d'aéronautique* of six fighter *escadrilles* with seventy-nine aircraft; and the 3er *Régiment d'aéronautique* of four reconnaissance-bomber *escadrilles* with forty-one aircraft. After the defeat of Belgium, some air personnel managed to get away to join the British, while those in the Belgian Congo joined the South African Air Force. Two fighter squadrons of Belgians were formed in the RAF, and 1,200 Belgian personnel served with the RAF.

BRAZIL

Brazil had formed a naval air service in 1913, and an army air service in 1919. But thereafter progress was slow, though the two forces amalgamated as the *Força Aérea Brasileira* in 1940. In 1942 Brazil declared war on Germany for the sinking of Brazilian ships by U-boats. Brazilian air bases were put at the disposal of the Allies, and the FAB received assistance principally from the United States, in the form of large numbers of aircraft. In 1944 a *grupo de aviação* (aviation group) of three eighteen-aircraft *esquadrões* (squadrons), equipped with Republic P-47 fighters, was sent to join the Allied air forces in Italy. Strength stood at about 1,000 aircraft at the end of the war.

BULGARIA

Bulgaria fought at first on the German side in World War II, and later changed over to join the advancing Russians. The Treaty of Neuilly had denied Bulgaria an air arm after World War I, but she renounced the treaty in 1937 and set about developing an air force within the army structure. Initial equipment was Polish and Czech. Bulgaria joined the Axis in time for German forces to use her territory as a springboard for the invasion of Greece in April 1941, and in return received substantial German military aid, especially for her air arm. This fought alongside the Germans in Russia, especially after 1943, and received in that year some one hundred ex-French Dewoitine 520 and 150 Bf 109 fighters to bolster its efforts against the Russians.

CANADA

Canada had an Aviation Corps during World War I, but in 1920 the Canadian Air Force was formed, largely with aircraft of the 'imperial gift'. In 1923 the force received its 'Royal' prefix. During the 1920s the force concentrated on more civil tasks, such as air mapping and communications work in the north of the country. Expansion followed the 1932 cuts in 1935, allowing additional aircraft to be bought and more squadrons to be raised. By the start of World War II the RCAF had 270 aircraft, but only forty of these could be considered militarily useful. There were eight regular and twelve reserve squadrons. One Hurricane squadron flew in the Battle of Britain, and by 1941 there were sixteen RCAF squadrons in Great Britain. The RCAF fought mostly in Europe and over the Atlantic, though one squadron was sent to Ceylon in 1942. Losses amounted to more than 17,000 men of the RCAF, and peak strength was ninety squadrons.

CHINA

China formed an Aviation Service in 1919 with British and French aid, though before this there had been a number of regional air units serving with local warlords, and nominal Chinese army and navy air arms. Most of the Aviation Service's equipment was of British and French origins until the early 1930s, and was widely used to combat insurgents. With the Japanese conquest of Manchuria, however, the Chinese asked for British aid in establishing a proper air force, and when this was refused, they turned to the United States, which agreed. By 1934 there was a Central Government Air Force with six fighter squadrons. In 1935 the Italians started to supply many aircraft types, and after 1937 the Russians also supplied advisers, aircraft and technicians. A seesaw technical battle was fought over China, usually in favour of the Japanese until the arrival of the American Volunteer Group in 1941. The AVG was reabsorbed into the USAAF in 1942, but thereafter the Americans supplied the Central Government Air Force with large numbers of aircraft and other equipment, as well as considerable technical help.

CZECHOSLOVAKIA

Czechoslovakia technically ceased to exist before World War II, as the result of Germany's annexation of the Sudetenland and then the establishment of a 'protectorate' over the rump of the country in early 1939. The Czech Army Air Force had been formed in 1918, and by 1928 had 400 aircraft in twenty-five squadrons. With the dismemberment of their country, many men of the Czech Army Air Force moved to Poland and France, serving in those countries' air forces after the beginning of World War II. After the fall of France, many Czechs escaped to Britain and joined the RAF, which eventually had three Czech fighter squadrons and one Czech bomber squadron. Other Czechs joined the Red Air Force, while others again joined the German-controlled Slovak Air Force.

DENMARK

Denmark had established small air units within the army and navy in 1912, but it was not until 1923 that the Army Flying Corps and Naval Flying Corps were formed. By 1926 the Naval Air Corps had two squadrons: 1 *Luftflotille* with reconnaissance seaplanes, and 2 *Luftflotille* with fighters. In 1932 the Army Flying Corps became the *Havaens Flyvertropper* (Army Aviation Corps) with four squadrons: 1 *Eskadrille* with fighters, 2, 3 and 5 *Eskadrilles* with reconnaissance aircraft. The planned fifth *Eskadrille* (no 4) was never formed for financial reasons. In April 1940, when the Germans invaded, the numerical and technical superiority of the Luftwaffe was so great that the Danish air arms surrendered immediately. Subsequently a few Danes got away to serve with the RAF.

FINLAND

Finland was recognised as independent by Russia in 1920, the year in which the *Lentojoukat* (Flying Corps) became the *Ilmailuvoimat* (Aviation Force), established with the assistance of the French. Initial equipment was about 150 aircraft, mostly of French and German origin. In the Winter War of 1939–40 the *Ilmavoimat*

Macchi C.200 fighters formed Italy's fighter backbone in 1940, 156 being in service. Manoeuvrability was excellent, but performance low because of the indifferent radial engine. Armament was two 12.7-mm machine guns.

(Air Force), as the force had been redesignated in 1928, performed remarkably well, exacting a high toll of the Russian bombers attempting to attack Finnish cities, and finishing the war with 104 serviceable aircraft. Finland then allied herself with Germany for the forthcoming war with Russia, and received German aid in return. By June 1941, the *Ilmavoimat* had some 300 combat aircraft deployed in its four *Lentorykmenttyi* (Flight Regiments). Again the Finns fought with distinction against the Russians, but were finally forced to seek terms in 1944, and then to change sides and fight against their former allies. During the 'Continuation War', as it was known to the Finns, the *Ilmavoimat* lost 536 aircraft, 209 in operations, and had shot down 1,567 Russian aircraft. Combat operations against the Germans cost them another fourteen aircraft.

FRANCE

France ended World War I with an air force of some 255 *escadrilles*, but this figure was quickly reduced to 180 *escadrilles* in Europe and France's African territories. Although new equipment was introduced in the 1920s and early 1930s, the *Aviation Militaire*, as the *Aéronautique Militaire* gradually became more popularly known in the 1920s, declined into an obsolescent force. On 1 April 1933 the force became known as the *Armée de l' Air* (Air Force). Two years later it was realised how elderly most of the force's aircraft were, and an immediate programme of new development was initiated, and some excellent types were produced in the last four years of peace. Too many types were designed and tested, however, and the French failed to get into production the chosen types in time for large numbers of them to have reached front-line units by 1939. Just before the outbreak of war, the *Armée de l' Air* had the following modern aircraft: Morane-Saulnier MS 405/406 fighter (465 in France), Potez 630 general-purpose aircraft (67), Potez 631 general-purpose aircraft (173), Potez 637 reconnaissance aircraft (60), Bloch 151/152 fighter (92), Bloch 131 reconnaissance aircraft (119), Lioré et Olivier 451 bomber (8), and Curtiss Hawk 75 fighter (156), for a total of 1,140 modern combat aircraft in metropolitan France. This total includes instructional aircraft and some still in the factories. After the German invasion of 10 May 1940, the *Armée de l' Air* fought bravely, and at times to great effect, but eventually the Germans had to win. By the time of the armistice of 25 June 1940, the French had lost about 1,200 aircraft, with 960 men killed and another 530 wounded. The air forces that remained in France became the 'Vichy French' Air Force, but was disbanded by the Germans when certain of its elements defected to the Allies when the latter landed in French North Africa in November 1942. The Free French Air Force was formed in Great Britain from French elements who had escaped at the fall of France, and began operations in 1942. It amalgamated with ex-Vichy units in 1943, and so the *Armée de l' Air* was re-formed. Known as the *Service Aéronautique* in World War I, the French naval air arm was renamed the *Aéronautique Maritime* in 1925, but played a relatively undistinguished part in World War II.

GREECE

Greece had early developed both army and navy air services, and the Royal Hellenic Navy Air Service and Royal Hellenic Army Air Force were strengthened by British aircraft after the end of World War I. When Greece was declared a republic in 1924, the 'Royal' prefixes were discarded. With money in desperately short supply in the late 1920s, the authorities had recourse to a strange expedient: a Greek Air Force Fund, with property, was endowed, the profits going to the air forces. The fund could also engage in other activities to raise money, including voluntary levies in major towns. In 1931 the two forces were amalgamated as the Hellenic Air Force, which once again received a 'Royal' prefix with the return of the monarchy in 1934. Equipment was obsolete by 1940, but nevertheless the Greeks severely handled the Italian invaders. This was not the case when the Germans took a hand in 1941, however, and the Greek air force was quickly worn down. Survivors escaped to Egypt, where Greek squadrons within the RAF were formed.

HUNGARY

Hungary emerged from the Austro-Hungarian empire's collapse in 1918, but was forbidden by the Treaty of Versailles from having an air force. Nonetheless, in 1936 Hungary began to develop a small air arm with German and Italian aircraft, and this soon became the Hungarian Army Air Force, which began to feature in Axis planning from 1940. The Hungarian Army Air Force used combat aircraft of German and Italian origins throughout World War II, when it was used almost exclusively on the Eastern Front. Heavy losses were suffered.

INDIA

India entered the field of military aviation late, the Indian Air Force being raised only in 1933, under RAF

One of Italy's best fighters, the Macchi C.202 combined the airframe of the C.200 with the Daimler-Benz DB01A inline engine. Performance was adequate, but armament (two 12.7-mm) was not. In the background is a Savoia-Marchetti S.M.82 trimotor heavy transport. In the foreground are British and French air force personnel.

control, to operate a flight of army cooperation aircraft. In 1940 this flight became a squadron, and large-scale expansion was intended. By 1943 the IAF had seven fighter and two dive-bomber squadrons, and was used almost exclusively on army support work in the Far East for the rest of the war.

ITALY

Italy was the first country to use aircraft in war, but like the other victorious nations in World War I, had to start cutting back her *Corpo Aeronautico Militare* (Military Aviation Corps) almost immediately. But in 1923 Mussolini came to power in Italy, and as a keen believer in the martial ability of Italy he immediately started to build up the armed forces. The CAM thus became the *Regia Aeronautica* (Royal Air Force), an independent air service. The *Regia Aeronautica* was extensively tested in peacetime record-breaking flights, and in wartime operations in Ethiopia and in the Spanish Civil War, though many wrong tactical and technical lessons were drawn, especially where the continued military use of the biplane was concerned. In 1940, when she declared war on France and Great Britain, Italy had some 2,600 aircraft in Europe and North Africa, with another 400 obsolete types in her East African empire. With the exception of her torpedo-bomber force, the Italian air arm was severely handled by the Allies, and was a sadly depleted force when Italy capitulated in September 1943.

THE NETHERLANDS

The Netherlands started into the field of military aviation in a serious way in 1911, and in 1913 formed the Aviation Division of the Royal Netherlands Army. The usual problems with finance were encountered in the 1920s and early 1930s, and it was only in 1938 that the poor state of the Air Division was fully appreciated. An immediate reorganisation and re-equipment was set in hand, one of the first moves being the redesignation of the Aviation Division as the *Luchtvaartafdeling* (Army Air Service). At the time of the German invasion the LVA mustered only some 125 aircraft, most of them made by Fokker. The force was divided into two *Luchtvaartregiments*, the 1st having reconnaissance and bomber aircraft, and the 2nd reconnaissance aircraft. Both regiments had a *Jachtgroep* (fighter group). As with other countries overrun by the Germans, the remnants of the Dutch air force fled to England, where the RAF was only too glad to have them. In the East Indies the air service of the Royal Netherlands Indies Army faced great odds with the Japanese, but fought well until driven from the skies. The *Marine Luchtvaartdienst* (Naval Air Service) played only a small part against Germany in 1940 before its survivors fled to France and England.

NEW ZEALAND

New Zealand's first air service, the New Zealand Permanent Air Force, was raised in 1923, though New Zealanders had fought with the RFC, RNAS and RAF in World War I. Initial equipment, as with Australia and Canada, was aircraft from the 'imperial gift'. The NZPAF was part of the army, while the New Zealand Air Force was a reserve force, using NZPAF aircraft for training. Although the NZPAF became the Royal New Zealand Air Force in 1934, it was not until 1937 that it finally split from the army. A large-scale expansion had started by the beginning of World War II, and despite the fact that New Zealand did much training work for the RAF, the RNZAF fielded twenty-seven squadrons: twelve fighter, six bomber, two flying-boat, two reconnaissance, one dive-bomber, one naval strike bomber and the remaining three transports. Most of the RNZAF's operations were in the South Pacific, though some elements fought in Europe and North Africa.

NORWAY

Norway entered the air force lists in 1915, when both the *Haerens Flyvapen* (Army Air Force) and *Marinens Flyvevaesen* (Naval Air Service) were formed. Progress in the 1920s and 1930s was slow, and at the time of the German invasion in April 1940 there was little that the two forces could put up in the way of effective resistance. Those who could finally escaped to great Britain. The Naval Air Service was relocated to Canada, where it trained on flying-boats before returning to join RAF Coastal Command. The Army Air Force stayed in Britain, its personnel forming two RAF fighter squadrons. In 1944 the two forces were amalgamated as the *Kongelige Norske Luftforsvaret* (Royal Norwegian Air Force) with three fighter, two bomber, one reconnaissance and one transport squadron.

THE PHILIPPINES

The Philippines formed an aviation department of the Philippine Constabulary in 1935, and this became the Philippine Army Air Force in 1940, with twelve Boeing P-26 fighters as equipment. All of these were destroyed on the ground during the initial Japanese strikes on the islands in December 1941.

POLAND

Poland began her air force in 1919, when seven squadrons were raised as part of the army, equipment being 100 French aircraft. This force was expanded during the war with Russia (1919–20), and proved very effective. During the 1920s and early 1930s, the Polish aircraft industry turned out excellent aircraft, but the position began to slip in the second half of the 1930s, however, and by the late 1930s most of the air service's aircraft were elderly. In 1938 the *Polskie Lotnictwo Wojskowe* (Polish Air Force) was formed as an independent air arm, with fifty-five fighters and seventy-six bombers as its main strength. This 'Dispositional Air Force' in 1939 had a Pursuit Brigade with five squadrons, a Bomber Brigade with eight bomber/reconnaissance squadrons, and one observation and four liaison squadrons, totalling 145 aircraft. There was also the Armies' Air Force, with detachments attached to each of seven armies. The detachments numbered about fifty aircraft: some twenty fighters, ten bombers and twenty general-purpose aircraft. The Poles fought back ferociously against the Germans, inflicting heavy losses on them, but within seventeen days it was all over.

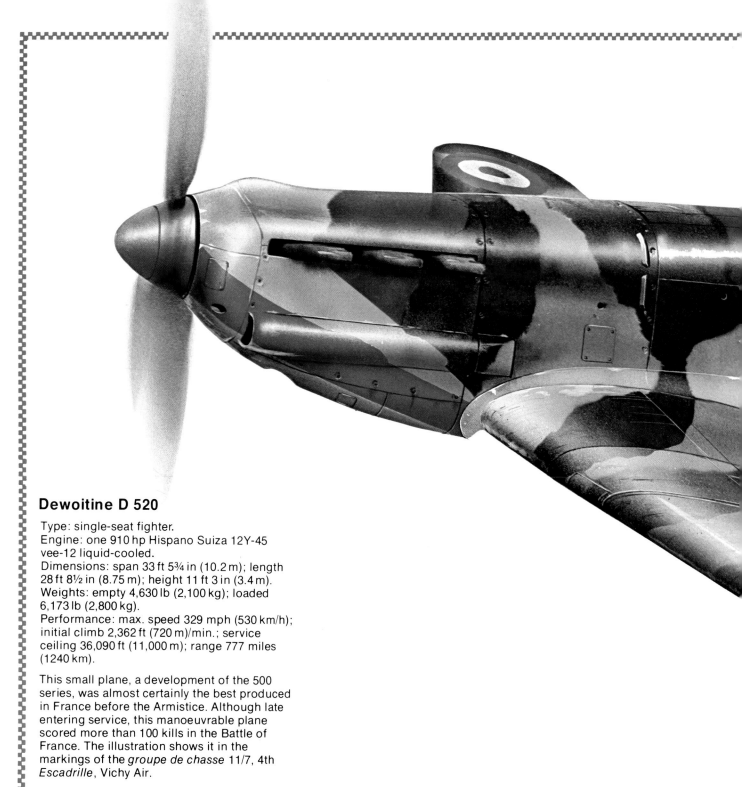

Dewoitine D 520

Type: single-seat fighter.
Engine: one 910 hp Hispano Suiza 12Y-45
vee-12 liquid-cooled.
Dimensions: span 33 ft 5¾ in (10.2 m); length
28 ft 8½ in (8.75 m); height 11 ft 3 in (3.4 m).
Weights: empty 4,630 lb (2,100 kg); loaded
6,173 lb (2,800 kg).
Performance: max. speed 329 mph (530 km/h);
initial climb 2,362 ft (720 m)/min.; service
ceiling 36,090 ft (11,000 m); range 777 miles
(1240 km).

This small plane, a development of the 500
series, was almost certainly the best produced
in France before the Armistice. Although late
entering service, this manoeuvrable plane
scored more than 100 kills in the Battle of
France. The illustration shows it in the
markings of the *groupe de chasse* 11/7, 4th
Escadrille, Vichy Air.

RHODESIA

Rhodesia provided bases for training under the
Empire Air Training Scheme, and the personnel for
two fighter and one bomber squadron in the RAF.

ROMANIA

Romania had an air corps in World War I, but the
country's swift defeat left little opportunity for it to
accomplish anything worthwhile. After the war,
though, a Directorate of Army Aviation was set up,
with nine squadrons disposed in three groups, one for
fighters, one for bombers and the last for reconnaissance aircraft. During the 1920s aircraft of British

and French origin were bought. During World War II
Romania fought at the side of the other Axis powers on
the Eastern Front, using German and Italian aircraft
for the most part. The Russian invasion of the country
in August 1944 signalled the end for Romania as an Axis
power.

SOUTH AFRICA

South Africa formed her South African Air Force in
1920 to use her 'imperial gift' of 100 surplus World War
I aircraft. Thereafter the SAAF bought British aircraft
on the whole, but also licence-built a number in the
country. An expansion programme was started in 1936,
and by September 1939 the SAAF had about 100

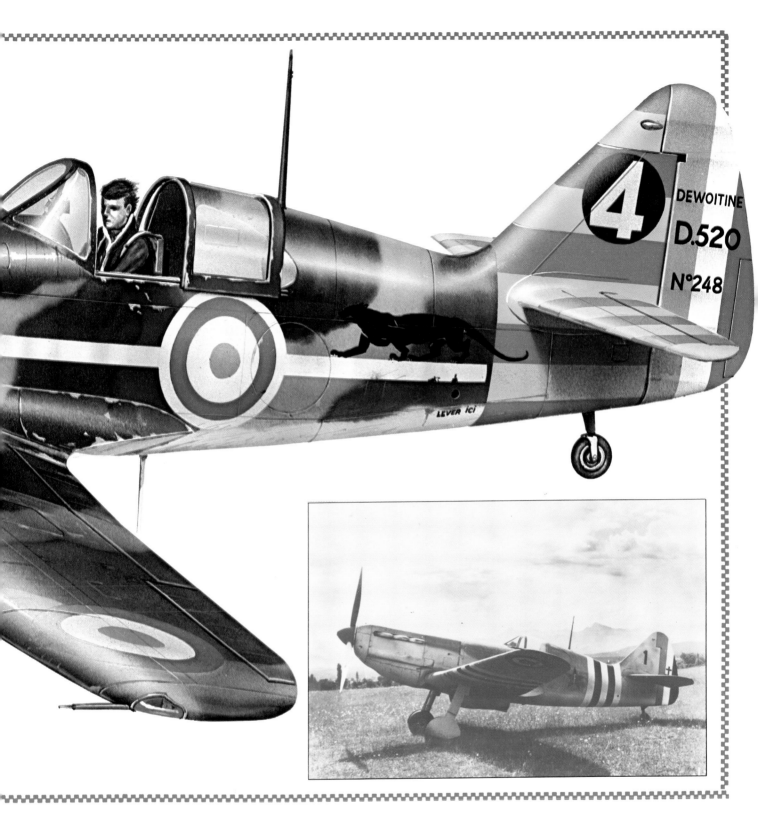

DEWOITINE
D.520
N°248

combat aircraft. Expansion continued throughout the war, and although the SAAF had no part in the Empire Air Training Scheme, SAAF airfields were used by the RAF for training. The SAAF played a vital part in winning the air war in East Africa, North Africa and then in Italy.

YUGOSLAVIA

Yugoslavia was another country to emerge from the remnants of the Austro-Hungarian Empire at the end of World War I, with the nucleus being formed by Serbia, one of Austria-Hungary's main opponents in the early part of World War I. A Yugoslav Army Aviation Department was formed in 1923, and used predo-

minantly French equipment. The air arm was granted a relative autonomy in 1930, but remained technically part of the army. By 1935 the Yugoslav Army Air Corps, as it had become, had the respectable force of forty-four squadrons with some 440 aircraft. Modern aircraft had been ordered from France, Germany, Great Britain and Italy, and an encouraging indigenous aircraft industry was getting on its feet. The Yugoslav Army Air Corps fought as best it could when the Germans invaded in April 1941, but were soon defeated by superior aircraft, numbers and combat experience. Many Yugoslavs managed to escape to Britain, and the RAF then formed Yugoslav bomber and fighter squadrons. Yugoslavia itself was partitioned, and in their portion the Italians formed a Croatian Air Force (of questionable loyalty) with Italian equipment.

CHAPTER TWELVE

THE DAYS OF BLITZKRIEG 1939·45

The *Luftwaffe* was expressly designed for tactical air operations, at least after the death of *Generalleutnant* Wever, and from the beginning of September 1939 to the end of September 1941, and perhaps to the end of December 1941, it reigned supreme over the skies of Europe. Indeed, the *Luftwaffe*'s single defeat in this period, the Battle of Britain, was the direct result of *Reichsmarschall* Hermann Göring's ambitions for his force, leading him to commit it to a strategic conflict for which it had neither the aircraft nor the tactics. This error left Britain in the war, and thus forced Germany to face a two-front war when she invaded Russia. This ultimately cost Germany the war.

But what is tactical air warfare? In short, the answer is that it is air operations designed to support the activities of the forces on the ground, by direct support action, air interdiction in forward and rear areas, and the disruption of the enemy's immediate ability to wage war, in both physical and morale terms.

When performed effectively by the ground and air forces, such tactics were highly efficient, and became quickly known in World War II as *Blitzkrieg* or Lightning War tactics. Much has since been said and written about the novelty of the tactics, but this is not in fact true. In 1918, Germany faced the problem of trying

to defeat Belgium, France and Great Britain on the Western Front before the arrival of large-scale, fresh American forces. Thus in the spring of that year five last-gasp offensives were launched in an effort to bring the Allies to their knees. The tactical cornerstone of these offensives were the novel *Sturmtrupp* or Storm-troop tactics devised by *General* von Hutier.

At the time, conventional tactics dictated that an assault should be prefaced by several days of intense artillery preparation and mining, after which the assault forces would edge forward massively and slowly. The trouble lay in the fact that the artillery preparation obviated any chance of surprise, and was at the same time ineffective. Thus the assault forces were usually met with a withering hail of fire, and the chances of more than local success were slim.

Hutier's tactics were based on the reintroduction of surprise. Accompanied only by a rolling barrage just to their front, and without the 'benefit' of a preliminary softening-up barrage, the stormtroops with their light scale of equipment and special training, dashed forward and smashed into the Allied front line, breaking through swiftly, bypassing any pockets of resistance and heading for the rear areas to take or disrupt the Allies gun lines, supply depots and communications.

The Heinkel He III in flight. This twin-engine medium bomber was one of Germany's mainstays in the Battle of Britain, where it suffered heavy losses. By mid-1940, it was being replaced by Ju 88s, and came to be used as a transport and glider tug on the Eastern Front, and for occasional night-bombing and mine-laying.

With the control of the Allied forces thus in disarray, the conventional infantry followed up, mopping up the pockets of resistance and consolidating, allowing the stormtroops to press on, supported from the air by special *Schlachtstaffeln* or Battle Squadrons.

It was these tactics that formed the basis for *Blitzkrieg*, updated in their equipment to take advantage of the latest technology, but still posited on the idea that speed and surprise would allow a quick breakthrough, disrupting the enemy's defensive plans and so facilitating a quick and inexpensive German victory.

How did such tactics work in practice? In place of the stormtroopers, the latest technology had provided armoured fighting vehicles (fully-tracked tanks, half-tracked personnel vehicles and wheeled armoured cars), which could move far faster than the foot-mobile stormtroopers. This speed would take them out of the range of horse-mobile artillery in a short space of time, and so other heavy support had to be found – and here aircraft entered the picture. Given the more sophisticated control possible with the use of radio communications, a *Luftwaffe* controller up with the leading elements of the *Panzer* and motorised regiments of the armoured spearhead could call in exactly the type of support needed by the ground forces. While Messerschmitt Bf 109 fighters prevented enemy aircraft from interfering overhead, and Bf 110 heavy fighters roamed farther to the enemy's rear, the controller could call in Henschel Hs 123 biplane ground-attack aircraft and Junkers Ju 87 dive-bombers to tackle enemy concentrations and strongpoints, while other dive-bombers and medium bombers destroyed bridges, roads, railways, supply dumps and the like in the enemy's rear, and also attacked the enemy's artillery positions, paving the way for a relatively unhindered advance by the *Panzer* forces, which could then launch great pincer movements to cut up the enemy. The Dornier Do 17, Heinkel He 111 and Junkers Ju 88 medium bombers also attacked the enemy's airfields, key marshalling yards, main industrial centres, and sometimes major cities in an effort to cow the civil population and so persuade the government to capitulate. Once the

enemy's air force had been eliminated, the Bf 109 and Bf 110 fighters were also free to cooperate with the ground forces, their cannon and machine guns proving very useful for harassing the enemy infantry and suppressing light anti-aircraft guns. The German *Flak*, moreover, was relatively mobile, and could thus keep up with the armoured units to provide local air protection and engage ground targets as the situation required.

As the *Panzer* forces pressed on, destroying the enemy's defence plans and cutting off great bodies of troops, the less mobile infantry formations followed and mopped up, sometimes against savage resistance.

All in all, the description of the *Luftwaffe* as the 'flying artillery' of the *Blitzkrieg* is apt, but does not reflect the scope and versatility of the aerial support offered to the ground forces.

For the Polish campaign, *Luftflotten* I and IV deployed some 1,581 first-line aircraft, a number swollen during the course of operations by army aircraft and home defence fighters. To resist this formidable aerial armada the Poles had only 154 bombers, 159 fighters and eighty-four observation aircraft – making 397 combat aircraft, plus thirty-six liaison aircraft for a grand total of 433 first-line aircraft.

Right from the start the Germans dominated, although the Poles at first fought back courageously and effectively. Indeed, the first aerial victory of the war was claimed by a Pole, Lieutenant Wladyslaw Gnys, who shot down a Ju 87 very soon after the start of hostilities, which had been marked by great German air raids. But on 7 September, one week after the start of the war, the rickety Polish early warning system collapsed, and the German air raids became doubly effective as the obsolescent Polish PZL P-7 and P-11 fighters failed to intercept. The Polish bomber force, with PZL P-23 and P-37 light and medium bombers, could do little to stem the German advance, and on 14 September it suffered a great blow when seventeen aircraft were destroyed on Hutnicki airfield by a bomber raid.

On 13 September the *Luftwaffe* raided Warsaw with 183 bombers, initiating a battle which ended effectively

One of the most famous and versatile combat aircraft ever built, the Supermarine Spitfire was the first all-metal, stressed-skin fighters produced in Britain. Pictured is the Spitfire I, which had eight .303 in. machine guns and a Rolls-Royce Merlin engine.

on 25 September with the razing of the city by 240 Ju 87s, 30 Ju 52/3m transports carrying incendiaries, and large numbers of medium bombers.

Polish reinforcements during the campaign had been seven fighters, sixteen bomber and reconnaissance aircraft, fifteen observation aircraft and sixty liaison machines, ninety-eight in all. Of the overall total of 531 aircraft on hand during the campaign, the losses totalled 327, about seventy shot down in combat, and the rest bombed or lost to 'friendly' ground fire. With the Russian invasion of eastern Poland on 17 September the remnants of the Polish Air Force were flown to internment in Romania, some 116 in number.

German losses were also heavy: 285 aircraft and 734 personnel. By type, the *Luftwaffe* lost seventy-eight bombers, sixty-seven single-engined fighters, sixty-three reconnaissance aircraft, thirty-one dive-bombers, twenty-two marine and miscellaneous machines, twelve transports and twelve twin-engined fighters. In addition, another 279 aircraft were 'lost to strength' being more than 10% damaged.

The German concept of *Blitzkrieg* had been amply proved, though, and the first aces of World War II made. On the German side the highest scoring pilot was *Hauptmann* Hannes Gentzen, with seven victories; on the Polish side, the most successful pilot had been Lieutenant Stanislaw Skalski with 6½ victories.

On the Western Front in France, occasioned by the

Below The Hawker Hurricane, most numerous of British fighters in the Battle of Britain, had more impact than the Spitfire, as its closely-grouped guns delivered more concentrated fire than the Spitfire's spread out guns. Slower, but more manoeuvrable than the Bf 109, it handled superbly and was a steady gun platform.

P7666

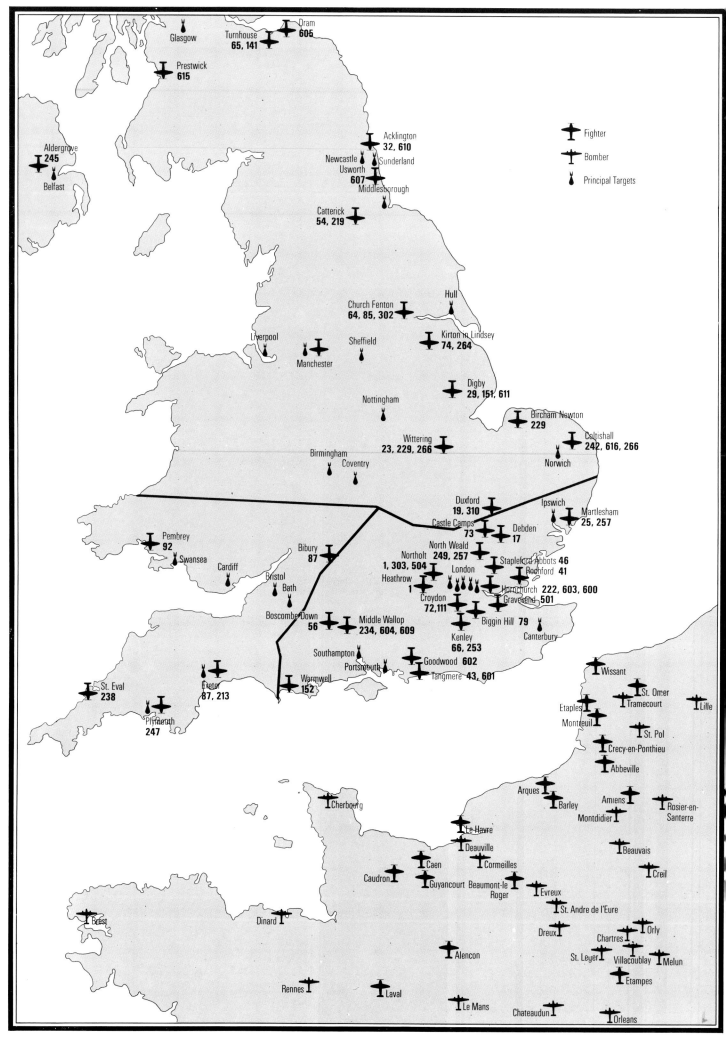

Glasgow

Turnhouse
65, 141

Dram
605

Prestwick
615

Aldergrove
245

Belfast

Acklington
32, 610

Newcastle
Usworth
607
Sunderland

Middlesborough

Catterick
54, 219

Hull

Church Fenton
64, 85, 302

Liverpool

Sheffield

Kirton in Lindsey
74, 264

Manchester

Digby
29, 151, 611

Nottingham

Bircham Newton
229

Wittering
23, 229, 266

Coltishall
242, 616, 266

Birmingham

Coventry

Norwich

Duxford
19, 310

Ipswich

Martlesham
25, 257

Castle Camps
73

Debden
17

Pembrey
92

Swansea

Cardiff

Bibury
87

North Weald
249, 257

Northolt
1, 303, 504

Stapleford Abbotts **46**

Rochford **41**

Bristol

Bath

Heathrow
1

London

Hornchurch **222, 603, 600**

Croydon
72,111

Gravesend **501**

Boscombe Down
56

Middle Wallop
234, 604, 609

Biggin Hill **79**

Kenley
66, 253

Canterbury

Southampton

Goodwood **602**

Portsmouth

St. Eval
238

Exeter
87, 213

Warmwell
152

Tangmere **43, 601**

Plymouth
247

Cherbourg

Wissant

St. Omer

Tramecourt

Lille

Etaples

Montreuil

St. Pol

Crecy-en-Ponthieu

Abbeville

Arques

Barley

Amiens

Rosier-en-Santerre

Montdidier

Le Havre

Deauville

Cormeilles

Beauvais

Caen

Creil

Caudron

Guyancourt

Beaumont-le-Roger

Evreux

St. Andre de l'Eure

Dinard

Dreux

Orly

Chartres

Brest

Alencon

St. Leger

Villacoublay

Melun

Etampes

Rennes

Laval

Le Mans

Chateaudun

Orleans

Fighter

Bomber

Principal Targets

168

eclaration of war on Germany by France and Great ritain after the invasion of Poland, air activity was esultory, both sides feeling their way into the war with reat caution. Air reconnaissance was widespread, and ometimes resulted in fierce air battles, however.

With the elimination of Poland, it was clear that the ext decisive campaign would be on the Western Front. ut while both sides were preparing themselves for this limactic battle, the Russians took the opportunity to y to seize various strategic portions of Finland in a aassive onslaught starting on 30 November 1939. Contrary to all expectations, the Finns were able to hold he Russians, and in a grisly 'Winter War' inflicted normous losses on the Russians before coming to erms on 12 March 1940.

The war started with large-scale air raids on Viipuri nd Helsinki by the Red Air Force, before any de-laration of war. Expecting a relatively simple victory, he Russians used only second-rate forces, supported y some 900 aircraft. To meet this threat the Finns had igh-grade infantry supported by about 145 operational ircraft, of which only 114 were serviceable.

Finland's first air success came on 1 December, when Lieutenant Eino Luukkanen in a Fokker D XXI fighter hot down a Tupolev SB-2 medium bomber. For the est of the year, though, poor weather prevented large-cale air activity, and it was not until January 1940 that he Finns' true mettle became apparent, to the extent hat the Russians committed 600 additional aircraft, ollowed in February by another 500 for the final .ussian offensive. The Finns received spasmodic re-nforcements from France, Great Britain, Italy and the United States. Even so, some 2,000 Russian aircraft vere opposed by only 196 Finnish aircraft, only 112 of hem serviceable. But by the time of the armistice, the 'inns had claimed 200 aircraft destroyed and 80 robably destroyed, compared with their own losses of 7 destroyed (only 42 in the air) and 69 damaged. It was lear proof that the leadership and flying skills of the .ed Air Force were not up to western standards, a fact hat Hitler found most encouraging.

Just before his blow in the West, Hitler decided to ecure his northern flank and the route of Swedish iron re to Germany via Narvik in Norway, by a swift onquest of Norway, with Denmark en passant. Den-nark fell with hardly a shot fired, thanks in no small neasure to the success of the first use of airborne roops, but the Norwegian campaign was altogether

more costly. The Norwegians, with British and French support, fought a campaign that they were almost certain to lose, but in the process cost the Germans dear. Once again, though, the efficiency of Germany's air arm, in the form of the 710 aircraft of *Fliegerkorps* X, proved decisive, and once German fighters were established in Norway, Allied day bombers suffered very heavily. Yet there were brighter spots. On the day after the campaign started, 9 April 1940, British Blackburn Skua dive-bombers sank the light cruiser *Königsberg*. But for most of the time until Norway's capitulation on 9 June 1940 the *Luftwaffe* dominated.

By this time, however, the world's attention was turned on France, where the Germans were about to cross the Seine after launching their major push to the west on 10 May. Belgium and Holland had quickly succumbed, the Anglo-French forces in the north had been cut off from the rest of France by Germany's strategic masterstroke, the drive through the Ardennes and north-west to the Channel coast, resulting in the evacuation from Dunkirk, and now the Germans were poised to administer the *coup de grâce* to hapless France.

For the western operation on 10 May, Germany had deployed 1,016 Bf 109s, 248 Bf 110s, 1,120 medium bombers, 385 dive-bombers, 640 reconnaissance, observation and transport aircraft, and 45 gliders. This serviceable strength of 3,454 aircraft was deployed as follows. In the north, *Generaloberst* Fedor von Bock's Army Group 'B' was supported by Kesselring's *Luftflotte* II: *Fliegerkorps* I (Ulrich Grauert) and *Fliegerkorps* IV (Alfred Keller), and the sea-mining 9th *Fliegerdivision*; in the centre, *Generaloberst* Gerd von Rundstedt's Army Group 'A' was supported by Sperrle's *Luftflotte* III: *Fliegerkorps* II (Bruno Lörzer) and *Fliegerkorps* VIII (Wolfram, *Freiherr* von Richthofen); in the south, *Generaloberst* Wilhelm, *Ritter* von Leeb's Army Group 'C' was supported by *Fliegerkorps* V (von Greim), part of *Luftflotte* III.

To meet this threat, the Dutch disposed of only eighty-two aircraft: ten Fokker C X reconnaissance bombers, twenty-nine Fokker D XXI fighters, twenty-three Fokker G I twin-engined heavy fighters, nine Fokker T V medium bombers and eleven Fokker T VIII-W floatplane torpedo-bombers. Belgium had 182 aircraft: fourteen Fairey Battle light bombers, ninety-eight Fairey Fox reconnaissance bombers, twenty-three Fiat CR 42 biplane fighters, fifteen Gloster Gladiator biplane fighters, eleven Hawker Hurricane

Opposite Map showing the location of Allied and Axis fighter and bomber stations during 1940.
Below The Junkers Ju 87 'Stuka' entered production in 1937 and earned itself a formidable reputation. This was dispelled in the Battle of Britain, where it suffered heavy losses and was withdrawn, to be used in less critical arenas where the Axis still enjoyed some air superiority.

Opposite page German pilots while away time playing cards, in between periods of fighting.
Far left A German pilot prepares for battle.
Left German ground crew hand crank the engine of a Ju 87 D Stuka.

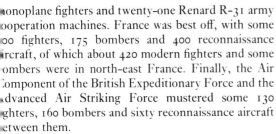

monoplane fighters and twenty-one Renard R-31 army cooperation machines. France was best off, with some 700 fighters, 175 bombers and 400 reconnaissance aircraft, of which about 420 modern fighters and some bombers were in north-east France. Finally, the Air Component of the British Expeditionary Force and the Advanced Air Striking Force mustered some 130 fighters, 160 bombers and sixty reconnaissance aircraft between them.

Thus some 3,454 German aircraft were faced by about 1,150 relatively modern Allied aircraft. The balance of forces was a clear indication of what was to come, for almost immediately the Germans secured air superiority, although only at the expense of heavy losses. On 10 May, for example, the *Luftwaffe* lost 304 aircraft and 267 aircrew, with another fifty-one aircraft damaged. The type lost in greatest numbers was the all-important Junkers Ju 52/3m, of which 157 were destroyed. Germany had started the war with only 552 of these aircraft, used for training, liaison, transport and other rear-service functions, as well as front-line duties such as paratroop-dropping and glider-towing. Other heavy losses were to the He 111 (fifty-one destroyed and twenty-one damaged), the Do 17 (twenty-six destroyed and seven damaged) and Fi 156 (twenty-two destroyed).

Although the German pre-emptive strikes in Belgium and Holland had enjoyed some success, those in France were a relative failure on 10 May, only forty-five French and fifteen British aircraft being caught on the ground. And though Allied fighters claimed ninety victories for twenty losses, the Germans were able to attain all their air objectives.

Typical of the German air effort was the concentrated bombardment on 13 May of French artillery positions covering the Meuse crossings between Sedan and Nouzonville to be used by *Panzergruppe* von Kleist. According to a strict schedule, some 310 medium and 200 dive-bombers of *Fliegerkorps* II and VIII poured down so much high explosive that the Germans were

able to get across the river against mediocre opposition.

The very next day the Allies riposted with attacks on the German bridges over the Meuse, but suffered terrible losses to the German *Flak* and fighters: thirty-six Battles and almost as many other British aircraft (amounting to 60% of the force committed), plus more than forty French bombers. At the same time the Germans were devastating the old quarter of Rotterdam.

By 15 May the Dutch air force had been eliminated, and the Belgian air force had lost thirty-nine aircraft in the air and 119 on the ground. The French and British air forces had also been hard hit, and despite the dispatch of another six Hurricane squadrons from England to France, the air battle was clearly lost. The Air Component was pulled out on 20 May, having lost 75 Hurricanes and forty-one Bristol Blenheim bombers, and abandoned 120 damaged Hurricanes.

A portent of brighter things for the future, however, was to be found over the evacuation beaches at Dunkirk between 27 May and 2 June. Here the *Luftwaffe* lost 189 aircraft in about 4,000 sorties (4.725%), while the RAF Fighter Command successfully covered the evacuation for the loss of ninety-nine aircraft in 2,739 sorties (2.766%). But while the *Luftwaffe's* main efforts were directed against Dunkirk, the French had rested, and on 5 June had a field day, claiming sixty-six German aircraft for the loss of only twenty-four of their own. The French had no bomber force left, however, and despite the valiant efforts of the fighter arm, the Germans were able to concentrate on ground-support with decisive results, forcing France to sue for an armistice on 17 June. This came into effect on 25 June. In the first month of the campaign the French admitted to the loss of 306 aircraft in the air and 329 on the ground, while British losses for the whole of May and June had been 1,019. Combined with Belgian and Dutch losses, this meant that the Allies had lost more than 2,000 aircraft during Germany's western drive. The *Luftwaffe*, though, had lost more than 1,200 aircraft in the air, and another 300 had been lost operationally, with a further high proportion of heavily damaged machines. The Germans had won the western campaign, and the *Luftwaffe* had again proved highly effective, but the cost had been very high.

Italy, eager to share in the spoils of a successful war, had entered the war on the side of Germany on 10 June, and this meant that after the fall of France, Britain was left alone to face the might of Germany from across the English Channel, and considerable Italian forces in the Mediterranean, North Africa and East Africa. In the short term, the main threat came from Germany, which was busily preparing plans for the invasion of England (Operation 'Sealion'). The plans were bedevilled by squabbles between the army and the navy as to the extent of the assault area, but both sides agreed that the *Luftwaffe* would first have to gain air superiority over southern England. Here Göring, ambitious as ever, stepped in and offered his *Luftwaffe* as the single means of defeating Great Britain – once his air force had crushed the RAF, Göring claimed, the British would be only too glad to come to terms with their capital and other cities and industries wide open to the threat of the *Luftwaffe*'s bombers. It was an ideal solution to the imbroglio in which the army and navy had found themselves. Göring was given his go-ahead, with *Adler-tag* or Eagle Day for the start of the main assault to waste British aircraft production facilities, fixed for 10 August, but later postponed to the 13th.

The *Luftwaffe* was about to undertake a strategic task for which it had neither the aircraft nor the tactics. The British, on the other hand, had the benefit of 'interior' lines of communication, ground-controlled radar interception techniques, increasing fighter production, and comparatively fresh pilots, although these were in direly short supply. The Germans, conversely, were tired and short of aircraft after the Battle of France, were about to operate beyond the realistic combat range of their aircraft, and were poorly informed of British capabilities.

The British defence was entrusted to RAF Fighter Command under Air Chief Marshal Sir Hugh Dowding: 10 Group (Brand) in the West Country, 11 Group (Park) in South-East England, 12 Group (Leigh-Mallory) in Central England and North Wales, and 13

Group (Saul) in northern England and Scotland. On 10 August Fighter Command's establishment strength was 1,106 aircraft and 1,588 pilots; the actual figures were 749 and 1,396. The fighter shortage was overcome quite quickly, but it was not until 12 October that there was a pilot surplus, allowing exhausted men to be rotated more rapidly.

On 10 August the three *Luftflotten* involved had an establishment strength of 3,609 aircraft, an actual strength of 3,358 and a serviceable strength of only 2,550. In Norway and Denmark was Stumpff's *Luftflotte* V, operating *Fliegerkorps* X (Hans Ferdinand Geisler). In Belgium and Holland was Kesselring's *Luftflotte* II with *Fliegerkorps* I (Grauert), *Fliegerkorps* II (Lörzer) and the 9th *Fliegerdivision* (Joachim Coeler), plus *Jagdfliegerführer* 2 (Theodor Osterkamp). In France was Sperrle's *Luftflotte* III, with *Fliegerkorps* IV (Kurt Pflugbeil), *Fliegerkorps* V (von Greim) and *Fliegerkorps* VIII (von Richthofen), plus *Jagdfliegerführer* 3 (Werner Junck).

The Battle of Britain, as this air campaign was to be called, was the world's first true air battle, and fell into five main phases. The first phase, between 1 July and 7 August, was intended to test Fighter Command by drawing its aircraft out by attacks on coastal convoys and ports by small groups of bombers heavily escorted by fighters. Radar interception techniques proved invaluable for the British, but German fighter tactics generally proved superior. In the phase the Germans lost 244 aircraft, with another eighty-eight damaged, to Fighter Command's 188 lost.

The second phase, between 8 and 23 August, was marked by further attacks along the coast, but mainly by attacks on radar stations and Fighter Command's forward bases. The German effort was marred by poor planning between the *Luftflotte* staffs. Fighter Command pilots also began to show distinct signs of battle fatigue. Comparative losses were 403, with another 127 damaged, to the *Luftwaffe*, and 303 to Fighter Command.

The third phase, from 24 August to 6 September, was again the elimination of Fighter Command in the air and on the ground, and the destruction of production facilities, by large bomber formations heavily escorted by fighters. Fighter Command continued as

before, with exhaustion becoming a desperate factor. Comparative losses were 378, with another 115 damaged, for the *Luftwaffe*, and 262 for Fighter Command. Yet the German effort had been checked, the vulnerability of the Ju 87 to good fighters amply proved, the range limitations of the Bf 109 exposed, and the general inferiority of the Bf 110 to single-engined fighters proved. The German bombers were also found to be incapable of carrying an adequate bomb load over a long range, too poorly armed for their own defence and vulnerable as all the crew were grouped in the extensively glazed nose compartment.

The fourth phase, from 7 to 30 September, was marked by a total change of objective. Berlin had been bombed on 25 August in retaliation for the 'bombing' of London on 24 August (a few German bombers had inadvertently dropped their loads on the outskirts of the capital, in direct contravention of Hitler's orders). Incensed, Hitler had ordered terror-bombing of London as soon as possible, which was 7 September. It was a fatal error, for Fighter Command, almost on its last legs, was reprieved, and then took the offensive against the daylight bomber streams heading for London. The day raids were stopped on 30 September, by which date the *Luftwaffe* had lost 435 aircraft, with another 161 damaged, to the RAF's 380. But now it was the Germans who were becoming exhausted.

The fifth phase, between 1 and 31 October, was the time of German fighter-bomber sweeps over southern England while the night *Blitz* against London was prepared. Losses for the *Luftwaffe* were 325 aircraft and another 163 damaged, while those to the RAF were 265. By the end of the month the Battle of Britain was over, leaving London and other British cities to face the *Blitz* before German air strength began to filter away to the east for the campaign against Russia. Hitler had cancelled Operation 'Sealion' on 17 September.

From the spring of 1941, the RAF began to take the air war back to Germany with fighter and bomber sweeps over occupied northern Europe to wear down the German forces there. But despite this effort, all but two *Jagdgeschwader* were finally removed for the Russian campaign, scheduled to begin on 15 May 1941. But the need to bolster Mussolini's Italian forces in the Mediterranean, and to overrun Yugoslavia and Greece,

delayed the programme until 22 June 1941.

To support the German ground forces in this campaign, the first stages of which were once again to demonstrate the efficiency of the properly run *Blitzkrieg*, there were the air units of four *Luftflotten*. In the north, *Luftflotte* V (Stumpff) provided the forces of *Fliegerführer* Kirkenes to support *General* Dietl's drive on Petsamo in the Arctic. *Generaloberst* Alfred Keller's *Luftflotte* I supported *Generalfeldmarshall* von Leeb's Army Group 'North' in the Baltic states with *Fliegerkorps* I (Foester) and *Fliegerführer* Baltic (Wild). *Generalfeldmarschall* Kesselring's *Luftflotte* II supported *Generalfeldmarschall* Fedor von Bock's Army Group 'Centre' in Belorussia with *Fliegerkorps* II (Lörzer), *Fliegerkorps* VIII (von Richthofen) and I *Flakkorps* (von Axthelm). And *Generaloberst* Alexander Löhr's *Luftflotte* IV supported *Generalfeldmarschall* Gerd von Rundstedt's Army Group 'South' in the Ukraine with *Fliegerkorps* IV (Pflugbeil) and *Fliegerkorps* V (von Greim), plus II *Flakkorps* (Dessloch). All in all the *Luftwaffe* deployed some 61% of its strength for Operation 'Barbarossa': 510 medium bombers, 440 single-engined fighters, 290 dive-bombers, 120 reconnaissance aircraft and forty twin-engined fighters.

22 June saw a classic *Blitzkrieg* assault, spearheaded by the *Panzer* forces with the *Luftwaffe* in front of them, and right from the start the results were staggering. On the very first day of the war, for the loss of a mere thirty-five of their own aircraft, the Germans destroyed no less than 1,811 Russian aircraft: 322 fell to fighters and *Flak* and 1,489 were destroyed on the ground. Some of these losses were attributable to other nations, for Romania had added her 230 aircraft, and the Finns their 299. A few days later the Hungarians, Slovakians and Italians also came into the Russian war. To meet this force the Russians had deployed some 7,000 aircraft in western Russia.

The first strike was made at 0315 by 637 bombers and 231 fighters against 31 Russian airfields. Only two aircraft were lost and this set the pattern for the future of air operations in Russia during 1941. By the end of the first week the Russians had lost 4,990 aircraft to the Germans' 179, and the *Panzer* spearheads, now all with *Luftwaffe* controllers, were driving forward remorselessly, although the Russians were far from beaten.

elow One of the *Luftwaffe's* ajor bombers, the Junkers 88, like the Mosquito, was sed in a variety of roles hich included level bombing, ose support, night fighting nd reconnaissance. Some ,000 of this aircraft were ilt.

CHAPTER THIRTEEN

THE JAPANESE AIR SERVICES 1919·45

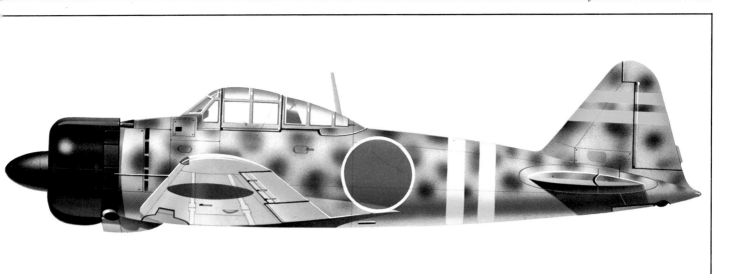

Below Comrades cheer a Japanese kamikaze pilot as his Mitsubishi A6M Reisen Zero fighter is taxied to take-off position on a Philippine airfield, during Japanese operations against the US invasion of Leyte in 1944. During October-November of that year, 424 suicide sorties were flown, and of the 249 planes expended 238 were Zeros.
Inset This illustration shows a Mitsubishi A6M3 Zero, built in 1943.

In 1919, the new importance of the Imperial Japanese Army's air arm, which had been growing steadily during World War I, despite its parent force's very minor part in that conflict, was signalised by its elevation to the status of Army Air Division under the command of Major-General Ikutaro Inouye.

Shortly after this, the Army Air Service was established as a result of the recommendations of a French air mission of sixty-three instructors led by Colonel Faure. Apart from advising on modern training and operational methods and organisations, the mission also recommended that the Japanese aircraft manufacturing industry, which was being built up with government aid, should concentrate on the production of proven European aircraft (most of them French) pending the design of indigenous Japanese aircraft. In this way, the Japanese were advised, they would secure an excellent grounding in modern construction methods before moving on to the more difficult and ambitious aspects of aircraft design. The army therefore adopted a number of French types as its primary equipment, among them the Spad 13 fighter, the Nieuport 24 advanced fighter trainer, and the Salmson 2 general-purpose and reconnaissance aircraft. Some British types were also adopted, including the Sopwith Pup and the Avro 504K primary trainer.

Further progress was made in 1925, when the Army Air Corps was established on 1 May. Ranking with the other arms of the army, it was put under the command of Lieutenant-General Kinichi Yasumitsu, head of the *Koku Hombu* (Air Headquarters). This new formation had some 500 aircraft and a personnel strength of 3,700 officers and men. The force shortly began to accept for service its first aircraft of Japanese design.

Further Japanese-designed aircraft came to the fore in the various 'brush-fire' wars in which Japan was involved during the 1920s and early 1930s, before large-scale operations in Manchuria and China convinced the Imperial Headquarters that the size of the Army Air Corps was inadequate to meet demands upon it, and so during the 1930s the force was built up and equipped with more modern aircraft, most of them Japanese in origin, although strong Western influences could be seen in their designs. It was this western influence, and the continued Japanese purchase or licence-production of European and American aircraft, that combined with a general feeling that the Japanese must be inferior, that led the politicians and commanders of the western powers who would face Japan in World War II seriously to underestimate the abilities of Japan's aircraft designers.

So it was that while this build-up of the Army Air Corps was being pushed ahead during the 1930s that major war with China and Russia flared up. Despite the importance attached to the Chinese war by the Japanese government, the army was in the short term more concerned with the expansion programme initiated earlier in the decade, and so concentrated its efforts to a support role in the north, using the forces located in the puppet state of Manchukuo, lately Manchuria, under the semi-autonomous control of the army's Kanto Command.

The border clashes with Russia, which soon turned into major confrontations, however, were taken far more seriously by the Kanto Command. And it was in these extremely costly battles that the aircraft with which the army's air units were to enter World War II were blooded or conceived. Concerned with the direct support of land units on the battlefield, and the

provision of tactical bombing support and recon naissance, the army decided that the type of aircraft needed were short-range machines, of relatively simple construction, with adequate performance and grea agility, and designed primarily for operations in the northern China area, where the atmosphere tended to be dry and cold.

This decision, as early as 1938, that Russia was to be regarded as the prime enemy, was to have a disastrou effect on the army's air effort in World War II. For it aircraft were on the whole not suited to operations in hot, humid climes, or to intensive flying over water.

With the end of the Manchurian incident, and the establishment of Manchukuo, the army decided that a increased air establishment was desirable. Thus it wa decided that between 1933 and 1935 an additional ter *Chutais* would be formed, bringing the total numbe available to thirty-six – fourteen fighter, twelve recon naissance, six light bomber and four heavy bomber.

As part of this expansion there was also to be a reorganisation, affecting principally the Kanto Com mand (*Kantogun*) which was to have a reconstitute *Hikotai* (Air Command) of three *Hiko Daitai* (Ai Battalions), later in 1933 renamed *Hiko Rentais* (Ai Wings). While this scheme was under way, though, the army again reconsidered, and decided on yet anothe expansion, this time to fifty-three squadrons, or anothe

Right The photograph shows Japanese pilots prior to a sortie.

176

eventeen, this figure to be achieved by 1938. These quadrons were to form sixteen *Hiko Rentais* in the apanese home islands, Korea, Formosa, and two in Manchukuo in support of the *Kantogun*.

Just as important, moreover, was the fact that at this me the army at last removed command of air units rom the ground formations with which they worked. The new command structure featured two new organizations: the *Koku Heidan* (Air Command) to control all ombat air units, and the *Hikodan* (Air Wing) to control wo to five *Sentais* or Groups. In the *Kantogun*, though, he command element was called the *Hiko Shudan* Joint Air Group). Command of the *Koku Heidan* was xercised by Lieutenant-General Yoshitoshi To-ugawa, who had made the first powered flight in apan.

The plan had been implemented in 1936, doubling he size of the army air service in only three years. But lmost immediately new schemes were under way for an xpansion by another eighty-nine squadrons within the ext six years, so that by 1942 there should be 142 quadrons – forty fighter, thirty-nine light bomber, hirty heavy bomber, twenty-nine reconnaissance and wo super-heavy bomber. Deployment was to be fifty-ight in Japan, fifty-seven in Manchukuo, sixteen in Korea and eleven in Formosa. Most notable in the new lan was the large number of bomber squadrons.

Quite apart from equipment, moreover, the nature of air operations in the late 1930s persuaded the army to introduce a new structure into its air service. Previously, the Army Air Corps had been composed of *Hiko Rentais* (Air Regiments) made up of a number of *Chutais* (Squadrons or perhaps Companies), the latter being equipped with fighter, bomber, reconnaissance or transport aircraft. Air warfare over China, despite the relative lack of opposition, soon convinced the army that a more flexible organisation, based on smaller units, was desirable. Thus the *Hiko Rentais* were replaced by *Sentais* (Groups), which were smaller and contained only aircraft of one function as their basic combat element. This system soon proved its efficiency in China, where the smaller and more flexible *Sentais* performed with proportionally greater success than the older *Rentais*.

The formation of air armies preceded the introduction of air corps, which were at first intended only as temporary command formations for reserve air units and for air regiments and air divisions staging up to the fronts' air armies. After their introduction, however, the air corps were seen to have a useful operational command function and became a permanent feature of the air armies, with specialisation into fighter, ground-attack and bomber roles depending on their equipment. The operational reserve, originally commanded by various corps, was an important adjunct to the frontal air armies: during important offensives it controlled as many as 2,000 aircraft. By 1943 the air corps had become a permanent feature of frontal aviation, the ADD and the PVO, but not in the Naval Air Forces.

The normal strength of the air corps was usually three or four air divisions, each containing some three or four air regiments. Some corps, though, had as many as seven air divisions, and others as few as one.

Throughout the war, the air regiment was the largest Red Air Force unit to have a fixed establishment, although this varied very considerably with the fluctuations of Russia's fortunes. During late 1941 and 1942, for example, the regiments were quite small; by 1945 they had increased in size by a large factor.

By 1944, each fighter and ground-attack regiment has an establishment of three squadrons, each made up of three flights (*zvenos*) each having four aircraft. Thus the fighter and ground-attack regiments had thirty-six aircraft. Bomber regiments, though, had only twenty-seven aircraft, the flights having only three aircraft each; reconnaissance regiments operated on the same establishment as bomber regiments.

Apart from the regiments in the air divisions, there were independent regiments, and sometimes divisions, attached to the headquarters of air armies. These were mostly reconnaissance units, reflecting the importance attached to tactical reconnaissance by front-line commanders.

At the lowest tactical levels, the squadrons and *zvenos* of fighter and ground-attack regiments were split up into *paras* of two aircraft (two *paras* forming a *zveno*), two *zvenos* forming a *gruppe* of eight aircraft.

During World War II, therefore, the Red Air Force as such was employed mostly as a tactical adjunct of the Red Army, providing it with tactical and long-range reconnaissance information, and finally ensuring the low- and medium-altitude air superiority over the battlefield that allowed the great ground-attack and medium bomber forces available to play a decisive part in the Red Army's efforts. To meet these requirements the Red Air Force was organised in an apparently

monolithic way, which has persuaded most postwar commentators into the simple error that the Red Air Force was an inflexible force commanded only by men of inferior abilities.

An examination of the Red Air Force's record during the war, however, will quickly dispel any such notion – Russia's air arm operated with great flexibility and imagination within the tasks laid down for it, under the command of some very able senior and middle-ranking commanders. By the end of the war, moreover, the standard of junior commanders had improved considerably, making them almost a qualitative match for their German opponents. Tactically, too, the Russians proved themselves ready to experiment and to profit from experience, so that by the middle of 1944 the ground-attack and medium bomber arms were sophisticated and highly successful support forces.

The *Sentai* consisted nominally of three *Chutais*, each deploying some nine to twelve aircraft, and the *Sentai Hombu* (Group Headquarters). The commander was usually a major or lieutenant-colonel. Next up the structural ladder was the *Hikodan* (Wing, or perhaps Air Brigade) commanded by a colonel or major-general. The *Hikodan* comprised a *Shireibu Hikodan* (Brigade Command Section), a reconnaissance unit of up to *Sentai* strength, and a combination of three *Sentoki Sentais* (Fighter Squadrons), *Keibaku Sentais* (Light Bomber Squadrons) or *Jubaku Sentais* (Heavy Bomber Squadrons).

Next up the command ladder was the *Hikoshidan* (Air Division), usually commanded by a lieutenant-general, and made up of two or three *Hikodans*. Finally there was the *Kokugun* (Air Army), again commanded by a lieutenant-general. Also possible within the rather stratified command structure were independent units such as the *Dokuritsu Shijugo Chutais* (Independent Squadrons) and *Dokuritsu Hikotais* (Independent Wings).

The whole organisation was run at the top by the Imperial Japanese Army itself, which was answerable to the *Daihonei* (Imperial General Headquarters), which could call upon the *Sanbo* (Chief of Army General Staff) as necessary. For air matters the *Sanbo* called upon the *Koku Sokambu* (Inspectorate General for Aviation) and the *Koku Hombu* (Air Headquarters). Of these last two the former was responsible for training of both flying and ground personnel, and the latter for design and research in all aspects of flying equipment, amongst other things.

This reorganisation was completed in 1939, in time to feature in the final stages of the confrontation with Russia, and in the continuing war against the Chinese. But in 1940 and 1941, the attentions of the Japanese high command were fixed ever more strongly outwards towards South-East Asia and the Pacific, where it seemed more and more likely that the Japanese empire would have to come to blows with the United States, Great Britain and her empire, and the Netherlands empire in the East Indies. Only if these areas, rich in many raw materials, especially tin, rubber and oil, were secured and the Allied powers held at bay, could Japan complete her war in China, essential for a number of political and economic reasons.

Given the limitations of its aircraft, which made it all but impossible for its aircraft to be deployed usefully in the Pacific Ocean theatre, the army was assigned primary responsibility for the Asia theatre, which included the Philippines and the Dutch East Indies. While large numbers of aircraft and units already tied

down in operations over China, the army could deploy only 700 of its 1,500 first-line aircraft for the southward drive. These forces were divided between two *Hikoshidans*: the 3rd for operations against Malaya, and the 5th for operations in the Philippines.

The 3rd *Hikoshidan* was composed as follows (450 aircraft):
3rd *Hikodan* (59th *Sentai* with Ki-27 and Ki-43 aircraft, 27th *Sentai* with Ki-51, 75th *Sentai* with Ki-48 and the 90th *Sentai* with Ki-48); 7th *Hikodan* (64th *Sentai* with Ki-27 and Ki-43, 12th *Sentai* with Ki-21-II, 60th *Sentai* with Ki-21-II and the 98th *Sentai* with Ki-21-II); 12th *Hikodan* (1st *Sentai* with Ki-27 and the 11th *Sentai* with Ki-27); the 15th *Dokuritsu Hikotai* (50th and 51st *Dokuritsu Dai Shijugo Chutais* with Ki-15 and Ki-46); the 81st *Sentai* with Ki-15 and Ki-46; and the 21st *Dokuritsu Hikotai* (82nd *Dokuritsu Dai Shijugo Chutai* with Ki-30 and the 84th *Dokuritsu Dai Shijugo Chutai* with Ki-27).

The 5th *Hikoshidan* had the following composition (250 aircraft):
4th *Hikodan* (50th *Sentai* with Ki-27, 8th *Sentai* with Ki-30 and Ki-48, and the 14th *Sentai* with Ki-21-I); 10th *Hikodan* (77th *Sentai* with Ki-27, 31st *Sentai* with Ki-30 and the 62nd *Sentai* with Ki-21-II); 10th *Dokuritsu Hikotai* (74th *Dokuritsu Dai Shijugo Chutai* with Ki-36, 52nd *Dokuritsu Dai Shijugo Chutai* with Ki-51 and the 76th *Dokuritsu Dai Shijugo Chutai* with Ki-15); the 16th *Sentai* with Ki-30; and the 11th *Hiko Chutai* with Ki-57.

Overall command of this major air effort was the responsibility of the Southern *Kokugun*, which thus controlled some sixty-eight of the army's 150 available *Chutais*. At the same time there continued at home the expansion initiated by the army in May 1937, with special emphasis on aircrew. By 1939 there were already in existence the Army Air Academy and the Army Juvenile Flying School, the latter accepting boys from the age of fifteen on; there were also four flying schools, located at Akeno, Hamamatsu, Kumgaya and Shimoshi.

In the following twelve months the army established another four schools: at Gifu for basic flight training, at Hokota for light bombing, at Mito for gunnery and communications, and at Paichengtso for navigation. At the same time the 101st to 108th *Sentais* were formed as operational training groups. It seems, therefore, as though the army had appreciated the need for replacement aircrews made all too apparent in the Mongolian border clashes. But the war in the Pacific was to show that they had no real conception of the needs of really prolonged operations such as would have to be fought against the Americans and British.

The army at first seemed to be on the right lines, the initial nine months of the Pacific war proving almost universally successful for Japanese arms. Despite these actual successes, however, it soon became apparent that all was not well, especially with the types of aircraft and their roles.

Firstly, non-combat losses to local climatic conditions at last revealed that the Manchurian theatre was not ideal for the exclusive combat evaluation of new types, and secondly the switch in priority, dating from 1936, from bomber development to fighter development, appeared a mistake. For although the bombers continued to perform with more than a little credit, it was seen that a more balanced policy would have been in order, with better protected bombers capable of delivering larger payloads becoming increasingly essential. Fighters, too, it was realised, would profit from

Opposite page Aircraft and aft flightdeck burn on the American aircraft carrier USS *Belleau Wood* (CVL-24) following a kamikaze attack in 1944. The ship was part of the invasion fleet off Leyte in the Philippines.

better armament and protection, even at the expense of manoeuvrability.

By late 1942 the two areas in which the Japanese army air service was involved most heavily, apart from China, where the Americans were having an increasingly successful time of it, were Burma and the New Guinea-Solomon islands theatre. In this latter area the Americans were making a determined effort to wear down the Japanese air strength with a war of attrition, and had by the middle of 1943 largely succeeded. Although their policy was not as clearly defined, the British were succeeding with a similar policy in Burma, especially during 1944.

It should be noted here, though, that right through this first stage of the war (in which the Japanese army and navy had at first swept all before them, then disagreed fundamentally on the right strategic stop-line before overextending themselves, before being checked and then pushed back by the Allies) the army's major preoccupation had been with the war in China and with the threat to the security of Manchukuo posed by the Russians, notwithstanding the non-aggression pact with that country. The extent of this preoccupation may be gauged by the deployment of the army's air units in July 1942:

the 1st *Kokugun* was charged with the defence of the Japanese home islands and of Manchukuo, for which it had the 17th, 18th and 19th *Hikodans*, and the 20th *Hikodan* of the 1st *Hikoshidan*;

the 2nd *Kokugun* was concerned with Manchukuo only, for which it had the 2nd, 6th and 8th *Hikodans* of the 2nd *Hikoshidan* with seven *Sentais*, the 9th, 10th, 13th and 14th *Hikodans* of the 4th *Hikoshidan* with ten *Sentais*, and the 15th and 28th *Dokuritsu Hikotais* with four *Dokuritsu Dai Shijugo Chutais*, plus the independent 2nd *Sentai* for strategic reconnaissance;

the 3rd (Southern) *Kokugun* looked after matters on the 'Southern Front' and in China, with the 4th *Hikodan* and 83rd *Dokuritsu Hikotai* of the 5th *Hikoshidan* (three *Sentais* and three *Dokuritsu Dai Shijugo Chutais*) located in Burma, the four *Sentais* and three transport squadrons of the same *Hikoshidan*'s 7th *Hikodan* in Malaya, the three *Sentais* and one *Dokuritsu Dai Shijugo Chutai* of the same *Hikoshidan*'s 3rd *Hikodan* in Java, the two *Sentais* of the same *Hikoshidan*'s 12th *Hikodan* in Sumatra, and the two *Dokuritsu Dai Shijugo Chutais* and two transport squadrons of the 21st *Dokuritsu Dai Shijugo Hikotai* in Indo-China; the three *Dokuritsu Dai Shijugo Chutais* of the 10th *Dokuritsu Dai Shijugo Hikotai* in the Philippines; and in China the 3rd *Hikoshidan* comprising the eight *Sentais* of the 1st *Hikodan* and the eight *Dokuritsi Dai Shijugo Chutais* of the 206th *Dokuritsu Dai Shijugo Hikotai*.

Thus about half the active strength of the army air service was deployed in Japan proper and in Manchuria, where it could play little direct part in the war being fought farther south.

The army was still planning expansion (there were the 101st, 102nd and 103rd Training *Hikodans* in Japan, and the 204th and 208th *Sentais* of the Hakujoshi Training *Hikodan* in Manchuria), but in the course of 1942 only thirty-three new *Chutais* were formed: twenty-three fighter, five light bomber, three reconnaissance and two ground co-operation. Thus at the end of 1941 the army had possessed some 150 *Chutais* (fifty-five fighter, thirty-three light bomber, thirty-two heavy bomber, twenty-nine reconnaissance and one transport); a year later it only had 170 *Chutais* (seventy-one fighter, thirty-seven light bomber, thirty-two heavy

bomber, twenty-nine reconnaissance and one transport).

Thus although they had swept all before them in the opening stages of their war, the Japanese found that their initial success was largely attributable to the fact that their aircraft, of the latest design, were superior to the obsolescent types which the Allies had deployed against them. In addition, the Japanese aircrew were almost universally superior to their Allied opponents because of the combat experience they had obtained against the Chinese and Russians.

After their first setbacks, therefore, the Allies deployed the very latest aircraft to the Pacific as quickly as possible, and once British and American pilots had come to grips with the tactical problems posed by the manoeuvrability and experience of their opponents, they soon proved themselves more than adequate matches for the Japanese. The boot was now on the other foot, and the Japanese pilots found that their lack of modern aircraft, with heavy armament, high speed, great strength, self-sealing fuel tanks and armour protection, gave the Allies a distinct qualitative edge.

Moreover, as the American air and sea stranglehold on Japan's sea routes began to have its effect, and as the American strategic bombing effort against Japan's industries, communications and cities bit deep, fewer and fewer aircraft, even of the obsolescent models, were forthcoming from the factories. And the virtual cutting off of the supplies of crude oil to the Japanese refining centres meant that aircrew, already in short supply, just could not be trained in the quantities, let alone the qualities, of the aircrew being lost to the growing number of Allied fighters and bombers.

By 1944, then, the Japanese army air service found itself in a vicious circle: Allied strength was inflicting severe losses on it, but new aircrew could not be trained,

Below Fast, light and manoeuvrable, the Mitsubishi A5M was the Imperial Japanese Navy's chief fighter in the Sino-Japanese war, and the most numerous aircraft at Pearl Harbor. A carrier-based fighter armed with two 0.303 in. machine guns, this was the predecessor of the famous A6M 'Zero'.

nor could new aircraft be put into large-scale production, because there were not the aircrew or the aircraft with which to meet and destroy the Allied air effort directed against the supplies of raw materials needed for aircraft production and aircrew training in Japan herself.

During 1944, therefore, in Burma, New Guinea, the Philippines, Formosa and China, the army air service was slowly whittled down and rendered all but impotent during 1945, despite the introduction of *Kamikaze* tactics, known as *taiatari* sorties in the army.

Unlike the army, the fortunes of the Imperial Japanese Navy's air arm suffered a decline immediately after the end of World War I, the only event of notable importance being the first deck take-off by a Japanese pilot, Lieutenant Kuwabara, from a specially constructed platform on the *Wakamiya Maru* on June 1920. Shortly after this, though, a British naval air mission led by the Master of Sempill arrived, and this revitalised Japanese naval aviation, as signified by the launching on 13 November 1921 of the *Hosho*, the first aircraft-carrier in the world to be designed as such from the keel up.

During the 1920s the Japanese naval air arm continued with wide-ranging experiments into the operation and use of naval aircraft, many of the tests being carried out by a series of aircraft designed in Japan by Herbert Smith, late of the Sopwith aircraft company. In fact, during the 1920s and early 1930s there was a thriving little community of foreign aircraft designers in Japan, principally from Great Britain, Germany, France and the United States, the most celebrated being Smith and Dr. Richard Vogt, later the designer of some excellent Blohm und Voss flying-boats back in Germany. These men provided the basic aircraft used by the Japanese in building up their air forces and their

Bottom A flight of Mitsubishi G3M medium bombers, code-name 'Nells'. These entered service in 1937 and were used in the war against China. They also took part in World War II, 1,000 being built by the end of 1943.

aircraft manufacturing industry, providing qualified leadership for the teams of Japanese designers, trained at first abroad and later at home, who would soon have the experience necessary to initiate and control the design of wholly Japanese aircraft.

It should be noted, moreover, that though during this period the Japanese also bought and licence-built a number of European and American aircraft, leading the western powers to think that they were incapable of designing adequate aircraft of their own, this was far from the case. Lacking any experience in engineering of this type, the Japanese were keen to buy and test all types of foreign aircraft, thus getting experience of all types of aircraft design and manufacture, before setting out on their own. Finally, however, they had a keen understanding of western aeronautical thinking, and were able to design and build aircraft of their own that were certainly reminiscent of western types, but individually engineered and usually lighter than their western counterparts.

Like the army air service, the naval air service adopted the useful competitive method of aircraft procurement, designs from a variety of companies being considered before a limited number of prototypes was ordered. These prototypes were then air- and ground-tested against each other to find the best all-round machine, which was then ordered into mass production, usually at a number of factories as the small companies then operating in Japan could not handle large orders on their own.

Although both Japanese air services had made good progress in the early 1920s, it was only in 1927, after the Emperor Hirohito had come to the imperial throne on the death of the Emperor Taisho, that the expansion of the two air services began to accelerate in earnest. By 1929 the army had realised its 1925 expansion programme, with eight air wings to cooperate with the most important army divisions. These 1st to 8th Air wings were based, respectively, at Kasumigaura (1st and 2nd), Yokaichi, Tachiarai, Tachikawa, Pyongyang (in Korea), Hamamatsu and Pingtung (in Formosa). The army's feeling about the utility of aircraft for anything but short-range tactical tasks may be gauged from the fact that of the 26 *Chutais* available, eleven were fighter units, eleven were reconnaissance units, and only four were equipped with bombers.

The navy had started on an ambitious expansion programme in 1920, but by 1927 this had achieved little. Then in that year the navy, like the army, established a *Kaigun Koku Hombu* (Navy Air HQ) to take over the administration of the navy's air arm. This move resulted almost immediately in the speeding up of the navy's expansion programme, and by 1931 all seventeen squadrons planned had been formed.

These were allocated to the six air corps (*Kokutai*) located at the six naval air bases, the last two of which, at Tateyama and Kure, had been commissioned in 1930 and 1931 respectively. The Kasumigaura *Kokutai* had seven squadrons, the Kure *Kokutai* $\frac{1}{2}$ squadron, the Ohmura *Kokutai* two squadrons, the Sasebo *Kokutai* $1\frac{1}{2}$ squadrons, the Tateyama *Kokutai* $3\frac{1}{2}$ squadrons and the Yokosuka *Kokutai* $2\frac{1}{2}$ squadrons. Of these seventeen squadrons, $4\frac{1}{2}$ were seaplane reconnaissance squadrons, $2\frac{1}{2}$ land-based attack, two each carrier-borne fighter, land-based reconnaissance and flying-boat squadrons, $1\frac{1}{2}$ each land-based reconnaissance and flying-boat squadrons, $1\frac{1}{2}$ each land-based and seaplane training squadrons, making only six of the squadrons land-based. Nonetheless, the Imperial Japanese Navy had begun to develop a keen appreciation of land-based aircraft for naval purposes of all types. (It should be remembered here that the Imperial Japanese Navy had its own infantry forces for operations in naval theatres of war, and this was one of the factors that led the navy towards its appreciation of the value of aircraft for both land and sea warfare.)

Just as the army was keen to expand its air service in the mid-1930s, so too was the navy. The new expansion would be possible with the generation of aircraft just coming into service after the requirements issued in 1932 by the then-new Naval Aircraft Establishment.

This first expansion plan had been the result of the London Naval Treaty of 1930, which had limited Japanese naval tonnage severely. In an effort to offset this, the navy wished to expand its air arm very considerably by the establishment of twenty-eight new land-based squadrons and the building of a 10,000-ton aircraft-carrier. For a number of reasons the Japanese government had refused to allow the building of the carrier, and had sanctioned only fourteen new squadrons. This programme would give the navy thirty-one squadrons by 1938, and these would form nine *Kokutais* (the existing six and three new ones at Ohminato, Saeki and Yokohama. The squadrons were to be 8½ torpedo-bomber, six seaplane reconnaissance, four large flying-boat, four fighter, three trainer, two small flying-boat and 1½ experimental.

While this programme was being implemented, the Shanghai Incident occurred, and the navy immediately called for extra strength as part of a second expansion – eight land-based squadrons, two 20,000-ton aircraft-carriers, three 13,000-ton seaplane carriers and new air corps at Kanoya, Kisarazu and Maizuru in Japan, and at Chinhe in Korea. By September 1937 the navy had thirty-nine land-based squadrons in thirteen *Kokutais*, these squadrons including three dive-bomber and 6½ twin-engined medium bomber units. At the same time the navy had some 2,710 aircrew to man its 563 land-based and 332 shipborne aircraft.

In 1934, in the United States, the Vinson Plan for naval expansion had been initiated, and in 1937 the Imperial Japanese Navy responded by forming another fourteen squadrons, building more aircraft and laying the keels of another two aircraft-carriers.

The programme was completed in 1940, giving the Imperial Navy 30½ land-based operational squadrons with 381 aircraft, 22½ training squadrons with 446 aircraft, and carrier-borne aircraft totalling 1,088. Twelve new *Kokutais* had been formed, bringing the total to twenty-five, of which fifteen were operational and ten training.

Yet more was to come when details of the second Vinson Plan were published in 1938 – a 34,000-ton aircraft-carrier, seventy-five land-based squadrons and more aircraft, in a five-year plan to begin in 1939. Its completion in 1944 would, it was anticipated, give the navy 128 squadrons with 2,294 land-based and 520 shipborne aircraft.

Vast though this programme was, especially in financial terms, the deteriorating position in the Pacific, where war with the United States and Great Britain loomed, made the navy call for completion of the plan in 1941. This tremendous target was very nearly achieved, moreover, in terms of aircraft: 1,095 aircraft in sixty-five land-based squadrons, and 690 aircraft on ships.

But although aircraft production had been excellent, crews and all equipment and spares were in short supply, despite the formation of six of the planned

182

sixteen new *Kokutais* (eight operational and eight training) at Bihoro in Korea, Hakata, Komatsujima, Tainang on Formosa, Tonkong on Formosa and Won-san in Korea. This raised the navy's strength to thirty-seven *Kokutai*, twenty-five of them operational ones.

The Imperial Japanese Navy responded very swiftly to the third Vinson Plan for US Navy expansion: a fifth expansion programme to raise strength to 160 squadrons with 5,500 aircraft. The programme started in autumn 1941, and had it been completed, would have given the Imperial Japanese Navy 132 operational squadrons with 2,696 aircraft, plus 2,040 ship-based and transport machines, 156 training squadrons with 3,670 aircraft, for a grand total of some 8,400 aircraft and 31,500 aircrew.

To match its vastly expanded strength, the Imperial Japanese Navy restructured its air organisation. At the top there was still the *Daihonei* (Imperial Headquarters), to which reported the *Gunreibu Socho* (Chief of the Naval General Staff). To this person was responsible the *Kaigun Koku Hombu* (Navy Air Headquarters), which was the controlling body for equipment of all types as well as for the training of all types of personnel. Operationally, the navy's aircraft were controlled by *Kantais* (Fleets), *Koku Kantais* (Air Fleets) and *Homen Kantais* (Area Fleets).

This reflects the growing importance of the air element in Japanese naval thinking, for before the January–April 1941 restructure the term *Kantai* had been reserved for major fleets of warships alone. Below this level, carrier-borne aircraft were part of *Koku Sentais* (Carrier Divisions, usually consisting of two aircraft-carriers. There was no fixed number of *Koku Sentais* to a *Koku Kantai*. Later in the war, it should be noted, this structure was altered, carrier-borne aircraft being allocated to *Kokutais* (Naval Air Corps), various numbers of *Kokutais* in turn being grouped to form *Koku Kantais*.

Land-based naval aircraft were formed into *Koku Kantais*, which in turn comprised one or more *Koku Sentais* (Air Flotillas), which were in turn made up of various *Kokutais*. The *Kokutai*, with up to 150 aircraft, was thus the basic organisational element in the Imperial Japanese Navy's air organisation.

At the time of the Japanese attack on Pearl Harbor, which started the war in the Pacific on 7 December 1941, the naval air arm was disposed as follows, under the overall command of the *Rengo Kantai* (Combined Fleet) of Admiral Isoroku Yamamoto:

the 3rd *Koku Sentai* was deployed to the 1st *Kantai*, with A5ms and B4Ys on the *Hosho*, A5Ms and B5Ns on the *Zuiho* and seaplanes on the fleet's battleships and cruisers;

various seaplanes were deployed to the 2nd *Kantai*'s cruisers ; the 12th *Koku Sentai* deployed its seaplanes aboard the seaplane carriers *Kamikawa Maru* and *Sanyo Maru* of the 3rd *Kantai*, and there were other seaplanes aboard the *Kantai*'s cruisers and the tender *Sanuki Maru*;

the Chitose *Kokutai* (G3Ms) and Yokohama *Kokutai* (H6Ks) formed the 24th *Koku Sentai* of the 4th *Kantai*, which also controlled the seaplanes aboard the fleet's

Right A Mitsubishi A6M 'Zero' fails to crash land on the deck of the battleship USS *Missouri* (BB-63) during the massive kamikaze attacks which took place on 27-28 April 1945 during the Okinawa campaign.

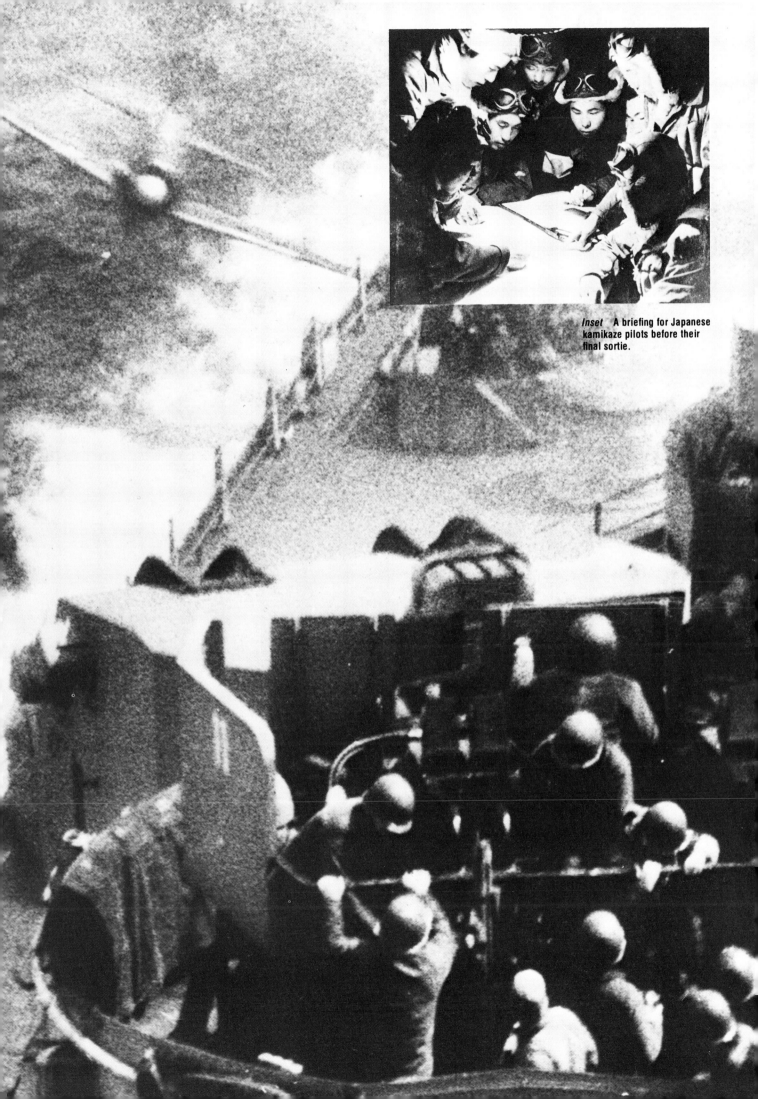

Inset A briefing for Japanese kamikaze pilots before their final sortie.

cruisers, minelayer and seaplane carrier *Kikokawa Maru*, and the seaplanes of the 16th, 17th, 18th and 19th *Kokutais*;

seaplanes were part of the 5th *Kantai*'s equipment aboard the seaplane carriers *Chichijima Maru* and *Kimikawa Maru*;

a few seaplanes were also allocated to the seaplane carriers *Sagara Maru* and *Kashii* of the *Nanha Homen Kantai* (Southern Area Fleet);

the 1st *Koku Kantai* deployed the A6Ms, D3As and B5Ns of the 1st *Koku Sentai* on the aircraft-carriers *Akagi* and *Kaga*, the A6Ms, D3As and B5Ns of the 2nd *Koku Sentai* on the aircraft-carriers *Soryu* and *Hiryu*, the A5Ms and B5Ns of the 4th *Koku Sentai* on the aircraft-carrier *Ryujo*, and the A6Ms, D3As and B5Ns of the 5th *Koku Sentai* on the aircraft-carriers *Zuikaku* and *Shokaku*; the 11th *Koku Kantai* controlled the 21st *Koku Sentai* (the 1st *Kokutai* with G4Ms, the Kanoya *Kokutai* with G4Ms, and the Toko *Kokutai* with H6Ks), the 22nd *Koku Sentai* (the Genzan *Kokutai* with G3Ms, the Mihoro *Kokutai* with G3Ms and a Special Detachment with C5Ms and A6Ms), the 23rd *Koku Sentai* (the 3rd Kokutai with A6Ms and C5Ms, the Tainan *Kokutai* with A6Ms and C5Ms, and the Takao *Kokutai* with G3Ms) and a special allocation of seaplanes on the seaplane carriers *Mizuho* and *Chitose*; and finally the *Shina Homen Kantai* (China Area Fleet) had a special detachment with B5Ns and some seaplanes.

Combat experienced after its operations in China, and possessing the right aircraft and training for long flights over water, the Imperial Japanese Navy was given a primary responsibility for operations in the Pacific, the 1st *Koku Kantai* being allocated the all-important task of crippling the US Pacific Fleet in Pearl Harbor on 7 December 1941, with the 11th *Koku Kantai* having the task, only slightly less important, of covering the operations of the army in South-East Asia.

The progress of the Japanese naval air arm, and indeed of Japanese arms in general, may be summarised by the activities of the 1st *Koku Kantai* in the first half year of war. After the tactically successful, but strategically incomplete, victory at Pearl Harbor, the 1st *Koku Kantai* went on to roam about the Pacific Ocean, and even venture into the Indian Ocean, striking at Wake Island, Rabaul, Amboina, the Marshall islands, Darwin and Ceylon before finally being halted in the Battle of the Coral Sea.

Final efforts took the Japanese into the Solomon islands, but then came the first, and as it turned out decisive, defeat in the Battle of Midway, where the 1st *Koku Kantai* lost four aircraft-carriers together with their aircraft, and perhaps most important, their irreplaceable aircrews.

It was after this battle that the Imperial Japanese Navy first began to realise that its pre-war expansion had taken the wrong lines for what was turning out to be a sustained war: having gambled on swift victory and not having secured it, the Imperial Japanese Navy was now finding that it did not have the reserves to match battle losses. And even the reserves that were available were not of the same calibre as those lost in operations

Right The front two rows of aircraft are Mitsubishi A6M 'Zeros', the outstanding Japanese combat aircraft of World War II. This fast, manoeuvrable fighter was the first carrier-based fighter to outperform corresponding land-based machines. It succeeded the Mitsubishi A5M 'Claude', seen in the third and fourth rows, which was an all-metal, stressed-skin monoplane.

up to the time of Midway, in which 216 aircrew had been lost.

The result of the Battle of Midway came as a profound shock to Imperial Headquarters, which judged, among other things, that one of the failings in the Battle of Midway had been the separation of the battleship force from the carrier force. Therefore the two were combined, as the 3rd *Kantai*, with the 1st *Koku Sentai* aboard the carriers *Shokaku*, *Zuikaku* and *Zuiho*, and the 2nd *Koku Sentai* on board the carriers *Ryujo*, *Junyo* and *Hiyo*. The rest of the navy's structure was also altered in July 1942, giving the following deployment (apart from the 3rd *Kantai*):

the 2nd *Kantai* had the 11th *Koku Sentai* operating from two seaplane carriers (*Chitose* and *Kemikawa Maru*);

the 4th *Kantai* had the 19th and 21st *Kokutais* operating from land bases, and seaplanes operating from the carriers *Kunikawa Maru* and *Kamui*;

the 5th *Kantai* had the 5th and Chichijima *Kokutais* operating from land bases, and seaplanes operating from the carrier *Kimikawa Maru*; the 8th *Kantai* had the 2nd *Kokutai* operating from land bases and seaplanes from the carrier *Kiyokawa Maru*;

the 11th *Koku Kantai* had four *Koku Sentais*, all operating from land bases – the 22nd with the Bihoro and Genzan (Wongsan) *Kokutais*, the 24th with the 1st, 14th and Chitose *Kokutais*, the 25th with the 24th, Tainan and Yokohama *Kokutais*, and the 26th with the 6th Kisarazu and Misawa *Kokutais*;

and the South-West *Homen Kantai* deployed a number of scattered air units – the 21st *Koku Sentai* (land-based Kanoya and Toko (Tongkong) *Kokutais*), the 23rd *Koku Sentai* (3rd and Takao (Kaoshun) *Kokutais*), the 1st Southern *Kantai* in Malaya and Indo-China with the 40th *Kokutai*, the 2nd Southern *Kantai* in the Dutch East Indies with the land-based 33rd, 34th, 35th and 36th *Kokutais*, and the 4th Transport Air Unit, the 3rd Southern *Kantai* in the Philippines with the land-based 31st and 32nd *Kokutais* and the 3rd Transport Air Unit, and in general reserve the 2nd and Yokosuka *Kokutais* and the 1st, 2nd, 5th and 6th Transport Air Units.

The new South-West *Homen Kantai*, it should be noted, had been formed after the Battle of Midway with the express mission of defending the Malaya, Indo-China, the Dutch East Indies and the Philippines from the Allied counter-offensive that could now be expected.

At the same time the 5th expansion programme, initiated on the eve of war, was radically changed, not at all realistically when the strain of the original 5th programme on the Japanese economy is recalled. The altered programme called for the construction of twenty-eight new aircraft-carriers (thirteen medium-sized *Hiryu* class, five large *Taiho* class, *Chitose* and *Chiyoda* converted from seaplane carriers into aircraft-carriers, three passenger liners to be converted, four battleships to be converted in 'hybrid' light aircraft-carrier/battleships, and the battleship *Shinano* to be converted into an aircraft-carrier). Only nine of these twenty-eight were completed by the end of the war, though. At the same time it was planned to build other warships, and also to raise the number of squadrons available to the Imperial Japanese Navy by the staggering figure of 659. These were to be as follows: (land-based) 100 fighter, sixty fighter-bomber, sixty twin-engined bomber, twenty-six patrol, eighteen floatplane bomber, twelve floatplane fighter, twelve flying-boat,

ten four-engined bomber, nine reconnaissance and four transport, these 311 squadrons to have 5,226 aircraft plus 2,229 reserve aircraft; (ship-based) eighty attack bomber, fifty-one fighter, twenty-one floatplane reconnaissance, eleven carrier reconnaissance and two floatplane fighter, these 165 squadrons to have 2,844 aircraft, giving a grand operational total of 476 aircraft and 10,299 aircraft; there were also to be 183 training squadrons with 4,939 aircraft, and some 936 transport aircraft.

The whole programme was planned for completion in 1947, when the Imperial Japanese Navy would have 787 squadrons with 19,083 aircraft, including units and aircraft currently on hand. The whole plan was in fact impossible, though by 1945 about half of it had been realised.

During 1942, moreover, further *Kokutais* were raised, giving the navy a strength of thirty-eight operational and twenty-four training *Kokutais* by the end of the year. There were at the same time alterations in nomenclature, the old place names for the *Kokutais* being replaced by three-figure numbers: the Chitose *Kokutai*, for example, became the 703rd *Kokutai*, and the Yokohama *Kokutai* the 801st *Kokutai*. The designations of the *Kokutais* that had already been numbered were also changed, the 19th *Kokutai* becoming the 952nd *Kokutai*.

Finally, in 1942, the South-West *Homen Kantai*, essentially an interim formation, was replaced by the South-East *Kantai*, a combination of the 4th *Kantai* and 11th *Koku Kantai*, to take part in the battles that were becoming increasingly bitter in the Solomons and New Guinea. For these battles the 4th *Kantai* had the 902nd and 952nd *Kokutais*, and the 11th *Koku Kantai* the 22nd *Koku Sentai* (252nd, 701st and 755th *Kokutais*), the 24th *Koku Sentai* (201st, 552nd, 703rd and 752nd *Kokutais*), the 25th *Koku Sentai* (251st, 702nd and 801st *Kokutais*), the 26th *Koku Sentai* (204th, 582nd and 705th *Kokutais*) and the independent 802nd *Kokutai*.

In real terms, this was the final stage of growth of the Imperial Japanese Navy's air arm, for thereafter, despite reorganisations and expansion to meet ever-increasing threats, the Japanese had lost the initiative with the Battle of Santa Cruz in October 1942, and were thereafter driven back onto the defensive. Once Guadalcanal had been evacuated in February 1943, the Allies mounted a major air effort in the New Guinea Area, and this cost the navy even dearer than the army. Slowly driven back in New Guinea, the Japanese lost aircraft and aircrew the whole time, a process repeated farther north as the carrier forces of the US Navy drove the inexperienced and poorly-equipped Japanese naval air forces from the skies over the Pacific islands that featured in Admiral Chester Nimitz's 'island-hopping' campaign towards the Philippines/Formosa area. Losses during the actual island campaigns were added to by frequent US carrier sweeps into Japanese-held areas.

The final knell for the Japanese naval air arm, whose crews and aircraft were wholly inferior to their American counterparts, was sounded in the 'Great Marianas Turkey Shoot' in the battle of the Philippine Sea during June 1944, losing most of the 450 aircraft involved.

Thereafter the naval air service battled on regardless, but despite the appearance of newer aircraft types, lack of skill and lack of production capacity meant that the naval air service, like that of the army, was slowly ground to virtual extinction in the closing months of the war in the Pacific.

CHAPTER FOURTEEN

THE RUSSIAN AIR SERVICES 1917·45

With the downfall of Kerensky's provisional government and the accession to power of the Bolshevik party in November 1917, the new master of Russia, Vladimir Ilyich Lenin, decided that the air units of the new state should be built up quickly, for political as well as economic reasons. The basic Tsarist units and organisations were to be retained in the short term, despite their many failings and shortcomings, but under Bolshevik control. Only in this way, Lenin reasoned, could the double threat of the non-Communist ('White') and foreign 'interventionist' war against the new 'Red' state be checked, the 'Red Air Fleet' being a principal prop of the Red Army, on which the main burden would fall.

The architect of the new force was Professor Zhukovsky, who drew up ambitious plans for the re-organisation of the Red Air Fleet and the industrial base on which it stood. In the long term, Zhukovsky planned, the Red Air Fleet would stand as one of the main bulwarks against foreign interference in Russia's affairs, and as a concrete proof of the Communists' educational, organisational, technological and industrial superiority.

Despite the enormous difficulties faced by the Communists in the civil and interventionist wars between 1917 and 1922, during most of which the central Communist state was assailed on four sides, by 1922 the air force had been increased in strength to some 400 aircraft. With the approach of victory in 1921, however, more concrete plans for the future were laid, signalised by the opening of the Zhukovsky Air Academy and a number of flying schools. But without any real aerodynamic background from which to develop their native talents, the Russians were at first willing to buy and to build foreign types, in the process gaining an empirical knowledge of western design and manufacturing concepts. At the same time, native designers were under training, and the first 'Communist' aircraft were being tested. This programme, though, only started to bear real fruit after 1924.

Given the chaos in which the Russian armed forces found themselves in 1917, it was hardly surprising that the first attempts to form a centralised Red Air Fleet were slow, even hesitant, the initial moves towards the necessary centralisation coming from Petrograd (soon

become Leningrad) before Moscow became the hub f military matters in December 1917.

On 20 December the earlier committee for aviation rganised by the War Commissariat of the Moscow Military District was replaced by the All-Russian Aviation Board, which operated under the aegis of the All-Russian Collegium for the Organisation of the Workers' and Peasants' Red Army, part of the Peoples' Commissariat for Military Matters. Under the Aviation Board, regional matters were administered by district oards, the whole structure being agencies of the Central Committee of the Communist Party.

So far the Communists had had relative peace in which to speed their activities. But with the signing of the Treaty of Brest-Litovsk in March 1918, by which Russia left World War I and the Germans ceased their eastward drive into Russia, there were clear signs of the wars to come. The Communists had fallen back as leanly as possible in front of the German advance, principally to preserve their forces for the internal struggle to come. By early 1918, for example, the Communists had been able to form about thirty-five squadrons from the remnants of the Tsarist air service, although the number of operational aircraft available in March was a maximum of 150 machines.

At the same time, naval flying units were also being re-formed, operating with the Lake Onega, Volga River and North Dvina River Fleets to start with, and then with the South Astrakhan, Dniepr, Don and West Dvina River Fleets. Other naval air units were formed to operate with the Baltic and Black Sea Fleets. Control of this service had by March 1918 centred on the Administration of the Naval Air Force, located in Moscow.

While these operational units were being formed, the central administration had been working at a feverish pace on the production of politically reliable personnel for the new force at a number of establishments, notably at Gatchina and Moscow. Naval training was undertaken at Oranienbaum, which was later supplemented by Nizhni Novgorod and Sevastopol.

Despite continued German encroachment into Russia, little could at first be done in 1918 because, although there were considerable forces under arms, they lacked the food, ammunition and other supplies necessary to fight any effective war.

The trouble lay in the fact that although there were any number of administrative departments, they all got in each other's way, causing a bureaucratic muddle there was no overall controller to clear up. Matters began to improve, however, with the appointment in July 1918 of Leon Trotsky to head a field staff charged with the overall direction of the armed forces, including the Central Administration of the Workers' and Peasants' Red Air Fleet, which had taken over from the All-Russian Aviation Board in May.

Trotsky's appointment did much to help clear up the mass of red tape which hindered the Russian military machine, especially after his elevation to the chairmanship of the Revolutionary Military Committee in September 1918. This body co-ordinated all the operational and administrative aspects of the Red Army and its support elements. Finally, in November 1918, the prosecution of the war was placed in the hands of the Council of Workers' and Peasants' Defence, whose chairman was Lenin, and two of whose members were Trotsky and Josef Stalin. The Council exercised control of the separate Red Army and Red Navy through the General Headquarters of the Revolutionary Military Committee.

The Red Air Fleet was not represented on the Revolutionary Military Committee, which ran the air service through the Field Administration of the Red Air Fleet, set up in September 1918. Actual command of

Ilyushin Il-2 Stormovik ground-attack aircraft flying at a typical low-level cruising altitude. Possibly the most important Russian aircraft of World War II, the Il-2 was built in greater numbers than any aircraft before or since, some 36,163 being made.

the field units, it should be noted, was nominally the job of new Communist commanders, although real command was exercised by ex-Tsarist officers, who acted only under the strictest control of political commissars.

By 1920 there were five Chief Aviation Administrations of the Front, subordinate to the Central Administration, whose task was to control the air units of the Chief Aviation Administrations of the Army, principally squadrons under the tactical command of army formations, as well as balloon units. In 1918 these squadrons, which were made up of two flights, each of some five aircraft, were sometimes combined into groups, with two squadrons to a group. These units were in theory categorised as fighter, reconnaissance, artillery observation or propaganda squadrons, but in fact served in any capacity. There were, however, no bomber squadrons.

In late 1919 this organisation was altered, larger numbers of aircraft being available. Aviation divisions, each containing four or more squadrons, were formed by the amalgamation of two aviation groups. Later still, air divisions were grouped together under a single command for special purposes. Naval air units were also grouped as divisions, with their subordinate units allocated to the Soviet fleets in the White, Baltic, Black, Azov and Caspian Seas.

Following the end of the civil and interventionists wars, the divisions once again gave way to squadrons. It should be noted here, however, that these wartime organisations were largely nominal, as the actual strength of the Russian air forces was only about one-third of the planned establishment at peak strength. Indeed, in the Baltic area, it is reckoned in April 1921

that the three naval air divisions had only nine aircraft and very few more pilots – in real terms only about one squadron.

During the civil war, the logistics of each squadron were semi-autonomous, with supplies and other equipment coming up to the front from each squadron's supply depot. At the front, the few half-trained mechanics did as much as they could with the aid of drafted unskilled personnel. More difficult repair jobs, though, were the responsibility of special repair trains, which operated some 50 miles (80 km) behind the front. These trains, with some twenty-five carriages and 110 men, were allocated one to each of the seventeen Soviet field armies, and could handle engine and airframe repairs to the tune of some six aircraft per month. The trains also supplied the squadron supply depots.

More difficult repairs still, however, had to be undertaken by aviation parks, of which there was meant to be one to each army. By the end of 1920, however, there were only seven aviation parks: at Kazan, Kiev (lately Vitebsk), Nizhni Novgorod, Petrograd, Samara, Tver and Yaroslav. The parks had some 300 men each, and undertook only jobs that required more than three weeks. By 1922, it seems, there were also parks in Orlov, Rostov, Sevastopol, Smolensk, Tambov and Tashkent. Finally, the worst repair jobs had to be sent off to Moscow, where the Central Aviation Park undertook the repair of aircraft that needed work just short of reconstruction, which was the task of the aircraft factories themselves.

The control of this whole organisation was the responsibility of the Supply Department of the Red Air Fleet Headquarters. At the end of 1919, however, it

Below Factory workers on an installation for a Petlyakov Pe-2 bomber, of which 11,426 were built. This aircraft was very versatile, being used as an attack bomber, interceptor fighter, dual trainer and reconnaissance.

...ecame the job of the newly formed *Glavkoavia* or ...hief Administration of the Aircraft Industry, which ...n the repair shops and even tried to extend its ...ntacles into the aviation parks. The situation was ...rther confused at the end of 1921 by the formation of ...e *Promvozduch* or Department of Industrial Enter-...rises of the Red Air Fleet, which ran the aviation ...pair facilities of the Red Air Fleet.

During the period under discussion, the strength of ...e Red Air Fleet increased methodically: in July 1918 ...rength was about 140 aircraft, rising to 350 by the end ...f 1920 and to 400 by the end of 1922. Most of this ...crease was the result of repairs to unserviceable ...sarist aircraft, the seizure of German aircraft aban-...oned when the German Army pulled back from the ...kraine, and imports from Germany, Italy and the ...etherlands. Production of Russian aircraft (of foreign ...esign) was very limited.

During the civil war, the workshops had their time ...ut out to repair a high proportion, about one-third, of ...e Red Air Fleet's strength that was unserviceable. To ...is end, some 1,574 aircraft and 1,740 engines were ...paired between 1818 and 1922, although these totals ...clude the same aircraft and engines mended on ...veral occasions.

The basic strength of the flying units, presumably of ...quadron establishment, was six aircraft. During 1918 ...ere were probably about sixty such squadrons, ...hough the figure fell during 1919 to about fifty ...quadrons. The total squadron strength varied between ...ese figures in 1920 and 1921, before rising finally to ...me seventy squadrons by the end of 1922. The basic ...ussian policy, moreover, was to raise squadrons with ...s many (or perhaps as few) aircraft as possible, and ...en build them up to establishment strength as more ...ircraft became available. This policy was maintained ...ght up to the end of World War II, in considerable ...ontrast with western practice, which was to make full-...rength squadrons combat ready in training for-...ations before committing them to the front.

Personnel was a constant problem for the Red Air ...leet, the more so as the few likely candidates were ...nder constant scrutiny for political reliability. Al-...hough the figures must be taken with a large pinch of ...alt, there is some truth in the official Russian figures, ...hich claim that the 300 trained pilots and observers in ...e Red Air Fleet during June 1919 had risen to 730 by ...e end of 1920. More realistic figures might be some ...75 pilots and 140 observers by the end of 1920, which ...eans that combat losses had been covered by the ...aining programme.

More importantly, perhaps, the whole nature of ...aining was overhauled in the winter of 1920–21, with ...r greater emphasis being placed on efficiency than on ...olitics, although the latter continued to feature prom-...ently in the training syllabus. The quality of in-...truction was greatly improved by the fact that German ...fficers were now being used under the terms of a secret ...usso-German military agreement. By 1921 there were ...welve flying schools, and by 1923 another six, with ...pecialist schools at another four locations. During the ...ost adverse conditions, therefore, the Red Air Fleet ...ad established itself in war, and although the com-...mand and logistics structures were not altogether ...atisfactory, improvements were on the way with the ...uild-up of the Red Air Fleet's training programme and ... more efficient indigenous aircraft industry.

With the coming of peace, the whole structure of the ...oviet armed forces came under review. With Trotsky

The Yakovlev Yak-1 was a solid machine with excellent handling, which later developed into the Yak-7, and finally the Yak-9, of which 16,769 were built.

fully involved in the organisation of the demobilisation programme, effective control of the Red Air Fleet (from this time onwards known increasingly as the Red Air Force) passed into the hands of Mikhail Frunze, and after the death of Frunze into the hands of Klimenti Voroshilov. Both Frunze and Voroshilov were ardent advocates of the offensive in warfare, and the tactics and organisation of the Red Air Force came increasingly to mirror this preoccupation.

From 1923, the controlling body of the Red Air Force became the Council of Labour and Defence of the Union of Soviet Socialist Republics. This body acted under the orders of the Commander-in-Chief of the Armed Forces. In parallel, the Revolutionary Military Council had a decisive political voice in the running of the Red Air Force through the agency of the Commissar of Military and Naval Affairs. Further to exacerbate the problems of command, the economics of the Red Air Force were controlled by the Soviet for the Preparation of the Red Army, one of the sub-committees of the Revolutionary Military Council.

Day-to-day running of the Red Air Force was at first the province of the General Staff, although after its formation in 1923 the Commissariat for Military and Naval Affairs (highly influenced by the German type of training most of its officers had received) gradually assumed control through the Commander-in-Chief of the Armed Forces, the head of the General Staff.

Actually within the Red Air Force, the highest command echelon was the Chief Directorate of the Air Force of the Red Army, which was established in 1923 as a department of the Commissariat for Military and Naval Affairs. The Chief Directorate was mainly re-sponsible for technical and administrative aspects of both the land and the sea air arms, and also had some influence in the tactical development of the land air arm by means of the fact that it controlled all aspects of training.

Actual field command of the Red Air Force's squad-rons, though, was exercised by the commander of the

Red Army Military District to which the various squadrons were assigned, by means of local Revolutionary Military Councils. The military district commander, moreover, could delegate control of squadrons to his subordinate formation commanders. The naval air arm suffered from a similar delegation of tactical control to fleet commanders.

During the first period of reconstruction, from 1923 to 1928, the Chief Directorate of the Air Force of the Red Army gradually developed in complexity, with the introduction of sections concerned with the major aspects of air force organisation, equipment, personnel and command. In this it was helped by the formation of the Red Air Force General Staff in the mid-1920s. This subordinate general staff was established to implement the orders of the Red Army General Staff so far as the Red Air Force was concerned.

At the same time, the political command of the Red Air Force was also ensured by the formation of the Political Department of the Red Air Force, successor to the Political Section of the Revolutionary Military Council, this in itself being a successor of the All-Russian Bureau of Military Commissars. A certain proportion of the political suspicion attached to the military commanders during the civil war period now began to disappear as a result of communist-trained commanders rising to higher ranks in all three services.

The head of the Political Department then became head of a military section within the Central Committee of the Communist Party. Here his influence was reduced, so far as the Red Air Force was concerned, to control of the party cells within the air force. It should be noted, though, that the secret police was very active in the ranks of the air force, as in the other armed services.

The period from 1923 to 1928 was marked in the field by a great number of tactical and organisational experiments, few of which were carried out fully, so great was

the flow of inspiration from above. In the later 1920s, though, the first full regulations for training and operational use of various categories of aircraft were issued, and from this time onwards a proper organisational structure was finally achieved: squadrons were allocated to specific functions as attack, bomber, fighter and reconnaissance units, attached to Red Army formations or directly controlled by the Red Air Force headquarters.

The squadron was established as the basic operational unit: it was composed of two or three flights, each of which had two or three sections. Thus the squadron had between eighteen and thirty-one aircraft. In 1928 air force brigades were established, each of these having between fifty and 120 aircraft. At first administrative centres for squadrons in a given area, the brigades gradually became tactical formations, and by the end of the 1920s had absorbed even the reconnaissance squadrons previously attached to army formations. Some of the brigades had as few as two squadrons, but by 1932 some had as many as six squadrons.

At this time the only aircraft left to the army formations were those in the independent flights known as 'corps detachments' of the Corps Aviation, which were administratively dependent on the brigades, but tactically deployed by army formations. These independent flights were usually of squadron strength, and were used mainly for artillery spotting, liaison and tactical reconnaissance.

As during the civil war, each of these flying units was supported by its own logistical tail, which it was hoped would ensure its flexibility in war. In an effort to improve mobility, moreover, between 1926 and 1931 the aviation parks were also required to undertake the provision and maintenance of motor transport with which the front-line squadrons could move quickly as the strategic situation demanded. But in 1932 it was

ealised that more benefit would be gained from an improvement in the basic services offered by the aviation parks, and so greater efforts were made to build up their numbers of trained personnel, especially in the more specialised trades, at the expense of the motor transport aspect, which could more profitably be left in the hands of the army.

In the years following the civil war, Russia was almost completely dependent for her military aircraft on imports, mostly from France, Germany, Italy, the Netherlands and the United Kingdom: between 1923 and 1928 the strength of the Red Air Force rose from 00 to about 1,100, of which 800 or more had to be bought from abroad. Of this 1928 strength, some sixty per cent were reconnaissance/light bomber types, twenty to twenty-five per cent fighters, twelve to sixteen per cent bombers and the remainder training, miscellaneous and reserve aircraft.

With the start of the first Five-Year Plan, indigenous aircraft production immediately began to rise, the Red Air Force numbering some 1,300 in 1931, rising to ,200 by the end of 1932, when Russian fears of Japan's expansion in Manchuria had given rise to very real thoughts of war in the east. Of this total of 2,200 some thirty per cent were bombers, with a high percentage of fighters and attack aircraft capable of operating in direct support of the ground forces. This was as Frunze and Voroshilov had planned, for the Red Air Force was seen as a direct adjunct of the ground forces.

Notwithstanding this, however, the Red Air Force had also been influenced by the strategic theories of the Italian General Guilio Douhet, and up to the time of the political purges that started in 1936 gave considerable thought and effort to the building up of strategic bomber forces with aircraft such as the Tupolev TB-3 (ANT-6). Another influence in this build-up of strategic air power was the continued German presence in Russian military matters – and the Germans, until the

death in 1936 of Lieutenant-General Walther Wever, were staunch believers in the future necessity of strategic air power.

Because of the Russian practice of starting new squadrons as cadres and then building up this nominally 'operational' unit with aircraft and pilots as they became available, it is difficult to assess the squadron strength of the Red Air Force at this time. In 1928, for example, on the eve of the establishment of air force brigades the Red Air Force claimed to have some ninety squadrons, yet only perhaps forty of these could in reality be considered operational and up to full strength. It was these squadrons which made up the fourteen brigades that existed in 1929, and by 1933 there were probably only twenty brigades with something like four squadrons to each brigade.

So far as personnel strength is concerned, the Red Air Force numbered about 10,000 in 1926, in which total there were some 800 pilots, 500 observers and 2,500 base staff. And although this marked a triple expansion compared with the numbers available in 1923, the Red Air Force was woefully short of flying personnel compared with western air forces.

Yet progress was being made, and in 1928 strength had grown to 15,000, by 1931 to 29,000 and by 1932 to nearly 50,000. The growing realisation of the importance of the air arm may be gauged from the fact that at the time the strength of the Red Army remained static. Given that there were no wars in the short term, though, Russia was in a strong position, for civilian training in flying clubs combined with the increased military training programme to give the Red Air Force an impressive pool of personnel under instruction for future expansion.

The growth of the Red Air Force in reality and in potential was mirrored by the growth of the aircraft and engine industries supplying it. By 1929 the number of major factories involved in aircraft and engine pro-

Below A graveyard of German aircraft destroyed in the climactic battle of Stalingrad, 1942, which resulted in great losses to both the *Luftwaffe* and the army. This battle was the biggest single defeat suffered by the Germans since the Napoleonic wars.
Inset Russian troops examine a Junkers Ju 87 dive-bomber. The Ju 87, with its cranked wings and high-pitched whine during the attack, proved vulnerable to Russian ground fire and fared badly against fighters such as the Hurricane and Spitfire.

duction had increased to eighteen, and by 1931 there were more than thirty such factories. The era of buying from abroad was over, at least as far as a bulk purchase was involved. From this time onwards the Russians concentrated on home production, although foreign aircraft and engines were still bought for evaluation, dissection and examination. The actual number of military aircraft built is, however, still uncertain, estimates varying enormously. In 1928 it seems that something like 330 military aircraft were built, this figure rising to about 500 in 1929.

With the ending of the first Five-Year Plan in 1933, the Red Air Force began to undergo a drastic alteration in most of its aspects, although this alteration was less the result of economic factors than of political and combat dictates and lessons. It was ultimately these factors that helped to produce the imbalanced air force with which the Russians faced the Germans in 1941.

After fifteen years of experimentation, the collective system of command was finally dropped in 1933, and in 1934 both the Council of Labour and Defence and the Revolutionary Military Council were abolished. Most of the latter's command and administrative roles were assumed by the Commissariat of Military and Naval Affairs, which became the Commissariat for Defence in 1934. Within this commissariat there was established an eighty-man committee with a broad consultative brief but no executive powers.

It seems likely that at the same time similar committees were established in the armed forces themselves. It thus seems that the Communist party had at last realised that command by a junta of military, political and economic interests was impractical, and that the more traditional military command structure, even if it was redolent of 'Tsarist' practices, was in fact superior in all practical ways.

But in 1936 Stalin instituted the great political purges which resulted in the deaths of a very high proportion of the armed forces' senior commanders, and with the purges there reappeared collective command notions, with military soviets appearing at formation command level, and with them the dreaded political commissars once again arrived on the scene.

Just as the purges, which were to cost the air force more than fifty per cent of its high command, including the commander-in-chief (General Alksins), were getting under way in the spring of 1937, the Red Air Force had been 'promoted' within the Russian military machine: in January the office of Deputy Commissar of Defence for the Air Force was created, thus giving the Red Air Force a measure of semi-autonomy within the armed forces. This office was directly represented in the Supreme War Council, set up by Stalin in 1938 to control the whole Russian military apparatus, especially in the very considerable expansion being undertaken as a result of combat lessons in Spain.

Further changes were made in 1940, when the Committee of Defence of the Council of People's Commissars was established to supervise and co-ordinate the various People's Commissariats and other military bodies involved in the highest military levels; the Red Air Force was again well represented on this new committee. At the time, it may be noted, the relative position of the air force may be gauged from that fact that one in every ten generals and admirals was an air force officer.

In July 1937, however, naval aviation had at last been separated from the main body of the Air Force as part of a major reshaping of naval command. The Commis-

Above left British and Russian aircrew with one of the Hawker Hurricanes of a British fighter wing operating in northern Russia during the winter of 1941–2. Some 2,952 Hurricanes were despatched to the Soviet Union, some receiving skis.
Above right Pokryshkin, Russia's second most successful ace, scored 59 victories. The aircraft in the background, with the victory markings, is a Bell P-39 Airacobra, which entered service with the RAF in 1941. About 9,500 were built, some 5,000 being supplied to the Soviet Union.
Left The wreckage of a Heinkel He 11 medium bomber. This, with the Dornier Do 17, was Germany's mainstay bomber, until it proved very vulnerable during the Battle of Britain in 1940 and was gradually replaced by Junkers Ju 88s.

sariat of Naval Affairs was divorced from the Commissariat of Defence, and given control of the new Naval Air Forces, control over which was exercised by a new Deputy Commissar of Naval Air Forces.

After a long reign as Commissar of Defense, Voroshilov was replaced in May 1940, largely as a result of the inadequacies of the armed forces revealed in the Spanish Civil War, the border clashes with Japan in Mongolia and the disastrous 'Winter War' against Finland.

The new commissar was Marshal Semyon Timoshenko, a veteran Soviet military man, who persuaded Stalin that the purely military deficiencies of the Russian war machine were largely attributable to poor command by officers appointed for political rather than military merit, and the general lack of morale among troops who were under constant political scrutiny, and spent nearly as much time in political indoctrination as in military training. This was a courageous thing for Timoshenko to do, but Stalin concurred, and in the summer of 1940 the collegiate command system was again abandoned in favour of a conventional system, and an intensive programme to improve morale and training was set in motion.

But efforts to rationalise the Red Air Force's structure had started as early as 1935: new technical and logistics departments had been established, and a new training command was authorised. At the same time, semi-independent commands for airborne forces, air defence and strategic bombing were set up, and the updating of the squadrons' and brigades' basic structures was taken in hand. Despite these wholesale internal reorganisations, though, tactical control of the majority of brigades and squadrons was still exercised by the ground force formations to which they were subordinated.

The only 'autonomous' element within the air force was raised in 1937: the AON or Special Duties' Aviation, which was controlled directly by Red Air Force headquarters in Moscow. The function of this force was long-range bombing missions and the delivery of the paratroops which the Russians were pioneering. The force's object was not strategic, however: the bombing raids and paratroop drops were to be deep in enemy territory, but were to be adjuncts to the main offensive by the Soviet ground forces, not strategic efforts to destroy the enemy's war-making potential.

The AON had been foreshadowed, it may be noted, by an 'independent' heavy bomber force set up in 1935. After the Russo-Finnish War of 1939–40, though, the AON was disbanded because of its poor performance, largely attributable in fact to the purging of its commander and his deputy at an earlier date. Headless, the AON had suffered heavy losses in operations over Finland, and in 1940 most of the surviving heavy bomber force, already obsolescent, was returned to ground force formation command.

Another force to receive great attention in the middle and late 1930s was the PVO or Air Defence Command. Operating within a high command structure which included anti-aircraft artillery, barrage balloons and the like, as well as an early-warning organisation designated VNOS, the PVO fighter squadrons were allocated to the defence of key cities and industrial areas. Actual control of the squadrons was vested in local air defence commanders or the commanders of military districts. The PVO was not part of the Red Air Force proper, though, and it was not until much later that the Red Air Force received its first interceptor squadrons.

While these major command reorganisations were being considered and carried out, the basic unit structure of the Red Air Force (detachments/independent flights, squadrons and brigades) did not undergo much change except in the establishment number of aircraft for each unit. A new unit was, however, introduced with the advent of the heavy bomber force. Two or

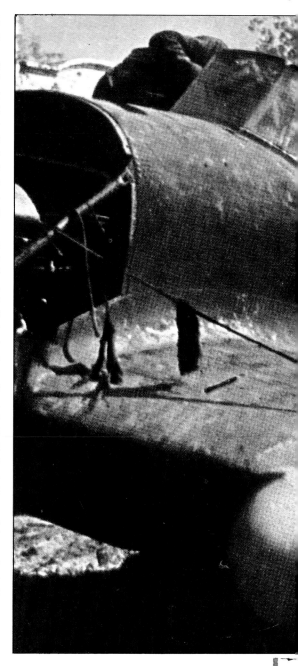

Below The Ilyushin Il-2 Stormovik, the Soviet Union's renowned ground attack aircraft. Even the massive armour plating of this aircraft did not make it invulnerable, as the photograph *right* shows.

three bomber squadrons were brigaded with several fighter squadrons, and brigades were unified under the command of new aviation corps. By the time of the German invasion in 1941, there were in all probability some six bomber corps. This type of formation was unique to the heavy bomber force until after the start of the Russo-German war in 1941.

Then in 1938 a major reorganisation of the Red Air Force was begun. Detachments became squadrons, squadrons became regiments, and brigades became divisions. Each division normally comprised three or four regiments, and each regiment about three or four squadrons. The only real reason for this reorganisation was apparently to bring Red Air Force structure into line with Red Army practice, and so facilitate command by ground force formations.

At the same time it was planned to establish air armies, composed of several air divisions. These air armies were to be allocated to the ground force 'fronts', each the equivalent of a western army group. While the plans for these formations was still under discussion, however, the Germans invaded Russia, and the plans had to be shelved until Russia had regained the initiative.

Between 1933 and 1938, the period of the second Five-Year Plan, the aircraft strength of the Red Air Force was increased from 2,200 aircraft to 5,400, and that of the Naval Air Forces from 400 to 800. Of approximately 5,000 aircraft possessed by the Red Air Force in 1937, some 4,200 were considered first-line machines, a high proportion compared with that in most western air forces. The whole question of aircraft strengths must be treated with great caution, however, for during this period the Russians became increasingly security-conscious, and put up a magnificent smoke-screen of conflicting reports of aircraft strength. Of the real strength, whatever it was, bombers made up perhaps forty-five per cent. At the same time in 1938, fighters made up about thirty per cent of the Red Air Force's first-line strength. What was lacking, however, were ground-attack aircraft, a fact that became painfully clear in the Spanish Civil War. General Smushkevich, Alksins' replacement as Russian commander in Spain, made repeated requests to the Soviet high

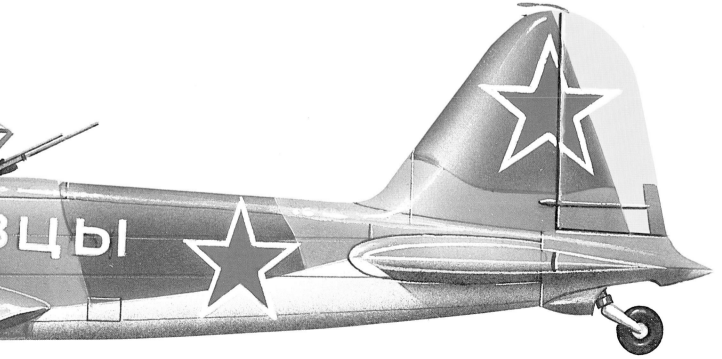

command for such aircraft, and immediately a major requirement for ground-attack aircraft was issued.

Within this organisational and numerical framework were the actual combat elements of the Red Air Force. Between 1933 and 1935 the number of brigades had grown from something over twenty-two to about fifty, with approximately 200 squadrons in the fifty brigades. By 1938 the Red Air Force had about sixty brigades, and the Naval Air Forces seven or eight; and a year later the Red Air Force's strength was probably in the order of eighty brigades.

To meet this growth in unit strength, the aircraft strength of the Red Air Force had also been built up, thanks to the efforts of the revitalised aircraft and engine industries: in 1940 there were up to 6,500 aircraft, 5,000 of them first-line machines; and by June 1941 Russian air strength had risen to 8,000 aircraft, with perhaps 6,000 of them classed as first-line machines. More than forty per cent of these aircraft were fighters, reflecting the Russian preoccupation with defence of the air space above their ground forces.

At the other end of the scale, quite surprisingly, were reconnaissance aircraft, which totalled only an inadequate five per cent of the Red Air Force's strength. As can be seen from the aircraft figures, the Russians had between 1939 and 1941 made a great effort to build up their air strength, and this is reflected in the growing in number of the air divisions available for combat service: the 1938 reorganisation of brigades into divisions had by 1939 turned the eighty brigades into some fifty divisions, a total which had by June 1941 been raised to over 100.

Thus, while the Germans were conquering most of western Europe, the Russians had doubled the size of their air force. But though strength was vastly increased, aircraft capabilities had not matched this. But approaching production stage in the Russian aircraft factories, most of them in European Russia, were several excellent new types.

Personnel strength had also risen considerably during the 1930s: by 1937 the Red Air Force could boast some 100,000 men, including 7,000 pilots. Figures for 1939 are largely hypothetical, but could well have been in the order of 135,000 men, including up to 10,000 pilots. By 1940 strength had risen to about 200,000, and at the time of the German invasion may have reached 500,000. Impressive as these figures undoubtedly are, they conceal the fact that quality was definitely inferior to quantity, even by the lower standards that the Russians set themselves compared with western air forces.

During 1936, for example, a programme to train 6,000 pilots was started – but only 3,500 suitable candidates could be found, even by scraping the bottom of the barrel. This same problem beset the Red Air Force right along the line, for the Russian educational system was just not up to providing enough young men with the right educational requirements for training as pilots, observers, mechanics, armourers, fitters, and the host of other specialised trades essential in any air force. Thus the only way to keep numbers up to the required establishment was to reduce standards, and in combat this proved disastrous.

In an effort to maintain standards, the Red Air Force received many special privileges, including high pay, better food and accommodation, adequate leave and even a 'military' rank structure from 1935. In 1940 general ranks were reintroduced, and by the end of the year there were thirteen air force lieutenant-generals.

This lack of trained personnel also affected the growth of the Russian aircraft and engine industries, which had fifty-four factories and major repair facilities in 1933. But by 1938 this had grown to twenty major aircraft and ten major engine factories, with increased numbers of accessory and repair factories. By 1941 the total had grown again, this time to twenty-eight aircraft and fourteen engine factories, plus four propeller and twenty-eight component factories. Contrary to popular belief, which has it that the whole of the industrial base for Russia's aviation industry was located in European Russia, and evacuated to eastern Siberia, in and beyond the Ural mountains, only after the start of the German invasion, the Russians had realised as early as 1937 that any future war would threaten European Russia, and had taken steps accordingly.

As war with Japan was also a distinct possibility, central Russia, just to the east of the Urals, offered the optimum site for the new industrial base that Russia was building. This location was also admirable from the purely economic viewpoint, offering the shortest routes for Siberian raw materials, Caspian oil, and European Russian manpower, skills and 'consumers'.

Thus by the time of the German invasion in June 1941, the Russians had established major aircraft production facilities at Tashkent in Turkestan, at Irkutsk, Omsk and Semeovka in Siberia, and at Novosibirsk and Komsomolsk in the Far East. Even then, these factories had half the production capacity of all the plants west of the Urals. Unfortunately, however, little had been done about the relocation of the aircraft engine industry to safer areas. In the event, though, Russia's production facilities, for all types of armaments, were saved from the German onslaught into European Russia by the herculean efforts of whole segments of the population under desperate conditions.

Such then was the Red Air Force at the time that Russia was invaded by the forces of Germany on 22 June 1941.

All Russia's prewar planning went by the board, however, in the weeks following the German invasion. Air regiments were decimated in the air and on the ground, and temporary organisational structures sprang up wherever they could. So great were the Red Air Force's losses, moreover, that even the most obsolescent military types, many civilian aircraft and every machine the factories could produce were swiftly rushed into front-line service.

Left Moscow's anti-aircraft defence was insufficiently organized, and sometimes had to rely on unsatisfactory methods. Here, one woman is operating a portable range-finder, while another uses binoculars.
Below Ilyushin Il-2s bank around for an attack. Waves of these aircraft, one of the first types to be armed with rocket projectiles, frequently attacked targets continuously for twenty minutes or until they had been destroyed.

At the same time, the training programmes for aircrew were curtailed and half-trained pilots and crew rushed to the front in an effort to make up the devastating losses being suffered at the hands of the Luftwaffe, by this time a highly trained and experienced force with modern aircraft. Notwithstanding these reinforcements, or even perhaps because of them, losses continued to rise in the late summer and autumn of 1941, by which time Russian air strength against Germany had fallen to as low as 2,250 aircraft.

In the dire days of 1941 and early 1942, the Red Air Force, together with the other Russian armed services, had to make do with the men and *matériel* available. But almost from the beginning of hostilities, when the German flood to the east was continuing with unabated momentum, the Russian high command began to digest the early organisational and strategic implications of the new war and alter the command structure accordingly.

As early as July 1941 operational command of the armed services was at last removed from the Commissariat of Defence and entrusted to the new *Stavka* or Supreme Headquarters. Two senior Red Air Force officers were attached to the *Stavka* to advise on air matters. The *Stavka* itself was concerned only with operational matters, and was subordinate to another body established at the same time, the State Committee for Defence, which was set up by the united decision of the Praesidium of the Supreme Soviet, the Central Committee of the Communist Party and the Council of People's Commissars.

In effect, it was the State Committee for Defence that ran the war for Russia, controlling as it did the Commissariat of Defence, the armed forces and the ministries concerned with war industry. Within the State Committee for Defence, the interests of the Red Air Force were entrusted to Georgi Malenkov. Stalin was chairman of the committee, and was soon appointed commander-in-chief.

The centralised control of the State Committee and of the *Stavka* was soon needed, for the three main sectors into which the front against Germany had at first been divided were soon broken down into twelve 'fronts' or army groups.

With the stemming of the first German onrush in the winter of 1941–42, the Russians at last had the opportunity to make a start on the reorganisation that early combat operations had shown to be essential. Luckily, the Spanish Civil War had shown what sort of aircraft would be needed in the future, and several types to meet these requirements were just coming to the fore. These were to prove an invaluable source of strength to the revised and revitalised Red Air Force in the years to come. In a way, moreover, the drastic losses of the first six months of war proved beneficial – the obsolescent types in current service had been destroyed for the most part, leaving the way open for the widespread introduction of newer designs. These had adequate performance and would soon appear in ever swelling numbers.

Organisational changes affecting the Red Air Force continued in late 1941 and early 1942, with the establishment of an independent long-range bomber force, there organisation of the fighter forces of the air defence forces, and the further removal of the airborne forces from Red Army control. All three elements were controlled directly by the *Stavka* by the end of 1942, although the Commissariat of Defence and the General Staff of the Red Army still had much say in their operational uses.

Mikoyan MiG-3

Type: single-seat fighter.
Engine: one 1,350 hp AM-35A.
Dimensions: span 33 ft 9½ in (10.3 m); length 26 ft 9 in (8.15 m); height reported as 8 ft 7 in (2.61 m).
Weights: empty, not known; max. load given as 7,390 lb and 7,695 lb (3,490 kg).
Performance: max. speed 398 mph (640 km/h), (also given as 407 mph); initial climb 3,937 ft (1,200 m)/min; service ceiling 39,370 ft (12,000 m); range 776 miles (1,250 km).

The MiG-3 was a refined version of the MiG-1 which had a rapid development. A single-seat fighter, the MiG-3 eventually proved to be no match for *Luftwaffe* fighters and by 1942, when they ceased production, they were being used for armed reconnaissance and support. The illustration shows a MiG-3 of the 341AP operating from Vnukovo, Moscow, during the winter of 1941–42. The lettering below the cockpit reads 'For the Fatherland'. The aircraft is in winter camouflage.

By the end of 1942, about seventy-five per cent of the Red Air Force's strength was devoted to the army air force, which operated in direct support of the Red Army, which the established military doctrine of the Russians had fixed as the decisive element in any war.

Naval aviation was controlled by the Commissariat of Naval Affairs under Marshal Zhavoronkov, although these forces, comprising some ten per cent of the total Russian military air strength, were subject to the direct control of the *Stavka*. It should be noted here, moreover, that the NKVD, Russia's internal security organisation, also had its own air force. Although intended primarily for internal operations, the units of this force were used at the front when the situation demanded.

The Long-Range Aviation or ADD was actually formed in April 1942 under the command of Major-General A. Golovanov, an officer whose closeness to Stalin ensured that the ADD enjoyed virtual autonomy within the Soviet armed forces, even to the level of having its own flying schools. The establishment of the ADD, however, must not be construed to mean that the Russians had at last accepted the idea of strategic bombing of the enemy's war-making potential. Far from it, the Russians had seen the Germans' failure in the Battle of Britain and in their air offensives against Leningrad and Moscow as clear proof of the fallacies inherent in the concept of strategic bombing. With the establishment of the ADD, though, the Russians put on a more formal footing their belief that the enemy's military rear areas and communications could be disrupted and even cut by the use of long-range bombers.

Right   Yakovlev Yak-9D fighters of an elite Guards fighter regiment. The Yak-9D was a medium-range fighter, small and manoeuvrable and easy to handle. It entered service in 1942.
Below left   Russian anti-aircraft guns were numerous, powerful and effective. The one shown here is a 76.2-mm model.
Below right   As they had no radar, the Russian warning systems were not very effective, employing equipment such as this acoustic director and height finder.

From very limited beginnings, including use of transport aircraft of the Civil Air Fleet, the ADD soon grew to considerable proportions. By 1944, it is estimated, it could muster some 1,500 aircraft in fifty air regiments. The aircraft total included long-range reconnaissance and transport aircraft, though, and so small had been the successes of the arm that late in 1944 the *Stavka* decided to disband the ADD as such, its aircraft and units thereupon becoming the 18th Air Army, under the direct control of the *Stavka*.

Although the Russian airborne forces were controlled by a separate headquarters, the VDV, during the war years they never had their own transport force except for a few squadrons for training purposes. For operational drops, though, the airborne forces had to rely on the aircraft of the ADD and the Civil Air Fleet. The success of the few drops attempted was negligible, though, and a reorganisation was carried out late in 1943 by General Kapitochin. This meant that by the end of the war, when they were hardly needed, the Russians had some twenty airborne brigades with artillery and armoured support, and relatively large numbers of aircraft in which to transport them. Like the Germans, though, the Russians increasingly used their airborne forces as conventional, but elite, infantry for desperate situations.

The Air Defence Forces or PVO controlled the defence of Russia's cities and industries against air attack, with the aid of fighters, artillery, searchlights, balloons and the rest of the paraphernalia of air defence. The whole was commanded by a colonel-general of the artillery arm. Although a point defence of major targets was the norm, the early-warning system was run on a zone system so that the command structure could switch the fighters allocated to one point to another should the situation warrant it. The PVO was directly subordinate to the *Stavka*, which was thus in an excellent position to assess the relative successes of the various parts of the PVO.

The most useful part was clearly the fighter arm, which by 1945 had grown to over 1,000 aircraft and so had the most important voice within the PVO. In coastal regions, key areas were defended by fighter units of the Naval Air Forces, and cities and key industries near the front line were also protected by fighter units of the Red Air Force. But at no time during World War II did the Russians ever establish an air defence air force as part of the Red Air Force.

Despite its almost catastrophic losses in the opening weeks of Operation 'Barbarossa', the Germans' drive in Russia in June and July 1941, the relative successes of the Red Air Force persuaded the *Stavka* to increase the air force's responsibilities *vis-à-vis* the other armed forces. This growing importance is reflected in the formation of the air armies in late autumn, 1941.

The air armies, which numbered perhaps seventeen or eighteen by the end of World War II, had no fixed establishment, their sizes varying with the demands made upon them. The smallest air armies numbered some 600 aircraft, and the largest over 2,000, the average being in the order of 1,250. The largest air armies numbered over twenty air divisions, whose primary tasks were air support of the ground forces to which they were attached.

In the closing stages of the war, one or two air armies were generally allocated to each front (army group). The commander of the air army was directly subordinated to the front's commander-in-chief, who thus controlled the tactical use of the air forces available.

CHAPTER FIFTEEN

THE AMERICAN AIR SERVICES 1918·1945

Loading bombs into a Boeing B-17F Flying Fortress. Powered by four Wright Cyclone radial engines, the 'Fort' gained a reputation for its strength and ability to absorb phenomenal damage and still get its crews home.

On 20–21 May 1918, US military aviation began a brief period of divorce from army authority when the Overman Act established two independent departments: the Division of Military Aeronautics, to supervise operational matters, and the Bureau of Aircraft Production, to look after aircraft procurement, supply and training. The two departments were collectively the Air Service, which had in 1918 a strength of 195,023 officers and men, compared with the Aeronautical Division's 1,218 officers and men in 1917.

Despite the Air Service's good performance in World War I, its strength and autonomy were short lived. By 1919 manpower had fallen to 25,603, and by 1920 to 9,050; and then on 4 June 1920 the Army Re-Organization Act once more made the aviation service part of the army, with an establishment of 1,511 officers and 16,000 men. The Army Air Service, as it now was, had the right to control research and development, and to select its own aircraft types.

The major source of trouble for the new Army Air Service came from within its own ranks, where Brigadier General William Mitchell was conducting an outspoken campaign to get the AAS made the chief guardian of the United States' physical security in place of the US Navy. A devotee of the concept of strategic air power, Mitchell in July 1921 sought to prove his ideas with carefully controlled attacks by Martin NBS-1 bombers on German ships now in American hands. The tests took place in Chesapeake Bay, and all were impressed when the 'unsinkable' battleship *Ostfriesland* was sunk after bombs had exploded in the water around her. The tests could hardly be conclusive, however, as the ships were stationary and throwing up no defensive gunfire. Nevertheless, it was an impressive feat, and one which should have given the protagonists of the battleship more food for thought than it did. These successes were repeated in September 1923, when more bombers sank two US battleships off Cape Hatteras.

Embarrassed, the War Department sent Mitchell off on a tour of inspection in the Philippines, a relative backwater at the time. Even so, he managed to put up the backs of the army establishment in the area by condemning General Sumerall's totally inadequate air defence plan for the Hawaiian islands.

Embarrassing as Mitchell might be, there was certainly much truth in his criticisms: at a time of financial stringency, Mitchell pointed out, there was little sense in storing 2,796 aircraft that were already obsolescent; and certainly the AAS's flying record needed considerable improvement, for between 1 June 1920 and 31 June 1921 the AAS had suffered some 330 crashes resulting in 69 dead and 27 severely injured.

By the middle of 1924 the AAS had 10,547 officers and men on its rolls, and an air strength of 754 aircraft (457 reconnaissance, 78 fighter, 50 bomber, 8 attack and the remaining 152 trainer). Although Major General Mason M. Patrick, the Chief of the AAS, thought that re-equipment was necessary, with a ratio of four fighters, bombers and other combat types to one reconnaissance machine, the funds were just not available. Therefore Patrick made the wise decision to spend what funds there were on research and development, to

Right Taken during a Japanese raid on the US-held Yontan Airfield, Okinawa, Ryuku Islands, the picture shows ack-ack tracer fire above US Marine Corps Corsair fighters.

keep the AAS fully up to date technologically. Then, in the event of a crisis, the best types under test could be placed quickly in production.

In April 1925 the AAS lost from a high position one of its most energetic officers, but in return regained a little tranquillity: Mitchell was removed from his position as Assistant Chief of the AAS to be Corps Air Officer in San Antonio, Texas. Then on 5 September of that year he commented to the press that the loss of the US Navy's rigid airship *Shenandoah* (ZR-1) two days before had been the result of naval high command negligence. Mitchell then went on to compound his error by slating the army high command for its lack of foresight in developing army aviation as a potent weapon. It was the last straw so far as the US Army was concerned, and Mitchell was court-martialled on eight charges. Suspended from duty, Mitchell shortly thereafter resigned.

Under Patrick's watchful eye, the AAS continued to evaluate small numbers of modern aircraft, such as the huge NBL-1 'Barling Bomber' and the Curtiss NBS-4 Condor bomber, but greater emphasis was placed on the development of aerodynamically refined fighters with powerful engines, such as the excellent Curtiss PW-8.

Throughout the early 1920s the AAS fought to regain its independence, but although it enjoyed the active support of House of Representatives' bodies such as the Lampert Committee and the Lassiter Board, the failure of the campaign was sealed when President Calvin Coolidge appointed the Morrow Board to investigate the matter in 1925. The board was opposed to an independent air service, but recommended that the AAS be upgraded to a corps to bolster its prestige. Thus on 2 July 1926 the Army Air Service became the Army Air Corps when the Air Corps Act came into effect. At this time personnel strength of the AAC was 9,674 officers and men, from an authorised establishment of 1,650 officers and 15,000 men. The Morrow Board had recommended, in addition to the manpower strength above, a five-year *matériel* expansion plan to provide 1,800 aircraft at its conclusion. The plan was in fact only implemented in July 1927, and thereafter suffered from cuts amounting in all to about 40%. Nevertheless, by June 1932, five years after the plan had been started, aircraft strength stood at 1,709, and manpower strength at 1,305 officers and 13,400 other ranks.

Like the Royal Air Force in retrenchment-bound Great Britain, the Army Air Corps concentrated on technical excellence to keep itself in the van of scientific progress, coupled with record-breaking flights to keep the service in the public eye and to prove the aircraft and their performances. Notable flights for these ends were relatively common in the late 1920s and early 1930s.

On 28 June 1927 the first nonstop flight from California to Hawaii was made in a Fokker C-2 by Lieutenants Lester Maitland and Alfred Hegenberger. Then in a Fokker C-2A Major Carl Spaatz, Captain Ira Eaker and Lieutenant Elwood Quesada established a world endurance record of 150 hours between 1 and 7 January 1929 with the aid of air-to-air refuelling. In September of the same year Lieutenant James Doolittle made the world's first blind solo flight with the aid of radio and Sperry gyroscopic flight instrumentation, only the first of the many records and feats achieved by the amazing Doolittle in the early 1930s.

Records continued to be made and broken, but then the Air Corps introduced into service in 1934 the

artin B-10 bomber, an ambitious design with twin
ngines, mid-mounted monoplane wing, retractable
ndercarriage, enclosed cockpit and a nose gun turret.
he B-10 had just beaten Boeing's B-9 for production
ders, and the fact that the Americans had two such
ombers came as a total surprise to all, for the two
ntenders for production orders had performances
perior to those of contemporary fighter aircraft.

Although the B-10 had an unprepossessing ap-
earance from the side, with its ungainly, protruding
ose turret and deep fuselage, from the front the sleek,
arrow lines of the fuselage gave the correct impression
f speed. The impression was confirmed in 1934, when
 squadron of ten B-10 bombers set off under the
ommand of Lieutenant Colonel Henry 'Hap' Arnold
n 19 July from Washington, DC to fly to Alaska and
en back to Washington state, a round trip of 8,290
iles (13,340 km) which was accomplished by 20
ugust. The reliability and performance of the B-10
ere amply proved.

The excellent performance of the B-10, combined
ith its bomb load of 2,260 lb (1,025 kg) led the many
vil and military adherents of the doctrine of strategic
r power, and an independent air service, to redouble
eir efforts to secure such a force. Among the leading
hts of the movement was Mitchell.

The 'Depression' started in 1929, and the US armed
rces were amongst the many national bodies to face
ts in their budgets. In December 1930, General
umerall, who had been criticised earlier for his lack of
r-mindedness by Mitchell, presented his last army
propriation request as chief-of-staff. For 1932 he
ked for $351 million, a cut of 3.134% compared with
e previous year. Although the cut was relatively small,

most of it was to come out of the Air Corps' slice of the
army's cake.

To the surprise of all, especially Sumerall and the
general staff, the Federal Budget Bureau instead increased the Air Corps' allocation, cutting instead the
ground forces and civilians employed by the army, to
the tune of $8 million. Matters were improved, how-
ever, by the arrival of Lieutenant General Douglas
MacArthur as chief-of-staff in 1931.

One of MacArthur's first jobs was an attempt to
finish off the ten-year wrangle that the army had been
having with the navy as to which service should defend
the coasts of the United States. Finally MacArthur and
Admiral William Pratt, Chief of Naval Operations,
came to the conclusion that the naval air forces would
operate at sea, and the 'army forces will be land-based
and employed as an essential element of the Army in the
performance of its mission to defend the coasts both at
home and overseas'.

Despite the protests of Major General Benjamin
Foulois, the new Chief of the Air Corps, the $15 million
sliced off the $331 million requested by the army for
1933 came out of the Air Corps' budget. It was at this
time, too, that Foulois and the Assistant Secretary of
War for Air, Trubee Davison, again called for the
independence of the Air Corps. Despite this pressure,
and more complaints from the powerful governor of
New York state, Franklin D. Roosevelt, about cuts in
the air components of the National Guard, for 1934
another $24 million was sliced off the military budget.

In November 1932, though, a new dawn seemed to
be just round the corner, for in that month Franklin
Roosevelt was elected president, and he was known to
favour a strong navy and a strong air service. A sign of

Opposite Captain Charles S.
Hudson, bombardier, in the
nose of a Boeing B-17G
Fortress. Note the
remote-controlled chin turrets
on this model.
Above Boeing B-17G Flying
Fortresses of the 381st
Bombardment Group.
Introduced at the end of 1942,
more G models were built than
any other bomber in history.
These could carry a maximum
bombload of nearly 17,600 lb
(8,000 kg) over short
distances, and was armed
with thirteen 0.50 in. machine
guns.

General Henry H. Arnold.

Below The Grumman F8F Bearcat fighter, one of the fastest and most manoeuvrable piston-engined aircraft, built too late for US Navy Service in World War II.

the times was the fact that in the next budget, the army was forced to take only a $51 million cut in its allocation demand instead of the $80 million recommended by the Federal Budget Bureau.

Although MacArthur was due to retire as chief-of-staff in December 1935 and become military adviser to the government of the Philippines, Roosevelt arranged things behind MacArthur's back so that the latter could take up his new appointment in October 1935. Mac-Arthur was not pleased that he had been superseded early by General Malin Craig, but so far as the Air Corps was concerned, MacArthur's last budget was excellent. Out of the total army allocation of $361 million, the largest for five years, the Air Corps was to receive $45 million, compared with slightly over $27 million the previous year.

Extra money meant that more aircraft and men could be contemplated, and from 1935 manpower gradually rose from the 15,000-man plateau on which it had been resting in the period from 1931 to 1934. Strength in 1935 was 16,247, rising to 17,233 in 1936, to 19,147 in 1937, to 20,089 in 1938, and to 23,455 in 1939. 1935 was also an important year for the Air Corps because it was at this time that the report of the Baker Board, issued in July 1934, was implemented. Set up in response to the demands of the independent air service proponents, the

Baker Board silenced them at least temporarily b advocating that although no separate air service shoul be formed, there should be a General Headquarters, Ai Force to control all the Air Corps' tactical air units. sound move in principle when it was implemented i 1935, the formation of the new HQ soon led in practic to friction, for while the GHQ, Air Forces controlle operations, the Office of the Chief of the Air Corp controlled procurement and training. The GHQ, Ai Force was established on 1 April 1935 at Langley Fiel Virginia, under the command of Brigadier Gener Frank Andrews.

A keen believer in the concept of strategic air power Andrews chose for his staff only officers he knew to b adherents of the doctrine. One of the first requests o the new GHQ was for the formation of East and Wes Coast Bomber Groups, each with 25 of the Boeing B-1 heavy bombers under development at the time. Thi first request was turned down by the army general sta on the grounds that the Douglas B-18 medium bombe (intended as a B-10 replacement) would be more tha ample when it appeared in squadron service in late 193 or early 1937. In reality, though, it was lack of fund which prevented large-scale B-17 procurement. At th beginning of World War II in Europe, the Army Ai Corps had only 23 B-17s in service.

Left A single-seater naval aircraft, the Grumman F4F-4 Wildcat fighter was one of the US Navy's fighter mainstays in 1942. Noted for their strength and manoeuvrability, they could operate from small escort carriers.

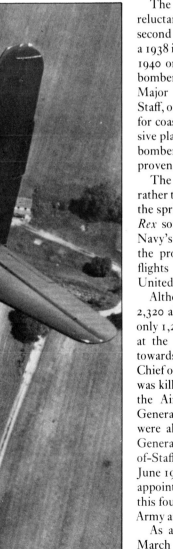

The American high command seemed strangely reluctant to allow real preparations for war in the second half of the 1930s, an impression strengthened by a 1938 instruction to the Air Corps that in the fiscal year 1940 only attack aircraft, light bombers and medium bombers were to be procured. This was explained by Major General Stanley Embruck, Deputy Chief-of-Staff, on the grounds that the army was responsible only for coastal defence, that heavy bombers implied offensive plans, and that in any case the superiority of heavy bombers over medium bombers was by no means proven.

The fact that the army was responsible for coastal rather than ocean defence was the result of an episode in the spring of 1938, when a B-17 'intercepted' the liner *Rex* some 600 miles (965 km) off the coast. The US Navy's *amour propre* was offended, and in the wake of the protests that followed, the army was limited to flights within 100 miles (160 km) of the coast of the United States.

Although the Baker Board had set a target strength of 2,320 aircraft for 1938, in this year the Air Corps had only 1,250 modern aircraft, with another 1,000 on order at the low production rate of 88 per month. Then towards the end of the year, on 21 September 1938, the Chief of the Air Corps, Major General Oscar Westover, was killed in an accident, and his successor, luckily for the Air Corps and the United States, was Major General Henry 'Hap' Arnold. Shortly after this there were also other high command changes, for in 1939 General George C. Marshall became US Army Chief-of-Staff, with Henry Stimson as Secretary of War in June 1940. In the spring of 1941, Robert A. Lovett was appointed Assistant Secretary of War for Air, and it was this four-man military/air service team that steered US Army and US army air services through World War II.

As a direct result of the annexation of Austria in March 1938, and then Hitler's speech demanding territorial concessions from Czechoslovakia, the latter broadcast from Nürnberg on 12 September. Roosevelt decided in late September or early November 1939 that war was inevitable, and that eventually the United States would have to play a part in it. More than ever aware of the importance of air power in the forthcoming war, Roosevelt sent his trusted aide Harry H. Hopkins to the west coast to set about speeding up aircraft production, centred in California and Washington.

Realising the way the wind was blowing, and the fact that as much as $500 million might shortly be made available for rearmament, the War Department set about exploring the possibilities. The Air Corps drafted plans for $400 million, and shortly after this the ordnance authorities put in a claim for $349 million. Although vastly increased allocations would no doubt be available, every department felt that it had been starved of funds more than others in the austere days of the early 1930s, and so should now receive an extra slice of the cake. Referred to Roosevelt in late October 1938, the problem was presented by Marshall with the warning that the implementation of a massive air programme to the detriment of other army branches 'would be contrary to the considered judgment' of the general staff.

Roosevelt was hardly to be deterred, however: he blithely talked of 20,000 aircraft per year, although he conceded that 10,000 might be a more reasonable figure, but finally settled on the 6,000 aircraft programme submitted by the Air Corps, at a total cost of $300 million, leaving the balance of the $500 million for the ground forces. The plan was put to the Congress on 12 January 1939 and passed on 3 April following.

The trouble with this plan lay in the fact that it was concerned almost exclusively with aircraft, without the training and other aspects of balance that would provide the Air Corps with the airfields, men and other equipment to service and fly them. Here Roosevelt's preoccupation with European affairs is recognisable: once the production plan had been authorised, Roosevelt expected that surreptitiously aircraft could be 'tapped off' from the production lines for sale to European powers such as Belgium, France and Great Britain. The notion came to light when the papers found that a French officer had been on board a Douglas aircraft that had crashed on a test flight. In the

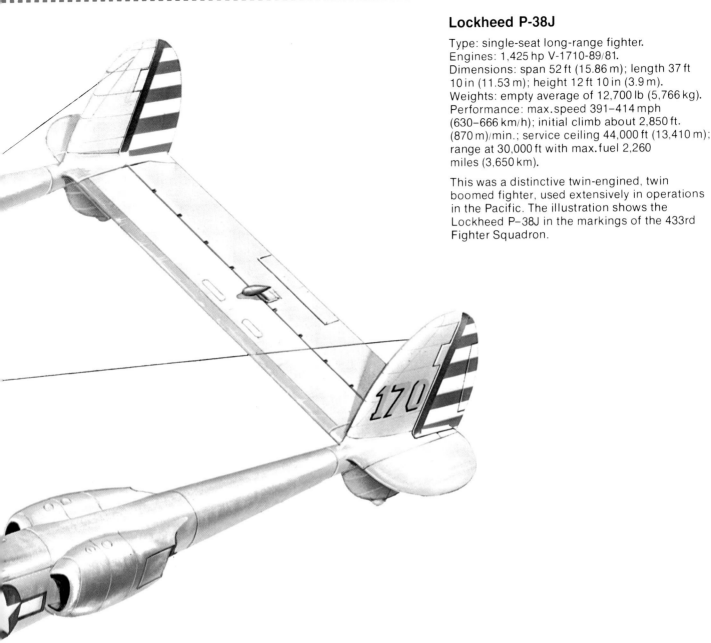

Lockheed P-38J

Type: single-seat long-range fighter.
Engines: 1,425 hp V-1710-89/81.
Dimensions: span 52 ft (15.86 m); length 37 ft
10 in (11.53 m); height 12 ft 10 in (3.9 m).
Weights: empty average of 12,700 lb (5,766 kg).
Performance: max. speed 391–414 mph
(630–666 km/h); initial climb about 2,850 ft.
(870 m)/min.; service ceiling 44,000 ft (13,410 m);
range at 30,000 ft with max. fuel 2,260
miles (3,650 km).

This was a distinctive twin-engined, twin
boomed fighter, used extensively in operations
in the Pacific. The illustration shows the
Lockheed P–38J in the markings of the 433rd
Fighter Squadron.

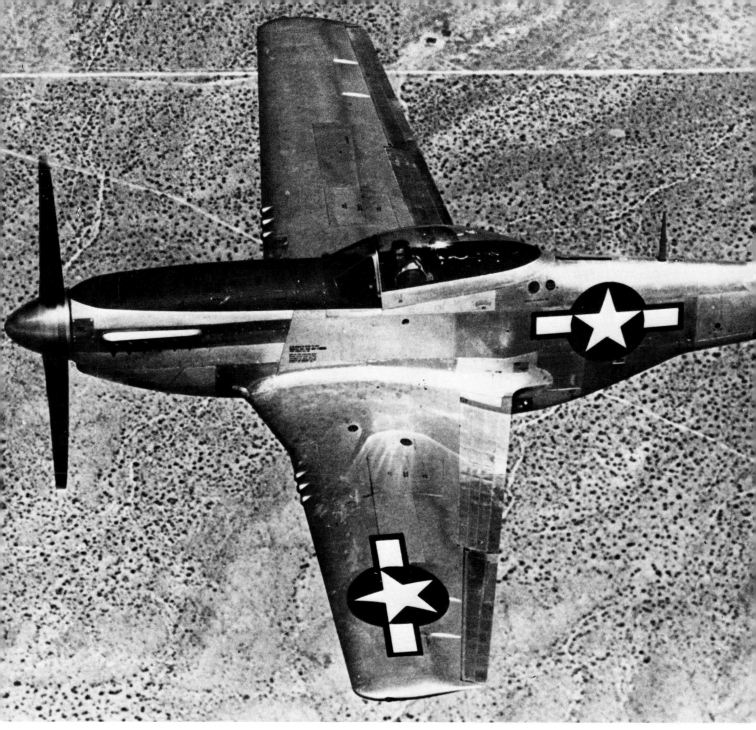

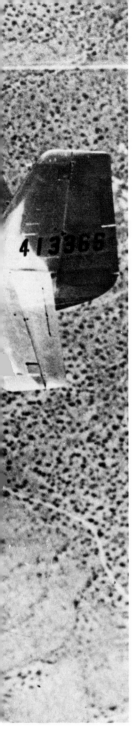

ensuing adverse publicity Roosevelt threatened Arnold with 'exile' to some remote spot, possibly Guam, and until September 1939 Arnold kept himself away from the White House.

Presidential, congressional and public sympathy with the aims of the Air Corps at the beginning of 1939 finally convinced even the most die-hard traditionalists in the army that a radically improved organisation for the Air Corps was essential. It had long been realised that the dual command structure of the Office of the Chief of the Air Corps (OCAC) and the GHQ, AF (controlling, at its inception, the Air Corps' three combat units: the 1st Wing on March Field, California; the 2nd Wing on Langley Field, Virginia; and the 3rd Wing on Barksdale Field, Louisiana) had produced an unwarranted and undesirable factionalism within the Air Corps, and that this unfortunate trait could only be cured by the appointment of a person or other staff to run both the previous authorities as subordinates. In February 1939, therefore, Arnold suggested that he be appointed Chief of Aviation, GHQ, with a staff to control both the OCAC and GHQ, AF. Arnold's suggestion was turned down, but from 1 March 1939 Arnold, in his capacity as Chief of the Air Corps, was authorised to 'supervise' the activities of the GHQ, AF.

But though internal organisation still left much to be desired, by 1939 the Air Corps at least had a clearer indication of what its military objectives and responsibilities were. Colonel J. W. Anderson of the general staff had been appointed to study the Air Corps' role in war, and had reported that the optimum use for aircraft was 'an active and aggressive defense involving operations beyond our territory'. This led General Craig to establish an Air Board to examine the Air Corps' role in 'hemisphere defense', with effect from 23 March 1939. By the time the board reported, Marshall had replaced Craig, and when Marshall informed Stimson on 1 September of the board's findings, he added that 'the report establishes for the first time a specific mission for the Air Corps'. In broad terms, the Air Board recommended, the security of the United States could no longer be ensured by the US Navy and the conventional coastal defences. This security could now only be assured by the establishment of a 'hemisphere defense' apparatus, in which the approaches to the United States via the North Atlantic, the Pacific and Latin America would have to be dominated by long-range heavy bombers. The board also recommended that outlying bases should be secured, so that aircraft based on them could operate at longer range from the United States. The heavy bomber, so ardently by the Air Corps, had been vindicated in theory.

But though military backing had been secured, the American people and their elected representatives in the Congress had yet to be convinced. Indeed, on 3 April 1940 the Congress had cut an army request for 166 aircraft to 57, and refused to entertain the notion of long-range bomber procurement as this was 'aggressive' in its connotations. But then Hitler launched his invasion of the Low Countries and France, and America was immediately converted. As Senator Lodge told Arnold, the Congress was now eager 'to provide all of the money necessary for the National Defense, and so all you have to do is ask for it'. Arnold did so, and in 'forty-five minutes I was given $1,500,000,000 and told to get an air force'. Roosevelt, thinking in terms of 20,000 aircraft as late as 1938, was now talking in terms of 50,000 aircraft per year. Money was now no object, and between July 1940 and June 1941 the Air Corps

spent $100 million just on research, $42 million alone going on development of the heavy bombers for which in 1938 the general staff had seen no foreseeable use.

Yet the military budget continued to increase. On 10 July 1940 Roosevelt asked the Congress for $4 billion for a 'total defense' programme, some $2 billion being for the procurement of 18,000 aircraft. The request was accepted, and the whole altered tenor of American public feeling may be seen from the fact that the provision of conscription, normally an anathema to the American people, was ensured by public demand on 16 September 1940.

This was not all, however, for on 14 May Roosevelt had called Marshall and Arnold to the White House to discuss the future growth of the Air Corps, not merely in terms of aircraft, as envisaged in 1939, but in all its requirements to make a balanced and effective force. It had already been planned to produce 4,500 pilots within two years, but this target was now scrapped in favour of one calling for the training of 7,000 pilots within one year – a threefold increase in the training programme. But then on 8 August the goal was raised to 12,000 pilots per year, and on 17 December to 30,000 pilots per year, a more than thirteenfold increase in one year. The object of the whole programme was to raise the strength of the Air Corps to fifty-four groups in 1941, and then eventually to eighty-four groups.

The deployment for hemisphere defence from August 1940 was made possible in the 'ships for bases' deal, in which 50 old US Navy 'flushdeck' destroyers, munitions, aircraft and credit facilities for the British were exchanged for 99-year leases on bases for the US Navy and Air Corps in the Bahamas, Bermuda, British Guiana, Jamaica, Newfoundland, St Lucia and Trinidad. The British also asked the United States for 2,000 aircraft per month, though this order had been increased to 3,600 aircraft per month by July 1942. The system on which the arrangement was based became legal as the Lend-Lease Act of 11 March 1941, the bill having been introduced on 10 January 1941. In April 1941 the United States extended its base plans into Greenland and Nova Scotia, as part of a plan to extend the US defence into the western Atlantic and free British forces for operational use in the European and North African theatres of operations. A Special Observer Group was also set up in London to keep the War

bove The North American
*-51D Mustang in flight. These
and other P-51 variants were
the war's best escort fighters,
flying from British bases to
targets right in the heart of
Germany.
ar left P-51D Mustang fitted
with six rocket-launching tubes.
eft Ordnance men load a
.00 lb bomb under a wing of
the Republic P-47 'Patricia
*Baby' of the 353rd Fighter
Group at a base in England,
April 1944.
ight Grumman Avenger
orpedo-bomber, October 1944.

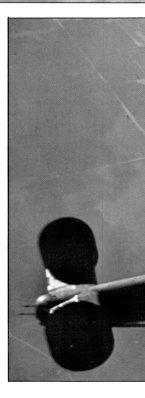

Department fully informed on the latest tactical and technical developments in Europe.

Meanwhile the Air Corps was faced by innumerable logistical and administrative problems in its expansion. Here it was greatly aided by Henry L. Stimson, who became Secretary of War in June 1940. Although the Air Corps Act of 1926 had provided for the Secretary to have an Assistant for Air, this post had in fact been vacant since 1932. Stimson thought the time more than ripe for an incumbent, and in November 1940 Robert A. Lovett was appointed to the office, becoming Assistant Secretary of War for Air in April 1941.

Ever since 1939, when the first Roosevelt expansion programme for the Air Corps was got under way, the advocates of an independent air service had redoubled their efforts, and although the actual establishment of an independent air service in such troubled times was unlikely, there was certainly a case for the Air Corps to enjoy greater autonomy within the army structure. Though out-and-out adherents to the concept of an independent air service maintained this posture despite its impossibility, more reasonable men called for greater autonomy. One of these latter was G. de Friest Larner of the National Aeronautics Association, who recommended that Arnold be made Deputy Chief-of-Staff for

Air, in a conversation with Robert P. Patterson, the Assistant Secretary of War. Patterson agreed with Larner, and told Stimson so on 18 September 1940, with a recommendation that there be a complete review of the Air Corps' position within the US Army.

Moves that would help this review had already been made, for on 26 July Marshall had established a General Headquarters under Major General Lesley J. McNair, to supervise the training of army units through the four field armies that had been established within the United States in 1932. Marshall had early come to the conclusion that the general staff was too unwieldy an organisation for the urgent task of training the US Army's expanding field formations. The establishment of an army GHQ of course raised the question of relations with GHQ, AF and, with the problem of whether or not to create a Deputy Chief-of-Staff for Air, this persuaded Marshall to call on the Air Corps' planning staffs for recommendations on 5 October 1940. Arnold replied that he thought three deputy chiefs-of-staff should be found, one for each of the main army branches, the Air Corps, the Ground Forces and the Service Forces. Each deputy would control his own staff, and issue orders in the name of the chief-of-staff, subject only to Marshall's overall authority. The De-

Left The Boeing B-17E, showing its clean lines, which were to become increasingly cluttered as the type was developed.

Left The Boeing B-29 Superfortress, technically far ahead of any other bomber of its time, was used only against Japan, where, in the inter-island vastness of the Pacific, its enormous range was desperately needed to bring the war home to Japanese industry. It set many trends in bomber design, including the use of remotely controlled defensive fire from gun barbettes.
Below Consolidated Vultee B-24 Liberators in flight. This aircraft was built in larger numbers than any other US aircraft, and is said to have destroyed more than 4,000 aircraft in its career.

puty Chief-of-Staff for Air, Arnold recommended, should be responsible for all units under the command of OCAC and GHQ, AF with the exception of those in combat theatres.

The plan was opposed by the general staff, and Marshall compromised on 30 October 1940 with the appointment of Arnold as Deputy Chief-of-Staff, but only in an acting capacity. The definitive rejection of the Air Corps' recommendations came on 19 November 1940, when GHQ, AF was subordinated to Army GHQ. The Air Corps' disappointment that there was to be no proper air staff or air unity was expressed on 26 December 1940 in a memo from Major General George H. Brett, Acting Chief of the Air Corps since Arnold's elevation to Deputy Chief-of-Staff for Air (Acting): consideration by the general staff of plans drawn up 'by the best qualified air staff available' would lead to 'interminable delay [and] the emasculation of basic plans and policies'.

Internally, however, the Air Corps' expansion was facilitated in late 1940 by the decision to form the Northeast, Southeast, Northwest and Southwest Air Districts. These districts became operational on 16 January 1941, under the GHQ, AF, and were responsible on a territorial basis for both administrative and tactical aspects of the expansion programme. The latter aspect was the result of the air districts' possession of both bomber and fighter units in the continental area and the fact that they were to provide fully trained units for overseas task forces. Administratively, the air districts were responsible for all air corps activities in their areas with the exception of certain service functions. Soon after their formation, the air districts started to search out new airfields, expanding existing ones and otherwise set about the training of the growing air service. OCAC still supervised training and *matériel* procurement.

Despite its failure to secure a more important niche in the US Army's hierarchy, the Air Corps gradually assumed a relatively dominant position as a result of world events. At the end of January 1941 secret military talks between the British and the Americans had begun in Washington, culminating in the ABC agreements: ABC-1 decided that if the United States entered the war, she would be responsible for the defence of the western hemisphere as a primary responsibility; seven alternative courses of action against Germany were also envisaged, although only two of them were early possibilities (a blockade of the Axis powers and a 'sustained air offensive to destroy Axis military power'). ABC-2 provided for full air cooperation.

Soon after this the War Department agreed that by the ABC agreements 'United States operations initially are limited to providing combat aviation in support of the British Isles', a fact emphasised by the dispatch of Arnold to the United Kingdom for talks in April 1941 and the appointment of Major General James E. Chaney, an Air Corps officer, to head the US Army mission in Great Britain.

Lessons of the war in Europe also suggested that air/ground defences of the continental United States should rely heavily on the Air Corps, and after experiments in the Caribbean and Alaska in March 1941 the Northeastern (subsequently Eastern), Central, Southern and Western Defense Commands were established, at first as additions to the four field armies, but later as full staffs. Controlled by GHQ, AF, these four defence commands later became the 1st, 2nd, 3rd and 4th Air Forces, in order to correspond with the four field

armies' numbering. It was only after prolonged wrangling, though, that the right of the Air Corps to supervise the defence areas was recognised.

This whole time pressure on the army to grant the Air Corps more autonomy had continued, against strenuous opposition from the army. Finally, however, Marshall became convinced that the subordination of the Air Corps to Army GHQ's overall control was hampering correct and speedy decisions. Stimson concurred as a result of a conference between 26 and 27 March 1941, and ordered moves be made 'to develop an organization staffed and equipped to provide the ground forces with essential aircraft units for joint operations, while at the same time expanding and decentralizing our staff work to permit Air Force autonomy in the degree needed'. This was to be achieved by the creation of a single air service command. So on 28 March 1941 Arnold, as Deputy Chief-of-Staff for Air, was ordered to coordinate all air matters. The new structure was revealed by the appointment of Lovett as Assistant Secretary of War for Air during April.

Further plans for a *de facto* if not *de jure* independent air force were worked out, not without acrimony, during April and May 1941, leading on 20 June 1941 to the formation of the Army Air Forces by Army Regulation 95–5: the new force was to be headed by the Chief of the Army Air Forces, who was also the Deputy Chief-of-Staff for Air, coordinating the work of the OCAC departments and the GHQ, AF, now re-designated the Air Force Combat Command (AFCC). Periodic reviews of various projects were to be undertaken by an Air Council consisting of the Assistant Secretary of War for Air, the Chief of the Army Air Forces (AAF), the Chief of the War Plans Division, the commander of the AFCC and the Chief of the Air Corps. There were thus still too many bodies with fingers in the AAF pie. The single most redeeming feature, though, was the fact that the Chief of the AAF had his own general staff organisation.

The new-found autonomy of the Chief of the AAF was recognised on 10 July 1941: the Joint Army-Navy Board added the Deputy Chief-of-Staff for Air and the Chief of the Navy Bureau of Aeronautics to its members, although only when air matters were being considered.

In the last months of peace, all concerned realised that the US Army chain of command was just too unwieldy for war operations: under Marshall as Chief-of-Staff were the Chief of the Army Air Forces (Arnold), GHQ (McNair), corps areas and the various chiefs of arms and services, all on a level. Arnold controlled two main bodies on the same level: AAFC (Lieutenant General D. C. Emmons) and OCAC (Brett); McNair controlled two main bodies on the same level: the field armies, and the defence commands. Although there was provision for co-ordination laterally, this could not be an adequate substitute for vertical chains of command. Brett's command, it should be noted, contained amongst other bodies the Materiel Division, the Air Service Command, the Ferrying Command, the Technical Training Command, the various Flying Training Centers, and the Proving Ground.

Although delayed by the attack on Pearl Harbor, the final revision of the command structure was published in War Department Circular 59 of 2 March 1942, made effective on 9 March 1942 by Executive Order 9082 from the president. The final structure was largely the

work of Major General Joseph T. McNarney, an Air Corps officer, aided by Colonel William K. Harrison of the War Plans Division and Lieutenant Colonel Laurence S. Kuter of the Air Corps. Under Marshall, as US Army Chief-of-Staff, were three Zone of Interior Commands: the Services of Supply (Army Service Forces) commanded by Lieutenant General Brehon Somervell, the Army Ground Forces commanded by McNair, and the Army Air Forces commanded by Arnold, by this time Commanding General, Army Air Forces with the rank of lieutenant general. It should be noted, though, that whereas Somervell and McNair were limited by their authority exclusively to the Zone of the Interior (the continental United States), Arnold was able to circumvent this limitation and deal directly with air units in the combat theatres by virtue of the fact that he was one of the three service representatives on the Joint Chiefs-of-Staff Committee. He was also a member of the Allied Combined Chiefs-of-Staff Committee, and was thus well placed to supervise the activities of all American air forces at home and abroad. This power extended to Arnold's staff, which served the triple function of controlling the logistical and training effort at home, of advising its head in high command matters, and of running the American air effort in every part of the world, even exercising direct command of the 20th Air Force in the Pacific during the strategic campaign against Japan from the Marianas islands.

Within the US Army structure, the Air Corps continued as the legal basis of the air service. But both OCAC and AFCC were abolished, their roles being assumed by AAF Headquarters. The end of AFCC had become inevitable shortly after the outbreak of war in December 1941, when the Eastern and Western Defense Commands had become the Eastern and Western Theaters of Operations, with the 1st and 4th Air Forces under command respectively. At the same time the 2nd and 3rd Air Forces became training commands, and thus part of OCAC rather than AFCC. With the final dissolution of the AFCC there disappeared the dual command structure that had beset the air service since 1935.

Within the AAF, therefore, the organisational structure on 9 March 1942 was a five-level one, with the Commanding General, AAF, at the top, the Chief of Air Staff and his deputy on the second level, the air staff departments on the policy or third level, the operations departments on the fourth level, and the commands and domestic air forces on the fifth level. The policy-level departments were A-1 (Personnel), A-2 (Intelligence), A-3 (Training and Operations), A-4 (Supply), as well as the Plans Department (sometimes called A-5) and Air Inspector. At the operations level, the departments were those of: the Director of Military Requirements (Air Defense, Bombardment, Ground Support, Base Services, War Organization and Movement, and Individual Training), the Director of Technical Services (Communications, Weather, Traffic Control and Re-

Left Members of the ordnance crew with the 93rd Group in Hardwick, England, loading bombs into a Consolidated B-24D Liberator. This B-24D is the 'Shoot Luke' which had been on 27 missions over enemy territory by April 1943.
Far left Liberators from the double assembly lines on Consolidated Vultee's Fort Worth plant get a final check by Field Operation crews; 18,188 of these aircraft were built.
Top left A massive attack using these firebombs in April 1945 hastened the end of the Nazi resistance at Royan, in France. The plane is a Consolidated B-24 Liberator.

gulation, Photography, and Technical Inspection), the Director of Personnel (Military and Civilian), the Director of Management Control (Air Adjutant General, Organizational Planning, Statistical Control and Legislative Planning), the Public Relations Officer, the Air Judge Advocate, the Budget Officer (Fiscal Office) and the Air Surgeon.

By the end of March 1943 operational lessons had led to a reorganisation of the Army Air Forces: at the top was still Arnold, the Commanding General. Below him were the Chief of the Air Staff and the Deputy Chiefs of the Air Staff, together with a parallel Management Control organisation consisting of Organizational Planning, Statistical Control, Manpower and Air Adjutant General departments. Then there was a third level, with twelve departments: the Assistant Chief of the Air Staff, Personnel (Military Personnel, Civilian Personnel, Special Services, and Air Chaplain); the ACAS, Intelligence (Operational Intelligence, Counter-Intelligence, Intelligence Information, Combat Liaison and Training, and Historical); the ACAS, Training (Aircrew Training, Unit Training, Technical Training, Training Aids, and Plans Analysis and Reports), with a primary supervisory responsibility for Flying Training Command, Technical Training Command, I Troop Carrier Command, and the continental air forces (the 1st and 4th AFs under Operational Theater control); the AC/AS, Materiel Maintenance and Distribution (Materiel, Supply and Services, Transportation, Air Ordnance, Air Chemical, Air Engineer, Air Finance, Air Quartermaster, Air Provost Marshal, Air WAAC, and Communication Equipment), with primary supervisory responsibility for the Air Transport Command, Matériel Command, and Air Service Command; the AC/AS, Operations, Commitments and Requirements (Requirements, Allocations and Programs, and Movements and Operations) with primary supervisory responsibility for the Proving Ground Command, Antisubmarine Command, Flight Control Command, and School of Applied Tactics (Combat Air Forces); the AC/AS Plans (Strategical, Policy, and Joint and Combined Chiefs-of-Staff Subjects); the Air Inspector; the Air Surgeon; the Budget and Fiscal Department; the Air Judge Advocate; Special Projects; and finally the various Commands.

Thereafter there were, of course, other changes, but the basic shape of the AAF command structure remained unaltered.

During the period between 1940 and 1945, personnel strength of the air service grew almost the whole time: 51,165 in 1940; 152,125 in 1941; 764,415 in 1942; 2,197,114 in 1943; 2,373,292 in 1944; and 2,282,259 in 1945. A peak strength was reached in March 1944 with 2,411,000 personnel, some 31% of the total US armed forces.

During World War II, the following air forces were operational within the AAF: the 1st AF in the north-east USA, the 2nd AF in the north-west USA, the 3rd AF in the south-east USA, the 4th AF in the south-west USA, the 5th AF in the South-West Pacific Area, the 6th AF in the Panama Canal region, the 7th AF in the Pacific Ocean Areas, the 8th AF in north-west Europe, the 9th AF in North Africa and England, the 10th AF in India and south-east Asia, the 11th AF in Alaska, the 12th AF in North Africa, Italy and England, 14th AF in China, the 15th AF in Italy, and the 20th AF in the Pacific Ocean Areas.

The basic operational unit of the Army Air Forces was the squadron (numbered 94th Fighter Squadron

etc); next up was the group (numbered 64th Troop Carrier Group etc); several groups constituted a wing or division (designated 13 Combat Bombardment Wing or 1 Bombardment Division etc); wings or divisions were controlled by fighter or bombardment commands (designated V Fighter Command etc); and commands formed an air force (at the time designated Twentieth Air Force etc).

The plan in the spring of 1942 was to form an air force of 115 groups, but this target was increased to 224 groups in July 1942, and then to 273 groups in September 1943. By the end of 1943 some 269 groups had been formed, but this number was reduced to 243 in April 1945 by a reorganisation. Of the 243 groups, though, 224 were serving abroad: twenty-six very heavy bombardment groups, $72\frac{1}{2}$ heavy bombardment groups, $28\frac{1}{2}$ medium and light bombardment groups, seventy-one fighter groups, thirty-two troop carrier groups and thirteen reconnaissance groups. In April 1945 1,224,000 AAF personnel were serving overseas, 610,000 of them against Germany and 440,000 against Japan.

By September 1945 the AAF had taken delivery of 158,880 aircraft, including 51,221 bombers and 47,050 fighters. The maximum aircraft strength reached was

Above top Ground crew checking the engine of a Curtiss P-40 of the 26th Squadron, 51st Fighter Group, China. The Curtiss P-40 series was the first mass-produced US single-seat fighter, and had the new liquid-cooled Allison engine.
Above The Curtiss P-40E in flight. This type served as a useful fighter-bomber in North Africa and Italy.
Right Armament man cautiously loading the 0.05 calibre machine guns of a Republic P-47 Thunderbolt, affectionately known as 'the Jug', which was the heaviest single-seat fighter of its time. The pilot of this plane is Lieutenant-Colonel Francis S. Gabreski, the leading ace in the European Theatre of Operations, with 28 victories.

79,908 (excluding gliders) in July 1944. The AAF dropped 2,057,000 tons of bombs and fired 459,750,000 rounds of ammunition. Combat sorties totalled 2,363,800, during the course of which losses were 121,867, including 17,021 officers and 20,040 other ranks killed. Aircraft losses were 22,948 on combat missions.

The other major air arm of the United States armed forces in World War II was that of the US Navy. Like every other air force, the Naval Flying Corps suffered severe trimming in the years after World War I, with its peak strength of 6,716 officers, 30,693 other ranks, 2,107 aircraft (including those of the US Marine Corps) and fifteen dirigible airships declining rapidly in the first eighteen months of peace.

Unlike the army, which beset itself with numerous problems as a result of its odd command structure, the US Navy relied on a simple vertical command structure headed by the Bureau of Aeronautics (BuAer), which was formed on 10 August 1921 to look after all matters concerned with naval aircraft, personnel and operations. BuAer was the aviation department within the office of the Secretary of the Navy, and was thus well placed to look after its own interests.

Nevertheless the 1920s were strange but exhilarating years, for although the tasks of the Naval Flying Corps were ill defined, and aircraft few, much experimentation was carried out, and the Naval Flying Corps with many record breaking flights.

Although naval aircraft had operated from land for the most part during World War I, there were many naval aircrew who believed that aircraft could and should operate from fleet warships, as well as from the aircraft-carriers that were slowly coming into commission. Keen to assess all ideas, the navy during the 1920s allowed detachments of aircraft to operate on its major warships, with excellent results. By the end of the 1920s the Naval Flying Corps was in evidence all over the US Navy: there were three aircraft-carriers, and patrol aircraft (many of them operating from seaplane tenders) were a common sight in US Navy manoeuvres. Such aircraft were also in evidence in the oceans of the world, for most battleships and cruisers had provision for catapult-launched floatplane patrol aircraft.

During the early part of the decade, advocates of the higher performance wheeled aircraft gradually began to win support in their struggle against the adherents of the flying-boats and floatplanes as the first such examples (Vought VE-7 fighters, for example) appeared. There were still good reasons to keep on with the development of floatplanes, though, as the excellence of such types as the Douglas DT-1 torpedo-bomber proved. But more to the public's taste were the trim navy racing aircraft flown by men such as Lieutenant Al Williams, the naval counterpart to the army's celebrated 'Jimmy' Doolittle.

In 1925 the same Morrow Board that had so affected development of the Army Air Corps recommended that the US Navy's air arm should be rapidly and radically expanded to make it the greatest naval air force in the world. By the end of the decade, though, the navy could muster only 660 combat, 162 training, 141 miscellaneous, 68 reserve, and 7 utility and transport aircraft, plus 2 nonrigid and 1 rigid airship. The most notable figure of this period, so far as US naval air strength was concerned, was the able head of BuAer from 1921 to the time of his death in the *Akron* (ZR-4) airship disaster of 1933, Rear Admiral William A. Moffett. Worried that the army might try to take over the naval air arm, as had

happened in Great Britain, Moffett ensured that the navy had its own bombers and the like, though these were normally disguised on floats to prevent army jealousy. Nonetheless, the decade was marked by army-navy squabbles that were only ended by the MacArthur-Pratt agreement of 9 January 1931, by which the army received responsibility for coastal defence and the Naval Air Corps was recognised as an element of the fleet, to operate with it and so help it carry out its primary tasks.

The need to rearm the American services was finally recognised in the late 1930s. By 1938 the Naval Flying Corps could muster some 2,000 aircraft, and in that year the Naval Expansion Act permitted the navy to possess at least 3,000 aircraft. In June 1940 the target strength was raised to 4,500, and soon after this the deteriorating world situation was reflected in author-ised increases to 10,000 and then to 15,000 aircraft.

By the time of Pearl Harbor the US Navy and Marine Corps between them mustered some 5,233 aircraft of all types, with 5,900 pilots and 21,678 enlisted men. There were eight aircraft-carriers in commission, with the appropriate carrier air groups. Designed for land- or shore-based operations were five patrol wings and two Marine aircraft wings.

During the war some 102 new carriers (77 of them escort carriers) joined the navy, and the peak air strength during the war was achieved on 1 July 1945, when the US Navy had 40,912 aircraft in its Air Force, Pacific Fleet and Air Force, Atlantic Fleet, created in 1942 and 1943 to administer the growing air strength deployed in these two major operational areas. During the war years the navy had accepted 18,081 fighters, 11,831 scout and dive-bombers, 8,982 torpedo-bombers, 7,963 patrol aircraft and 3,052 observation aircraft.

Surprisingly, losses were very low, with only 2,360 aircraft lost in all. Of these, only 664 were lost to enemy action, a fact partially attributable to the strength of the Naval Flying Corps fighters, which had grown in number between 1941 and 1945 from 514 to 13,940.

The Marine aviation force was controlled by a Director of Aviation, Marine Corps Headquarters, the Division of Aviation being established in April 1936, although Marines had been operational in the air since World War I. In December 1941 the Marine Corps had 251 aircraft (seventy-eight of them in the Pacific, including forty-eight in the Hawaiian islands). The Division of Aviation reached its manpower peak in January 1945 with 125,162 men. During the war the Division suffered 794 killed in action, 319 missing, 1,375 killed on operational flights, and 1,136 wounded, shooting down 2,355 Japanese aircraft in the process.

Major General Lewis H. Brereton, Commanding General of the 9th Air Force, Lieutenant General Carl Spaatz, head of US Strategic Air Forces, and General Dwight D. Eisenhower, Chief of Allied Forces in the European Theatre of Operations, during an inspection of 9th Air Force B-26 medium bomber stations in England.
Left Martin B-26 Marauder bombers of the US Army 9th Air Force bombing the Nazi-held Schipol Aerodrome, Amsterdam, Holland. This was the chief medium bomber of the 9th Air Force. and by VE-day it had set a record for the lowest loss-rate of any US army bomber in Europe.

221

CHAPTER SIXTEEN

BOMBER OFFENSIVE IN EUROPE
1939·45

An Avro Manchester runs up its Rolls Royce 'Vulture' engines as dusk falls. Roy Chadwick designed a four-Merlin-engined development of this unsuccessful bomber, because the Vulture was so unreliable. This development became the Lancaster, arguably the finest heavy bomber in Europe in World War II. In the background is one of the best of the previous generation of bombers, the Vickers Wellington.

During World War I, bombing had been essentially a tactical weapon, designed to support the operations of the ground forces which would, all agreed, decide the outcome of the war. Yet during the course of the war, it became increasingly clear that the combatant nations' civil populations were just as important as their fighting men: it was these which supplied the food, weapons and all else necessary for the fighting troops to carry out their tasks. These civil populations were thus a 'legitimate' target for offensive action, provided only that a means of taking the war to them could be found. The best means seemed to lie with seapower, which in the end proved decisive: the Germans' increasingly widespread use of U-boats to attack Britain's, and to a lesser extent France's, sealanes nearly proved decisive in bringing the Allies to their knees, but also brought the United States into the war; on the other hand, the exercise of Allied surface seapower to blockade Germany meant that by 1918 the civil population of that

hapless country was beginning to feel the pangs of starvation. Combined with the land defeat of their army from August 1918 on, this starvation, and the rising death toll it exacted, finally compelled the Germans to sue for terms in November 1918.

On the periphery of these major operations, though, most of the major combatants had seen that airpower too could play a part in the strategic war against the fighting troops' home bases. On the Allied side, France had early developed a major tactical/strategic bomber force, Italy had her formidable Caproni force, and Russia had her *Ilya Muromets* four-engined bombers. It was Germany and Great Britain who made the greatest efforts, though. In her Imperial Navy's airship fleet, most of the craft being of Zeppelin construction, Germany had the making of a fine bombing force, as the civilians of London and other major urban areas in the south of England began to find in 1915 and 1916. But though the airships had useful bombloads and ranges,

Above RAF bomber crews going to their Vickers-Wellington machines to prepare for a dawn take-off. This aircraft was a formidable bomber, and had an extremely durable, geodetic construction.

they proved vulnerable to the British defences once these latter began belatedly to appear. The Germans thus turned increasingly to the heavy bomber, culminating with the mammoth Zeppelin (Staaken) multi-engined types at the end of the war. Fortunately for the Allies, though, Germany was too late: a great deal of time and effort had been wasted in the development of a number of types that were extensively tested over the Eastern Front, so that when the final types were selected for major production and deployment against Great Britain the war was virtually over.

Nevertheless, the threat of the German bombers had caused virtual panic among certain parts of the civil population, and the loss to industry, when their work forces had to take cover in the face of an imminent air raid, had been considerable. The first British response had been to reorganise the air defence completely, in the course of which the Royal Air Force was born, and then to realise that the air war could profitably be taken to Germany from bases in eastern central France. Thus there was born the Independent Force, the world's first true strategic air force. Circumstances prevented this from playing a decisive part in the closing stages of the war. Nevertheless, though, the concept of strategic bombing had been widely tested in World War I.

Thereafter bombing became one of the great 'bogey' weapons of the 1920s and 1930s, most civilians thinking that the bombers would be unstoppable in the future, if World War I had not been the 'war to end all wars': air fleets, it was believed, would fly over major cities right after the outbreak of hostilities, crushing buildings with high explosive and incendiary bombs, and wiping out the civilian population with gas, another military legacy of World War I. Latent fears of such a military future

were brought out into the open by the military teach ings of men such as the Italian General Giulio Douhe the imaginative writings of men like H. G. Wells, whos book *The Shape of Things to Come* played an importar part in forming civilian attitudes towards civil defence and the apparent total success of operations such as th Japanese bombing of Shanghai and the German razin of a small Spanish town that was immediately o everyone's lips – Guernica.

Despite this, however, the opening of World War I saw little activity on the part of the 'heavy' bombers largely because few such types had actually bee brought into service, but also because government were chary of letting their air forces loose on civ targets for fear of political and propagand repercussions.

Germany, initially a keen adherent of the strategi bombing concept, had opted for tactical bombing afte the death of *Generalleutnant* Wever, the chief of ai staff, in 1936, and the continued development of heav bombers proceeded with only very low priority. Gör ing, Milch and Udet all felt that Germany's productio facilities would be better used turning out large num bers of twin-engined tactical bombers than consi derably smaller numbers of four-engined long-rang strategic bombers. Similar thoughts also bedeville Allied rearmament programmes, although not to s great an extent. Thus political antipathy combined wit military inability to prevent long-range strategic bomb ing of civilian targets as a deliberate policy of war at th beginning of World War II.

Tactical bombing flourished, on the other hand, a the civilians and military alike of Poland, Belgium Holland and France discovered in the period betwee

eptember 1939 and June 1940. With its attack on Warsaw on 13 September 1939 the *Luftwaffe* began the orld's first air campaign against a fortified city, rought to a successful conclusion on 25 September hen the remnants of Warsaw were virtually in-nerated. Nevertheless, the *Luftwaffe* tried to restrict s operations to tactical efforts in direct support of the rmy, although the world indignation about the bomb-ng of the old quarter of Rotterdam on 14 May 1940 has ended to conceal this fact. Nevertheless, it should be oted that although the Germans had warned of the ombing of Rotterdam unless the Dutch capitulated, he bombing itself was a mistake, radio communications ailing to inform the German commander that the raid ad been cancelled.

So far little had been attempted in the way of long-ange bombing. There had been a portent of what was o come, though, on 18 December 1939, when a force of wenty-two Vickers Wellington bombers of the RAF ad been intercepted over the Heligoland Bight by a orce of *Luftwaffe* Bf 109 and Bf 110 fighters, which romptly shot down twelve and crippled three of the Vellingtons, which were operating without fighter over, the defensive fire of the tightly packed Welling-on formation being reckoned sufficient. The defeat had n immediate and lasting effect on RAF Bomber Command's thinking: from this time on the British eavy bombing effort would take place only by night nless heavy fighter escort could be provided. As there vere no such things as long-range escort fighters until he beginning of 1944, this meant that the British long-ange heavy bombing effort was perforce a night effort.

Political decisions meant that neither side attacked nd targets in the others' homelands, and so during the early part of the war, long-range efforts were restricted to attacks on warships and convoys in coastal waters and anchorages. The Wellington force decimated in the Heligoland Bight action, for example, had been on its way back from attacking shipping in Wilhelmshaven Roads when the German fighters revealed the British bombers' vulnerability to beam attacks. British and French bombers had, it must be admitted, operated over Germany with some frequency – but only to drop many millions of propaganda leaflets! Even in these low-intensity operations, though, the limitations of the French bombers, with the exception of the latest Lioré et Olivier LeO 451s, and of British types such as the Armstrong Whitworth Whitley, Bristol Blenheim, Handley Page Hampden and even the Vickers Welling-ton were fully revealed. Thus the introduction of four-engined heavy bombers, able to carry substantial offen-sive loads over long ranges while defending themselves with turret-mounted machine guns, was pressed on with utmost priority. This type of bomber had been called for in the mid-1930s, and two major types, the Short Stirling and Handley Page Halifax, were showing promise, as was a twin-engined type, the Avro Man-chester. Ultimately, the Rolls-Royce Vulture engines of the Manchester proved too troublesome, and a four-engined derivative was developed as the Lancaster, Britain's best heavy bomber of the war.

Ultimately it was the decision of Hitler, supported by Göring, to switch the German bomber effort from Fighter Command to London, that lost the Germans the Battle of Britain and revealed the *Luftwaffe's* mistake in abandoning the concept of the heavy bomb-er. Only one German bomber had inadvertently drop-ped its load on London on 24–25 August, but in

Above An RAF Bomber Command Handley Page Halifax in flight during a daylight attack on the synthetic oil plant at Wanne-Eickel, in the Ruhr. From 1940, this heavy bomber, in its many diverse roles, made a great contribution to the Allied victory in World War II. It operated over Germany, and was the only RAF four-engined bomber in the Middle East. *Above left* Loading a heavy bomb into a Handley Page Halifax.

etaliation Churchill sanctioned a major raid on Berlin
or the next night. Although only twenty-nine of the
ighty-one British bombers sent out found the target,
Hitler was so enraged that he immediately rescinded his
rohibition of a *Terrorangriff* or terror campaign
gainst the British and ordered attacks on the capital,
which finally started on 7 September. Heavy losses were
immediately incurred, and the last major daylight raid
was made on 27 September. The Germans now pre-
ared for the night *Blitz* against London and other
major industrial cities.

Though lacking the heavy bombers to make their
ffort decisive, the Germans nevertheless caused great
damage in England. Two special navigational aids were
used: *Knickebein* or Bent Leg, a system using intersect-
ing radio beams, was soon discovered and 'bent' to
produce navigational errors, and *X-Gerät* or X-
Apparatus, which was not effectively jammed until the
pring of 1941. This latter device was used by a special
athfinder force, *Kampfgruppe* 100, which set the target
n fire thus providing a marker for the main body of
ombers. The greatest success of the campaign oc-
urred on 14 November 1940, when *Kampfgruppe* 100
marked Coventry with great accuracy, and some 450
ombers devastated the city.

At about this time Britain's first effective night-
ighter, the Bristol Beaufighter, armed with cannon and
quipped with AI (airborne interception) radar, began
o enter service. As more of the fighters entered service,
German losses began to climb, and although these only
eached the bearable level of 3.5%, the number of
ircraft being dispatched against Britain began to tail off
during May 1941 as the Germans redeployed for their
Mediterranean and Russian adventures. Nevertheless,
he significance of night-fighters on air warfare may be
auged from the growing number of kills claimed by
RAF night-fighters: twenty-two in March 1941, forty-
ight in April and ninety-six in May.

The *Blitz* may be said to have finished with the two
aids of 10 and 13 May 1941, in each of which some 550
ombers took part. The whole campaign had lasted
ome eight months and cost the Germans 600 bombers.
The cost had been high for the British too: 40,000 dead,
6,000 wounded and enormous physical damage caused
o urban and industrial areas. To fight the bombers very
reat effort had to be diverted from other areas that
eeded all the men and money they could get. There
an be no denying, however, that the *Blitz* had failed in
ts main objective of forcing Britain out of the war.

While the *Blitz* was still continuing, RAF Bomber
Command had received its first four-engined heavy
ombers, and these Stirlings made their first raid on the
ight of 10–11 February, when four of them raided
Rotterdam to attack the dock area. The ill-starred
Manchester was also soon in service, followed by the
Halifax on 10 March. Bombers of this last type made
he first four-engined bomber raid on Germany on 12
March. Thus started what was to be Britain's only way
f taking the war to Germany proper for the next few
ears. Almost immediately, though, the build-up of
aids on Germany was slowed by the diversion of
onsiderable efforts against the battle-cruisers *Gneise-
au* and *Scharnhorst*, which arrived in Brest after a
ortie into the North Atlantic. During the next two
months the Brest docks received 1,161 missions.

On 11 June the RAF started its first major campaign
gainst Germany, with twenty major raids on con-
ecutive nights against the Rhineland and Ruhr,
Germany's industrial heart. High hopes had been

pinned on this effort, but subsequent analysis by the
RAF's operational research staff revealed that only very
few aircraft had even got close to the target areas, let
alone bombed them. Night navigation was poor except
in bright moonlight, and this gave the German defences
just the conditions they needed.

Worried by the growing strength of Bomber
Command's raids, though, the Germans were setting
up elaborate night-fighter defences under the command
of *Generalmajor* Josef Kammhuber. On taking over,
Kammhuber inherited an organisation of *Flak* guns,
searchlights and single-engined fighters. These last
operated with tactics known as *helle Nachtjagd* or
Illuminated Night-Fighting: lacking airborne radar,
the fighters had to wait for the searchlights to illuminate
a target for them, and then attack conventionally. As
may be imagined, successes were few, thanks to the
inefficiency of the tactics and the small number of
fighters available.

Kammhuber took over in May 1940, and soon began
to develop the *Himmelbett* or Four-Poster Bed tactics:
every twenty miles (32 km) from Liège to Schleswig-
Holstein there was set up a radar control station. The
location of this fighter belt, running across all Bomber
Command's main routes, was kept clear of the larger
cities, and hence of the main *Flak* areas, so that the
fighter could operate without fear of their own artillery
defences. Each *Himmelbett* station had one *Freya* area
search radar and two *Würzburg* precision radars. Once a
British bomber had been located with *Freya*, it was
picked up by one of the *Würzburg* sets. The controller
could then vector in his orbiting fighter to an interception, the fighter's position being determined by
the other *Würzburg*. Once they were close enough, it
was hoped, the crew of the night-fighter would pick up
their target visually and close in for the kill. By the
middle of 1941 Kammhuber had some 250 aircraft at
his disposal: I., II., and III./*Nachtjagdgeschwader* 1,
I./NJG 2 and I./NJG 3 with Dornier Do 17, Junkers Ju
88 and Messerschmitt Bf 110 aircraft.

With the exception of I./NJG 2, these were defensive
units. I./NJG 2, though, was used for intruder (*Fern-
nachtjagd*) missions against bomber streams over England. The overextended needs of the *Luftwaffe* during
the late summer of 1941, however, meant that I./NJG 2
was returned to more conventional night-fighting
duties with its Ju 88s and Do 17s. By July 1941 the
reorganised night-fighter arm had claimed some 250
victories.

Opposite The pilot waves
from the Boeing B-17G
Fortress, which was
nicknamed 'General Ike' and
christened in April 1944 with a
bottle of Mississippi water by
Eisenhower. The B-17G was
the US army's mainstay heavy
bomber in Europe during
1944–5.
Above Bristol Type 152
Beaufort torpedo bombers in
flight. This four-seat torpedo
bomber was used as a
mine-layer, and bombed many
ships including the battle
cruiser *Scharnhorst*.

Bomber Command was still expanding the scope of its activities, and the Kammhuber Line, as the belt of *Himmelbett* control boxes was known, was extended south to the Swiss frontier and north to Denmark. It was clear that the main limitation of the system was that each box could engage only one bomber at a time, so Bomber Command introduced 'stream' tactics, in which concentrations of bombers flew through the *Himmelbett* belt as tightly as possible, giving the Germans the minimum chance of engaging more than just a very few aircraft. Kammhuber responded by widening his belt so that the bombers had to fly through what was in effect three belts. At the same time two new radar equipments were introduced into German service: *reise Würzburg* or Giant *Würzburg*, a more flexible ground radar to replace the old *Würzburg*, and *Lichtenstein BC* AI radar, which greatly increased the success rate of the aircraft into which it was fitted from the beginning of 1942.

The increasing successes of the night-fighters at last persuaded the British to use 'Window', tinfoil strips dropped in bundles to swamp the Germans' radar screens with radar echoes and make the detection of aircraft very difficult. The device was an immediate success, and allowed Bomber Command virtually to destroy Hamburg in four raids at the end of July and beginning of August 1943.

Kammhuber was relieved, and new tactics adopted: *wilde Sau* and *zahme Sau*, or Wild Boar and Tame Boar. For the former, a special unit was raised in the form of *Jagdgeschwader* 300: operating Bf 109s and Fw 190s, the pilots of this unit operated over German cities, picking up British bombers in the light of searchlights and of the fires of the target. The *Flak* shells in the area were all fused to detonate below a given height, the *wilde Sau* single-engined fighters operating above this. The radar-equipped twin-engined fighters could engage in these activities, but were more gainfully employed in the *zahme Sau* tactics. Here the controllers in each *Fliegerdivision*'s area brought in the fighters to where the 'Window' reflections were thickest, in the correct

assumption that this would be hiding large numbers bombers. Once in the 'Window' saturated area, t *zahme Sau* fighters had to pick up their target aircra visually. This tactic meant that different night-fight units could be brought in to engage the bomber strea the whole way to and from the target while they were German radar range. The tactic was also aided by t introduction of new radar equipments: *Lichtenste SN-2* AI, working at frequencies not affected 'Window'; *Naxos*, homing on the emissions of t British H2S blind-bombing and navigational radar; a *Flensburg*, homing on the emissions of the Briti 'Monica' tail-warning radar.

Once a target had been found, a favourite Germ tactic was to close up underneath and behind t bomber. Here the chances of being spotted were sma and if the crew of the bomber proved vigilant, there w little chance of a diving escape, and not many bombe had ventral guns. Many of the night-fighters ha *schräge Muzik* or Shrill Music (jazz) armament i stallations: two cannon in the fuselage, disposed to fi obliquely upwards and forwards, and these prove lethal in such tactics. Alternatively the pilot had mere to pull up the nose of his aircraft and rake the bomb with the fixed forward-firing cannon armament.

By September 1943 the *Luftwaffe* had six *Nach jagdgeschwader*: NJG 1 with four *Gruppen*, NJG 2 wi three *Gruppen*; NJG 3 with four *Gruppen*, NJG 4 wi four *Gruppen*, NJG 5 with five *Gruppen*, and NJG with four *Gruppen*. This was the basis for the Germa night-fighter arm for the rest of the war, although mar other less well established units were added right at t end, when changes of designation and lack of record make it difficult to keep track of them all. Some of the were, however, notable: NJG 100 and NJG 200 ha independent *Gruppen* on the Eastern Front, with the radar and controllers made very mobile by their lo cation in trains; NJG 101 and NJG 102, each with thr *Gruppen* after September 1944, were derived from t operational training squadrons at the night-fight school at Schleissheim, and were located at Ingolsta

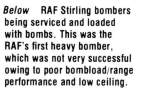

Below RAF Stirling bombers being serviced and loaded with bombs. This was the RAF's first heavy bomber, which was not very successful owing to poor bombload/range performance and low ceiling.

and Kitzingen respectively; JG 301 and JG 302 were like JG 300 short-lived *wilde Sau* units; NJG 10 was an experimental unit to test new radar under operational conditions; and NJG 11, with two *Gruppen*, formed from ex-*wilde Sau* pilots (10/NJG 11 was the war's only jet night-fighter squadron, equipped with Me 262s and commanded by *Oberleutnant* Welter).

'Window' was used for the rest of the war, and so *zahme Sau* tactics continued to be the German night-fighters' standard operational method, at times scoring very heavily. On 30–31 March, 1944, for example, the majority of the 107 British bombers lost that night fell to the *zahme Sau* night-fighter units. But from that time onwards the night-fighter arm, together with the rest of the *Luftwaffe*, went into a decline: RAF night intruders operating with the bombers were cutting down the

German night-fighters, the German radar was jammed ever more successfully, the quality of replacement aircrew was lower than desirable, and finally fuel shortages grounded almost the whole arm from the beginning of 1945.

Meanwhile, Bomber Command had continued to grow, despite its early lack of success. By September 1941 there were some forty heavy bombers, sixty Whitleys, 120 Hampdens and 200 Wellingtons available, though of this total of 420 raids by more than 150 bombers were only very rarely made. The efficiency of the force was improved at this time by the advent of 'Gee', a radio navigational aid, and of large bombs, weighing some 4,000 lb (1,814 kg).

Up to 8 July 1941, Bomber Command's main target was supposed to be German oil production facilities,

Above The Avro Manchester bomber, with its twin Rolls-Royce Vulture engines, was not a success, but led to the superb four-engined Lancaster.

but in fact only 8% of the force's effort had been devoted to this, with some 30% of the effort instead given to the futile exercise of destroying the invasion craft gathered in northern European ports for the proposed invasion of southern England the year before. Another major target was the U-boat bases in western France, another campaign that was almost completely unsuccessful. The trouble lay largely with the fact that crews just could not navigate successfully by night, it being reckoned in the autumn of 1941 that only three out of ten crews were dropping their bombs within five miles (8 km) of their target area. Combined with the growing success of the German night-fighters (Bomber Command lost 516 aircraft in 10,179 night missions, or 5.07%, compared with seventy-three in 912 day missions, or 8%, in the period between August and November 1941), this meant that the British night bombing effort was wasteful in terms of the resources involved.

The introduction of 'Gee' and a later generation of navigation aids, plus newer aircraft (in November 1941 Bomber Command's German offensive was virtually halted to allow the new four-engined bombers to be introduced in substantial numbers) meant that the future was brighter. Then on 22 February 1942 Air Chief Marshal Sir Arthur Harris succeeded to the control of Bomber Command in place of Air Marshal Sir Richard Peirse, whose period as commander had ended on 8 January 1942. Harris was a keen adherent of the strategic bombing theory as propounded by Marshal of the Royal Air Force Lord Trenchard. A forceful character who also had the ear of Churchill, Harris on 13 February secured approval from the war cabinet for his own bombing policy: the main target would become German cities, under a policy of 'area bombing' of civilian urban centres. The reasoning behind this was that the German workforce would be destroyed or so dislocated that industry would seize up, and thus halt Germany's war machine. Of course German industry would also be hit, as much of it was located in urban areas, but this was only a bonus – the real object of the exercise was the German civil population.

Statistically, the campaign can be summed up quite simply: during the main period of the 'area bombing' campaign between 13 February 1942 and 6 March 1944, RAF Bomber Command dropped some 194,000 tons (197,114 tonnes) of bombs on German cities, destroying 23,000 acres (9,200 hectares) of forty-two German cities, and causing about 500,000 casualties; Bomber Command's losses had been 4,285 bombers.

This can, of course, be only part of the story. The first great event in the campaign was the first '1,000-bomber' raid, which blasted Köln on the night of 30–31 May 1941. This was as much a propaganda as a purely military raid, and served to convince some of Harris's opponents of the value of his policy. The damage caused was considerable, but the raid was brought up to the 1,000-aircraft mark only by the inclusion of training and Coastal Command aircraft, which caused serious dislocation of their plans. For the first time the 'bomber stream' tactic was used, in which a tightly controlled stream of aircraft bombed the marker fires started by the leaders using 'Gee'. Though the *Himmelbett* system was swamped by the stream of bombers coming through it at one point, the great number of bombers provided good targets, and forty-one were shot down.

In June 1942 Essen and Bremen also received major raids, but luckily for the Germans cloud obscured both targets, which thus escaped lightly. June saw 4,800

Left An RAF crew with the coastal command Boeing Fortress II. These aircraft were used for long-range maritime patrol.
Below A camouflaged bomb dump at an American air base in England.

missions dispatched, and losses of 212, or 4.4% for the month. For the rest of the year Bomber Command continued to keep up its area raids, at the same time experimenting with small daylight raids against special targets. The most successful of these occurred on 17 April, when twelve of the new Avro Lancaster heavy bombers flew at low level to the MAN diesel engine factory in Augsburg. Severe damage was caused, but eight of the bombers were shot down. By October some forty-five such raids had been made, many of them against the U-boat yards at Danzig, Gdynia and Lübeck. By this time, too, the de Havilland Mosquito was in service, and proving a great nuisance to the Germans. Fast and manoeuvrable, it could nevertheless carry a useful bombload, and the German efforts to deal with small groups of these aircraft on 'nuisance raids' greatly hampered their main efforts.

At the beginning of 1943 Bomber Command had some 738 'main force' bombers and twenty-three Mosquitoes. To counter this force the Germans had

about 390 night-fighters. The average bombload that could be carried on a single raid by Bomber Command was thus about 2,100 tons (2,134 tonnes).

On 5 March 1943 there started the so-called Battle of the Ruhr, when 480 acres (192 hectares) of Essen were destroyed. In this and another four major raids on Essen before the end of July 1943, 2,070 sorties were dispatched, but this centre of the Krupp industrial empire still continued to turn out vast quantities of heavy armaments. The most successful raid of the battle was that against Wuppertal on 29 May, when 70% of the 657 bombers sent out bombed within three miles (4.8 km) of the aiming point, destroying some 1,000 acres (400 hectares). During the battle Aachen, Bochum, Duisburg and Düsseldorf were also heavily damaged, but industrial output fell only 10%. Yet the cost was great: in the forty-three raids Bomber Command had made over 18,000 sorties, and lost 872 with another 2,126 damaged. June was the worst month with 275 aircraft lost and 662 damaged.

Below Lockheed developed the Model 414 Hudson bomber to meet a British requirement for a maritime patroller, and these served with several RAF commands in many theatres of war. The one pictured was for maritime use in India.

But in July and August Harris's theory seemed to be vindicated by the virtual destruction of Hamburg in the aptly named Operation 'Gomorrah'. In the second raid there occurred the first firestorm of the war, in which the heat of burning houses caused great air currents to provide further oxygen for the firestorm, which in turn raised wind speed higher. It is believed that temperatures exceeded 1,000° C and wind speeds 200 mph (320 kph). Some 30,000 civilians were killed in the one firestorm, and in the operation Hamburg and its industries virtually eliminated: at the end of August only 35% of the city's work force were available. This success by Bomber Command is largely attributable to good weather, and ideal target area, and the use of 'Window': 3,095 sorties had been dispatched, and losses amounted to only eighty-seven aircraft or 2.8%. Another 174 bombers had been damaged. If Bomber Command had been able to keep up this type of success, the area bombing policy might have decided the Germans to sue for terms.

But the battle of Hamburg was followed by the unsuccessful Battle of Berlin, which took place between 18 November 1943 and 24 March 1944. In this some sixteen major raids by 9,111 sorties were made, but Harris's dream of destroying Berlin and thus ending the war at a stroke was sadly unrealised: the joint Bomber Command and US 8th Army Air Force raids failed entirely, for although forty-eight factories were destroyed and another 259 damaged, civilian losses were only 10,000, and the Allies lost 581 four-engined bombers, or 6.4% of those committed. At the same time nineteen other raids were launched against more German cities. These involved 11,113 sorties and 565 losses (5.1%), but nowhere was significant damage on the scale of that in Hamburg and in Kassel (raided on 22 October 1943, when the world's second firestorm was raised) achieved.

On 30 March 1944, just before Bomber Command passed to the tactical use of General Eisenhower for the Allied build-up towards the D-Day landings, Bomber Command suffered its worst ever defeat, in a raid on Nürnburg. The German night-fighter force was available in strength, and was at a peak of efficiency. Some 794 bombers were sent out, but the damage caused was very small. Losses were heavy: ninety-four Lancasters and Halifaxes (11.8%), most of them victims of the 294 night-fighters; twelve more aircraft were lost in crash landings and another seventy-one were damaged, for a total casualty rate of 22.3%.

In preparation for D-Day, the Allied strategic bomber forces operated in France for the most part, some 250,000 tons of bombs being liberally dropped to cut and otherwise destroy the Germans' lines of communication with France's north coast. In this the Allies were wholly successful. During the invasion period the heavy bombers were used for tactical purposes, and it was only after the breakout from the Normandy beachhead lodgement area that the bombers were returned to their primary missions, with emphasis on the strategic target against which they should have been concentrating all along: Germany's fuel industries. For the rest of the war these were cut to pieces, materially speeding up the end of hostilities. Bomber Command, though, never ceased with its area bombing tactics, which culminated in one of the most useless and ghastly raids of all on 13–14 February. In this raid, against Dresden, 804 bombers raised the worst firestorm of the European war. Dresden's military value was negligible and it was packed with refugees fleeing the Russians. Over

Below Maintenance and 'cosmetic' work on a Boeing B-17G Fortress.
Opposite A page of German propaganda from *Signal*, on the futility of the British bombing efforts.

100,000 people died in this one horrendous night. Bomber Command lost only three aircraft.

During the war Bomber Command's casualties totalled 7,449 night bombers, together with 47,130 aircrew killed in operations and another 8,000 or more in training accidents and non-operational flights. Yet strategic bombing as advocated by Harris had singularly failed to win the war single-handed.

Bomber Command's partner in the strategic air war against Germany was the United States Army Air Forces. Convinced of the relative futility of the area bombing theory, compared with their own ideas of high-altitude raids against specific industrial targets by day, the precision of the Norden bombsight ensuring accuracy, and the cohesion of their bomber formations giving the German fighters little chance to get in among the bombers to shoot them down in substantial numbers, the commanders of the 8th Army Air Force early in 1942 started planning the operations of their forces once these had been established in Great Britain.

During 1942 these forces were slowly concentrated, and the 8th AAF was able to undertake its first mission on 17 August 1942, when twelve Boeing B-17s, escorted by nine RAF Supermarine Spitfire squadrons, attacked marshalling yards near Rouen in France. More than half of the 16.5 tons (16.76 tonnes) dropped fell on the target, encouraging the USAAF in its belief in the efficacy of daylight precision bombing. Other raids on targets in occupied Europe gave the 8th AAF experience of modern tactics and methods, while avoiding the main German fighter defences.

In January 1943, however, all was judged right for the first raid on Germany: on the 27th sixty-four B-17s, unescorted by fighters, attacked Wilhelmshaven, bombed successfully and returned for the loss of only three aircraft. Wilhelmshaven was raided again in February, and this time seven aircraft were lost. Bremen was also visited, and severe damage caused to the U-boat building yards for the loss of only two of the ninety-seven aircraft involved.

But then another raid on Bremen showed the Americans what they were up against. This time, on 26 April 1943, the target was the Focke-Wulf aircraft factory. Of the 107 bombers dispatched, fifteen were shot down by the defending fighters, and another forty-eight damaged. Despite this success, the Germans clearly felt that the American effort would grow, for day fighters were slowly removed from the Eastern Front and from the Mediterranean theatre for the defence of Germany, to the detriment of the German air effort in these areas.

The Casablanca Conference was held in January 1943 between Prime Minister Churchill, President Roosevelt and the Combined Chiefs-of-Staff Committee, the conduct of the war was reviewed. The results, so far as the air effort was concerned, were embodied in the 'Pointblank' Directive: the British were to attack the Germans' will to continue the war with the saturation bombing of German cities by night; the Americans were to attack the Germans' ability to continue the war, with precision raids against key industrial plants, especially those concerned with aircraft production in any way. Overall, though, the order of priorities for the Allied strategic bombers was first, German submarine construction yards, followed by the German aircraft industry, transportation, oil production facilities, and finally any other targets in Germany's war industry. In general, though, this plan did not work, principally because the two relevant commanders-in-chief, Sir Arthur Harris and Ira C.

Eaker, chose to interpret the 'Pointblank' Directive in different ways. As the war continued the order of priorities changed, with German submarine construction capability receiving less and less priority as the threat of the U-boat arm diminished after May 1943.

The Americans saw Germany's air potential as their main target, therefore, and it was this that persuaded the Americans to choose the Messerschmitt factory at Regensburg, and the ball-bearing factories of Schweinfurt, as the targets for their first deep-penetration mission into Germany. Some 363 B-17s set out on 17 August 1943, and did considerable damage to their targets, but only at terrible cost. The Germans had seen the raid developing, and thus met it in strength. Over Germany fifty-nine B-17s were shot down, and of the 123 survivors of the Regensburg half of the raid, who had flown on to North Africa, fifty-five were found to be too badly damaged for local repair. These were staggering losses, which the 8th AAF was hard pressed to explain away.

On the night of this same day Bomber Command made its first night precision attack, when 597 heavy bombers struck at the V-weapons experimental establishment at Peenemünde. The target was accurately marked by pathfinders, and the main force kept up to the mark with instructions from an orbiting 'master bomber' running the attack from the air. This technique had been tested operationally for the first time only ten days before, but proved an invaluable aid to bombing accuracy. Unfortunately, though, this was the day that the Germans started their *zahme Sau* tactics, and forty bombers were shot down and another thirty-two damaged (12% of the total dispatched). Allied heavy bomber losses for the day were thus ninety-nine destroyed and more than one hundred damaged.

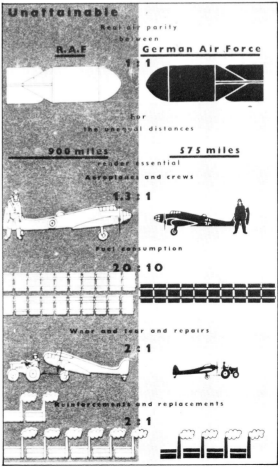

Determined to secure revenge on the Germans for the 17 August *débâcle*, the Americans returned to Schweinfurt again on 14 October. Again the target was badly damaged, but this time the losses were even worse. Of the 291 B-17s sent out, twenty-eight were shot down *en route* to the target and another thirty-two on the way back; and of the 231 bombers to get home, 138 were damaged. The loss rate had been 20.6%, compared with the earlier raid's 16.25%. Such losses could not be tolerated, and the 8th AAF immediately discontinued deep-penetration missions by day until strength was restored and escort-fighters.

By the beginning of 1944 the long-legged North American P-51B Mustang had arrived to supplement the shorter-ranged Lockheed P-38 Lightning and Republic P-47 Thunderbolt escort squadrons. So the new Strategic Air Forces command, headed by General Carl Spaatz under the direct supervision of the authorities in Washington and comprising the 8th AAF in England and the 15th AAF in Italy, decided on a trial of strength with the *Luftwaffe*, hoping that a war of attrition would crush the German day fighter arm, leaving the American air forces to roam the skies of Europe at will. There were more than 2,000 B-17s and Consolidated B-24s in England and Italy, and these would tackle the German aircraft production centres and depots. Their escorts would chop down the German fighters as they tried to intercept the great daylight bomber formations.

The offensive got off to a bad start on 11 January 1944, when bombers and escort failed to link up over Brunswick, and sixty of 667 bombers were shot down. This was seen only as a temporary setback, however, and the Americans pressed on with their programme.

The main effort, since known as the 'Big Week', began on 20 February 1944, In this and the following five days, five major raids were launched against twenty-six German aircraft factories, causing enough damage to reduce aircraft production by an immediate 20%. Although American losses were relatively heavy, at 228 of the 3,800 four-engined bombers dispatched (6%), plus twenty-eight single-engined fighters, the Germans lost far more heavily, with 355 of the 1,000 fighters available for defence of the *Reich* lost, together with 360 aircrew killed and wounded. Clearly such aircraft losses, in the order of 35.5%, could not be tolerated. The 'Big Week' could therefore rightly be claimed a considerable American victory.

The key to American successes of this type was the superlative P-51 Mustang, in its Merlin-engined escort fighter models. So long as the USAAF's B-17s and B-24s were escorted by these aircraft, which could operate to very long range with the aid of drop tanks, and then outfly the German defending fighters after they had jettisoned their tanks, deep-penetration daylight missions were entirely feasible. Although the Americans were to cooperate in the Battle of Berlin, the US senior commanders were loathe to do so because not until March 1944 were the two necessary groups of P-51 available for the 1,200-mile (1,930 km) raid. In all, the 8th AAF made five daylight raids, and the importance

Below A B-17 Fortress after the war; several versions of this outstanding aircraft were used for search rescue, training, photographic and other purposes.

f the P-51 cover can best be illustrated by the losses on March, when only one hundred of the 796 fighters ispatched to escort the 730 bombers could get through Berlin and back. With the escort stretched far too in, the German *Gefechtsverbände* were able to fight eir way into the US bomber boxes and slaughter large umbers of them. On this raid the USAAF suffered its orst losses on any single raid, sixty-nine of the ombers failing to return, 9.45% of the total dispatched.

Like Bomber Command, the US Strategic Air orces were switched to Eisenhower's command for actical purposes at the end of March. Here the US eavy bombers proved decisive in a number of ways efore returning to their strategic tasks. In the interval, ne 9th AAF in North Africa had launched its celerated raid against the Romanian oilfields at Ploiesti on August 1944. The force dispatched was made up of 77 B-24s, and only 123 of these returned home, the oss rate being 30.5%. The German *Flak* and fighter efences, with considerable warning of the Americans' rrival, had prepared excellent defences. Oil production as reduced only slightly. Towards the end of May the trategic Air Forces were able once again to undertake art of their strategic missions, with German oil roduction facilities receiving the highest priority. On 7 uly more than 1,000 bombers from the 8th and 9th AFs raided four oil producing plants in the Leipzig rea with great effect. It was over this area, considered f prime importance by the Germans, that the first Messerschmitt Me 163 rocket-propelled point inter

ceptors were met.

All the while the German fighter force was being decimated by continued air raids with strong fighter escort, and the bombers began to roam almost at will. Between July and September 1944, aviation fuel production fell from 35,000 tons to 7,000 tons per month, further reducing the part the *Luftwaffe* could play in the war. At the same time the German railway system was cut to shreds, making the movement of coal for synthetic oil production and more conventional uses all but impossible.

The first Messerschmitt Me 262 jet interceptors were met for the first time in September 1944, but only in very small, and therefore ineffective, numbers. By the first part of 1945, though, the numbers of Me 262s available had grown, and on 18 March the largest such group to engage the Americans at one time, thirty-seven in all, took on the 1,122 bombers and 632 escort fighters attacking Berlin. Bomber losses were eight, and none of the Me 262s was caught by the P-51 escort. Finally, the best defence of the Me 262 force was found to be a waiting game over the German airfields, for the Me 262 had only a short endurance.

From the D-Day landings onwards, the US Strategic Air Forces could muster some 3,500 heavy bombers. The USAAF's losses in the European theatre totalled some 8,067 heavy bombers, although the main objects of the strategic campaign were finally realised only after the success of the D-Day landings had made the defeat of Germany inevitable.

Below A squadron of the successful B-17s en route to Germany. More than 12,700 Boeing B-17s were built, of which 8,700 were the B-17G model. The B-17E became the first weapon of the US 8th Bomber Command in England, serving for three years from 1942 as a day strategic bomber.

CHAPTER SEVENTEEN

TACTICAL AIR POWER 1941·5

With their victory in the Battle of Britain behind them, at the end of 1940 the British were able to turn their attention to more positive offensive action against the Germans. The bombers were already starting to foray into Germany and occupied Europe, but the Battle of Britain had left the RAF with a strong Fighter Command, for which an offensive use had now to be found. Accordingly, on 20 December 1940 the first 'Rhubarb' operation was flown by a pair of Supermarine Spitfire fighters. The object of the 'Rhubarb' type of activity was to keep the *Luftwaffe* in occupied Europe on its toes by means of nuisance raids flown at low-level by small numbers of aircraft attacking targets of opportunity.

During 1941 this type of operation was extended considerably in scope, but successes were limited as by May 1941 there were only two *Jagdgeschwader* left in occupied Europe.

Also pioneered at the beginning of 1941 were 'Circus' operations, in which a small medium bomber force was sent over the Channel with strong fighter escort, the idea being to draw up the *Luftwaffe*'s fighters and so destroy them in a war of attrition. The nature of this campaign was revealed in the very first such operation, flown on 10 January 1941 by six Bristol Blenheim bombers and an escort consisting of three Spitfire and three Hawker Hurricane squadrons: for the

Egyptian pilots in North Africa with their Gloster Gladiators. This aircraft, which was Britain's last biplane fighter, entered service in 1937, and Gladiators of the Auxiliary Air Force intercepted the first bombing raid on Britain, over the Firth of Forth in 1939.

loss of one Hurricane over the Pas-de-Calais area, the British disposed of only two Messerschmitt Bf 109 fighters. Throughout 1941 the bomber element of these 'Circus' operations was strengthened, but losses were too high for the results achieved, and the combined 'Rhubarb' and 'Circus' campaign may most charitably be judged as an effective means of keeping up British morale by taking the war to the Germans. By the middle of June 1941, the RAF had sent out 104 'Rhubarb' and only eleven 'Circus' operations, operating at the limit of the fighters' ranges. The largest of these had been a 'Circus' involving thirty bombers and almost 300 fighters: the Germans had responded, losing only sixteen fighters to the RAF's twenty-five.

At the same time the Germans were about to bring into service the excellent Focke-Wulf Fw 190 radial-engined single-seat fighter, which was more than a match for the mark of Spitfire currently deployed by Fighter Command. Unlike the Germans, who intercepted 'Rhubarbs' and 'Circuses' only when they felt they had the edge, the British kept standing patrols of fighters in the air over southern England to try to intercept the *Jabo* (*Jagdbomber* or fighter-bomber) sneak raids favoured by the Germans during the first half of 1941. Flown by Bf 109s and Fw 190s, these raids had considerable nuisance value, and caused the RAF to use up large quantities of fuel and valuable airframe and engine hours. Even when intercepted, the German fighter-bombers could usually evade the British fighters once they had dropped their bombs.

Realising in May that the German forces in Western Europe were being thinned for other ventures, the RAF stepped up its offensive day operations over occupied Europe in the hope of drawing back part of this redeployed German strength. Thus in the six weeks up to the end of July 1941, by which time Germany had launched the invasion of Russia, the RAF dispatched 374 bomber sorties covered by no less than 8,000 fighter sorties. For the loss of fourteen bombers and 123 fighters, the RAF shot down only eighty-one German fighters, and failed singularly in its attempt to lure the German air forces back to the west.

Germany was raided on 12 August, when fifty-three Blenheims attacked targets in the Köln area, with 1,500 fighter sorties being dispatched over occupied Europe as a diversion. Notwithstanding, twelve of the Blenheims were shot down. Such operations were not worth the cost to the British, the more so when the Fw 190 began to appear in some numbers during September. The immediate effect was that the RAF lost 108 fighters during September and October to the Germans' forty-three. The position continued to deteriorate during the rest of the year, bringing the RAF's fighter losses for the previous twelve months to 849 aircraft and 462 pilots in 150,828 sorties. Fighter Command pilots claimed the destruction of some 800 German aircraft, but real losses were far lower.

Far from forcing the *Luftwaffe* to return aircraft to western Europe, the RAF campaign, coupled with the fear of a mass German return, kept seventy-five fighter squadrons tied down in Great Britain when these units could far more profitably have been sent out to the North African, Mediterranean and Far Eastern theatres. By the end of the year the *Luftwaffe* had some 25% of its strength deployed on the 'southern front' in the Mediterranean and North African areas, and in the Far East the Japanese had just unleashed considerable air, land and sea forces on the mediocre British forces in the area.

In the Mediterranean, operations had started immediately after Italy's declaration of war on the Allies on 10 June 1940 with Italian raids on Malta, Corsica and southern France, and with British raids on the Italian bases round El Adem in North Africa. Initial British reinforcements for this double theatre were Hurricane fighters flown out via France and Malta, but with the fall of France in June this route had to be replaced by others: Malta received spasmodic supplies of fresh aircraft from aircraft-carriers that ventured as close as they could, while North Africa and the Middle East were dependent for their reinforcements on a hastily improvised air route across Africa from Takoradi in the Gold Coast! The first aircraft reached Egypt by means of this latter route on 26 September.

With the exception of their bombers, the Italians had no aircraft in the *Regia Aeronautica* to match the British

Above top A Junkers Ju 88 prepared for a bombing mission from Sicily against Malta.
Above A Focke-Wulf Fw 58 Weihe light transport and liaison aircraft, North Africa. These entered service in 193 and were often used as crew-trainers.

pes, and soon the RAF had air superiority over the Mediterranean and North Africa, with its growing force of bombers and torpedo-aircraft playing an important part in strangling Italian seaborne supplies and reinforcements for North Africa. In this campaign Malta, aptly called Britain's 'unsinkable aircraft-carrier', lying on the Italians' shortest route to Tripoli, was an asset worth its weight in gold. Try as they might, the Italians just could not crush Malta, and finally the *Luftwaffe* had to move *Fliegerkorps* X into Sicily to help. The corps arrived in January 1941 with 132 medium bombers, seventy-two dive-bombers and thirty-six twin-engined fighters. The strength of the German presence was immediately felt on Malta and by the Royal Navy, and the initial assault against the former on 10 January was largely responsible for the safe arrival in North Africa of the first convoy bringing in German ground and air forces. At the same time, Bf 109 single-engined fighters arrived in Sicily and began to cut down the Hurricanes defending Malta.

At the end of October 1940 the Italians had invaded Greece, only to be repulsed by the Greek Army, supported by the Greek air force supported by hastily flown in British aerial reinforcements. By the beginning of 1941 these reinforcements, to the tune of three fighter squadrons and several bomber squadrons, had wrecked the Italians in Greece, but left the British in North Africa vulnerable to Rommel's first offensive, which pushed the British back into Egypt.

In the Balkans, moreover, the Germans had swiftly prepared to conquer Yugoslavia and Greece before turning their attentions to Russia. Air support for the offensive, which was launched on 6 April 1941, was provided by the 1,200 aircraft of *Luftflotte* IV and 650 aircraft of the *Regia Aeronautica*. There was little the Yugoslavs, Greeks and British could do but start a fighting retreat. As in Poland, Scandinavia and western Europe, the *Blitzkrieg* appeared invincible, and the Yugoslavs' 210 fighters and 170 bombers were soon destroyed. Before pulling out of Greece, the RAF lost seventy-two aircraft in the air, with another seventy-one damaged aircraft burned to prevent them falling into German hands. German losses were slightly higher.

An interesting but unfortunate incident at this time was the British conquest of Syria from the French. The French had some 290 aircraft in the country, and in the course of the fighting, in which the French several times decimated British air formations, 127 modern fighters and bombers, and another fifty-two obsolescent types, were destroyed. This campaign began on 8 June 1941,

Above top Arming a Bf 110, Messerschmitt's twin-engined fighter.
Above Junkers Ju 52/3m transports and two Messerschmitt Bf 110 fighter escorts on a Tunisian airfield. The trimotor Ju 52/3m carried up to 18 paratroops and took part in many airborne invasions.
Left The Hawker Typhoon 1B proved to be a potent anti-tank, -train and -shipping aircraft, with four built-in Hispano 20mm cannon, 8 rockets and bombs.

by which time all major German air formations in the Balkans and Mediterranean had been withdrawn for the Russian campaign, leaving only those in North Africa to continue the fight against the RAF. The withdrawal of the Sicily-based *Fliegerkorps* X was a particular relief to Malta.

As the land war seesawed back and forth along the north coast of Africa, with the side in the ascendent usually having local air superiority, Malta continued to be the linchpin of British strategy in the theatre, and held out against considerably greater pressure during 1942 once German air formations had returned. Nevertheless, air reinforcements in just sufficient numbers continued to get in from aircraft-carriers, and a threatened Axis airborne invasion in the spring of 1942 did not materialise. Thus Malta was able to continue its war against the Axis supply lines across the Mediterranean, gradually throttling them in the second half of 1942.

On 19 August 1942 there occurred the biggest RAF tactical air operation of the war in northern Europe to date, when the exploratory landings in Dieppe by 6,000 British, Canadian and a few American troops were made. British and American day bomber forces, the first with medium and the second with heavy bombers, flew diversionary raids elsewhere in the hope of drawing off the German fighter force, while fighter cover over the landings themselves was provided by 2,340 British and 123 American sorties. The Germans were not to be confused, however, and in major air fighting throughout the day the RAF lost 106 aircraft, the Americans eight, and the Germans forty-eight aircraft destroyed

plus another twenty-four damaged. The landings ha[d] been a disaster, but all three services quickly absorbe[d] the implications of this small-scale reverse and pr[e]pared in a more satisfactory fashion for the maj[or] landings that would take the Allies back into Europe [in] 1944.

Back in North Africa, the British had secured a[ir] superiority in time for the decisive 2nd Battle of [El] Alamein, which started on 23 October. Thereafter th[e] Allies' air superiority was emphasised by the Angl[o-] American landings in North-West Africa in Novembe[r.] It was notable, however, that the Germans still had [a] qualitative edge, as the Allies found out when the[ir] bomber forces had to operate beyond the range [of] fighter escorts. In the open terrain of North Afric[a,] Allied fighter-bombers, armed with 40 mm canno[n] bombs and later rocket projectiles, proved devastati[ng] against Axis armour, and the Allied light and mediu[m] bomber forces made German and Italian movement b[y] day all but impossible, as well as striking crippli[ng] blows at their supply dumps. The problems of the Ax[is] were magnified by the increasing successes of th[e] torpedo-bombers operating from Malta and Nort[h] Africa, which coordinated their activities with bombe[rs] and submarines to prevent all but a dribble of suppli[es] reaching Tunisia and Tripolitania. With the Allied ri[ng] closing in on the last Axis positions in Tunisia in th[e] first part of 1943, the Germans tried to fly in reinforce[-] ments, but the giant air transports were shot down i[n] droves by Allied fighters. On 5 April 1943, for exampl[e,] eighteen transports were shot down, and on 22 Apr[il] almost all of a force of twenty great Messerschmitt M[e]

Below The superlative de Havilland Mosquito was a bomber constructed of wood. Designed not to need defensive armament, its very high speed would be its only protection. Development of the aircraft led to day and night fighters, strike fighter-bombers and reconnaissance versions; such was the design's adaptability. Pictured here is an N.F. 30 night fighter.

23s was shot down. The Axis hold in Africa was crumbling fast, greatly aided by the activities of the Allied fighter-bombers whose part in the campaign, already significant, became decisive after 24 March 1943, when British fighter-bombers, attacking in great numbers, destroyed the Axis artillery positions covering the Tebaga Gap route past the Mareth Line position.

With the defeat of the Axis forces in North Africa, the Allies' next move was into Sicily on 10 July 1943, into the toe of Italy on 3 September, and then into Italy proper at Salerno on 9 September. The struggle for Italy was to last the rest of the war, and was desperately hard fought. In the air, however, the Allies had things all their own way, and the tactical use of airpower was extensive.

The largest air battles of the war, and the most widespread use of tactical airpower, occurred in Russia. The largest air battles took place right at the beginning of the campaign, with the Germans destroying almost incredible numbers of poorly flown and led Russian aircraft, very many of them obsolescent. Although greater numbers of aircraft were destroyed in the first few days of the war, these were mostly on the ground. By the end of the month, with the German ground forces approaching Minsk towards the northern end of the Army Group 'Centre' front, the Russians began to commit very large numbers of aircraft in desperate efforts to halt the Germans. On 30 June, for example, *Jagdgeschwader* 51 claimed 114 Russian bombers shot down. Farther towards Leningrad, JG 54 claimed sixty-five Russian bombers shot down while attacking the bridges over the Dvina river just taken by the Germans. It was the same story all along the German line, with most of the Russian attackers shot down. A clear instance can be found on 6 July, when sixty-five of seventy-three Russian bombers attacking the German bridgehead at Ostrov were shot down.

During this period JG 51, commanded by *Major Werner Mölders*, became the first fighter formation to claim 1,000 victories in World War II on 30 June; by 8 September this same *Jagdgeschwader* had claimed its 2,000th victim; and by 10 September JG 51 had claimed 1,357 aircraft shot down and another 298 destroyed on the ground since the beginning of the Russian campaign only just under twelve weeks earlier.

In spite of the Germans' great successes up to the end of September 1941, Russia was by no means out of the war, and from this time onwards her air force, essentially a tactical force in concept and training, gradually began to have an effect. With most of its obsolete *matériel* 'obligingly' destroyed by the Germans, the Red Air Force was able to bring forward newer, and superior, types of aircraft during the winter of 1941–42: these included the Lavochkin LaGG-3, Mikoyan-Gurevich MiG-3 and Yakovlev Yak-1 fighters, the classic Ilyushin Il-2 *Shturmovik* ground-attack aircraft, and the Petlyakov Pe-2 light bomber. The LaGG and Yak fighters were the precursors of great families of fighters, and the Il-2 and Pe-2 continued throughout the war, being modified as necessary though generally keeping the same basic designations.

It was at this stage that the Germans began to realise their error in failing to develop a long-range heavy bomber, for this type (now christened the *Uralbomber*) was now essential if the *Luftwaffe* was to make any impression on the great war factories springing up in and beyond the Ural mountains, just out of reach of the current generation of German medium bombers which

was, with the exception of the great Junkers Ju 88, reaching obsolescence. Frantic efforts were made to develop such a bomber, but the Germans were too ambitious, and rushed the best of the types, the Heinkel He 177 *Greif* (Griffon) into service before the teething problems with its two sets of twin-coupled engines had been straightened out. Thus the type was never really satisfactory.

There are a few factors concerning the air war in Russia that should be mentioned. Tactical air operations were the most important part of the air war over the Eastern Front, and such operations usually took place at medium to low altitudes, and rarely above 16,400 feet (5,000 m). Concerned with the direct support of their armies, the Russians tried to base their airfields as close to the front as possible, so that their aircraft could make as many sorties a day as possible. Operating only at these relatively low altitudes, the Russian escort fighters were agile, tough and adequate performers, the last fact being apparently unknown to many, who compare the high-altitude performance figures of western aircraft with the medium altitude performance of the Russian machines; as the Germans found to their cost, the Russian fighters could generally equal the best the Germans could produce at the formers' preferred altitudes. There can be no denying of the Germans' general technical and tactical superiority right to the end of the war in aerial matters. But eventually Russian production and training allowed the Russians to swamp the *Luftwaffe* fighter defences, giving the Red Air Force the ability to operate as it wished. The Germans were always able to secure air superiority on small sectors of the front, but the Russians almost invariably attacked across a broad front, overtaxing the *Luftwaffe*'s ability to respond. This goes a long way towards explaining the Germans'

Above A Z.501 Gabbiano biplane reconnaissance/bomber pictured at the seaplane base at Preveza on the west coast of Greece, with two attacking Bristol Beaufighters in the background.

xtraordinarily high victory scores, often disbelieved by ceptics, but in all probability substantially correct. At ow level the Russians reigned supreme, their Il-2s, Pe-s and later Tu-2s proving superior to anything the Germans could produce. (The Il-2 was built in greater umbers than any other aircraft of any period, some 6,163 being produced; the Pe-2 was made in greater umbers than any other twin-engined bomber of World War II other than the Junkers Ju 88 and ickers Wellington, the respective figures being 11,426, 4,676 and 11,461.)

In February 1942 some 90,000 men of the German II nd X Corps were cut off at Demyansk, south of Lake lmen, by a rapid Russian advance, and the *Luftwaffe* ow attempted the world's first major airlift of supplies o this beleaguered force, which Hitler designated a fortress' rather than a 'pocket'. In a fascinating oper-tion the *Luftwaffe* just succeeded, between 18 Feb-uary and 19 May flying in 64,844 tons of food, weapons nd ammunition, five million gallons of fuel, and 30,500 einforcements. In the same period 35,400 wounded vere evacuated, and 265 aircraft of all types were lost. The isolated force was finally relieved by a specially ormed ground formation.

Demyansk was a great success, but had the unfor-unate side-effect of persuading *Reichsmarschall* Her-nann Göring that his *Luftwaffe* could succeed in any irlift. This factor became important at the end of 1942, or right at the apex of the German drive towards the Volga the 6th Army was cut off in Stalingrad when the wo halves of a great Russian pincer movement met in heir rear. Göring assured Hitler that the *Luftwaffe* could supply the isolated garrison with the 500 tons of food, ammunition and supplies needed daily until a relief force could smash its way through.

The operation began on 24 November with the eleven *Gruppen* of Ju 52s and two *Gruppen* of Ju 86s located at Tatsinskaya (320 aircraft in all), joined on 30 November by the 190 He 111 aircraft of six bomber and two transport *Gruppen* located at Morosovskaya, all these aircraft flying in to Pitomnik airfield in Stalingrad. Deliveries were far short of the 500 tons a day promised when the Russians attacked again on 16 December and forced the abandonment of Tatsinskaya on 23–24 December, sixty transports being lost there. Both Tatsinskaya and Morosovskaya were finally abandoned in January 1943, the Ju 52s then operating from Ssalsk and the He 111s from Novocherkassk, both some sixty miles (100 km) farther from Stalingrad than the first airfields. During January a second airstrip was prepared at Gumrak within the Stalingrad perimeter, and ad-ditional aircraft were sent in for the airlift, but the weather, Russian defences and other operational rea-sons helped to keep the tonnage wholly inadequate. On 16 January Pitomnik was overrun, with Gumrak also falling on 22 January. The airlift had failed, at a cost of 490 irreplaceable transport aircraft, and on 2 February *Generalfeldmarschall* Friedrich Paulus and the 90,000 survivors of the 6th Army, once 300,000 men strong, surrendered to the Russians.

Germany was now on the strategic defensive in Russia, but in July 1943 made a last effort to regain the initiative with a massive pincer offensive designed to pinch out the Russian salient around Kursk. But the Russians, warned by spies, were ready for the offensive, and inflicted a crushing defeat on the Germans in the greatest armoured battle of all time. At the same time the Germans had planned a great pre-emptive strike against the Red Air Force's bases in the area by 800 bombers, dive-bombers and Henschel Hs 129 tank-busting aircraft, supported by 270 fighters. It was intended as a decisive air battle, and in fact was one.

The Russians, knowing of the German plans, plan-ned their own pre-emptive strike by some 500 bombers and fighters. They failed, however, to take into account the fact that the Germans had early-warning radar. Thus the bomber and ground-attack aircraft were scrambled away from the impending raid, which was then attacked by the German fighters. The Germans had a field day, shooting down 120 bombers in the first attack. In the rest of the day the German fighters claimed another 312 victories, with another 205 on the next day.

The bomber and ground-attack units were thus able to undertake the missions planned, and at first deci-mated the Russian armoured troops with heavy cannon, and infantry and other unprotected troops with the new SD types of fragmentation bombs. Nevertheless the Russians poured in more and more men and *matériel*, and finally ground down the German offensive, just as the Germans had decided to halt to allow the removal of forces for the Italian theatre, where the Allies had just landed in Sicily.

Opposite A store of unexploded bombs with a Disposal Unit officer examining one.
Below A Fiat C.R.32 after having been shot down. This aircraft was the forerunner of the Fiat C.R.42 Falco, which, although slow by World War II fighter standards, had classic biplane handling and manoeuvrability qualities that caused many to regret underestimating its abilities as a fighter.

After Kursk the Russians had things relatively their own way in the air and on the ground, though the German defence was superb. But there was no way that the Germans could halt the monumental Russian drives, especially as they had to thin their forces in the East to meet the Allied threat in Italy from July 1943, and in North-West Europe after June 1944. At the same time the Russians introduced newer types of aircraft, such as the excellent Lavochkin La-5 and Yak-9 fighters, which meant that with the improving standard of Russian flying skills, the Red Air Force was able to dominate the air over major battlefields. An example of the case in point can be found in the almost ludicrous position of *Luftflotte* VI, which had to face an onslaught by the 7,000 aircraft of five Russian air armies with only forty fighters on 22 June 1944, when the Russians opened their massive drive from Belorussia into Poland and the Baltic states. From this time on there was nothing that the *Luftwaffe* could do to stem the Russian advances, despite reorganisations and re-equipments, and the exhortations of everyone from Hitler down-wards.

The story of tactical air operations in the West is much the same type of story, with the Germans being overwhelmed by the size and skill of the two main Allied tactical air formations, the British 2nd Tactical Air Force, and the US 9th AAF, both formed in November 1943. The strength of these forces lay in good medium bombers, mostly of American origins, and excellent fighter-bombers armed with cannon, rocket projectiles and bombs.

The Germans were taken completely by surprise when the Allies landed in Normandy, and the great air effort covering the invasion force was largely un-necessary. The *Luftwaffe* responded quickly, however, and by nightfall on 6 June 1944 some 200 aircraft had arrived from Germany, the vanguard of far larger forces. Gradually the air battle over the Allied lodge-ment increased in tempo, with the Germans wholly unable to inflict decisive damage, but losing whole bomber *Gruppen* in the process to the vastly superior Allied strength. When the Allies broke out of the beach-head, rocket-firing fighter-bombers decimated the Ger-man armour attempting to prevent further advance, while the heavy bomber forces, used for tactical sup-port, blasted open paths for major advances. Through-out this campaign the tactical air forces proved an invaluable adjunct to the land forces, preventing vir-tually all German movement by day, and cutting down obstructions to Allied progress.

At the end of the year the *Luftwaffe* made its last great effort in support of the desperate Ardennes offensive (the so-called Battle of the Bulge), flying 500 support sorties on the first day, 16 December. But the main blow was saved for 1 January, when a pre-emptive strike against Allied airfields was planned. Some 900 fighters and fighter-bombers took part in the attack, which was directed mostly against the 2nd Tactical Air Force's airfields. Allied losses were about 150 aircraft destroyed and 80 damaged, but the Germans lost more than 300, most of these to the German *Flak* guns, who could not believe that so large a force coming from the Allied lines at low level was German, and so opened fire. After this Hitler decided that the Eastern Front was more important and so five *Jagdgeschwader* were sent off to the East. For the rest of the war Allied tactical aircraft roamed the skies above Germany virtually at will.

Left A Gloster Gladiator in North Africa. These biplane fighters gave good account of themselves in the Mediterranean until more modern types could be released from a hard-pressed Britain.
Below A hot—air generator being used to start the motor of this He III on a snow-covered German airfield.
Opposite The Savoia-Marchetti S.M.79 Sparviero was a good medium bomber. At the outbreak of World War II, this aircraft comprised over half the Italian Air Force's bomber fleet, and were to be one of the war's most successful torpedo-bombers.

CHAPTER EIGHTEEN

NAVAL AIR POWER IN THE PACIFIC 1941·5

Unlike the war waged in the western hemisphere between the Axis and Allied powers, over Europe and the vast land masses of North Africa and European Russia, the Pacific war in the eastern hemisphere was fought over great stretches of ocean containing only small specks of land. So unlike the western war, in which what might be termed 'army' aircraft were paramount in tactical operations, the eastern war, at least that part of it in the Pacific, it was naval aircraft that were predominant. In the open spaces between the Hawaiian islands in the east, the Philippine islands in the west, the Aleutian islands in the north, and the New Guinea and Solomon islands line in the south, it was aircraft-carriers, the new 'capital' ships of World War II, that dominated naval warfare, their aircraft being necessary to cover the landings that provided each side with its bases for progress across the ocean, and to protect the supply ships and other vessels operating between the rear and forward areas, and moving raw materials across the seas to major industrial centres. On the American side (for the Pacific war was overwhelmingly a conflict between the Americans and the Japanese), it was the naval forces and their aircraft that made possible the seizure by the ground forces of

islands ever nearer to Japan for the strategic air bases that permitted the final crushing of Japan's industries and cities by heavy bombers.

Like Germany, Japan was at first able to exploit to the full the vital elements of strategic, tactical and technical surprise in her tide of conquest across the Pacific. So far as the air side of the war is concerned, the machine that best sums up the reasons for Japan's initial tactical success is the Mitsubishi A6M, in 1941 and 1942 unquestionably the best carrierborne fighter in the world, with phenomenal agility, good performance and firepower, and a range that led many Allied commanders to believe that the Japanese had twice as many A6Ms as they did, because they could not credit that the same aircraft could be operating against targets 1,000 miles (1,610 km) apart on consecutive days. The Allies' reaction to the Zero also gives an indication of their initial setbacks, for the type had been operating in China since August 1940, and full reports had been made by Colonel Claire Chennault amongst others. Chennault was in China aiding Chiang Kai-shek's air force in its hopeless fight against the superior Japanese, but his reports to Washington were filed away without comment. The western nations involved in the Far East

The crippled carrier USS *Lexington* (CV-2) after being hit by two bombs and two torpedoes. An approaching destroyer is almost obscured by smoke.

had fallen victim to their own propaganda that the Japanese were basically inferior, and that Japanese aircraft were merely inferior derivatives of western design philosophies.

The Imperial Japanese Navy's prime responsibilities in the forthcoming war were the Pacific areas (with the attack on Pearl Harbor and the overrunning of various American-held islands being the most important tasks) and the air and naval support of the army's invasion of the Philippines. Secondary responsibilities included the escort of troop convoys for the invasions of southern Siam and Malaya. The army, on the other hand, had as its prime tasks the protection of the puppet state of Manchukuo (Manchuria) from any Russian moves, the continuance of the war in China, and the conquest of the Philippines and Malaya. Once these last two had been achieved, the army would move forward into Burma and the Dutch East Indies.

For its Pacific tasks the Imperial Japanese Navy deployed its 1st *Koku Kantai*: seven aircraft-carriers comprising four *Koku Sentais*. The carriers *Akagi* and *Kaga* formed the 1st *Koku Sentai*, *Soryu* and *Hiryu* the 2nd *Koku Sentai*, *Ryujo* the 4th *Koku Sentai*, and *Zuikaku* and *Shokaku* the 5th *Koku Sentai*. The 1st *Koku Kantai* had 418 aircraft – 130 fighters, 126 dive-bombers and 162 level/torpedo-bombers.

For the Philippines operation, which needed naval air support as the army's aircraft lacked the range to operate from the nearest Japanese bases, the Imperial Japanese Navy's land-based 11th *Koku Kantai* was allocated: the 21st *Koku Sentai* with the 1st, Kanoya and Toko *Kokutais*; the 22nd *Koku Sentai* with the Mihoro and Genzan *Kokutais* and the *Koku Sentai* Special Attachment; and the 23rd *Koku Sentai* with the 3rd, Tainan and Takao *Kokutais*. The 11th *Koku Kantai* had 557 aircraft, including 220 fighters and 283 Mitsubishi twin-engined bombers.

It is generally assumed that the war in the Pacific began with the 1st *Koku Kantai*'s devastating attack on the US Pacific Fleet's base at Pearl Harbor in the Hawaiian islands on 7 December 1941. In fact the war had started a few hours earlier with the Japanese landings in Siam and Malaya on 8 December (the apparent contradiction in dates is explained by the two locations being on opposite sides of the International Date Line). For the loss of only twenty-nine aircraft from the carriers *Akagi*, *Kaga*, *Soryu*, *Hiryu*, *Zuikaku* and *Shokaku*, the US Pacific Fleet lost four battleships sunk and three badly damaged, with several other smaller ships also damaged. The two redeeming factors in this otherwise black day were the facts that the Japanese did not attack the fuel oil tanks and repair facilities in Pearl Harbor, and that the fleet's three aircraft-carriers were absent and therefore unattacked: *Lexington* was ferrying aircraft to Midway island, *Enterprise* was returning to Pearl Harbor, and *Saratoga* was in California. These three major striking elements were thus left to start taking the war to the Japanese.

The 11th *Koku Kantai*'s first major strike against the American aircraft in the Philippines, planned for dawn on 8 December, had to be postponed because of fog, but even so the attacking force arrived at noon and caught the American air forces, based for the most part on Clark Field north of Manila, totally unawares, though news of the Pearl Harbor attack had already been received. The 108 Mitsubishi G3M and G4M bombers made excellent practice on the neatly lined-up American aircraft and destroyed about half of the 180 US aircraft in the Philippines. Amongst the lost aircraft were seventy-five of the Americans' latest combat types, Boeing B-17 bombers and Curtiss P-40 fighters.

The Japanese bombers returned on subsequent days, but their next most decisive raid against the Philippines took place on 10 December, when Cavite Navy Yard in Manila was all but destroyed, ending any chance that US naval and air strength would be able to turn the tables in the Philippines. On the same day there also occurred an event of great moment for the traditionally regarded capital ships (battleships and battle-cruisers), when one of each type, the British *Prince of Wales* and *Repulse*, were sunk off the coast of Malaya by torpedo attacks from the eighty-four Mitsubishi bombers of the 22nd *Koku Sentai*'s Genzan and Mihoro *Kokutais*, and part of the 21st *Koku Sentai*'s Kanoya *Kokutai*. Under the command of Rear Admiral S. Matsunaga, the Japanese had for the first time accomplished the sinking of capital ships at sea to air power alone.

For the Japanese, success could best be obtained by the classic use of the precept 'concentration in time and space'. This would ensure local superiority in strength, tactical surprise, and the maintenance of strategic momentum to the south, where the capture of the oil-rich Dutch East Indies was of overriding importance. Air power was of prime importance in keeping up the speed of the advance, and so forward airfields had to be captured as quickly as possible. This was the reason for the campaign's first airborne operation, when 334 naval paratroops were dropped on Manado airfield in northern Celebes by twenty-eight bombers on 11 January 1942. The airfield was soon taken, and only four days later the air arm of the Imperial Navy was operating from it.

Still pushing south, the Japanese first bombed Java on 3 February 1942 with a view to wiping out Allied air strength on this key island. At the beginning of the war the Dutch had deployed some 200 aircraft in their islands, and to the survivors of these were added some US B-17s and P-40s, and about one hundred Hawker Hurricanes of the RAF in the Far East. By the end of the first week in February, the Japanese had shot down some seventy Allied aircraft over Java and Sumatra.

Further losses followed in the next twelve days, and then on 19 February the Japanese started their major effort to wipe out the Allied air forces with major raids from Amboina, Bali, Borneo, Celebes and Sumatra. The carriers which had struck at Pearl Harbor were also in the area, and launched a 188-aircraft raid on Port Darwin, the main Allied base to the south of the Dutch East Indies; eighty-five land-based bombers also struck at Darwin. It was the end of the Allied air effort in the area, for seventeen aircraft were lost and many others damaged. In addition, eleven ships were sunk. The Japanese lost only one A6M.

By 1 March, when the Japanese invaded Java, the Allies had only fifty serviceable aircraft with which to try to prevent the activities of 500 Japanese machines. By 8 March the air effort was over, the Allies having lost since 8 December some 470 British, 190 Dutch and 340 American aircraft. So far the Imperial Japanese Navy had lost only 250 aircraft in all, and the Imperial Japanese Army about 125.

After striking at Port Darwin, the 1st *Koku Kantai* had moved west into the Indian Ocean, to launch attacks against Ceylon and British shipping in the area. The five Japanese carriers had 117 A6M fighters, and 260 B5N and D3A bombers, against which the British had 107 land-based aircraft and eighty-five shipborne aircraft on one obsolescent and two modern carriers. Between 5 and 9 April severe fighting occurred, in which the British lost nine warships (including the old carrier *Hermes*) and fifty-six aircraft (forty-three in the air and the rest on the ground) before the Japanese pulled back out to prepare for the operations designed to extend the perimeter of Japan's 'Greater South-East Asia Co-Prosperity Sphere' into New Guinea and the Solomons.

Halted in their overland drive on Port Moresby on the south coast, the Japanese prepared an invasion force to land on the south coast, the whole operation being planned for early May. The move was to lead to a decisive moment between the Japanese and American carrier forces.

Below A burned-out B-17C Flying Fortress on Hickam Air Field, Pearl Harbor, following the surprise Japanese air attack of 7 December 1941. Two thirds of the American naval aircraft were destroyed, leaving only sixteen serviceable Army Air Force bombers.

Meanwhile, the US carrier force had been taking the war to the Japanese since February 1942. *Saratoga* had been badly damaged by a torpedo on 11 January, so *Yorktown* had been detached from the Atlantic Fleet to bring the Pacific Fleet up to a strength of three carriers. The first strike took place on 1 February, when *Enterprise* and *Yorktown*, under the command of Vice Admiral William F. Halsey, attacked targets in the Gilbert and Marshall islands. Twenty days later *Lexington*, under the command of Vice Admiral Wilson Brown, attempted a raid on Rabaul, but was beaten off by Japanese air attacks. Halsey was at the time returning from Pearl Harbor, to strike at Wake Island on 24 February and Marcus Island on 4 March. While this was happening, *Lexington* was joined by *Yorktown*, and the two carriers then struck at Lae and Salamaua on 10 March, sinking several small ships and other naval vessels. This early stage of American counter-strikes ended on 18 April when the newly arrived *Hornet* steamed to within 800 miles (1,290 km) of Tokyo to launch sixteen USAAF twin-engined North American B-25 medium bombers under the command of Lieutenant Colonel James H. Doolittle against the Japanese capital. It was a stroke of propaganda genius.

Admiral Isoroku Yamamoto, Commander-in-Chief of the Combined Fleet, had prepared a two-pronged plan for the move south to extend Japan's defensive perimeter: the small carrier *Shoho*, plus cruisers and destroyers, would escort an invasion force to Tulagi in the Solomons, while a larger force, centred on the fleet carriers *Shokaku* and *Zuikaku*, would provide long-range cover for the Port Moresby invasion force. Local command was exercised by Vice Admiral Shigeyoshi Inouye, commander of the 4th Fleet.

The Americans had broken the Japanese naval code, and thus knew what was afoot. Accordingly, Task Force 17 (*Yorktown* and *Lexington*) under the command of Rear Admiral Frank J. Fletcher, was sent by Admiral Chester W. Nimitz, Commander-in-Chief, Pacific Ocean Areas, to intervene. The result was the Battle of the Coral Sea, which had several stages between 4 and 8 May 1942. For the loss of *Lexington* and damage to *Yorktown*, TF17 sank *Shoho*, badly damaged *Shokaku*, and decimated the Japanese carrier air groups. Tactically the battle may be regarded as a draw, the Americans losing a more important carrier, and the Japanese more aircraft (sixty-one to thirty-nine), but strategically this novel battle, the first in which the surface combatants never came within sight of each other, was a decided American victory: the Japanese gave up their attempt to take Port Moresby. For the first time, too, there had been a carrier-*versus*-carrier battle, and the Japanese vessels, under the tactical command of Rear Admiral Takagi, seemed to come off worse.

Determined to bring the US Pacific Fleet to a decisive battle, in which the Americans' still depleted strength could be crushed, Yamamoto now planned a complex campaign. While small forces, including two carriers, struck at the Aleutian islands as a diversion, the Japanese main force, including the fleet carriers *Akagi*, *Kaga*, *Hiryu* and *Soryu*, would cover an invasion force directed against the Americans' key outpost of Midway Island. This carrier force, which should have included *Zuikaku* and *Shokaku*, the one without adequate aircraft and the other badly damaged, was commanded by Vice Admiral Chuichi Nagumo, of Pearl Harbor fame; two other carriers, both of them light, were available, but were allocated to the powerful

Midway invasion force and the covering body of battleships. Nagumo had 272 aircraft aboard his carriers.

Again warned by intercepted Japanese signals, the Americans had just enough time to prepare their meagre forces. Under Nimitz's overall command, tactical command was exercised by Fletcher aboard *Yorktown* (TF17), hastily repaired after the Battle of the Coral Sea, with Rear Admiral Raymond A. Spruance's TF16 (*Enterprise* and *Hornet*) under command. Fletcher had 233 aircraft.

Thus the scene was set for the climactic Battle of Midway, under the command of two great admirals, Yamamoto and Nimitz. The battle began on 4 June and ended on 6 June, after four confused phases which the Americans won against all odds in a quite decisive manner. Midway may be likened to the 2nd Battle of El Alamein and Stalingrad as one of the great turning points of the war. For the loss of one carrier and 147 aircraft, the Americans sank no less than four Japanese fleet carriers, all of them veterans of the Pearl Harbor attack, and destroyed 332 aircraft. It was a blow from which the Japanese, and especially their naval air arm, were never to recover.

The way things were now to go was clearly demonstrated in the Solomons. Despite their failure in the Battle of the Coral Sea, the Japanese had pressed on with the Solomons half of the plan, and had built up a strong presence on the islands. The Americans responded on 7 August 1942 with the landing of the US 1st Marine Division on Guadalcanal and neighbouring Tulagi and Florida islands. The Japanese responded quickly, and in the first two days of the invasion the shipping off the beaches was attacked by some seventy naval bombers. The invasion was enjoying the support of three carriers, and the Grumman F4F Wildcat fighters from these joined AA guns in bringing down thirty-six bombers and several of their escorting fighters. These early heavy losses caused the 11th *Koku Kantai* to pause for reflection over the next few days, by which time the Americans had made operational Henderson Field on Guadalcanal, an airfield started by the Japanese themselves. The airfield was soon the base of navy and marine Wildcats and Douglas SBD Dauntlesses, which were later joined by army Bell P-400 Airacobras.

By the end of August, therefore, the south-eastern end of the Solomons was the scene of almost constant air battles, the Japanese naval aircraft having to operate from the Rabaul area, some 650 miles (1,050 km) distant. Thus the Japanese pilots had long flights to the combat area, where in general they prevailed, but then faced the long haul home, possibly with damaged aircraft. Understandably, non-combat losses gradually eroded the strength of the 11th *Koku Kantai*.

On 24 August the Japanese Navy attempted to reinforce the troops on Guadalcanal, the convoy of destroyers being escorted by three carriers (*Ryujo*, *Shokaku* and *Zuikaku* with 174 aircraft) under the command of Nagumo. The US TF61 (*Saratoga*, *Enterprise* and *Wasp* with 253 aircraft), under Fletcher's command, was ordered to intercept, and did so in the Battle of the Eastern Solomons with *Saratoga* and *Enterprise* (174 aircraft). The Japanese lost the small carrier *Ryujo* and ninety aircraft, while the Americans suffered damage to *Enterprise* and the loss of twenty aircraft. The transport convoy turned back.

In a make or break effort in October, the Japanese committed considerable forces in an effort to destroy

Location of Major Air and Naval Operations in the Pacific

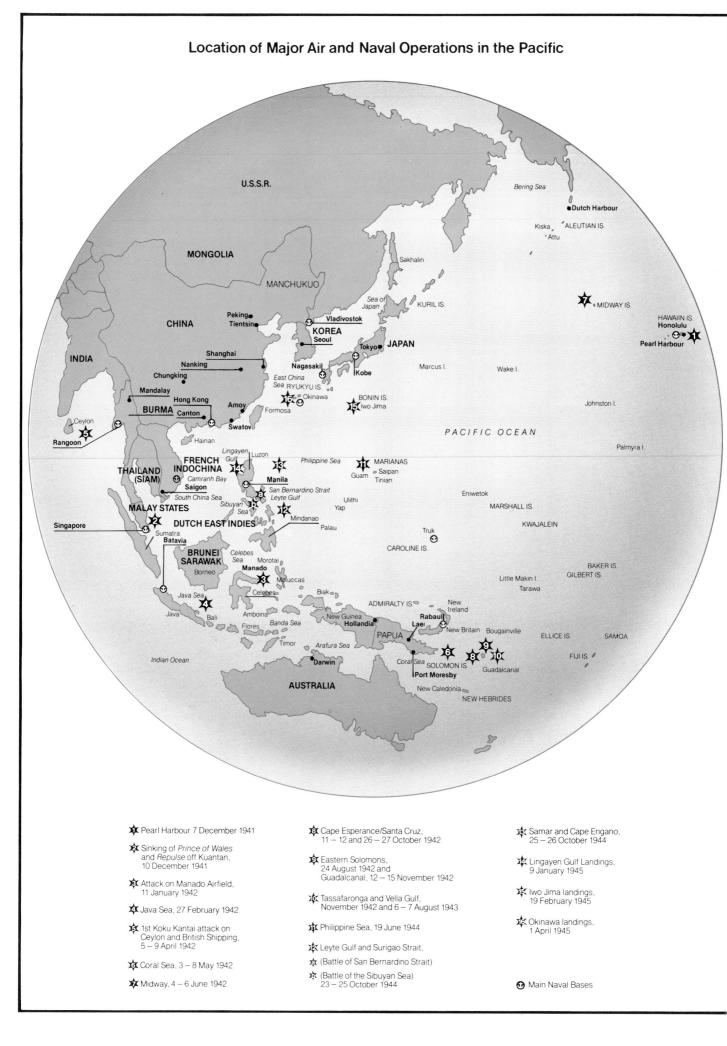

he sea and air strength of the US Navy, and so allow their land forces to expel the US ground forces from the eastern Solomons. Admiral Nobutake Kondo had over-all command, and direct control of the light carrier *Junyo*, while subordinate air command was exercised yet again by Nagumo, with the carriers *Shokaku*, *Zuikaku* and *Zuiho*. The Japanese had 207 aircraft. On the American side, Halsey had been promoted to area command, and Rear Admiral Thomas C. Kincaid had replaced Fletcher in command of the carriers *Enterprise* and *Hornet*, the only two such ships left to the Pacific Fleet, with 169 aircraft. Kincaid was ordered in to the attack to prevent the Japanese from reinforcing the land-based aircraft attacking Guadalcanal with carrier-borne machines. In the Battle of Santa Cruz on 26 October, both forces launched their aircraft at the same time, the strike forces passing each other in the air. *Zuiho* was damaged, and *Shokaku* very badly damaged, but the Americans lost *Hornet*, the aircraft destroyed on each side being one hundred and seventy-four re-spectively. *Enterprise* was also damaged, and Kincaid had to withdraw. Though they had clearly won, the Japanese made a great error in failing to pursue and sink the crippled *Enterprise*. It was, however, a pyrrhic victory of the Japanese, for yet again they had lost too many aircraft and highly trained aircrew.

Carrier aircraft continued to play a small but impor-tant part in the rest of the campaign, which ended in February 1943, but from now on the most important part was played by land-based aircraft. Newer Amer-ican aircraft and the increasing skill of army, navy and marine corps pilots gradually eroded Japanese naval air strength up to the end of the campaign. Thus the naval

air arm lost almost 2,000 aircraft and many experienced pilots and crew between December 1941 and February 1943, some three-quarters of these in the skies above the Solomons and New Guinea.

The pace of air operations over New Guinea speeded up at the beginning of 1943 as the army forces in the area were reinforced, but now the USAAF and Royal Australian Air Force had evolved the diving-pass tactics that allowed them to use their speed to get through the Japanese naval air arm's fighters to the bombers below without involvement in dogfights with the more manoeuvrable Japanese fighters.

In the middle of March the Japanese navy believed the time ripe for a major air offensive in the Solomons. Virtually the last aircraft and trained aircrew available were sent ashore from the navy's four serviceable carriers, bringing the air forces in the New Guinea and Solomons area up to 375 navy and 200 army aircraft. The Allies had 850 aircraft in the Solomons and 500 in New Guinea, but failed to make decisive inroads against the Japanese attacks, shooting down only forty aircraft for the loss of the same number themselves. Neverthe-less, Japanese losses were high, for another sixty or more aircraft were lost operationally but not in combat. Japanese successes were few, more trained aircrew had been lost and, perhaps most important of all, Admiral Yamamoto was killed when his bomber transport was specially intercepted and shot down by USAAF Lock-heed P-38 twin-engined fighters over Bougainville on 18 April 1943. The Imperial Japanese Navy had thus lost its foremost strategist.

It was now the turn of the US Navy to take the air war to the Japanese with a revitalised carrier force,

Below Admiral Maro A. Mitscher talks to Colonel James Doolittle, left, while his men gather round on the flight deck of the USS *Hornet* (CVA-8). In the background can be seen one of the sixteen B-25 Mitchell bombers which were used to bomb Tokyo in 1942.

Above A North American P-51 Mustang in flight. This long-range escort fighter, built up until the end of 1945, was one of America's best fighters, with an excellent airframe and Rolls-Royce Merlin engines.

thanks to the sterling efforts of the US shipbuilding industry. On 1 September 1943, 275 missions were flown against Marcus Island, only 1,000 miles (1,610 km) from Tokyo, as a diversion while a seaplane base was secured on Baker Island in preparation for the forthcoming landings in the Gilbert Islands.

Carefully built up again, the Japanese carrier air groups were once more ruined when 173 aircraft were landed at Rabaul from the Truk-based carriers on 1 November 1943. The US Navy consistently refused to do this, a point emphasised on the same day when aircraft from *Princeton* and *Saratoga* attacked Japanese airfields on Bougainville. Three days later the air groups from the two carriers lost only five out of forty-five attacking bombers, plus five of the new Grumman F6F Hellcat fighters, in a strike on Rabaul, despite the fact that seventy Japanese fighters intercepted. Six cruisers and two destroyers were crippled in Rabaul harbour, effectively destroying Japanese naval power in the area. One week later the aircraft of five US carriers struck again at Rabaul. This time only one destroyer was sunk and another damaged, though the attacking force had been 148 bombers escorted by 127 fighters. Again about seventy Japanese fighters intercepted, shooting down thirteen US aircraft for the loss of six of

their own aircraft. A strike was launched at the US carriers, but the forty bombers and seventy fighters failed to score any hits, the first time that this had happened, and lost heavily. This short campaign over New Britain, centre of Japan's power in the area, had cost the Japanese almost half of the 192 aircrews they had landed from the carriers, and so the painful process of building up the carrier air groups had to begin once again.

Bougainville had been invaded on 1 November 1943, the western end of New Britain on 26 December, the Admiralty Islands to the north-west of New Britain on 29 February 1944 and the St. Matthias group on 20 March, effectively isolating the main base areas of Rabaul on New Britain and Kavieng on New Ireland, which were left for the rest of the war to 'wither on the vine'. In this area, an extension of what the Japanese believed to be the optimum defence line, the Imperial Navy had lost 2,940 aircraft between August 1942 and February 1944, while the Imperial Army had lost more than 1,000 during 1943 alone. The useless addition to Japan's empire had indeed been a graveyard of the Japanese air services. And whereas these losses amounted to about one-third of Japan's aircraft production for the period, and a high proportion of aircrew 'pro-

uction', at a time when Japan was trying desperately to expand her forces to meet the growing Allied threats, similar US losses were more than made up by massive aircraft and aircrew production.

US Navy strategy in the Central Pacific called for the seizure of a chain of islands eventually leading to the Japanese home islands. The first link in this chain was the Gilbert group of islands, invaded on 20 November 1943. Naval support was furnished by Vice Admiral Spruance's 5th Fleet, which had by October reached a strength of seven battleships, eight carriers, seven heavy cruisers, three light cruisers and thirty-four destroyers. Army air support was provided by Major General Willis A. Hale's 7th AAF, which had been operating in the Solomons but had now been switched to bases in the Ellice Islands south of the Gilberts. The centrepiece of the naval air component was the Fast Carrier Task Force.

Before the landings, naval aircraft struck at airfields in the Gilberts and Marshalls, the island group next to the north, during November, while after the landings close air support was provided by six escort carriers with 147 aircraft. The Japanese managed to damage the light carrier *Independence* on 20 November, but thereafter the US air forces destroyed virtually all Japanese aircraft in the area. The escort carrier *Liscome Bay* was lost on 24 November to a Japanese submarine-launched torpedo. Admiral Mineichi Koga, Yamamoto's successor, kept his meagre air resources on the ground at Truk to protect his fleet, which he felt was incapable of tackling the 5th Fleet.

Nimitz then moved his forces forward to the Marshall Islands, where the same pattern of operations was repeated from 30 January 1944. While the actual landings were supported by light carriers and escort carriers, Vice Admiral Marc A. Mitscher's Fast Carrier Task Force set off to attack the Combined Fleet's main base at Truk. The carrier centrepiece of this force was TF58, consisting by this time of six fleet and six light carriers. With no operational carriers, there was little that Koga could do to hamper the US operations in the Marshalls, and now he waited for the arrival of Mitscher's force. The Combined Fleet was rapidly dispersed to safety before Mitscher arrived on 17 February. During the next two days the Americans dispatched 1,250 sorties against Truk, destroying 275 of the 370 Japanese naval air arm aircraft located there, and sinking ten warships and thirty-three other vessels, totalling more than 200,000 tons. The strike had clearly

demonstrated the futility of Truk as a main base, and as the Combined Fleet fell back towards the Philippines, Truk was also left to 'wither on the vine' for the rest of the war. The strike had been magnificently successful, and was repeated in the Palaus on 30 and 31 March. Here some twenty-six ships of 107,000 tons were sunk, and more naval air strength was destroyed in the air and on the ground by the Fast Carrier Task Force's fighters.

Japan's naval air arm was now in desperate straits. The 1st *Koku Sentai*'s aircraft and aircrew had been lost in the Rabaul-based air operations; a similar fate had overtaken the 2nd *Koku Sentai* at Truk; the 4th *Koku Sentai* had been decimated in the Battle of Midway and then lost in the Battle of the Eastern Solomons; and the 5th *Koku Sentai* was still being built up after its losses in the Battle of the Eastern Solomons and the Battle of Santa Cruz, as well as land-based losses in the Solomons campaign.

The 1st and 2nd *Koku Sentais* were re-formed in January and March 1944 respectively, and the new 3rd *Koku Sentai* (for the carriers *Chitose* and *Chiyoda*, which had been completed in January 1944 and October 1943) was raised in February 1944. New attack aircraft, in the form of the Nakajima B6N torpedo-bomber and Yokosuka D4Y dive-bomber, were available, but the fighter element still had to use the now elderly Mitsubishi A6M, although in updated models. The aircraft were perhaps adequate, but the aircrew were not, for Japan's flying schools just had not been able to maintain both quality and quantity in the replacements they were having to turn ever more speedily. Once they had finished working-up as far as was possible in the time available, the three carrier divisions linked up at Tawi-Tawi, between Mindanao in the Philippines and Borneo. Here they were joined by the new flagship of the 1st Carrier Strike Force, *Taiho*. The choice of Tawi-Tawi as a base was conditioned as much by its closeness to the oil wells of Borneo as by strategic considerations. The carriers could, and did at a pinch, burn crude oil when supplies of refined oil became unobtainable.

By this time the Americans had serving with the Pacific Fleet fifteen fast carriers with 895 aircraft for strategic use, eight escort carriers with 196 aircraft for support of invasions, five more escort carriers with 135 aircraft as a floating reserve, and one hundred more aircraft aboard transport carriers.

Nimitz's next move up the chain of islands towards Japan was the invasion of Saipan on 15 June 1944 by

Below The wreckage of a Republic P-47 Thunderbolt. Production delivery of this aircraft began in 1943, and it became the first long-range fighter to escort the B-17 and B-24 heavy bombers. The Thunderbolt was a huge, formidable bomber which could carry drop tanks, flying all the way to the target.

V Amphibious Corps. Before the actual assault, Mitscher's air units had pounded the island, and others in the Marianas group, destroying 200 aircraft.

But other moves were afoot. The Japanese regrouping, set in motion by Admiral Soemu Toyoda, commander of the Combined Fleet since the death of Koga in an aircraft accident on 1 April, was part of a plan to lure the American carriers into the Woleai-Palaus-Yap area to the east of Mindanao, where land-based aircraft could help the Combined Fleet to destroy the Americans. For this reason the Combined Fleet elements had rendezvoused off the Sulu archipelago, south-west of the Philippines, on 16 May. But on hearing of the Saipan landings, Toyoda ordered his local commander, Vice Admiral Jisaburo Ozawa, to head for the scene of action. His departure was immediately known to the Americans, whose submarines had been shadowing the force. Nagumo, it is interesting to note, was Commander-in-Chief of the Marianas area, base for the Central Pacific Fleet of a few minor warships.

Thus was set the scene for the fifth great carrier battle of the Pacific war, the Battle of the Philippine Sea. Ozawa had five fleet and four light carriers, five battleships, eleven heavy and two light cruisers, and twenty-eight destroyers. Japanese air strength was 473 aircraft. The American force to meet this was Admiral Spruance's 5th Fleet, which had seven fleet and eight light carriers, seven battleships, eight heavy and thirteen light cruisers, and sixty-nine destroyers. American air strength was 956. To the Japanese strength should also be added about one hundred land-based machines on Guam, Rota and Yap.

Contact was made on 19 June, and the battle lasted two days. The whole episode was a disaster of unparalleled proportions for Japan, and has gone down in history as the 'Great Marianas Turkey Shoot': for the loss of some fifteen aircraft, on the first day the Americans shot down 243 carrierborne and fifty-eight land-based Japanese aircraft; on the second day, for the loss of twenty aircraft in combat and another eighty which ran out of fuel and ditched, or crashed while trying to land in the dark, the Americans destroyed another sixty-five Japanese aircraft. On 19 June the Japanese had also lost the carriers *Taiho* and *Shokaku* to submarine-launched torpedoes; and on 20 June the US carrier aircraft had sunk the carrier *Hiyo*. The Japanese *matériel* losses were thus catastrophic, but just as vitally, they had lost virtually the last 460 trained and experienced pilots the naval air arm possessed. The Americans, on the other hand, had lost few men: of the 209 men on the eighty aircraft that had ditched, 160 were rescued. And after the battle the surviving six Japanese carriers had only fifty aircraft left, whereas the fifteen American carriers had more than 700. As a fighting force the Japanese carrier fleet was effectively finished.

In the aftermath of this Battle of the Philippine Sea, the two remaining major islands of the Marianas group, Guam and Tinian, were invaded. The group was secured on 10 August, but even before this engineers had started work on great heavy bomber airfields on Saipan and Tinian.

There now occurred a change in command, though the ships of the command remained unchanged. Spruance and the staff of the 5th Fleet set about planning the seizure of Iwo Jima and Okinawa, while Halsey took over what was now redesignated the 3rd Fleet, TF58 (the Fast Carrier Task Force) becoming TF38. Mitscher remained in command of this last force.

As a prelude to the navy-controlled invasion of Yap,

TF38 swept through the Yap, Ulithi and Palaus area on 6 September, and the coast of the Philippines between 6 and 13 September, destroying military targets and aircraft wherever it went. Yap no longer seemed a target of importance, and was so bypassed, the American fleet base being moved to Ulithi after its capture on 23 September.

Just before this, on 15 September, the American strategic plan had been altered. Instead of a divided thrust towards Japan, with MacArthur's South-West Pacific Area forces moving up through the Philippines and Nimitz's Pacific Ocean Areas' forces moving into Formosa or China (possibly) and then Iwo Jima and Okinawa, the two plans were to be combined into a joint (and earlier) attack on the Philippines and then the Iwo Jima/Okinawa landings before the final descent on Japan herself.

As a prelude to the initial Philippines operation, against the island of Leyte on 20 October, TF38 struck at Japanese air power in Okinawa in the first week of October, and then turned its attention to Formosa between 13 and 16 October. For the loss of only slightly over one hundred aircraft, which could easily be replaced from the eleven ferry carriers operating with the 3rd Fleet, the Americans destroyed almost 500 Japanese naval and more than 150 army aircraft. Only two American cruisers and the carrier *Franklin* were damaged.

The Leyte landings went ahead on 20 October,

Right A Japanese kamikaze attack on the USS *Columbia* (CL-5) during operations against the US invasion force in Lingayen Gulf, Philippines. The aircraft, a Yokosuka D4Y4, has been specially adapted for suicide missions. *Below* Damage-control crews on the flight deck of the USS *Yorktown* (CV-5) working to save the ship following direct hits by bomb and torpedo during Japanese air attacks. Shortly after this photograph was taken, the ship was sunk and the destroyer alongside her, the USS *Hamman* (DD-412), was broken in two.

without the fear of Japanese air intervention from other island groups. But in the Philippines the Japanese had just under 400 aircraft. On 24 October some 200 of these were committed to an attack on the beach-head: sixty-six were shot down. Meanwhile the main surface elements of the Combined Fleet were closing in on the invasion force, divided into four main groups. TF3 concentrated on Vice Admiral Takeo Kurita's Force A of the Main Striking Force, which contained the two super-battleships *Yamato* and *Musashi*. But only after two days of bombardment was *Musashi* disposed of. Japanese land-based aircraft had during this time sunk the light carrier *Princeton*. This Battle of the Sibuyan Sea was only one of four main actions that together constitute the Battle of Leyte Gulf, the greatest naval battle ever fought and the battle that ended the Combined Fleet as an effective weapon. Air power played no part in the Battle of San Bernardino Strait, and in the Battle off Samar air power was only involved inasmuch as the Japanese Force A sank the escort carrier *Gambier Bay* with gunfire.

On 25 October, in the northernmost of the actions, the Battle of Cape Engaño, carriers were vital. Coming down from the north was Ozawa's 1st Carrier Strike Force as a decoy for the main American strength. It was a decoy as it had virtually no aircraft after the Battle of the Philippine Sea. Rushing forward to meet it were the ten carriers and twenty-two destroyers of Mitscher's TF38, and the six battleships, four cruisers and eight destroyers of TF34, under Halsey's command. The Japanese could not fight off the American aircraft with gunfire alone, and the carriers *Zuikaku*, *Zuiho*, *Chitose* and *Chiyoda* were sunk.

The battle of Leyte Gulf had cost the Japanese four carriers, three battleships, six heavy cruisers, four light cruisers, eleven destroyers, one submarine and about 500 aircraft. American losses were one light carrier, two escort carriers, two destroyers, one destroyer escort and some 200 aircraft.

Thereafter the threat to the US Navy from Japanese aircraft was basically from *kamikaze* aircraft, which did indeed cause considerable losses at times. The first planned *kamikaze* attack took place on 25 October, when the escort carrier *Santee* was hit by an A6M. AA fire, radar picket ships and fighter patrols helped to check the threat, but it was impossible to obviate it entirely, and up to 12 December seven fleet carriers were damaged. Seven other warships were sunk, and another twenty-three damaged. At times, though, poor weather and large concentrations of ships, such as during the Lingayen Gulf landings (9 January 1945), the Iwo Jima landings (19 February 1945) and the Okinawa landings (1 April 1945) provided excellent scope for the *kamikazes*.

During 1945 the US carrier force continued to grow, and raided throughout the area left to Japan with increasing impunity. It was also joined by four British carriers. Between 10 and 22 January 1945, for example, fourteen fast carriers, with 925 aircraft, moved into the South China Sea and sank more than 300,000 tons of shipping. Yet despite the fact that this sea was surrounded by Japanese air bases, it was not until 21 January that the force was found and *kamikazes* damaged two carriers and one destroyer.

TF58, now back under Spruance's command, raided Tokyo on 16 and 17 February, destroying 200 aircraft in the air and many more on the ground, for only sixty losses. Thereafter the carriers operated ever closer to Japan for the rest of the war.

CHAPTER NINETEEN

ARMY AIR POWER IN THE PACIFIC 1941·5

The Japanese Army's main preoccupation at the start of the Pacific war still lay in China and Manchukuo, though it realised that in a war with the western powers the speedy seizure of the Philippines, Malaya, the Dutch East Indies and Burma was essential. Only thus could these strategic areas, brimming with many of the raw materials Japan needed for her economic survival, be secured before Allied strength increased radically. The differing importance allocated by the Imperial Army to the various parts of its sphere of responsibility may be gauged by the numbers of first-line aircraft allocated to each: 600 to China and Manchukuo, 550 for Malaya (where the army would have the support of 150 naval aircraft), 175 for the Philippines (where the army would have the vital support of 300 naval aircraft, much longer-ranged than the army aircraft), and only fifty in Japan herself (the navy, on the other hand, had 350 aircraft in the home islands and the Marshalls).

Of the 2,620 first-line aircraft deployed by the Japanese, the army contributed 1,375.

The Allies, as they would become after the outbreak of hostilities, could muster only 1,284 aircraft in the Far East and Pacific. The United States contributed 385 in the Hawaiian Islands and as part of the Pacific Fleet, 180 in the Philippine Islands, and twelve each on Midway and Wake Islands; the British mustered some 330 aircraft in Malaya; the Australians had 165 aircraft in Australia, Malaya, the East Indies and the Solomon Islands; and the Dutch could deploy 200 aircraft in their East Indies. The trouble lay in the fact that most of these Allied aircraft were obsolete, or at best obsolescent.

For its two main southern thrusts, the Imperial Army mustered two *Hikoshidans*. The 3rd *Hikoshidan* was allocated to the Malayan operation, and had the 3rd, 7th and 12th *Hikodans* with eleven *Sentais*, plus the 15th and 21st *Dokuritsu Hikotais* with four *Dokuritsu Dai Shijugo Chutais*. The 4th *Hikoshidan* was allocated to the Philippines campaign, and had the 4th and 10th *Hikodans* with seven *Sentais*, plus the 10th *Dokuritsu Hikotai* with three *Dokuritsu Dai Shijugo Chutais* and a *Hiko Chutai*.

The army air arm's war started on 8 December, when bombers from bases in Siam struck as the RAF airfields in northern Malaya, destroying sixty of the 110 British and Australian aircraft in the area. For the rest of the month the aircraft of the 3rd *Hikoshidan* kept up a relentless pressure on the Allied aircraft and bases in Malaya, allowing their fast-moving ground forces the

freedom to act with little interference from Allied aircraft. By the end of the month, army bombers were operating from captured bases in the north of Malaya, supplementing the naval air effort against Singapore.

By this time Allied air strength in Malaya was down to 160 aircraft, all gathered on the four airfields on Singapore island. Air reinforcements were, however, received: sixty-four medium bombers from Australia, Egypt and Great Britain; a small number of Consolidated PBY reconnaissance flying-boats from Gibraltar and Java; and finally fifty-one Hawker Hurricane fighters from Great Britain, these arriving by sea on 13 January 1942. These were totally insufficient to turn the tide, though, and by the end of the month, when most of the surviving Allied aircraft were flown out to Sumatra, only about twenty-five of the Hurricanes were still operational. The few Hurricanes left fought on, making their last sortie before pulling out to Java on 9 February. The great fortress of Singapore fell on 15 February, after a Japanese assault across the Straits of Johore under cover of an intensive army bomber bombardment.

With the end of Japan's initial advance to establish the defensive perimeter for her 'Greater South-East Asia Co-Prosperity Sphere', the Allies at last had a little time to take stock of the situation and determine how best they could strike back at the Japanese, and then fight their way back into the conquered territories and thence to Japan. From this point, at about the end of March 1942, the Japanese revised their overall strategic plan: instead of a perimeter resting in Burma, the Malay barrier, the Dutch East Indies, northern New Guinea, the Bismarck Islands, the Gilbert Islands, Wake Island and their own Pacific possessions, the Japanese now opted for a new perimeter including southern New Guinea, the Solomon Islands and Midway Island. It

A North American B-25 Mitchell of the 14th Air Force bombs the 9,000 ft Yellow River bridge in China. Note the anti-aircraft tower in the bottom of the picture. The B-25 was heavily defended, with a normal bombload of 3,000 lb (1,360 kg). Over 4,5●● were built.

was a disastrous change, and gave the Allies their first chances of success.

On 11 March 1942, General Douglas MacArthur, commanding the American and Filipino forces in the Bataan peninsula, the only major part of Luzon left in Allied hands, was peremptorily ordered by President Franklin D. Roosevelt to hand over his command and leave the Philippines for Australia. Here he was to set up a combined headquarters to control all Allied forces in the South Pacific, or the South-West Pacific Area. This US Army-controlled area was to be one half of the giant force that was to prepare and run the Allied counter-offensive against Japan, the other half being the three US Navy-dominated Pacific areas controlled by Admiral Chester W. Nimitz's Pacific Ocean Areas. After a considerable amount of strategic dispute between the army and the navy, it was eventually decided in June and July 1942 that the American, Australian and New Zealand drive was to be a double one, with Nimitz pushing eastwards across the Pacific from the Hawaiian Islands through the central island groups towards the Philippines and Formosa, while MacArthur drove into New Guinea, along this great island's north coast towards the east, and then poised his forces for the jump north towards the Philippines.

If nothing else, the success of the Japanese southward drive had convinced the Americans of the need for powerful air support for their ground forces, and one of the first tasks facing MacArthur was the establishment of a powerful tactical air force. The possibilities of aircraft manufacture in Australia were very limited, and so the great majority of aircraft and supplies had to be brought in from the United States, several thousand miles away across the Pacific. This logistical backing was eventually to grow into a huge and smooth running complex, but during 1942 matters were very difficult as the service echelons struggled to set up the basis of this organisation.

To head this new force, a joint American and Australian formation designated the 5th Army Air Force, MacArthur selected a tried and trusted subordinate, Major General George C. Kenney. During the second half of 1942, Kenney set about setting up and training his force with considerable energy. There was an enormous amount to be done, quite apart from the logistical side. The right aircraft had to be found, converted to local standards of operational serviceability and effectiveness; new tactics had to be devised; and then the aircrews had to be trained thoroughly before they could stand a chance against the excellent Japanese air forces, elements of the Imperial Navy based on Rabaul in New Britain, and the air component of the Imperial Army's 18th Army, based in New Guinea.

Kenney had anticipated that he would have the second half of the year in which to accomplish his training programme, but Japanese moves against Port Moresby in July forestalled this. Realising that in the short term he would have to rely on the aircraft which had proved inferior to the Japanese ones, but which were still the only types available in any numbers, Kenney had pinned his hopes on superior firepower and highly trained pilots, and set about producing an appropriate 'school' programme. But the Japanese thrust towards Port Moresby, with its attendant threat to northern Australia, meant that the fledgling 5th Air Force had to be committed to major operations long before Kenney adjudged it properly operational.

At first the Japanese had things all their own way,

Above A flight of Republic P-47 Thunderbolts. These were the heaviest single-engine fighters of World War II, and were powerfully armed. Vast numbers of the P-47D version served in the European and Pacific theatres until the end of the war.

just as they had earlier in the year. But gradually the increasingly hard school into which the 5th Air Force's pilots had been thrown began to yield results as the survivors learned how to stay alive and strike back.

At first Kenney had tried to husband his new striking forces, but soon these too had to be thrown into the battle, and from this point onwards the tide began to change against the Japanese. Flying Bristol Beaufighters, North American B-25 Mitchells and Martin B-26 Marauders, the Allied strike forces hit at Japanese air bases in New Guinea and New Britain, harassed the coastal shipping on which Japanese communications were dependent, and then hit at the Japanese forces struggling in terrible plight in the jungles of the Owen Stanley mountains. At first the bomber forces also suffered heavy losses, but the offensive meant that the Japanese had first to stop their fighters flying beyond the Owen Stanleys so that they could protect base areas, and then the war of attrition in the air swung decisively in the Allies' favour. And with the cessation of escort for the bombers pounding Port Moresby, the Allied fighters began to extract a terrible toll on these lightly protected aircraft. By the end of November, the Japanese were beginning to feel as the Allies had in the opening months of the year. In the autumn of 1942, moreover, the first Lockheed P-38 Lightning twin-engined fighters, generally far superior to Japanese fighters except in dogfighting ability, arrived in the South-West Pacific Area, and helped turn the qualitative tide against the invaders.

As the Japanese ground forces fell back from their abortive offensive towards Port Moresby in September, the aircraft of the 5th Air Force gradually took to the offensive in a major way against ground targets, although the part they could play in the final defeat of the

panese at Buna and Gona on the north coast was
verely limited by the close proximity of the two sides'
round troops to each other. Nonetheless, by the end of
42 the American and Australian units of the 5th Air
orce were beginning to emerge as formidable tactical
perators, much feared by the Japanese.

It should be noted, though, that by the end of 1942
e Japanese were still firmly entrenched in their
efensive perimeter' as envisaged before the war – the
tacks on Port Moresby and Guadalcanal had been
tras, and although very costly in men and *matériel*,
eir defeats had not dented the perimeter in the
ightest. Yet the Allies had gained valuable experience,
hich was to prove decisive in the battles that lay ahead
the Allies pierced the perimeter.

Clearly MacArthur's next target was the twin base
ea of New Britain and New Ireland, with their major
ases of Rabaul and Kavieng, by means of a naval-
ntrolled advance up the Solomons chain, and an
my-directed advance up the New Guinea coast before
landing across the Vitiaz Strait near Cape Gloucester.
he plan was later changed so that these base areas were
erely isolated and left 'to wither on the vine' while the
llies moved forward towards the Philippines.

By the end of 1942 Kenney's air strength had grown
nsiderably, and in the first few months of 1942 his
ansport aircraft were able to give MacArthur's ground
rces a strategic mobility that the Japanese could not
pe to match, by flying in large bodies of troops to
portant locales, constantly threatening the Japanese
the rear. On 9 January 1943, for example, Kenney's
rcraft flew in a brigade of Australians to Wau, where
eir airhead threatened the Japanese base of Salamaua.

Despite the diversion of some effort to airborne
operations and the resultant need for airborne supply
operations, Kenney, by now a lieutenant general, was
able to send the 5th Air Force into action against the
Japanese on an ever-increasing scale. The first five
months of the year were devoted to the attrition of
Japan's air formations in the New Guinea area. The
fighter battle was an extremely bitter one, with both
sides pouring in reinforcements as quickly as they
could. Here at last the growing experience of the Allied
pilots, combined with the arrival of ever increasing
numbers of the latest aircraft, such as the Republic P-47
Thunderbolt, meant that the Japanese could find no
long-term answer.

By February 1943 MacArthur's forces were posing a
distinct threat to the major Japanese forward base at
Lae in the Huon Gulf, and the Japanese decided that
the base must be reinforced as quickly as possible,
before it was cut off by the Allied advances. Accordingly
a troop convoy of seven merchant ships would load the
51st Division at Rabaul between 23 and 27 February,
and then head for Lae under the escort of eight
destroyers, covered by some forty naval and sixty army
aircraft. The whole operation was planned down to the
last detail, with the troop convoy to arrive at Lae on 3
March, unload immediately, and return to Rabaul by 8
March.

At first all went well for the Japanese. But on 1 March
the convoy was spotted by a patrolling Consolidated
Liberator: seven merchantmen, eight destroyers
and the special service ship *Nojima*. This was just what
Kenney had been waiting for, and plans for an anti-
shipping strike were immediately set in operation.

Below The Bell-39 Airacobra made up a large part of the US Army Air Force's fighter strength in the first half of World War II. Used in the Mediterranean, New Guinea and the Solomon Islands in 1942, this aircraft was only moderately successful.

Several attack methods had been tried, and the most satisfactory adopted and trained for, so the squadrons to be used were ready for what was to be the 5th Air Force's most decisive battle – the Battle of the Bismarck Sea.

Spotted shortly after it left Rabaul on 1 March, the convoy came under attack from B-17s on the next day. This attack damaged two transports and sank the army transport *Kyokusei Maru*.

3 March, however, was the day that sealed the fate of the convoy. Now within reach of the main strike units based in the Port Moresby area as they reached the area of the Huon Peninsula, the Japanese received the full force of a series of coordinated attacks by torpedo-bombers, attack aircraft, medium bombers and their escorting fighters. During the morning the destroyer *Arashio* was hit three times and steaming out of control collided with the already damaged *Nojima*, which sank. *Arashio* sank a few hours later. Almost immediately afterwards, the flagship *Shirayuki* was crippled and abandoned. At the same time another destroyer, *Toki-tsukaze*, was severely damaged, as a result of which she sank a short time later.

More importantly for the Japanese, however, were the six surviving troopships, with their 6,000 desperately needed reinforcements for Lae. The attacks that had so hurt the escort had sunk or crippled all six of these merchantmen, and the whole convoy had broken up.

As another strike was prepared, the five surviving destroyers, *Asashio, Uranami, Shikinami, Yukikaze* and *Asagumo*, were scouring the area of the battle for survivors. The strike force returned on the afternoon of 3 March and took up where it had left off. But this time their efforts were not as successful, and only the destroyer *Asashio* was sunk. The last four destroyers continued to search for survivors during the afternoon, with considerable success. Sent out from Kavieng to help, the destroyer *Hatsuyuki* joined with *Uranami* in ferrying some 1,500 survivors back to Rabaul after refuelling the three destroyers that remained on the scene still looking for survivors. Overnight they picked up more men before racing to Kavieng. Japanese submarines rescued the last 275 men to be found.

Nevertheless, some 3,000 men had been lost, as well as seven transports, the special service vessel and four destroyers. It was a decisive victory for the 5th Air Force, and put an end to this attempt to reinforce Lae, as well as causing the Japanese to abandon such methods of reinforcing their garrisons in the future. Of the original 7,000 troops destined for Lae, only 850 had arrived there.

In the air the battle had also resulted in a decisive Allied victory: for the loss of two bombers and three fighters, the aircraft of the 5th Air Force had shot down some twenty-five of the defending Japanese fighters before the battle ended on the morning of 4 March.

For the rest of the year from June to December, the 5th Air Force went from strength to strength as a support formation unequalled in the Pacific and possibly anywhere in the world. The pattern evolved was as follows. Firstly, fighters and light bombers roamed over the area which MacArthur next intended to assault, gaining air superiority by decimating the Japanese air defence on the ground and in the air. At the same time, heavy bombers raided Japanese bases supporting the area to be assaulted, often in collaboration with aircraft from naval strike forces. This effectively prevented reinforcements reaching the threatened area. Secondly,

fighters and light bombers again attacked the assault area, with the intention this time of damaging ground installations and making it impossible for the Japanese to ship in troops or supplies from neighbouring areas. The area to be assaulted was thus isolated, damaged and deprived of air support. Finally, as the assault troops moved in, ground targets became the primary objective up to and during the actual battle for the area. So good did the ground/air liaison become that aircraft could be called in to deal with trouble spots only yards from the Allied front line. If the landing was an airborne one, as many along the coast of New Guinea were, the practice was the same, but in this instance the trooping aircraft shuttled back and forth to the assault area from their bases bringing in supplies and reinforcements. Engineer units on the ground started work building an airstrip as soon as the ground forces had captured a suitable site, so that light aircraft and troop-carriers could operate right from the front line as quickly as possible. The Japanese could find no counter to all this, and their air strength was steadily whittled away by the growing power of the 5th Air Force. Kenny's forces continued to support MacArthur's land forces in their advance right to the western end of New Guinea, and then in their campaigns in the Philippines right up to the end of the war. Their skill as support forces became legendary, with refinements being constantly introduced to improve the chances of the ground forces fighting below.

The South-West Pacific Area was only one of the places in which 'army' aviation played an important part. There was also China, where an interesting strategic campaign began.

Wary of Japanese intentions against China, and against the possessions of the western powers in the Far East, the US government had given its silent approval in September 1941 to the formation of the American Volunteer Group, about one hundred ex-Army, Navy and Marine Corps pilots who were to fly Curtiss P-40 fighters supplied to China under the Lend-Lease Act in defence of major Chinese cities, notably Chiang Kai-shek's capital, Chungking. The American Volunteer Group's aircraft were serviced by American ground-crew, and the group's commander was Captain Claire L. Chennault, who held the rank of colonel in the Chinese air force. Chennault trained his force on the deserted British airfield of Toungoo in Burma. By

December the American Volunteer Group was in action against the Japanese, and for the first time the latter began to meet effective air opposition over China. Despite the relative obsolescence of their aircraft compared with those of the Japanese, Chennault's pilots were able to inflict far more serious losses than they themselves sustained, and gradually evolved to perfection the diving tactics that were only later to be adopted elsewhere in the theatre against the more nimble Japanese fighters. An astute and practical man, Chennault realised that his hand-picked pilots were in a better position to take on the Japanese than the average US pilot, and sent a number of messages to the authorities back in the United States about the calibre of Japanese fighters and their pilots. As noted earlier, these reports were uniformly ignored by men who had made the classic error of believing their own propaganda.

With the start of the major Japanese drive in South-East Asia in December 1941, Chennault's two main priorities were clear: the defence of Chungking, and the defence of Kunming, the Chinese end of the Burma Road, the only supply route into China still left to Chiang Kai-shek. Courageously supported by Chiang, though, Chennault decided to protect Kunming and, at the request of the British, sent one of his three squadrons to help in the air defence of Rangoon. The third squadron was kept in reserve, to be rotated with those at Kunming and at Mingaladon, the latter being the base for the air defence of Rangoon. The Kunming squadron went into action on 20 December, shooting down six Japanese bombers without loss; and the Mingaladon fighters entered the fray three days later, disposing of several Japanese aircraft with only slight losses to themselves.

The Japanese kept heavy air pressure on Rangoon during January and February 1942, and the British fighters were gradually whittled down and crushed. The Americans, however, were able to use their superior tactics to inflict heavy losses, over one hundred Japanese aircraft, for the loss of only fifteen of their own aircraft.

Left Two Boeing B-29 Superfortresses release incendiary bombs on a Japanese target, 1945. The photograph was taken through the nose of a Superfortress. *Below* A string of parachute fragmentation bombs is released by a North American B-25 over the Byoritsu oil refinery, Formosa. Smoke trails from the B-25 No.192, which has been hit by flak from a camouflaged battery.

Mitsubishi K-67 Hiryu

Type: heavy bomber.
Engines: two 1,900 hp Mitsubishi Ha-104 18 cylinder two row radials.
Dimensions: span 73 ft 9¾ in (22.5 m); length 61 ft 4¼ in (18.7 m); height
18 ft 4½ in (5.6 m).
Weights: empty 19,068 lb (8,649 kg); loaded 30,346 lb (13,765 kg).
Performance: max. 334 mph (537 km/h); initial climb 1,476 ft (450 m)/min.;
service ceiling 31,070 ft (947 m); range with full bomb load 621 miles
(1,000 km).

This type entered service in 1944, proving to be fast and manoeuvrable,
and is regarded as the Japanese Army's best all-round bomber of World
War II. The Ki-67 Hiryu (Flying Dragon) was nicknamed 'Peggy' by the
Allies. This type began its career as a torpedo bomber in the Philippine
Sea battle and later operated against Iwo Jima, the Marianas and in the
defence of Japan.

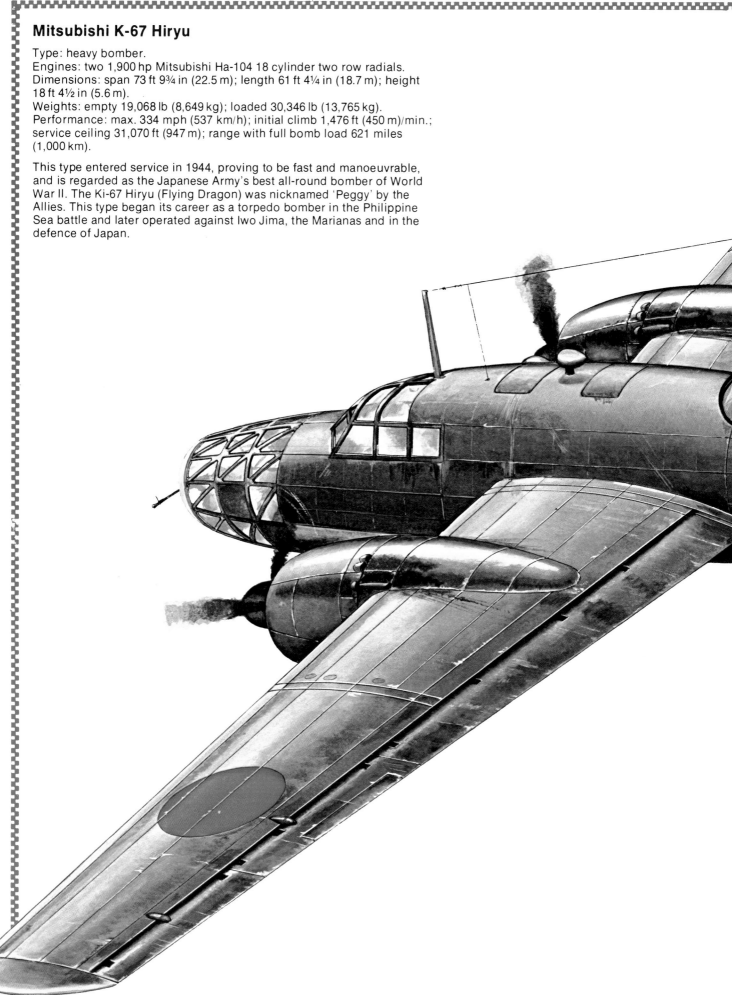

The approach of Japanese ground forces late in February forced the Allied aircraft to fall back to Magwe by 1 March, and from here Chennault's pilots kept up their good work for three weeks, giving the Allied ground forces very useful ground support as well as mauling any Japanese bomber formations that came within range. But on 21 March the Japanese launched a heavy raid on Magwe and managed to catch the Allied aircraft on the ground. Chennault now had only three fighters left in Burma, and these he withdrew to Loiwing, just over the border in China. The British survivors were withdrawn to India, leaving the ground forces with only marginal air support as the range at which the aircraft had to operate meant that their battlefield endurance was small. By May, however, as the Japanese were consolidating their hold on Burma, some Supermarine Spitfires arrived in the theatre, giving the RAF near parity of fighter quality for the first time. But as the RAF's position improved, that of Chennault deteriorated: the Burma Road had finally been closed by the Japanese arrival in Lashio, the road's Burmese terminal, and Chennault now found himself short of fuel, ammunition and spares.

There was now only one possible way in which supplies could be dispatched into China: by air. The Americans were the only people with the resources for such an undertaking, and they set about it with a will. Never before had an airlift of the required proportions been attempted, and never before had any such airlift been tried in conditions as difficult as those in this corner of Lieutenant General Joseph Stilwell's China-Burma-India Theater. A great complex of bases had to be built in north-east India, with railways to bring in the supplies from Calcutta, and the whole organisation built up in India and China. The transport aircraft could not fly directly to Kunming, as the Japanese would have been able to intercept them from bases near Myitkyina, so the airlift, which began in June, was forced to operate 'over the hump' of the Himalayas in south-east Tibet, where the mountains rise to some 21,000 feet (6,400 m). To protect the bases from which the airlift operated in India, the US 10th Army Air Force was established under the command of Major General Howard C. Davidson. Yet the difficulties in which the Allies found themselves in 1942 meant that precious few extra transport aircraft could be allocated to the CBI theatre. Thus the 'hump' airlift was at first a puny child, although by the end of the year the organisation had reached the state that extra allocations of aircraft could be coped with immediately, and the volume of the airlift stepped up whenever the resources were available.

Chiang had hoped much of the airlift, and Stilwell's admission that he had been unable to prevail upon the US Joint Chiefs-of-Staff for the allocation of large numbers of transport aircraft helped to worsen the two men's relationship. At the same time Chennault and Stilwell became more and more antagonistic towards each other, as a result of Chennault's insistence that the majority of 'hump' tonnage should be supplies for his forces. These had been reorganised on 4 July 1942 as the US China Air Task Force, with Chennault elevated in rank to brigadier general. Stilwell put Chennault's back up by insisting that the land and air forces should receive equal shares of the supplies flown in, a policy with which Chennault disagreed as his increasingly strike-orientated forces were in a better immediate position to take the offensive against the Japanese in China and northern Burma, particularly the former.

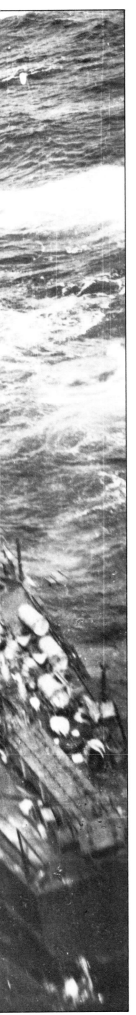

Even with the restricted tonnage allocated to him, Chennault was well pleased with the success of his force, which was still handling the Japanese very severely. Combat experience provided part of the reason for this, but so too did the arrival of more modern combat aircraft: the combination meant that the Americans enjoyed a kill : loss ratio of some 10:1. Chennault, convinced that in his China Air Task Force he had a weapon that could win the war in China unaided, grew increasingly hostile towards Stilwell as the latter steadfastly refused to allow the air forces to receive more than half the 'hump' tonnage. With the operations of his strike forces thus severely curtailed, Chennault gradually won the support of Chiang, principally because the latter was growing ever more displeased with Stilwell. The clincher came when Chennault won the backing of President Roosevelt, and on 11 March 1943 the China Air Task Force was enlarged and redesignated the US 14th Army Air Force, with Chennault rising in rank again to major general. With the 'hump' tonnage dispute now settled in Chennault's favour, the 14th Air Force went from strength to strength during the year, gaining air superiority over most of southern China, and launching raids on the Japanese as far afield as Formosa.

Although the weight of these offensive operations in 1943 was borne by medium bombers and 'heavies' such as the Consolidated B-24 Liberator, Chennault expected in the spring of 1944 to receive a number of the new Boeing B-29 Superfortress strategic bombers, with which he hoped to carry the war to the Japanese homeland. The supply problem to China was still acute, and at first these giant bombers would operate from Indian bases against targets in South-East Asia, gaining combat experience over secondary targets, before staging through Chinese airfields *en route* to Manchuria and Japan, and finally moving in to Chinese airfields when the supply situation made this possible. To this end the building of several new airfields, five in India and four in China, had been undertaken by the manual labour of some 750,000 local men, women and children. Other airfields were planned for China as the situation warranted.

Well aware of what was likely to happen, the Japanese had decided on an all-out offensive in southern China to destroy the Allied air bases whose aircraft had been so potent a thorn in their sides for the last year.

Thus the Japanese spent the first five months of 1944 readying themselves for this offensive. Meanwhile the first operational B-29 had landed at Kwanghan airbase in China on 24 April 1944. The first B-29 raid had yet to be launched, however.

The Japanese ground offensive, controlled by General Yasuji Okamura, Commander-in-Chief of the China Expeditionary Army, opened on 7 May: the 250,000 men of the 11th Army drove south-west from Hankow towards Changsha, and the 50,000 men of the 23rd Army advanced from Canton directly westwards. Chinese resistance was distinctly spotty at first, and after a stiffening in August began to crumble again later in the year. Chennault's 14th Air Force operated with almost complete freedom against the Japanese ground forces, but could not halt the drive. By the end of November the Japanese had taken seven of the 14th Air Force's twelve airfields, but were halted in December.

The strategic bomber offensive, however, was in the meantime getting under way after its prolonged gestation. In late April, B-29s of the newly-activated XX Bomber Command, commanded by Major General Curtis E. LeMay and part of the 20th Army Air Force, arrived in India in some numbers, and launched their first combat raid, against the railway network in Bangkok, Siam, on 5 June. Ten days later the B-29s hit at Japan for the first time. Some sixty-eight Superfortresses took off from the air bases around Calcutta, staged through the bases near Chengtu in China, and attacked the steel plant at Yawata in Kyushu island. This was the first American raid on Japan since the celebrated 'one-off' Doolittle raid of April 1942. During the rest of 1944, XX Bomber Command continued to step up its raids on targets in Kyushu, Formosa and southern Manchuria, all key industrial areas for the Japanese war effort. With 'hump' tonnages still insufficient to support a major effort from Chinese bases, the B-29s continued to operate from Indian bases, staging through the Chinese bases to refuel and arm.

Japanese air opposition to the B-29s was limited, but at first technical problems with the B-29s resulted in a number of losses. The trouble lay in the fact that the bombers incorporated a large number of new features, such as pressurisation on a large scale, remote-controlled turrets and advanced engines, and the teething problems with these took some time to be eradicated. Under LeMay's energetic promptings, though,

Left A Japanese Destroyer escort on fire after an attack by North American B-25s of the 345th Bomber Group, off the China coast in 1945.

Right Mitsubishi A6M5a 'Zero' fighters of the 653rd Naval Air Corps at Olita airbase, Japan, 1944. Towards the end of the war, naval bombers were used to try to halt US strategic bombing of Japan.

the technical 'bugs' were gradually removed, and the B-29s acquired an enviable reputation for serviceability as well as performance. The type's performance meant that it was very difficult for the Japanese to intercept, and even then its formidable defensive armament of twelve 0.5-in (12.7-mm) machine guns and one 20-mm cannon meant that it was a difficult type to shoot down, even with heavy cannon.

At the beginning of 1945 XX Bomber Command was moved to the Marianas, leaving Chennault with only his 14th Army Air Force in China. Yet this was a formidable support force, and for the rest of the war it performed excellently in cooperation with the Chinese ground forces.

Okamura had realised that his position was now untenable, and had decided on a strategic withdrawal towards the north. Although this movement started well, the Chinese were soon harrying the retreating Japanese, aided ably by the 14th and 10th Army Air Forces.

The attempt to use China as a springboard for one half of the strategic air campaign against Japan had been only a qualified success, principally as a result of logistical difficulties, and the distance of Japan from even the nearest Chinese airbases. The development of

tactical air power, in the form of the 10th and 14th Army Air Forces, had been very successful, on the other hand, as had the gradual evolution of the airlift 'over the hump', until land communications with China from Burma had been restored in January 1945.

While it was possible from fairly early in the war to take the offensive against the Japanese from bases in China and India, the situation in the central Pacific was more difficult, for here there were few land masses large enough for the establishment of major airbases for operations against Japan. Yet in the successful mounting of strategic bombing of Japan lay one of the United States' main hopes of winning the war economically: for a minimum loss of life, heavy bombers far superior and far more numerous than their Japanese opposition could strike at the Japanese homeland, destroying the will of the people to resist, destroying them and their homes as a major element in Japanese war industry, and also destroying industrial facilities on which Japan's long-term ability to wage an extended war was based.

In the circumstances the assessment of Japan's will to fight on was sadly wrong, but in essence the strategic plan was entirely valid. What was needed, though, was a platform for the strategic bomber campaign. China went some way towards meeting the US Army Air

orces' needs, but the problems of this theatre far utweighed any possible benefits to the strategic bombg campaign. In retrospect, perhaps, the importance of he bombing campaign from Indian and Chinese bases ay in the way in which they helped to iron out the perational 'bugs' with the B-29 bombers on which the ampaign was based. Important results had been chieved by the bombers of XX Bomber Command, ut these alone could not bring down Japan. Therefore nother base was necessary, and the only feasible area or the establishment of a vast strategic bombing omplex was that offered by the Marianas islands.

The Marianas were thus the object of the drive across he central Pacific by Admiral Chester W. Nimitz's acific Ocean Areas. Saipan, invaded on 15 June 1944, nally fell on 13 July; Guam, invaded on 21 July, fell on o August; and Tinian, invaded on 25 July, fell on 2 August. As soon as each island fell, army engineers noved in and set about lengthening and strengthening he runways of the Japanese airfields on the islands, and he construction of numerous other runways and other acilities for the tens of thousands of men that would be eeded for the servicing, flying and running of the ircraft and their logistical backing. Soon the islands egan to take on the appearance of almost nothing but

airfield as two major complexes were rushed into readiness on each of Guam and Tinian, and one on Saipan. But even as the engineers and other rear area troops hastened about their tasks, the first USAAF aircraft began to arrive. These were Boeing B-17 Flying Fortresses and Consolidated B-24 Liberators, which could operate from the existing Japanese runways. Although these two heavy bombers did not have the payload and range combination for major offensive operations against targets in the Japanese home islands, they could fulfil a very useful role in attacking Japanese bases in the Bonin islands and on Iwo Jima, preventing aircraft from these bases interfering with the work in the Marianas, and preparing for another American forward move.

Each of the five base complexes in the Marianas was intended to handle 180 B-29s, so that XXI Bomber Command, part of General Nathan F. Twining's 20th Army Air Force, would eventually deploy some 900 strategic bombers on the islands. This force, it was reckoned, would cripple Japanese industry in a relatively short time. Major General Haywood S. Hansell, commanding XXI Bomber Command, received the first B-29s into the Marianas during October, and an intensive programme of operational training was

Below A Martin B-26 Marauder ready for take-off. This two-engined medium bomber which entered service in 1941. In 1943 it became the chief medium bomber of the 9th Air Force in the European Theatre of Operations, and saw extensive South West Pacific service.

instituted. All was adjudged ready for the onslaught against Japan in late November, although several operational-training missions against Truk had been flown, the first on 28 October.

Meaning to start as they intended to go on, the staff of the 20th Army Air Force decided that the first raid on Japan proper should be against Tokyo, the most heavily defended target in the country. Led by Brigadier General Emmett O'Donnell, 111 B-29s set off for Tokyo, but only twenty-four of the bombers actually dropped their bombs over the Japanese capital.

After this first raid, whose primary objective had been an aircraft factory on the outskirts of the city, the B-29s of XXI Bomber Command struck at Japan about every five days with anything between one hundred and 120 aircraft. But success was slow to come, as the winds at bombing altitude made accuracy difficult for the bomb aimers. Moreover, losses were heavy. Iwo Jima was still in Japanese hands, and as the bombers passed the island *en route* to Japan, fighters rose to maul the bombers. Over Japan itself, moreover, an élite force of experienced pilots had been gathered in expectation of the raids, and these 250 or so pilots, flying the best aircraft Japan had, took a heavy toll of the American bombers. And on their way home, the tired crews, who might be flying damaged aircraft or be short of ammunition, then had to run the gauntlet of the Iwo Jima fighters once again. Many bombers, damaged by the Japanese fighters' fire, crashed in the sea on the long haul home from Iwo Jima to the Marianas. Although the Japanese losses to the bombers were also serious, the bombers were by the end of the year suffering losses in the order of 6%, one per cent higher than the maximum acceptable rate for a sustained offensive.

The strategic bombing campaign, of which so much had been hoped and expected, was clearly in trouble, and there were many worried faces in the Marianas and in Washington. Inevitably there had to be a reappraisal of the whole scheme, and in January and February 1945 the Joint Chiefs-of-Staff spent a considerable amount of effort on the way in which matters might be improved. The problem was that the weather was a fixed quantity: at the standard high bombing altitude, the wind was very strong; the cold and dampness of the air resulted in the wings and engines icing up, thus reducing performance significantly, and the optical sights on which the Americans relied also icing up, further reducing bombing accuracy; and the radar aids carried were not sufficiently accurate to enable pinpoint bombing to be hoped for.

Although Japanese fighters had proved troublesome in 1944, by 1945 they were no more than an irksome nuisance. Nevertheless the situation of the 20th Army Air Force bomber crews was further improved in April by the appearance of the first escort fighters to operate over Japan, starting on the 7th. This was made possible by the capture of Iwo Jima, where VII Fighter Command was established soon after the island's fall. Flying Republic P-47 Thunderbolt fighters and North American P-51 Mustang long-range fighters, which far outclassed anything the Japanese could put into the air, VII Fighter Command pilots soon established total air superiority over Japan, eliminating all but the last vestiges of Japan's once all-conquering fighter arm. This complete command of the air meant that the bombers of the 20th Army Air Force could now begin once again to operate by day, although only at medium altitudes to avoid the poor weather at high altitude and the anti-aircraft fire at low altitude. As XX Bomber

Left A flight of 58th Bombardment Wing Superfortresses dropping huge two-ton bombs on the Japanese city below. Two of the missiles can be seen beneath the upper plane. Powered by four massive 2,200 hp Wright Cyclone engines, this aircraft could carry 12,000 lb (5,443 kg) of bombs.
Far left The Phu Lang bridge, Indo-China, after a direct hit by GP bombs, 1945.
Below left Bomb damage in Tokyo, Japan, after an incendiary attack by a Boeing B-29 Superfortress.

homeless, and other millions starving because just about all means of communication had been destroyed. Any western country would have sued for terms long before reaching this stage, yet the oddities of the Japanese system meant that this was out of the question: the country would fight on to the last unless the Americans could come up with something else.

No immediate solution appeared possible, but because the Marianas offered a better base than China, XX Bomber Command was shifted from Chengtu to the Marianas, and because he had achieved some measure of success, LeMay was shifted from command of XX to XXI Bomber Command, his command of XX Bomber Command being taken over by Brigadier General Roger M. Ramey. Pondering what might be done to increase XXI Bomber Command's results and reduce its losses, LeMay and his staff decided during February and March 1945 to adopt the tactics that had proved successful with XX Bomber Command in China: low-level attacks with incendiary bombs rather than high-level ones with high-explosive bombs.

LeMay's new tactics were immediately vindicated. Some 334 B-29s took off for Tokyo on 9 March of which 302 attacked the target, dropping 1,667 tons of incendiaries from 7,000 feet (2,134 m). Returning crews told the intelligence officers debriefing them that Tokyo had caught fire, and the results of the follow-up photographic reconnaissance mission were eagerly awaited. The photographs proved beyond doubt the correctness of LeMay's tactics: $16\frac{1}{2}$ square miles of Tokyo had been destroyed. Only fourteen aircraft had been lost over the target, and although this was quite high, the results were well worth it. Tokyo had suffered 83,000 dead in the firestorm resulting from the raid, with 100,000 injured and many more made homeless.

To prepare the way for the planned invasion of Okinawa, scheduled for 23 March, it had been decided that five Japanese cities should be destroyed: Tokyo, Nagoya, Osaka and Kobe. Five raids were made, as the first raid on Nagoya was only marginally successful, and during the course of this campaign thirty-two square miles of the industrial cities were destroyed by some 10,000 tons of incendiaries. Just as important, perhaps, was the fact that only twenty-two B-29s were lost – a rate of only 1.4% of the 1,595 sorties dispatched. The lowering of the loss rate is attributable in part to the fact that the raids were night operations, in which the Japanese could offer little resistance, and in part to the fact that Iwo Jima had been neutralised as a Japanese fighter base by the American conquest of the island between 19 February and 24 March. Quite apart from the elimination of the Japanese fighters, the island's capture also meant that the airfields there could be used as emergency landing strips for crippled bombers returning from the target. Indeed, on 17 March sixteen B-29s made emergency landings on the island. By the end of the war some 2,251 B-29s landed on Iwo Jima, saving the lives of some 24,761 aircrew.

The dramatic decline in the B-29 loss rate continued in further operations, falling to .08% per mission in June, to .03% in July and .02% in August. To provide the B-29s with a minimum of protection against attacking fighters, the tail guns were reinstated in May. At the same time more and more aircraft were becoming available, with missions of over 400 aircraft being launched from May onwards. Almost all the major targets allocated by the strategic planning staffs had been destroyed by the middle of June, so a campaign against some sixty smaller targets began on the 15th.

Command had arrived in the Marianas in April, this meant that virtual round-the-clock bombing could be carried out. The airfields in the Marianas had been added to, and with the arrival of yet more aircraft from the United States, the bombers roamed at will over Japan, virtually destroying all of Tokyo, Nagoya, Kobe, Osaka and Yokohama. The residential areas of most large cities had been destroyed, leaving millions homeless, and food distribution had almost completely broken down as a result of the mining of Japan's ports, preventing any shipping movements, and the almost total destruction of the rail network by bombers

The single most devastating raid made by the 20th Army Air Force was that against Tokyo on the night of 25–26 May 1945. Unfortunately for the Americans, it was also the 20th Army Air Force's single most costly raid. Some 498 B-29s were dispatched on the raid, and of these 464 bombed their primary target. The results were devastating: in an enormous firestorm, some 18.9 square miles of Tokyo were destroyed. Yet twenty-six B-29s were lost to Japanese countermeasures, which included fighters, anti-aircraft guns, rockets and special incendiary devices. Returning aircraft reported ninety-four attacks by Japanese fighters, and seventeen of these were claimed as shot down. But the loss rate had been 5.6%, and 254 aircrew out of 5,586 had become casualties. Apart from those B-29s actually shot down, another one hundred, or 21.3%, were damaged by anti-aircraft fire. Another problem to be faced by the crews was the massive air turbulence and updraughts caused by the firestorms in the city. This had long been a problem, although few (if any) aircraft had actually been lost in such circumstances.

By July 1945 the B-29s from the Marianas had burned the heart out of Japan. The country was on its knees, with its industries and cities destroyed, millions

CHAPTER TWENTY

THE ACES
1939·1945

Airmen painting 'kill' markings on the tail of a Messerschmitt Bf 109 fighter, one of the greatest combat aircraft in history. Many versions of the Bf 109 were used in a variety of roles, from 1938.

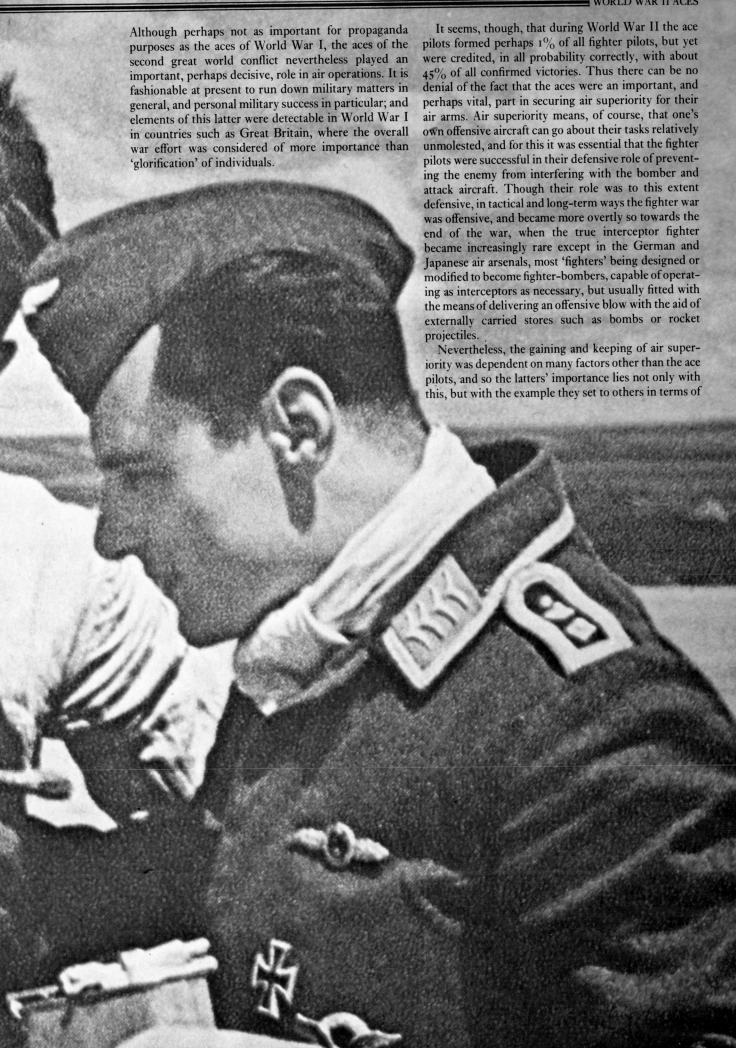

Although perhaps not as important for propaganda purposes as the aces of World War I, the aces of the second great world conflict nevertheless played an important, perhaps decisive, role in air operations. It is fashionable at present to run down military matters in general, and personal military success in particular; and elements of this latter were detectable in World War I in countries such as Great Britain, where the overall war effort was considered of more importance than 'glorification' of individuals.

It seems, though, that during World War II the ace pilots formed perhaps 1% of all fighter pilots, but yet were credited, in all probability correctly, with about 45% of all confirmed victories. Thus there can be no denial of the fact that the aces were an important, and perhaps vital, part in securing air superiority for their air arms. Air superiority means, of course, that one's own offensive aircraft can go about their tasks relatively unmolested, and for this it was essential that the fighter pilots were successful in their defensive role of preventing the enemy from interfering with the bomber and attack aircraft. Though their role was to this extent defensive, in tactical and long-term ways the fighter war was offensive, and became more overtly so towards the end of the war, when the true interceptor fighter became increasingly rare except in the German and Japanese air arsenals, most 'fighters' being designed or modified to become fighter-bombers, capable of operating as interceptors as necessary, but usually fitted with the means of delivering an offensive blow with the aid of externally carried stores such as bombs or rocket projectiles.

Nevertheless, the gaining and keeping of air superiority was dependent on many factors other than the ace pilots, and so the latters' importance lies not only with this, but with the example they set to others in terms of flying and operational skills, as well as a combination of sustained and 'immediate' courage. Many of the aces were also excellent commanders and leaders of men, an important factor in raising the general level of efficiency in their squadrons. This last aspect of air fighting cannot be taught to a novice by a 'chairborne' commander.

Statistically, the first fact to stand out in an examination of World War II's leading aces is the enormously disparate scores of each country's leading aces, and the extremely high score of the top German pilots compared with those of every other country.

For example, the top ranking German ace, *Major* Erich Hartmann, is credited with 352 victories, whereas the Allies' highest scoring fighter pilot, Guards Colonel Ivan Kozhedub, is credited with only sixty-two victories. Moreover, thirty-five German aces in all are credited with a score of 150 or more each, and another seventy-two scored between one hundred and 149 victories. These 107 German aces between them shared 15,615 victories in World War II, and another thirty-eight in Spain scored by four of them. In World War II, therefore, the top 107 German fighter aces averaged 145.935 victories each, which is 2.354 times as many as the single highest scoring Allied ace.

When the figures of these German aces gradually became known after the war, the immediate reaction was to scorn them as wildly inaccurate, and even today many regard the figures as little more than fiction or propaganda masquerading as fact. Yet the German figures have since been revealed as accurate, for they were prepared at unit level, and thus could not have been tampered with by the propaganda authorities controlled by Goebbels. Detractors of the German figures have tended not to look at the historical facts that made the German scores possible. Firstly, there is the fact that the German fighter pilots, unlike their Allied counterparts, did not fly to a system of 'operational tours', in which a pilot flew a certain number of operational missions in a front-line area, and were then rotated, for rest, to a less intensive area, or to a staff appointment, or to a school in which their expertise was passed on to the men under instruction.

The Germans, on the other hand, continued in intensive combat operations until they were killed, injured or captured, with only short periods of leave. Thus the average *Luftwaffe* pilot had an operational life perhaps twice as long as his Allied opposite number, giving him considerably more scope for the shooting down of aircraft. A large number of the better German pilots had as many as 1,000 combat sorties to their credit, whereas the leading British pilots, who generally had more sorties to their credit than their American allies, rarely exceeded 500 operational sorties.

Secondly, there is the fact that the Germans were generally operating against large numbers of aircraft, especially on the Eastern Front, giving them greater opportunity than Allied pilots for continued successes. For whereas Allied pilots were able to score heavily at times when the Germans were present in large numbers, as in the Battle of Britain, or over Malta, for the greater part of the war the Allies had few aircraft at which to direct their efforts. A clear example can be found in North-West Europe, where the pilots who had scored heavily during the Battle of Britain returned from prolonged leave in the spring of 1941 to find that the Germans had all but gone, leaving only two *Jagdgeschwader* and a few bomber units in occupied Europe. Thus Fighter Command's aces had little

28 FIGHT

Lieut. Mölders †
101 victories

Major Graf
202 victories

Capt. Marseille †
158 victories

Major Gollob
150 victories

Lieut. Dickfeld
130 victories

Lieutenant Setz
133 victories

Lieut. Clausen
120 victories

Captain Bär
122 victories

Captain Philipp
113 victories

Captain Hackl
112 victories

Maj. Müncheberg
116 victories

Lieutenant Bauer
106 victories

Captain Steinhoff
110 victories

Lieut. Berenbrock
105 victories

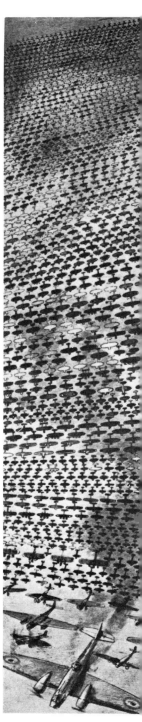

...BROUGHT D(

PILOTS...

Lt. Heinz Schmidt
107 victories

Captain Brändle
105 victories

Lieut.-Col. Lützow
101 victories

Major Ihlefeld
104 victories

Major Oesau
102 victories

Major Wilcke
132 victories

Lieut. F. K. Müller
100 victories

Lieutenant Tonne
101 victories

Sergeant Crinius
100 victories

Sergeant Reinert
103 victories

Lieut. Beisswenger
103 victories

Sgt. Zwernemann
102 victories

Lieutenant Rall
101 victories

Serg.-Major Stotz
100 victories

9 PLANES

AT MEANS ➡

chance of raising their scores significantly until the Germans returned in force again in 1944.

Mutatis mutandis, the same applied to the other Allied air forces: when the targets were there, the leading pilots scored heavily, but for most of the war there just were not the volume of targets the Germans and Japanese always had. In the West the Germans always had a sufficiency of targets, the trouble here being that these targets were usually aircraft with a performance comparable to those of their own fighters, and flown by pilots who were not markedly inferior to German pilots.

This was all different on the Eastern Front. Here, right from the start of the war in June 1941, the Germans were always outnumbered, and so had a plethora of targets. And at the start of the campaign,

---

Assuming that of

3,239 machines

brought down in air battles one third (1,080) were two-engine bombers and two thirds (2,160) fighter planes, we obtain the following equation:

3,239 planes brought down = 40 squadrons

= 4,320 engines

capable of approximately **4.5 million h.p.**

Calculating an average of 1 ton of aluminium for a fighter and only 2.5 tons for a bomber the loss of 3,239 planes by the enemy means a loss of

4,860 tons of aluminium

Taking the ratio of aluminium to bauxite as 1 : 4 this means

19,440 tons of bauxite

filling **1,940 railway trucks**

or **39 goods trains**

To smelt 4,860 tons of aluminium

121.5 million kilowatt hours

were required, the daily consumption of current in an industrial country with a population of 100,000,000. Reckoning for the manufacture of the fighter, including engines and fittings, 60,000 working hours and for a bomber 150,000 working hours 3,239 planes lost means:

291.6 million working hours

Counting 10 working hours a day in a six-day week this amounts to the output of

100,000 workers for 291.6 working days

or of **50,000 workers for 583 working days**

= 1 year 10 months

or of **31,300 for 3 years**

To this must be added the labour required for the production of raw materials (light metals, steel, etc.)

Above Major Erich Hartmann, scored 352 victories.

Russian aircraft were on the whole inferior to the Messerschmitt Bf 109E and 109F, and Focke-Wulf Fw 190A fighters deployed by the Germans, while at the same time the Russian pilots seemed capable of flying their aircraft 'straight and level', and little else. Evasive combat manoeuvres, aerobatics and other operational requirements seemed to be totally lacking. This meant, of course, that the Germans could start building up enormous individual and unit scores, as the figures demonstrate (see Chapter Seventeen).

Gradually, however, the skills of the Russian pilots improved, although with few exceptions, right up to the end of the war the best Russian pilots were equal in skill only to the moderate German fighter pilots. This should not be taken to mean, however, that the Germans had an easy time of it on the Eastern Front, or that their lot was easier than that of their comrades on the Western and North African Fronts. For there can be no doubt but that the skill of the Russians in general improved markedly as the war went on, and the very herds of Russian aircraft that presented such excellent scoring possibilities also meant extreme danger for the outnumbered Germans. With so many hostile aircraft ranged against them, there was a good chance that even a pilot mediocre by the Russians' reduced standards could get on the tail of the best German pilot and shoot him down. And with the war gradually turning against the Germans, the fighter pilots (with all other aircrew) were called upon to undertake as many missions as they could in an effort to stem the Russian advances. This meant extreme tiredness, exhaustion even, with the result that there was a tendency for pilots to lose the 'edge' that meant the difference between life and death.

Nevertheless, it was on the Eastern Front that the highest scores were achieved. The first man ever to score one hundred victories was *Major* Werner Mölders, when he shot down his 100th aircraft on 15 July 1941. First to 150 was *Major* Gordon Gollob, on 29 August 1942; to 200 *Hauptmann* Hermann Graf on 2 October 1942; to 250 *Major* Walter Nowotny on 14 October 1943; to 300 *Hauptmann* Erich Hartmann on 24 August 1944; and the only man to reach 350 was Hartmann again, on 8 May 1945.

The Eastern Front was also notable for other impressive feats. In 1942, *Hauptmann* Emil Lang, a veteran *Lufthansa* pilot, joined JG 54 at the age of thirty-three, which is distinctly on the old side for a fighter pilot. In one three-week period he amassed no less than seventy-two victories, and on one day shot down eighteen Russian aircraft, a feat never equalled

As impressive was the achievement of *Major* Erich Rudorffer, who on 6 November 1943 shot down thirteen Russian aircraft in one sortie, an extraordinary feat of ammunition economy and marksmanship. And amongst day fighter pilots, *Leutnant* Günther Scheel is remembered for the fact that in an operational life of only seventy missions, he achieved seventy-one victories, the best success ratio enjoyed by a fighter pilot.

The number of factors contributing to the German fighter pilots' considerable scores on the Eastern Front must not, however, obscure the fact that even when allowance has been made for these factors, the inescapable conclusion remains that the German fighter pilots were for some reason markedly superior to their Allied counterparts.

These then were the ten highest scoring fighter pilots of the war:

1. *Major* Erich Hartmann (352 victories), who served with JG 52 and included ninety twin-engined and one four-engined aircraft in his total;

2. *Major* Gerhard Barkhorn (301), who served w JG 52 and JV 44;

3. *Major* Günther Rall (275), who served with JGs 11 and 300, scoring all but three of his victories the Eastern Front;

4. *Oberleutnant* Otto Kittel (267), who served with 54;

5. *Major* Walter Nowotny (258), who served with 54 and *Kommando* Nowotny, scoring all but thr (which were scored in an Me 262) of his victories the Eastern Front;

6. *Major* Wilhelm Batz (237), who served with JG and scored all but five of his victories on the Easte Front;

7. *Major* Erich Rudorffer (222), who served with J 2, 54 and 7, and scored 136 of his victories in t East, sixty in the West and twenty-six in Nor Africa;

8. *Oberstleutnant* Heinz Bär (220), who served wi JGs 51, 77, 1 and 3, as well as JV 44, and scor ninety-six victories in the East, seventy-nine in t West and forty-five in North Africa (he was also t top scoring jet pilot, with sixteen victories on t Me 262);

9. *Oberst* Hermann Graf (212), who served with J(51, 52, 50, 11 and then back to 52, and scored all b ten of his victories in the East; and

10. *Major* Heinrich Erhler (209, possibly 220), wl served with JGs 5 and 7.

Other Germans to score more than 200 victories we *Major* Theodor Weissenberger (208), *Oberstleutna* Hans Philipp (206), *Oberleutnant* Walter Schuck (20(*Oberleutnant* Anton Hafner (204), and *Hauptman* H(mut Lipfert (203).

The ablest of these men was clearly Hartmann, wl was born in April 1922. It was not until 10 October 19 that Hartmann received his first operational posting, 9./JG 52 in the Ukraine, commanded by the successf *Oberleutnant* Hermann Graf. Hartmann was slow (the mark, scoring his first kill on 5 November 1942, a reaching only seven 'kills' in April 1943, by which tin he had flown one hundred combat missions. Ther after, though, Hartmann's score rose rapidly. He was cool pilot and excellent marksman, though this latt did not prevent him from trying to close the range much as possible to ensure hits and economise ammunition. By the time of the Battle of Kursk he w with 7. *Staffel*. Hartmann became *Staffelkapitän* 4./JG 52 in October 1944, and *Gruppekommandeur* II./JG 52 in February 1945. Hartmann surrendered the Americans at the end of the war, but was the handed over to the Russians, who sentenced him to te years' imprisonment. He returned to Germany in 195

Operating against the Western Allies, only eigl German fighter pilots scored more than one hundre victories:

1. *Hauptmann* Hans-Joachim Marseille (158 victories who served with JG 27;

2. *Oberstleutnant* Heinz Bär (124), who served with variety of units on the Eastern and Western Front

3. *Oberstleutnant* Kurt Bühlingen (112), who serve with JG 2;

4. *Generalleutnant* Adolf Galland (104), who serve with JGs 27 and 26, and JV 44;

5. *Major* Joachim Müncheberg (102), who served wit JGs 26, 51 and 77, scoring another thirty-thr victories in the East;

6. *Oberstleutnant* Egon Mayer (102), who served wi

JG 2;

7. *Major* Werner Schroer (102), who served with JGs 27, 54 and 3, scoring another twelve victories in the East; and

3. *Oberst* Josef 'Pips' Priller (101), who served with JG 26.

It is worth remembering with these aces that three of them had short operational lives: Marseille from April 1941 to September 1942, Galland from September 1939 to November 1941, then from January 1945 to May 1945 (in the intervening period he was *General der Jagdflieger*), and Müncheberg up to March 1943.

The most successful of the 'Western' aces was Marseille, who had only a short service career. Born in December 1919, Marseille first entered combat with *Lehrgeschwader* 2 and 4./JG 52 in the finishing stages of the Battle of Britain. Although he shot down seven British fighters, Marseille was himself shot down four times. In April Marseille was posted to I./JG 27 in North Africa, and it was in this theatre that he excelled, his magnificent eyesight (especially at long range) and marksmanship often being commented on. On 8 June 1942 he became *Staffelkapitän* of 3./JG 27, and on 1 September of the same year shot down no less than seventeen Allied aircraft in one day, possibly the most outstanding fighter feat of the war. Marseille achieved his 100th victory on 18 June 1942, but died on 2 September, the day after his elevation to *Staffelkapitän*.

As the Allied strategic bomber campaign against Germany began to exact its toll, the *Luftwaffe* placed increasing emphasis on the destruction of four-engined bombers. The *Luftwaffe's* leading aces in the destruction of American bombers (B-17s and B-24s) were:

1. *Oberleutnant* Herbert Rollwage of JG 53, amongst whose 102 victories were forty-four four-engined bombers;

2. *Oberst* Walter Dahl of JGs 3 and 300, among whose 128 victories were thirty-six four-engined bombers, and *Major* Georg-Peter Eder, with thirty-six confirmed four-engined bombers and thirty-two probables;

4. *Major* Anton Hackl and *Hauptmann* Viktor Bauer, each with thirty-two four-engined bombers;

6. *Oberleutnant* Kurt Welter, with thirty four-engined bombers;

7. *Hauptmann* Hugo Frey, *Major* Rolf Hermichen, *Major* Werner Schroer and *Major* Hermann Staiger, each with twenty-six four-engined bombers; and

1. *Hauptmann* Werner Gerth and *Oberstleutnant* Egon Mayer, each with twenty-five four-engined bombers.

Another fifteen pilots shot down between twenty and twenty-four four-engined bombers totalling 318 aircraft. Notables among these last were Kurt Bühligen and Heinrich Bär, who scored twenty-four and twenty-one respectively.

The night counterpart to the 8th and 15th Army Air Forces' day bombing was the area bombing of RAF Bomber Command. This was always treated seriously by the Germans, and twenty-four aces scored fifty or more night victories.

1. *Major* Heinz-Wolfgang Schnaufer (121)

2. *Oberst* Helmut Lent (102, plus another eight by day)

3. *Major* Prinz Heinrich von und zu Sayn-Wittgenstein (eighty-three)

4. *Oberst* Walter Streib (sixty-six)

5. *Hauptmann* Manfred Meurer (sixty-five)

6. *Oberst* Günther Radusch, *Hauptmann* Heinz Rökker and *Major* Rudolf Schoenert (sixty-four each)

9. *Major* Paul Zoerner (fifty-nine)

10. *Hauptmann* Gerhard Raht (fifty-eight)

The remaining fourteen aces to score between fifty and fifty-seven victories amassed 752 'kills' between them.

The highest award given to German soldiers during World War II was the Knight's Cross of the Iron Cross (*Ritterkreuz des Eisernen Kreuzes*). This had four grades: the Knight's Cross, the Knight's Cross with Oakleaves (*Eichenlaub zum Ritterkreuz*), the Knight's Cross with Oakleaves and Swords (*Eichenlaub mit Schwertern zum Ritterkreuz*) and the Knight's Cross with Oakleaves, Swords and Diamonds (*Eichenlaub mit Schwertern und Brillanten zum Ritterkreuz*). There was also a special version, the Knight's Cross with Golden Oakleaves, Swords and Diamonds, which was awarded to only one military man, the celebrated Stuka pilot Hans-Ulrich Rüdel.

Only twenty-seven men received the highest grade, the Knight's Cross with Oakleaves, Swords and Diamonds. *Generalleutnant* Adolf Galland, *Oberst* Gordon Gollob, *Oberst* Hermann Graf, *Major* Erich Hartmann, *Oberstleutnant* Helmut Lent, *Hauptmann* Hans-Joachim Marseille, *Oberst* Werner Mölders, *Major* Walter Nowotny, *Oberst* Hans-Ulrich Rüdel and *Major* Heinz-Wolfgang Schnaufer were the ten *Luftwaffe* recipients.

In alphabetical order, the following pilots received the Knight's Cross with Oakleaves and Swords (with the number of victories each achieved in brackets): *Oberstleutnant* Heinz Bär (220), *Major* Gerhard Barkhorn (301), *Major* Wilhelm Batz (237), *Oberstleutnant* Kurt Bühligen (112), *Major* Anton Hackl (192), *Oberst* Hajo Herrmann (9), *Oberst* Herbert Ihlefeld (130), *Oberleutnant* Otto Kittel (267), *Oberst* Gunther Lützow (108), *Oberstleutnant* Egon Mayer (102), *Major* Joachim Müncheberg (135), *Oberst* Walter Oesau (123), *Oberleutnant* Max-Helmuth Ostermann (102), *Oberstleutnant* Hans Philipp (206), *Oberst* Josef Priller (101), *Major* Günther Rall (275), *Oberleutnant* Ernst-Wilhelm Reinert (174), *Major* Erich Rudorffer (222), *Major* Prinz Heinrich von und zu Sayn-Wittgenstein (83), *Major* Werner Schroer (114), *Leutnant* Leopold Steinbatz (99), *Oberst* Johannes Steinhoff (176), *Oberst* Werner Streib (66), *Oberst* Wolf-Dietrich Wilcke (161), and *Major* Josef Wurmheller (102). Another sixteen *Luftwaffe* personnel won the Knight's Cross with Oakleaves and Swords, making the *Luftwaffe* total forty-one of the 154 such decorations awarded.

Of the lower grades, the *Luftwaffe* gained 192 of the 860 Knight's Crosses with Oakleaves; and 1,730 of the 7,500 Knight's Crosses.

The *Luftwaffe* had more than 5,000 aces, and German pilots claimed destruction of more than 70,000 enemy aircraft, 45,000 of these on the Eastern Front.

By comparison with the leading German scores, the victory tallies of the Royal Air Force's leading aces appear meagre. But it must be borne in mind with these men that they just did not have the scoring opportunities of their German opposites. They lacked the targets, and frequently they were not at the front, instead being rested or used for other purposes.

By its nature, the Royal Air Force was a multi-national force, and this is reflected in the scores of its leading aces in World War II:

Above *Major* Walter Nowotny, scored 258 victories.

1. Squadron Leader M. T. St. J. Pattle, Distinguished Flying Cross and bar, (South African) is credited with at least forty-one victories;
2. Group Captain J. E. Johnson, Distinguished Service Order and two bars, DFC and bar, (British) scored thirty-eight victories;
3. Group Captain A. G. Malan, DSO and bar, DFC and bar, (South African) scored thirty-five victories;
4. Squadron Leader P. H. Clostermann, DFC and bar, (French) scored thirty-three victories;
5. Wing Commander B. E. Finucane, DSO, DFC and two bars, (Irish) scored thirty-two victories;
6. Squadron Leader G. F. Beurling, DSO, DFC, Distinguished Flying Medal and bar, (Canadian) scored thirty-one victories;
7. Wing Commander R. R. S. Tuck, DSO, DFC and two bars, (British) scored thirty victories;
8. Wing Commander J. R. D. Braham, DSO and two bars, DFC and two bars, Air Force Medal, (British) scored twenty-nine victories;
9. Squadron Leader N. F. Duke, DSO, DFC and two bars, AFC, (British) scored twenty-eight victories;
10. Group Captain C. R. Caldwell, DSO, DFC and bar, (Australian) scored twenty-eight victories;
11. Group Captain F. H. R. Carey, DFC and two bars, AFC, Distinguished Flying Medal, (British) scored at least twenty-eight victories;
12. Squadron Leader J. H. Lacey DFM and bar, (British) scored twenty-eight victories;
13. Wing Commander C. F. Gray, DSO, DFC and bar, (New Zealander) scored twenty-seven victories;
14. Flight Lieutenant E. S. Lock, DSO, DFC and bar, (British) scored twenty-six victories; and
15. Wing Commander L. C. Wade, DSO, DFC and two bars, (American) scored twenty-five victories.

There were, in addition, another twenty-eight RAF pilots who scored between twenty and twenty-four victories, 232 who scored between ten and nineteen victories, and 664 with between five and nine victories.

Pattle is perhaps the least known of the major aces. A South African, Marmaduke Thomas St. John Pattle, known as 'Pat', tried to join the South African Air Force in the first half of the 1930s, but was refused entry. He travelled to Great Britain and joined the RAF in 1936, finishing his training in 1937. In 1938 he was posted to the Middle East with No 80 Squadron, one of whose flight commanders he had become in 1939. The squadron was equipped with Gloster Gladiator biplane fighters. A shrewd tactical thinker, Pattle had formulated his own individual tactics by the time war with Italy broke out in June 1940. In the Middle East and later in Greece, Pattle shot down at least fifteen Italian

aircraft, and had revealed himself to be a masterly sho and an expert tactician, with an uncanny instinct abou when he should fire.

Shortly after 10 February 1941, No 80 Squadro converted to Hurricanes, in which Pattle also excelle before being posted to take over command of No 3 Squadron in the middle of March. Soon after thi Germany invaded Yugoslavia and Greece, and Pattl now had the opportunity to prove he was as good as th vaunted Germans. His score continued to rise, but o 20 April Pattle was shot down in combat with Bf 110s his aircraft falling into Eleusis Bay. Although officiall credited with forty-one victories, his real score was i all probability about 60, and may have been as high a seventy-five, which would make him by far the highes scoring Allied ace of the war.

The highest scoring British pilot was James Edga 'Johnnie' Johnson, who was born in 1915 at Lough borough in Leicestershire. Like Pattle, Johnson was a first refused entry into the armed forces, but wa accepted into the RAF Volunteer Reserve in 1939 receiving his flight training during that year and th first half of 1940. Although he was posted to No 1 Squadron in the closing stages of the Battle of Britain he was immediately forwarded to a resting squadron No 616. After a period in hospital due to an old shoulde injury, he finally got into combat during January 1941 By the middle of the year his score stood at six. In Jul 1942 Johnson was promoted to the command of No 610 Squadron, and with this exceptional mixed-nationalit unit his score began to rise fast.

In March 1943 Johnson was given command of th Kenley Wing of Spitfires, and between March an September Johnson's score rose by 19. Following thi tour, Johnson was rested, and only returned to comba in March 1944, when he was given command of No 14 Canadian Wing. Johnson flew his 515th and las mission over Arnhem on 27 September 1944, scorin his 38th victory. In 1945 he was promoted to grou captain and given command of the Spitfire-equippe No 125 Wing, which fought in the closing stages of th war, though Johnson himself saw no action. All hi individual victories had been against Fw 190 and Bf 10 fighters, and Johnson must be regarded as the leadin British fighter-*versus*-fighter tactician of World War II

The following are the American pilots who score twenty-five or more victories in World War II:

1. Major Richard I. Bong, Medal of Honor, USAAF with forty victories;
2. Major Thomas B. McGuire, Medal of Honor USAAF, with thirty-eight victories;
3. Captain David McCampbell, USN, with thirty four victories;
4. Colonel Francis S. Gabreski, USAAF, with thirty

one victories;

5. Lieutenant Colonel Robert S. Johnson, USAAF, with twenty-eight victories;

6. Lieutenant-Colonel Gregory Boyington, USMC, with twenty-eight victories (twenty-two in the Pacific, and six while serving with the American Volunteer Group in China);

7. Colonel Charles H. MacDonald, USAAF, with twenty-seven victories;

8. Major George E. Preddy, USAAF, with twenty-six victories;

9. Major Joseph J. Foss, USMC, with twenty-six victories; and

10. Lieutenant Colonel Robert M. Hanson, USMC, with twenty-five victories.

The most successful American fighter pilot of the war, Richard Ira Bong, was also one of the most flamboyant. Born in September 1920 in Superior, Wisconsin, Bong enlisted in the Army Air Corps in May 1941. After training in California and Arizona, Bong was commissioned in January 1942. After further combat training on the new Lockheed P-38 Lightning, Bong was posted to the 9th Fighter Squadron, part of the 49th Fighter Group, based in Australia. Then in November 1942 Bong was transferred to the 35th Fighter Squadron of the 35th Fighter Group, with whom he scored his first five victories. In January 1943 he was once more posted back to the 9th Squadron, with which he remained until the following November, when he was posted again, this time to the HQ of V Fighter Command as Assistant Operations Officer, his special responsibility being replacement fighter aircraft. Despite this staff job, Bong continued to fly combat missions, and by the time he was sent back to the US to instruct on the latest combat techniques, Bong's score stood at twenty-eight.

In September 1944, Bong was back with V Fighter Command in New Guinea as Gunnery Training Officer. Bong continued to fly in combat although he did not have to, and added another twelve Japanese aircraft to his score over Borneo and the Philippines before being ordered back to the US in December 1944. He was killed on 6 August 1945 when the jet engine of the P-80 he was testing failed.

Other nations of course produced their own aces, and there follows a list of the greatest aces by nation:

Australia: Group Captain Clive R. Caldwell with twenty-eight victories

Austria: *Major* Walter Nowotny with 258 victories

Belgium: *Commandant* Comte Ivan du Monceau de Bergendal with eight victories

Canada: Squadron Leader George F. Beurling with thirty-one victories

China: Colonel Liu Chi-Sun with eleven victories

Czechoslovakia: 2nd Lieutenant Rotnik Rezny with thirty-two victories

Denmark: Group Captain Kaj Birksted with ten victories

Finland: Flight Master Eino I. Juutualainen with ninety-four victories

France: Squadron Leader Pierre H. Clostermann with thirty-two victories

Germany: *Major* Erich Hartmann with 352 victories

Hungary: 2nd Lieutenant Dezjö Szentgyörgyi with forty-three victories

Ireland: Wing Commander Brendan E. Finucane with thirty-two victories

Italy: *Maggiore* Adriano Visconti and *Capitano* Franco Lucchini each with twenty-six victories

Japan: Sub-Officer Hiroyoshi Nishizawa with 103 victories

Netherlands: Lieutenant Colonel J. van Arkel with five air victories and twelve V-1 flying bombs

New Zealand: Wing Commander Colin F. Gray with twenty-seven victories

Norway: Captain Svein Heglund with fifteen victories

Poland: Wing Commander S. F. Skalski with nineteen victories

Romania: Captain Prince Constantine Cantacuzene with sixty victories

South Africa: Squadron Leader Marmaduke T. St. J. Pattle with forty-one victories

United Kingdom: Group Captain James E. Johnson with thirty-eight victories

United States of America: Major Richard I. Bong with forty victories

Union of Soviet Socialist Republics: Guards Colonel Ivan N. Kozhedub with sixty-two victories

Yugoslavia: Lieutenant Cvitan Galic with thirty-six victories.

An indication of the scope of the air war may be found in the numbers of aircraft built and lost during the war:

	built	*lost*
Germany (1939–45)	118,778	50,000
German-occupied countries	8,139	
Italy (1940–43)	*c.* 11,000	4,000
Japan (Army, 1941–45)	28,000	*c.* 8,000
Japan (Navy, 1941–45)	32,422	10,370
United Kingdom (1939–45)	128,775	45,000
United States (1940–45)	272,000	22,600
Union of Soviet Socialist Republics (1941–45)	158,218	47,000 or more
	757,000 or more	164,000 or more

Twenty types of aircraft were built extending to more than 10,000 examples.

CHAPTER TWENTY-ONE

HIROSHIMA & NAGASAKI
THE FINAL
AIR CAMPAIGN
1945

After the conquest of Okinawa, the daunting prospect facing the US forces in the Pacific was that of the invasion of Japan. How else could the war be ended, as the Japanese appeared irremediably committed to a policy of no surrender? Long before the actual seizure of Okinawa, American planning staffs had been preparing for this climactic final campaign of World War II: Operation 'Olympic' was to put the 6th Army ashore on Kyushu starting on 1 November 1945, and Operation 'Coronet' was to see an invasion of Honshu by the 1st and 8th Armies on 1 March 1946. Although the strategic bombing campaign from the Marianas had all but destroyed Japan's industries, and therefore her ability to wage a modern war, the Americans fully expected to suffer more than one million casualties before Japan's military resistance could be broken. The cost to the Japanese would, of course, be far higher by several millions: the lessons of the American drive across the Pacific and into the Philippines had made that absolutely clear.

The prospect was an appalling one, but how else could the Allies bring the war with Japan to a conclusion? Japan refused to allow the reality of her inevitable defeat, and seemed determined to go down fighting in one of the bloodiest campaigns that would ever have been fought. Unknown to the planners, though, by the middle of 1945 there was in existence the possibility of a new weapon that might bring Japan to her knees without the necessity for American troops to invade the Japanese homeland. For some time before the war, scientists had been investigating the theoretical possibilities of using radioactive heavy elements, such as uranium, as the 'fuel' for explosive devices of almost inconceivable power. Working in the utmost secrecy, with only a few government and armed forces officials 'in the know', a large team of Allied scientists had spent

Below The devastating effect of the atomic blast can be seen in this panorama of the Nagasaki Medical College Grounds, Nagasaki, Japan, taken a month after the bomb was dropped.

Above The Boeing B-29 Superfortress, nicknamed 'Bock's Car', which dropped the atomic bomb on Nagasaki.

a large part of the war trying to perfect such a weapon, using uranium or plutonium as the key ingredient of their mix. The research and development teams were at last ready for the first practical test of their work in July 1945. An experimental atomic device was assembled at the top of a pylon in the New Mexico desert near Alamogordo, and triggered off by remote control on 16 July. A light 'brighter than a thousand suns' burst over the scene. A few moments later, the observers felt the enormous blast that shook the air and ground. As conditions returned towards normal, a huge mushroom-shaped cloud of fire, smoke and dust could be seen rising over the site of the explosion. Later examination of the area around the bomb revealed that the desert had been fused into a crude form of glass by the heat of the explosion, and the enormous power of the new weapon began to be appreciated.

Clearly there was in this experimental device the makings of an efficient weapon: a single bomb that could be carried by air to devastate remote targets. The problem now facing President Harry S Truman was whether or not to use the A-bomb, as the new weapon was designated. For some time the 509th Composite Group, USAAF, had been training secretly in the desert areas of Utah, practising the delivery of un-specified weapons by small numbers of aircraft with very considerable accuracy. Thus Truman knew that both the weapon and the means to deliver it were to hand. The debate was a heated one, with political, military and moral aspects to be considered. Only a few highly placed individuals were in on the secret and the debate, but finally most of the senior officers, supported by Secretary of War Henry Stimson, came to the

conclusion that the weapon should be used against Japan, in the hope of bringing the war to an end and avoiding the bloodbath of an invasion. Ultimately the decision rested with Truman, and finally he decided to allow the bomb to be used. At the Potsdam Conference during July 1945, Truman told Clement Attlee, the British prime minister, of the successful test of the bomb, and his decision to use it. Knowing that the success of the atomic device would open the way for the use of the weapon in combat, the Allied leaders had warned Japan in the Potsdam Declaration of 7 July that a refusal to surrender would lead to the 'inevitable and complete destruction of the Japanese armed forces and ... the utter devastation of the Japanese homeland'. No reply was received from the Japanese authorities, and so Truman ultimately gave his permission for the first A-bomb to be used operationally.

The target selected for this historic occasion was the city of Hiroshima. This had a population of some 300,000, although the number had been swollen by refugees from other cities. As though destined for this special niche in history, Hiroshima had been spared the worst of the bombing that had befallen other Japanese industrial cities. The 509th Composite Group had meanwhile been transferred to the Marianas, where its presence, and use only on familiarisation flights, caused much comment amongst the more conventional bomber forces located on the islands. The parts of the bombs to be used were brought in by sea and assembled in secret, and then 6 August was fixed as the date for the raid on Hiroshima. The aircraft selected for the mission was a B-29 named 'Enola Gay' after the mother of the pilot and group commander, Colonel Paul Tibbetts.

Escorted by other aircraft carrying observers, 'Enola Gay' took off and set course for Hiroshima. Arriving over the target area, the bombers were picked up by the Japanese air raid organisation, which sounded the alarm. But seeing that there were only a few aircraft above them, most of Hiroshima's citizens failed to take cover. Far above, the bomber made its run, dropped the A-bomb and turned for home at maximum speed as ordered. The bomb dropped steadily to exactly the right height and place, and then exploded with a force equivalent to about 20,000 tons of TNT. The devastation on the ground was almost beyond belief: the centre of the city was totally destroyed, and spreading out from the epicentre of the explosion were rings of damage from blast and fire. The exact casualty figures are still not known, but it seems that 78,150 people died in the initial blast, and that 70,000 more were injured. Some of these are still dying from the effects of the radiation released by the explosion.

Although the news of the disaster had a very considerable effect on the thinking of Japan's leaders, there was a certain amount of confusion and incredulity about the facts. But then, only three days later, a second bomb was dropped, and this dispelled any doubts about the nature of the Americans' latest weapon. This time the B-29 'Bock's Car' dropped its bomb over Nagasaki, a city with a population of some 250,000. Luckily for those below, the worst effects of the explosion were mitigated by the fact that the city is built on a series of hills, and this did much to divert and check the blast. Nonetheless, some 40,000 people were killed and 25,000 others injured.

Japan was now convinced of the urgent need to end the war. The Emperor Hirohito took the unprecedented step of intervening in politics to insist upon a surrender. Certain elements of the armed forces refused to consider any such action, and an attempted coup had to be put down, but negotiations with the Allies started immediately by radio. Although termed an unconditional surrender, there were several clauses included to alleviate the problems that would be caused: Japan was not to be divided, and the emperor was to stay on the throne.

The official cease-fire came into effect on 15 August, although many units refused to believe it and so fought on for a few more days, claiming that the 'Imperial Rescript' read out by the emperor over the radio was an Allied trick. Gradually, however, peace began to drift down over the battlefields of the Pacific, East Asia and South-East Asia. In Manchuria, however, war was still in full swing, with the Russians crushing the Kwantung Army in a campaign of great skill and speed, ably supported by large numbers of tactical aircraft.

General Douglas MacArthur and the first occupying troops arrived in Japan on 28 August, bringing home to most Japanese the real meaning of their defeat. Hostilities formally ended on 2 September, with the signing of the surrender documents on board the battleship *Missouri* in Tokyo Bay. MacArthur headed the Allies deputation, which included many released prisoners of war, with the Japanese Foreign Minister, Mamoru Shigemitsu, signing on behalf of the Imperial Government. At the cost of some 120,000 Japanese dead, the war against Japan had been ended without the need for what would have been an even costlier invasion and conventional ground campaign.

Above right When the first atomic bomb hit its target, Hiroshima, a column of smoke rose 20,000 feet above the city and spread over 10,000 feet at the base.
Above left The ground crew of the Boeing B-29 'Enola Gay' which bombed Hiroshima. The pilot, Colonel Paul W. Tibbets, centre.
Above left, top The Flight Crew of Ship 77 which flew the atomic bomb mission over Nagasaki on 9 August 1945.

INDEX

Numbers in italics refer to illustrations

ACKNOWLEDGEMENTS

The writer owes a debt of considerable gratitude to the authors of the following works:

Bekker, Cayus: *Luftwaffe War Diaries*, London, 1966

Boyd, Alexander: *The Soviet Air Force since 1918*, London, 1977

Brown, David, Christopher Shores and Kenneth Macksey: *Guinness History of Air Warfare*, Enfield, 1976

Craven, W. F. and J. L. Cate: *The Army Air Forces in World War II*, Washington, 1948–55

Collier, Basil: *The Defence of the United Kingdom*, London, 1957

Constable, T. J. and R. F. Tolliver: *Horrido*, London, 1958

Cynk, Jerzy B.: *History of the Polish Air Force 1918–1960*, Reading, 1972

Emme, Eugene: *The Impact of Air Power*, New York, 1959

Francillon, René: *Japanese Aircraft of the Pacific War*, London, 1970

Frankland, Noble and Sir Charles Webster: *The Strategic Bombing Offensive*, London, 1961

Freeman, Roger: *The Mighty Eighth*, London, 1970

Higham, Robin: *Air Power*, London, 1972

History of the United States Air Force 1907–1957, US Strategic Bombing Survey Reports, New York, 1958

Imrie, Alex: *Pictorial History of the German Army Air Service*, London, 1971

Johnson, J. E.: *Full Circle*, London, 1964

Killen, John: *The Luftwaffe*, London, 1967

Kilmarx, Robert A.: *A History of Soviet Air Power*, London, 1962

Manson, Kenneth: *Aircraft of World War I*, London, 1967

Manson, Kenneth: *Aircraft of World War II*, London, 1972

Mason, Francis K.: *Battle of Britain*, London, 1969

Morison, Samuel E.: *The US Naval Operations in World War II*, Boston and London, 1947–62

Neumann, G. P.: *The German Air Force in the Great War*, Bath, 1969

Penrose, Harold: *British Aviation: The Great War and Armistice*, London, 1969

Penrose, Harold: *British Aviation: The Pioneer Year*, London, 1969

Price, Alfred: *Pictorial History of the Luftwaffe*, London 1969

Raleigh, Sir Walter and H. A. Jones: *The War in the Air* (six volumes), London, 1922–37

Richards, Denis and Hilary St. G. Saunders: *Royal Air Force 1939–1945*, London, 1953–54

Robertson, Bruce and others: *Air Aces of the 1914–1918 War*, Letchworth, 1959

Saunders, Hilary St. G.: *Per Ardua*, London, 1944

Sekigawa, Euchiro: *Pictorial History of Japanese Military Aviation*, London, 1974

Sherod, Robert: *History of Marine Corps Aviation in World War II*, Washington, 1952

Siefring, Thomas A.: *US Air Force in World War II*, London, 1977

Sims, Edward H.: *The Fighter Pilots*, London 1967

Tantum, E.H. (editor): *The Rise and Fall of the German Air Force*, Old Greenwich, 1969

Taylor, John W. R. and J. D. Rawlins: *Pictorial History of the RAF*, London, 1968–70

Thetford, Owen and Peter Gray: *German Aircraft of the First World War*, London, 1962

USAF Historical Studies: The German Air Force in World War II, monograph series: various authors, New York, 1960s onwards

United States Strategic Bombing Survey, various authors, Washington, 1945–47

Van Haute, André: *The French Air Force*, London, 1974–75

Wragg, David W.: *World's Air Forces*, Reading, 1971

rkagraphic 168;

amber, Jim 14–15, 15 (inset), 106–7, 142, 262–3;

ritish Aerospace 40, 51;

undesarchiv 8, 9, 12–13, 13 (b), 20 (t:1 and r and c), 113, 114–5, 118–9, 120–1, 122–3, 124–5 (b), 125(t), 126–7 (t and b), 128, 132–3, 132 (inset), 164–5, 169, 172–3, 244–5 (b);

hoi, Kai 162–3, 198–9, 210–11;

ooksley, Peter G. 34–5, 38, 46–7, 102, 234 (inset);

efence Department 204–5;

ear, Michael 43;

ox Photos 211 (inset);

ujifotos Japan 180–1 (t and b), 184, 263 (inset), 265;

rumman Aerospace Corporation 208 (b), 209;

nperial War Museum 7, 10–11, 16 (t: l and r and b), 17 (t and cr and b: r and l), 18–9, 18 (t), 22–3, 27 (t and cl), 28 (t), 28–9, 30–31 (t), 32–3, 34–5 (inset), 36, 41 (t and b), 44 (l and r: t and b), 45 (l: t and b and r: t and b), 48–9, 49 (t and c), 50, 52–3, 52 (t), 55 (t and b), 57, 58 (t), 58–9, 60–1, 62, 63, 64, 72, 74 (b), 82 (inset: t and b), 82–3, 84, 85 (t), 86–7, 88, 89 (t and b), 90–1, 94, 95, 100–1, 104 (b), 108, 108–9 (b), 136, 144 (t), 145, 146–7, 148, 149 (t and b: l and r), 150 (t and c and b), 151 (b and inset), 152 (t and c and b), 153 (t and b), 154–5, 156–7, 158–9, 160–1, 189, 224, 225 (l and r), 228–9, 229 (t), 232, 236–7, 240, 241, 242, 243, 244 (t), 245 (t), endpapers;

Levy, Harold 42 (t), 70 (t1 and r);

McDougall, Harry 103;

Moore, J. G. Collection 78–9, 130, 131, 140–1, 143, 170, 171 (l and r), 176–7, 202–3, 207, 222–23, 226, 227, 230 (t and b), 231, 234–5, 238 (t and b), 239 (t and c and b), 270–1;

Musée de l'air title page 26 (t and b), 27 (cr and b), 30–1 (b), 37, 81 (t and c and b), 92–3, 163 (inset);

Novosti, P.A. 66–7, 186–7, 188, 190–1, 191 (inset), 192 (t and b), 193, 196 (t), 196–7, 200, 201 (t and b);

Pilot Press 138–9 (t and b), 166–7, 175, 194–5 (b);

Quarto 250;

Radio Times Hulton Library 17 (c1), 22 (t), 24–5, 56, 65, 73, 74 (t), 80, 85 (c and b), 104 (t), 110–11, 116 (l and r), 129, 144 (b);

Rockwell Int. 212 (t and b1), 252 (t);

Signal 105, 194–5 (t), 233, 272–3, 273;

Taylor, John W. R. and Michael 42 (b), 167, 214–5 (t and c);

United States Army Air Force Collection 68–9, 70 (b), 206, 208 (t), 212 (br), 215 (b), 216–7 (t), 216 (b), 217 (b), 218 (t and b), 219, 220–1, 221 (t), 256–7, 258–9, 259, 260, 261, 264, 266–7, 268 (t and b), 269, 278–9, 280, 281 (l: t and b and r);

United States Navy Collection 174–5, 178, 182–3, 182 (inset), 213, 246–7, 248–9, 251, 252–3 (b), 254–5 (b), 255 (t);